UN Peacekeeping in Africa

A project of the International Peace Institute

UN Peacekeeping in Africa

From the Suez Crisis to the Sudan Conflicts

Adekeye Adebajo

LYNNE
RIENNER
PUBLISHERS

BOULDER
LONDON

The views expressed in this volume reflect those of the author and not necessarily those of the International Peace Institute (IPI). IPI welcomes consideration of a wide range of perspectives in the pursuit of a well-informed debate on critical policies and issues in international affairs.

Published in the United States of America in 2011 by
Lynne Rienner Publishers, Inc.
1800 30th Street, Boulder, Colorado 80301
www.rienner.com

and in the United Kingdom by
Lynne Rienner Publishers, Inc.
3 Henrietta Street, Covent Garden, London WC2E 8LU

Library of Congress Cataloging-in-Publication Data
Adebajo, Adekeye, 1966–
UN peacekeeping in Africa : from the Suez crisis to the Sudan conflicts
    / Adekeye Adebajo.
        p.   cm.
Includes bibliographical references and index.
ISBN 978-1-58826-757-3 (hardcover : alk. paper)
ISBN 978-1-58826-782-5 (pbk. : alk. paper)
    1. United Nations—Peacekeeping forces—Africa—History. 2. Peacekeeping forces
—Africa—History. 3. Peace-building—Africa—History. 4. Conflict management
—Africa—History. I. Title.
JZ4997.5.A35A34 2011
355.357096—dc22

                                                                2011020126

British Cataloguing in Publication Data
A Cataloguing in Publication record for this book
is available from the British Library.

Printed and bound in the United States of America

The paper used in this publication meets the requirements
of the American National Standard for Permanence of
Paper for Printed Library Materials Z39.48-1992.

5 4 3 2 1

To Adebayo Adedeji, Mary Chinery-Hesse, Francis Deng, and James Jonah, all board members of the Centre for Conflict Resolution in Cape Town, South Africa, who have served the United Nations with great dedication and distinction as prophets of Pax Africana

And to the memories of Karen Ballentine and Marlye Gelin-Adams, two dear colleagues at the International Peace Institute, New York, with whom I learned so much about UN peacekeeping in Africa

We come from Africa . . . on this historic occasion to pay tribute to
that founding ideal, and to thank the United Nations for
challenging, with us, a system that defined fellow humans as lesser
beings. . . . The youth . . . are . . . bound to wonder why it should be
that poverty still pervades the greater part of the globe; that wars
continue to rage; and that many in positions of power and privilege
pursue cold-hearted philosophies which terrifyingly proclaim: I am
not your brother's keeper! For no one, in the North or the South,
can escape the cold fact that we are a single humanity.

—Nelson Mandela, president of South Africa,
at the UN General Assembly, October 1995

Contents

Preface

In 1991, while a graduate student at Oxford University, I took a course by a genial historian, Geoffrey Best, on "The Politics of the United Nations and Its Agencies." In the "city of lost causes," I also witnessed Africa's first UN Secretary-General, Egyptian scholar-diplomat Boutros Boutros-Ghali, deliver the Cyril Foster lecture on "The Diplomatic Role of the UN Secretary-General" in 1996, and a Kenyan scholar, Ali Mazrui, give the Evan Luard memorial lecture on "The UN and the Muslim World" a year earlier. These were all formative experiences that stirred my intellectual interest in the world body. Like many Africans of my generation, however, it was the genocide in Rwanda in 1994—when an estimated 800,000 people were killed while the UN shamefully withdrew most of its peacekeepers—that shaped my thinking about the global apartheid that lies at the heart of the world body. The concept underlines the political and socioeconomic inequities within the UN and suggests that some lives often appear to be worth more than others in a grisly aristocracy of death. This watershed event strengthened my resolve to study and improve the peacekeeping efforts of fledgling regional organizations in Africa to *complement* rather than to *replace* UN peacekeeping on the continent.

Encouraged by an early mentor, Ibrahim Gambari, Nigeria's permanent representative to the United Nations at the time, my first practical experience with the UN occurred when I served for three months in 1994 as an electoral observer in South Africa. There, I personally witnessed the revered Nobel Peace Prize laureate Nelson Mandela's victory as the first democratically elected leader of a liberated South Africa. Many of the diplomatic battles to impose sanctions on apartheid South Africa had been fought within the institutions of the UN led by dedicated African diplomats, often supported by other members of the global South, the Eastern bloc, the Nordics, and later Canada. Between 1994 and 1995, I served with the UN mission in

Western Sahara—Africa's "last colony"—where I again witnessed a visit by Boutros Boutros-Ghali. Tragically, the self-determination referendum being prepared for that country has still not been held, sixteen years later. My third UN stint involved spending six months as a geographical observer in Iraq in 1997, traversing that country's eighteen governorates while monitoring implementation of the country's humanitarian oil-for-food program.

Between 1999 and 2003, I worked at the International Peace Institute (IPI)—then known as the International Peace Academy (IPA)—in New York, which provided me a front-row seat to the "sacred drama" that is the United Nations. As director of IPI's Africa program, I sought, with my dedicated African colleagues, as well as the organization's dynamic Canadian president at the time, David Malone, to serve as a bridge between the UN and Africa's regional bodies and actors. We produced academically rigorous and policy-relevant knowledge on security issues on the continent with the world's largest UN peacekeeping presence. My time at IPI also coincided with the leadership of the second African Secretary-General, Ghana's Kofi Annan, whom I encountered at annual IPI board dinners, which he attended as the honorary board chairman at the time.

Returning to my own continent in 2003 as executive director of the Centre for Conflict Resolution (CCR) in Cape Town, South Africa, I sought to continue strengthening the conflict management capacity of African institutions and actors and to establish CCR as one of the very few centers of excellence on the United Nations in Africa. The Centre has published a thirty-chapter volume on the UN's relations with Africa and another on Africa's stake in UN reform efforts in 2004–2005. CCR has also worked with UN bodies in supporting the world body's work on mediation, peacebuilding, human rights, and the impact of conflicts on women and children. With its great convening power, IPI has always generously provided CCR with an influential platform to disseminate its work—produced on the ground in Africa—among the UN community in New York.

* * *

Many personal debts have naturally been accumulated over this period. As always, first I wish to acknowledge the incredible support of my family—"Auntie," Tilewa, Kemi, and Femi—who sustained my efforts. I would also like to thank the teacher of my UN course at Oxford, Geoffrey Best, who consistently encouraged me to pursue both the theoretical and practical aspects of the UN. At IPI, David Malone (himself, a leading scholar on the UN Security Council) was a formidable mentor. Angela Ndinga-Muvumba, Aida Mengistu, and John Hirsch were pillars of the Africa program. Olara Otunnu (a former IPI president), Margaret Vogt (the first director of its Africa program), and Musifiky Mwanasali (a committed scholar-practitioner) had earlier laid the foundation for IPI's Africa program. I also benefited immensely at the institute from the knowledge of a "golden generation" of young, dynamic researchers that included Karen Ballentine, Simon Chesterman, Waheguru Pal Singh Sidhu, and Chandra Sriram, who produced a bountiful harvest of research.

John Hirsch generously read the manuscript of this book and offered useful suggestions for strengthening the work, as did two anonymous external reviewers. Sierra Leone's former UN undersecretary-general for political affairs and a thirty-year veteran of the world body, James Jonah, deserves special gratitude for contributing a substantive foreword that places the study in a solidly pan-African context, having already provided useful comments on several chapters. I must also thank all the other mentors, friends, teachers, and colleagues who generously read earlier drafts of parts of the manuscript, offered insightful suggestions, and, I hope, helped me to avoid errors of fact and judgment: Hamid Abdeljaber, Ngozi Amu, Patrick Cammaert, Devon Curtis, Francis Deng, Gwinyayi Dzinesa, Page Fortna, Solomon Gomes, Alem Habtu, Ruth Iyob, Erik Jensen, George Joffé, Gilbert Khadiagala, Lansana Kouyaté, Daniel Large, David Malone, Ian Martin, Aida Mengistu, Musifiky Mwanasali, Chris Saunders, Sharath Srinivasan, Paul Williams, and Dominik Zaum. I have also benefited over many years from the insights, many reflected in this book, of the following collaborators on UN-related issues: Adebayo Adedeji, Olu Adeniji, Martin Agwai, Aldo Ajello, Henry Anyidoho, Mats Berdal, Mohammed Ibn Chambas, Simon Chesterman, Mary Chinery-Hesse, Sam Daws, Berhanu Dinka, Felix Downes-Thomas, Comfort Ero, Emmanuel Erskine, Ibrahima Fall, Ibrahim Gambari, Trevor Gordon-Somers, David Keen, Abdul Lamin, Chris Landsberg, Garth Le Pere, Elisabeth Lindenmayer, Victor Malu, Khabele Matlosa, Gloria Ntegeye, Chikadibia Isaac Obiakor, Francis Okelo, 'Funmi Olonisakin, Chris Olukolade, Adetunji Olurin, Ahmedou Ould-Abdallah, Salim Ahmed Salim, Amos Sawyer, Tor Sellström, Martin Uhomoibhi, Margaret Vogt, and Agostinho Zacarias.

I wish to place on record my immense gratitude to the International Peace Institute for sponsoring this publication, written by a member of its "extended family." Adam Lupel, the institute's editor, deserves particular praise for his unstinting support, cajoling, and encouragement, which ensured that this project was successfully completed. Ellie B. Hearne, IPI's former publications officer, ably assisted Adam with the preliminary editing, formatting, and compilation of the bibliography, for which I am most grateful. IPI's former vice president, Ed Luck, was an early and consistent supporter of the project and has been a close collaborator (along with the UN Secretary-General's special adviser for the prevention of genocide, Francis Deng) on other projects. Adonia Ayebare, former director of the Africa program, similarly backed this project strongly and consistently. I am also grateful to IPI president Terje Rød-Larsen, under whose leadership the book is being published.

I thank Lynne Rienner, Karen Williams, and their team in Boulder, Colorado, with whom I have published three earlier books. Russell Clarke and Bridget Impey at Jacana in Johannesburg, South Africa, also deserve praise for their role in shepherding the production of an African edition of the book. Finally, at the Centre for Conflict Resolution, Cape Town—my current employer—I would like to thank the staff and board (particularly board chair Yasmin Sooka, herself a "UN insider") for the support that allowed me to complete the project. I must especially acknowledge the tremendous research support of CCR researchers Dawn Nagar and Elizabeth Otitodun and the tireless efforts of the Centre's librarian, Margie Struthers. I also wish to thank the main funders of CCR's Africa program, who are supporting dissemination of the African edition: the governments of Denmark, the Netherlands, and Sweden, three countries that have traditionally provided substantial support to UN peacekeeping efforts in Africa.

Foreword

Terje Rød-Larsen
President, International Peace Institute

The International Peace Institute (IPI) is proud to present this book by Adekeye Adebajo on *UN Peacekeeping in Africa*. In this sweeping volume of fifteen case studies, Adebajo brings a combination of practitioner insight and academic analysis to bear on the successes and failures of UN peacekeeping in Africa, especially during the post–Cold War period.

During 2000–2003, Adekeye Adebajo was the director of the Africa program at IPI (then known as the International Peace Academy). Much of the analysis of the strengths and weaknesses of UN peacekeeping in Africa in this volume began with IPI's work with the Organization of African Unity and Africa's major subregional organizations from the mid-1990s onward. As Adebajo recalls, peacekeeping in the 1990s was often ad hoc for both the UN and African organizations. The subregional organizations (the Economic Community of West African States, the Southern African Development Community, and the Intergovernmental Authority on Development), originally established to promote economic integration, were suddenly called on to respond to the new challenges of intrastate conflicts that were often fueled by mineral resources in states from Sierra Leone to Angola to the Democratic Republic of Congo (DRC).

Such challenges stood in marked contrast to the UN's first generation of relatively simpler, interstate peacekeeping experiences. The new generation of peacekeeping required the five permanent members of the Security Council to work together with African regional organizations to adapt quickly to their new peacekeeping responsibilities. In looking at these cases, Adebajo has highlighted the need for scholars and practitioners to develop a comprehensive analytical overview that includes an appreciation of all these domestic, regional, and external forces.

Adebajo's book traces the trajectory of UN peacekeeping from the tragedies of Somalia and Rwanda in the 1990s to the most recent operations in Burundi, the DRC, and Sudan. The UN has largely recovered from the setbacks of the 1990s by undertaking several reform initiatives—from the 2000 "Brahimi Panel" to the New Horizon agenda in recent years—to strengthen its capacity to deploy peacekeeping operations in Africa more effectively. At the same time, the number of conflicts on the African continent actually declined following peace agreements and democratic elections in places like Liberia and Sierra Leone, while most of Southern Africa has remained at peace following UN missions in Namibia and Mozambique. There is also stronger cooperation between the UN and the African Union, as reflected in their partnership to develop a new peace and security architecture, including the African Standby Force, and to address postelection challenges from Guinea to Côte d'Ivoire.

Due in part to their success, several large UN peace operations in Africa have now shifted focus from peacekeeping to peacebuilding and postconflict reconstruction, as reflected in the revised roles of the UN in Southern Sudan, Sierra Leone, and Liberia. Adebajo argues that by working in a pragmatic and cooperative spirit, international and African officials can overcome many—if not all—the dysfunctions, operational failures, and shortcomings of earlier peace operations in Africa.

The International Peace Institute continues its work today both on peace operations and the unique security challenges on the African continent. As IPI's longest-running regional program, the Africa program maintains an ambitious agenda of cooperation and capacity-building efforts with the African Union. Meanwhile, IPI's work on UN peacekeeping enters its forty-first year focused on strengthening partnerships between the UN and other peacekeeping stakeholders, while developing innovative policy ideas and tools to improve the overall effectiveness of UN and other multilateral peace operations.

As Adebajo reminds us, UN Secretaries-General Boutros Boutros-Ghali and Kofi Annan, as well as a host of distinguished African political and military leaders serving as UN special representatives or force commanders, have been at the helm of most UN peacekeeping operations in Africa. Africa has not been merely the passive recipient of international support but has also made "immense conceptual and practical contributions to the birth, development and growth of UN peacekeeping over the last five and a half decades." For all these reasons it is particularly valuable to have the perspective that this volume provides.

Foreword

James Jonah
Former UN Undersecretary-General for Political Affairs

This book, written by an African author who over the years has passionately analyzed the involvement of the United Nations on the African continent, is a remarkable addition to the literature on UN peacekeeping operations. Having served on UN missions in Western Sahara, South Africa, and Iraq, Adekeye Adebajo brings to this vital task a wealth of experience with how the United Nations works, combined with a profound knowledge of many of the UN's peacekeeping actors. His book represents the first comprehensive historical and analytical review of the engagement of the UN's peacekeeping efforts in Africa. Audacious and vigorous in articulating an African perspective on these various peacekeeping operations, the book is a breath of fresh air. Adebajo tackles head-on many of the myths surrounding UN peacekeeping in Africa and lays bare the often parochial national interests of the major powers involved. It is understandable that the reflection of a strong African perspective may contradict or diverge from the analyses and approaches that are common in the academic literature. But this makes it all the more important for scholars, politicians, diplomats, and others to absorb the assessment and understanding of a knowledgeable African analyst.

The book serves as an excellent point of departure for reviewing the enormous impact of UN peacekeeping in Africa. It is helpful that Adebajo commences his exercise with the first-ever armed UN peacekeeping mission—in the aftermath of the Suez crisis of 1956—allowing us to see how the concept of peacekeeping has evolved over the past five and a half decades. The UN Emergency Force I (UNEF I) (1956–1967), deployed in the Sinai, allowed Britain and France to withdraw relatively gracefully from the Canal Zone that they had occupied. It was also the first time that a UN Secretary-General—Sweden's Dag Hammarskjöld—made use of the provisions of Article 98 of the UN Charter to plan and execute a peacekeeping operation.

It is often forgotten in today's climate that the first peacekeeping operation after the outbreak of the Suez crisis of 1956—as distinct from UN observer missions—was authorized by the UN General Assembly and not by its powerful Security Council. Under the broad powers of the General Assembly as set out in Articles 10 and 11 of the UN Charter, the General Assembly was barred from taking any action in the field of security. But the Uniting for Peace resolution of 1950, which was intended to prevent the Soviet Union's use of its veto in the Security Council to stop the US-led force in Korea (a force that had been authorized during the absence of the Soviet Union from the Council), allowed the General Assembly to take action on peace and security matters and thus magnified its role. This was a godsend to emerging African states, as the new situation made it possible for them to play a far more critical role within the UN than their size or influence would otherwise have allowed.

But the empowerment of the new African states was soon tempered by the UN Operation in the Congo (ONUC) in 1960–1964. This mission raised particular challenges for African states as they witnessed the two superpowers—the United States and the Soviet Union—using Africa as a battleground for their ideological and geostrategic struggles. The death in 1961 of Congolese premier Patrice Lumumba—who was supposed to be under the protection of the UN—and the failure of the United Nations to assist in halting the attempted secession of the diamond-rich Katanga province convinced African leaders that there were enormous risks in inviting the UN to deploy its peacekeeping forces to the continent. It was this fundamental concern that prompted Ghana's Kwame Nkrumah and others to call for a continental military force, the African High Command, and to advocate for the creation of the Organization of African Unity (OAU), which was born in 1963. A consensus emerged among African leaders that henceforth African problems were to be resolved by Africans themselves. This attitude, known as the "Congo allergy," prevailed for nearly three decades, as a result of which no major UN peacekeeping mission was deployed in Africa between 1964 and 1989.

Although some scholars refer to "complex peacekeeping operations" as a development of the post–Cold War period, ONUC was in fact the force behind this concept. UNEF I had been a rather simple operation: an interposition force was deployed between two hostile armies, and as long as those opposing armies respected the authority of the UN force, relative peace could be maintained. Under those circumstances, peacekeeping was seen as a regime that would support peacemaking activities. ONUC, on the other hand, was a messy operation that was deployed in a country bedeviled by secessionist tendencies and civil conflict. The command structures of the warring parties were weak, and there was a lack of respect for the UN's own command structure. This represented a "complex peacekeeping operation."

In the wake of ONUC, the Soviet Union and France, by their refusal to contribute toward the costs of further peacekeeping operations, created a financial crisis that almost destroyed the UN in the mid-1960s. The United States threatened to invoke the sanctions of Article 19 of the UN Charter, which would have deprived these two veto-wielding permanent members of the Security Council of their votes in the General Assembly. To resolve the crisis, the famous Committee of 33 on Peacekeeping Operations was created in 1965. This body spent many years attempting to resolve the three issues that were raised as a result of ONUC: the authorization, financing, and management of peacekeeping operations. The Soviet Union strongly opposed any role for the UN Secretary-General in the management of peacekeeping operations, arguing that all such management should be left to the UN's nearly defunct Military Staff Committee. In contrast, almost all of the Western powers were opposed to any peacekeeping role for the Military Staff Committee. This serious dispute precluded any peacekeeping operations, with the sole exception of the Cyprus mission, which was authorized in 1964 under special arrangements such as limited mandates and financing by voluntary contributions. It was only with the establishment of UNEF II in the Sinai in 1973 that the technical and political issues of peacekeeping were resolved in a landmark report of the UN Secretary-General to the Security Council.

The end of the Cold War did not immediately energize the major powers to deploy peacekeeping operations in Africa. Indeed, Egyptian UN Secretary-General Boutros Boutros-Ghali, at the outset of his term of office in 1992, complained bitterly that the Western powers were interested in tackling "rich men's wars" in the Balkans to the detriment of Africa's "poor men's wars" in places like Somalia and Liberia. Truth be told, the Western powers were dragged "kicking and screaming" into supporting efforts to authorize peacekeeping operations in Africa. The halfhearted approach that they took to grappling with the tragic genocide in Rwanda (in which about 800,000 people were killed, despite the presence of a UN peacekeeping mission) was telling. Then, the experience of the United States as a troop-contributor to the UN peacekeeping force in Somalia in 1993 led to the Bill Clinton administration's May 1994 issuance of Presidential Decision Directive 25, which signified the US determination to end UN peacekeeping operations in Africa due to the costs and dangers involved. By the turn of the century, however, the Security Council displayed a new propensity to deploy peacekeeping forces to Africa. There have been some successful peacekeeping cases on the continent, such as Namibia, Mozambique, and eventually Sierra Leone and Burundi, but there also have been serious failures and mistakes, for example, Somalia, Rwanda, and Angola.

Decades of UN peacekeeping in Africa have broken new ground in the conduct of peacekeeping operations. In the early phase of UN peacekeeping operations in Liberia, the world body cooperated for the first time with the forces of a subregional organization when the Security Council authorized a small UN observer force in 1993 to work alongside the Nigerian-led Economic Community of West African States Ceasefire Monitoring Group in the disarmament and demobilization of rebel forces. Similarly, the United Nations and the African Union—which succeeded the OAU in 2002—deployed a hybrid force in Sudan's volatile Darfur region in 2007. The operation of this latter force was experimental, and lessons learned in the operation may improve future coordination and control between the United Nations and regional organizations. However, the refusal of the Security Council to financially support any peacekeeping operation that it does not control continues to hamper the effectiveness of regional peacekeeping operations, as evidenced by East African efforts (involving Ugandan and Burundian troops) in 2010–2011 to stabilize Somalia through the African Union mission in Somalia. Without a strong regional capacity, it is difficult to envision reliable and effective peacekeeping operations in Africa.

I am hopeful that this book will trigger wider debates and discussions on the whole range of issues examined by the author. Even though conflicts in Africa have been reduced over the years, there are still dangers ahead as witnessed by the sporadic violence in Sudan's Darfur region and the DRC's Kivu province, the postelection violence in Côte d'Ivoire beginning in December 2010, and the fragile postreferendum situation in Southern Sudan since January 2011. There is more than enough substance in the pages that follow to assist efforts to strengthen the capacity of both the United Nations and regional organizations, as well as Africa's evolving peace and security architecture.

1

Introduction:
Blue Berets, Burning Brushfires

As Secretary-General I was duty-bound to carry out the resolutions
of the Security Council to the letter. But as a lifelong student
of international law, I lamented this situation, which both
disparaged international law and displayed the United Nations
not as an organisation of sovereign states equal under the
Charter but as a political tool of the major powers.
—*Boutros Boutros-Ghali, UN Secretary-General, 1992–1996*[1]

This book is about the games that great powers play. These games often
determine the outcomes of United Nations (UN) peacekeeping missions in
Africa and elsewhere. After the first armed UN peacekeeping mission was
deployed to end the Suez crisis of 1956, the politics of the Cold War would
truly overshadow future missions, as most dramatically illustrated by the
Congo crisis four years later. The first armed UN mission in Egypt had been
created as a result of the machinations of Britain and France. Future peacekeepers would also succeed or fail based on these same machinations, for
good or for ill. The Suez crisis of 1956, to a large extent, set the tone for the
later Congo crisis. The United States and Britain lined up on the side of
pro–Western Congolese leaders and sought to use the UN peacekeeping mission to oppose the "radical," nationalist prime minister, Patrice Lumumba, in
order to prevent the spread of Soviet communism (which was supporting
Lumumbist elements) to this huge country at the heart of Africa. France
refused to pay any peacekeeping dues and, later, from the 1970s, would
attempt to draw the Congo into its neocolonial francophone sphere of influence in Africa.

More positively, the end of the Cold War and increased cooperation
between the United States and Russia facilitated the deployment of UN
peacekeepers to Namibia, Angola, Mozambique, and Somalia. None of these

missions would have been possible during the Cold War era of proxy wars waged by the superpowers. During UN missions in Sierra Leone and Côte d'Ivoire after 2000, the British and French still demonstrated some residual colonial attitudes of guilt and possessiveness in their former colonies. Historical ties largely determined US support for the UN mission in Liberia, a close Cold War ally during the 1980s. The Russians, under Mikhail Gorbachev, were able to nudge former Marxist allies in Angola and Mozambique to the negotiating table as they sought improved ties with the West in the late 1980s. China similarly pushed the government of Sudan—its third-largest trading partner in Africa—to accept a UN peacekeeping force in the volatile Darfur region in 2007. The games that these powers play, which I have described elsewhere as creating a system of "global apartheid,"[2] must always be placed at the center of any analysis of UN peacekeeping missions, for it is often these games that help determine the course and outcome of these interventions. The apartheid system that I describe here is of course different from the legalized racism in South Africa or the pre–civil rights United States and focuses more on the fact that the majority of populations in much of the Third World live in widespread poverty as a result partly of the global structures of political and economic power. Like domestic structures in racist societies in South Africa and the United States of the past, however, the consequences of apartheid are similar in terms of darker populations in the Third World suffering the worst forms of an oppressive, unjust system. Peacekeeping has often operated on the basis that those who mostly pay the piper also call the tune, and Western interests (the Permanent three [P-3] of the United States, Britain, and France) have tended to dictate where and when these missions are deployed and for how long.[3]

The five veto-wielding permanent members (P-5) of the anachronistic UN Security Council—the United States, Russia, China, Britain, and France—still largely reflect the alliance of victors dating from the end of World War II in 1945. The Council must thus be urgently democratized to ensure stronger permanent membership from Africa, Latin America, and elsewhere. While the formal use of the veto by the P-5 has declined, it is still effectively used in the closed-door consultations of the Council, which is where much of its serious business occurs. Many of the archaic procedures and policies of the Council are well known to the five permanent members, who also have privileged access to UN documents through Secretariat staff. Decisions are often based on complex and not always visible trade-offs between members of the P-5 that have been worked out over many years. Since no written records of these closed-door consultations are kept, the five permanent members represent the Council's institutional memory, giving them a huge advantage over the ten rotating members—sometimes dismissed as "tourists" by P-5 members—who only serve two-year terms.[4] In this study, I have sought to assess the views of key P-5 representatives.[5]

The need for a book that assesses UN peacekeeping in Africa over the past five and a half decades is clear: between 1948 and 2011, about 40 percent (27 out of 65) of the UN's peacekeeping and observer missions were deployed in Africa; nearly half of the fifty UN peacekeeping missions in the post–Cold War era have occurred on the continent; the "Katanga rule" (peacekeepers using force in self-defense and to assist missions to fulfill their tasks) and the "Mogadishu line" (peacekeepers avoiding "mission creep") were both influenced by African cases; Africa hosted the most numerous and largest UN peacekeeping missions in the world in December 2010; much of the UN's socioeconomic and humanitarian efforts are located in Africa; and the world body has established subregional offices in West Africa, the Great Lakes region, and Central Africa, as well as peacebuilding offices in Liberia, Guinea-Bissau, Central African Republic (CAR), Sierra Leone, and Burundi. Two Africans—Egypt's Boutros Boutros-Ghali and Ghana's Kofi Annan—were Secretaries-General during the critical post–Cold War years of 1992 and 2006, while Boutros-Ghali, Annan, Algerian diplomat Lakhdar Brahimi, and Sudanese scholar-diplomat Francis Deng were involved in leading some of the most important conceptual debates and initiatives on UN peacekeeping and interventions after the Cold War. In June 2011, six out of fourteen UN peacekeeping missions were in Africa (Western Sahara, Liberia, Côte d'Ivoire, the Democratic Republic of Congo [DRC], South Sudan, and Darfur), while about 70 percent of its personnel were deployed on the continent. Sixty percent of the UN Security Council's deliberations also focus on Africa.

But despite the importance of the UN to Africa, there has been no exclusive study that has assessed the UN's peacekeeping role on the continent over the past five and a half decades. This book represents an effort to fill this gap. Other studies by Mats Berdal, William Durch, Lise Howard Morjé, Roland Paris, Paul Diehl, Alex Bellamy and Paul Williams, and Page Fortna[6] have covered some of this ground but have not focused exclusively on African cases and are not based on the same practical experiences and African insights.[7] In fact, although many of the peacekeeping missions in the world in recent times have been deployed in Africa and other developing countries, this literature, though generally insightful, has been Western-centric and self-referential, almost as if the thinking and experiences of scholars and practitioners living on continents where the missions take place are not worth reading. Many Western scholars also often pull their academic punches when discussing the role of their governments in abysmal failures such as Somalia and Rwanda. I have tried to criticize these great powers where necessary, and to praise them where appropriate. It is, however, important that Western scholars avoid labeling the genuine criticisms of scholars from the "global South" who wish to expose the transparent double standards of the powerful as "polemical." As Palestinian American scholar

Edward Said frequently noted, "speaking truth to power" should be a mission of all independent scholars,[8] and peacekeeping is one of the areas where standards of "global apartheid" are most frequently applied with tragic consequences.

Concepts and Contingencies

The historical approach that I adopt in this book highlights the crucial role that contingencies play in analyzing unique cases like the fifteen that are assessed here.[9] I argue that one of the most crucial factors in explaining the various outcomes of these cases can often be found in contingencies. While concepts derived from past peacekeeping experience are useful to bear in mind, they must always be carefully applied. These cases demonstrate the importance of focusing attention on the significant role of domestic, regional, and external actors, while not treating regions as autonomous subsystems of the global order.

The relationship between international, domestic, and regional security has been the subject of close study by, among others, Barry Buzan. Buzan described three levels of analysis in security studies: state (local), subsystem (regional), and system (international).[10] This analytical framework requires one to understand the distinctive security dynamics at all three levels before assessing how they interact. I focus on these three interdependent levels in five African subregional systems. I have not formally adopted or tested Buzan's concept of the regional security complex, however, due to its limitations in these cases; I instead seek to demonstrate that contingencies at these three levels—rather than any established security patterns or theories—were critical factors in explaining the outcomes in the fifteen UN peacekeeping cases presented here.

The choices of national actors, regional states, and external great powers often shaped how these fifteen peacekeeping missions started, developed, and ended. By examining interests, motivations, and policies in detail, these historical narratives help us to explain the complex processes through which UN peacekeeping succeeded or failed in each case. Intraregional relations often depended as much on contingent circumstances as on long-standing patterns of interests and alignments. Geographic contiguity and the destabilizing effects of war eventually determined the policies of several national actors, subregional states, and external powers.

I also seek to demonstrate that only by achieving a degree of consensus at all three interdependent levels were peacekeeping successes facilitated in some of these fifteen cases. This calls attention to the need for more scholars to study the complex interaction at all three levels in order to capture the dynamics that lead to peacekeeping successes and failures. All three levels are interconnected: without the commitment to disarmament of powerful warlords such as Angola's Jonas Savimbi and Liberia's Charles Taylor, it proved difficult for UN peacekeepers to achieve peace in both countries; without the healing of subregional divisions, the peacekeeping interventions lacked subregional legitimacy, and warring factions often continued to enjoy military support from regional or external states; without external support from great powers, UN peacekeeping often lacked adequate resources and military effectiveness.

My focus on contingencies does not mean that some findings from the fifteen African cases cannot be used to derive broader lessons for other cases outside the continent. The argument here is that any lessons must not be seen as a panacea or formula to be applied to all cases. One must always take into account contingent factors of "spoilers," domestic and regional interests, and the role of external actors through a comprehensive understanding and investigation of each specific case.

In this book, I adopt a historical and analytical approach. The five main chapters focus on fifteen case studies in five African subregions: North Africa (Egypt and Western Sahara); the Great Lakes region (the DRC, Rwanda, and Burundi); Southern Africa (Namibia, Angola, and Mozambique); West Africa (Liberia, Sierra Leone, and Côte d'Ivoire); and the Horn of Africa (Somalia, Ethiopia-Eritrea, South Sudan, and Darfur). These diverse cases all offer important lessons for peacekeeping and reflect the largest and most important operations in Africa in the past fifty years.

Justifying the Historical and Comparative Approach of the Book

I have consciously set out to analyze these important peacekeeping missions in five African subregions in order to enable policymakers to draw valuable policy lessons from the cases. The cases are idiosyncratic, and an understanding of each one is important in its own right. Some of the Western scholarship on UN peacekeeping in Africa has theoretical ambitions that often seem detached from the reality of peacekeeping missions on the ground.[11] Even some of the most reputable of these analysts lack a proper grasp of the important domestic and regional intricacies of the cases with which they deal, resulting in flawed and sometimes superficial analyses in which Africa is used as an exotic backdrop to draw theoretical generalizations invented in Western laboratories. The approach here seeks to do the opposite by drawing together the complex domestic, regional, and external dynamics that shape peacekeeping outcomes in UN missions in Africa based on the insights of both Western and African analysts. This is, of course, not to suggest that African insights are inherently better than Western ones, but that a combination of both perspectives will enrich analysis in this critical area.

Some of the recent studies in the field have asked useful questions about the division of labor between the UN and regional organizations; how to measure success and failure in peacekeeping missions; and the impact of peacekeeping on local populations.[12] These studies, however, still lack a basis in rigorous examination of the domestic, regional, and external factors that shape peacekeeping missions. Some of the US-inspired political science methods applied to peacekeeping often appear to be blunt tools that produce analyses that are sometimes esoteric, jargon-laden, and somewhat detached from peacekeeping realities on the ground.[13] As American Cold War historian John Lewis Gaddis famously noted, the failure of political scientists to predict an event as momentous as the end of the Cold War surely leads to a questioning of the presumed tools of these academic alchemists.[14]

Assessing UN peacekeeping in Africa therefore requires a similar nuanced understanding of the domestic, regional, and external intricacies of the cases being investigated. Idiosyncrasies such as a profound understanding of the motives of recalcitrant warlords such as Angola's Jonas Savimbi and Liberia's Charles Taylor; the roles of Nigeria and South Africa as regional hegemons and Uganda and Rwanda as regional spoilers; and the machinations of external "godfathers" such as the United States, Britain, France, China, and Russia in their historical spheres of influence are critical factors that are often missed in theoretical approaches. Much of the most insightful work on the UN has been published by insider practitioners such as Conor Cruise O'Brien, Brian Urquhart, Rajeshwar Dayal, Marrack Goulding, Boutros Boutros-Ghali, David Hannay, Kishore Mahbubani, Chinmaya Gharekhan, Shashi Tharoor, John Bolton, and James Jonah,[15] and it is still critical to combine academic rigor with policy insights in this important area of endeavor. Peacekeeping in Africa is clearly too important to leave to theoreticians in Western academic laboratories.

The main issue here is not that African peacekeeping has startling revelations and insights that may not exist in any other part of the world. It is that in order to draw lessons from African and other cases elsewhere in the world, one must first properly understand the specific domestic and regional dimensions of the cases that are being explained. If these complex dynamics are not well understood, the wrong lessons may be drawn from the cases. Thus, I do not argue that key lessons are to be derived from African cases that cannot simply be drawn from cases in the Balkans, Asia, or Latin America. My expertise and interest happen to be in Africa, and I have therefore focused on fifteen cases on my own continent. But I have first sought to understand the domestic and regional dynamics of each case, before relating them to the UN and the external level. In my view, a theoretical knowledge of peacekeeping will prove inadequate to explaining key outcomes in UN peacekeeping missions without a sound grasp of often intricate domestic and regional dynamics.

Key Peacekeeping Issues

Since the UN's peacekeeping successes and failures are often contingent on the domestic, regional, and external dynamics of conflict situations, it is important to pay particularly close attention to the *politics* of peacekeeping and not just to focus on its technical and logistical constraints. While these technical and logistical deficiencies are often important, the existence of political consensus among domestic, regional, and external actors—particularly the powerful members of the Security Council—is often more significant in determining the success or failure of UN peacekeeping missions in Africa. Technically deficient peacekeeping missions can still succeed with strong political support, while the most technically brilliant peace operations are likely to be undermined by a lack of political commitment on the part of key national, regional, and external actors. The UN succeeded in Namibia, Mozambique, and, eventually, in Sierra Leone and Burundi, despite logistical and financial constraints, while well-resourced missions in Somalia and Angola (the UN Angola Verification Mission [UNAVEM III]) were spectacular failures.

In determining success in UN peacekeeping missions, I have adopted the simple and straightforward definition of a peacekeeping mission as one that brings peace and stability to a particular case by implementing the key tasks of its stated mandate (e.g., ceasefire; disarmament, demobilization, and rehabilitation; elections) even if these are not fully completed before the mission concludes. It is important, however, in measuring success, that there is some stability in the country after the peacekeepers have left, even if all their tasks have not been completed. Based on a thorough assessment of these fifteen cases,[16] three key factors stand out as having most often contributed to success in UN peacekeeping missions in Africa: (1) the interests of key permanent members of the UN Security Council must be aligned to efforts to resolve the conflict in question, along with a willingness to mobilize diplomatic and financial support to peace processes; (2) the willingness of belligerent parties to cooperate with the UN to implement peace accords is critical and, in cases where such cooperation is not forthcoming, the development of an effective strategy to deal with potential spoilers who are prepared to use violence to wreck peace processes; and (3) the cooperation of regional players in peace processes is important, as well as their provision of diplomatic and/or military support to UN peacekeeping efforts.

It is the alignment of interests at these three interdependent levels—domestic, regional, and external—that has often shaped the course and outcome of the fifteen cases examined here. I have particularly highlighted the critical role of the most powerful members of the UN Security Council, as they are the only actors who have the power to start or end peacekeeping missions by the world body. They also play a crucial part in the two other factors: the Security Council must work to ensure the consent of domestic parties in implementing peace agreements, and the Council has the authority to develop incentives for cooperation or sanctions for noncompliance. The five permanent members of the Security Council have also frequently played a key role in our third factor—regional cooperation—as they often have clout over regional actors, which they can employ to encourage cooperation (sometimes even funding regional contingents to deploy to peacekeeping missions) or to sanction countries supporting spoilers by "naming and shaming" them through UN reports, or by applying diplomatic or economic pressure on them.

Three other subfactors are worth noting in determining the success of UN peacekeeping missions: (1) the absence of conflict-fueling economic resources in war zones; (2) the cessation of military and financial support to local clients by external actors; and (3) the leadership of peacekeeping missions by capable UN envoys. It is also important to note that the presence or absence of these factors does not automatically determine the outcome of peacekeeping missions. All of these factors will likely not be met in every case of success or failure.

A historical background of previous UN missions in Africa is essential to understanding the context of the current UN missions on the continent, and it is also important to note Africa's innovative contributions to global peacekeeping. The UN mission to Egypt after the Suez crisis in 1956 effectively represented the birth of armed international peacekeeping. Four years later, the UN's credibility was badly shaken by its controversial intervention in a turbulent civil war in the DRC between 1960 and 1964. The organization was struggling to keep peace in the same country in another protracted civil war five decades later. A huge country at the heart of Africa, the DRC crystallizes the difficulties that the UN has experienced in its peacekeeping efforts on the continent since 1956. In this book I examine historical case studies in Suez and the Congo and draw lessons for the thirteen post–Cold War peacekeeping cases in Africa.[17] Significantly, all but three of the post–Cold War cases (Namibia, Western Sahara, and Ethiopia-Eritrea) are cases of civil war, reflecting the changing nature of post–Cold War peacekeeping across the globe. The varied cases, most of which have seen the large-scale deployment of troops, have been selected for the significant lessons that they provide for UN peacekeeping in Africa and beyond.

Africa has thus been a giant laboratory for UN peacekeeping and has repeatedly tested the capacity and political resolve of an often self-absorbed Security Council whose five veto-wielding permanent members were often too divided during the Cold War to make decisions on peacekeeping. The end of the Cold War by 1990, and the increased cooperation of the Security Council raised great expectations that the UN would finally be able to contribute decisively to ending wars in Africa. Under the loose heading of peacekeeping, the UN launched an unprecedented number of missions in the post–Cold War era. But despite the great expectations that with a more united Security Council, the Blue Helmets would fill Africa's post–Cold

War security vacuum, hard times appeared after disasters in Angola in 1992, when warlord Jonas Savimbi brushed aside a weak UN peacekeeping mission to return to war after losing an election; in Somalia in 1993, when the UN withdrew its peacekeeping mission after the death of eighteen US soldiers; and in Rwanda in 1994, when the UN shamefully failed to halt genocide against about eight hundred thousand people and instead withdrew its peacekeeping force from the country. These events scarred the organization and made its most powerful members wary of intervening in Africa: an area generally of low strategic interest to them.

Based on the cases discussed in this book, there is a pressing need to establish a proper division of labor between the UN and Africa's fledgling security organizations, which need to be greatly strengthened. Rwanda's Arusha agreement of 1993, the DRC's Lusaka accord of 1999, and the Algiers accords of 2000 that ended the Ethiopia-Eritrea conflict, all clearly revealed the military weakness of the Organization of African Unity (OAU)/African Union (AU), whose members lacked the resources to implement agreements they had negotiated without UN peacekeepers. In Sierra Leone and Liberia, the UN took over peacekeeping duties from the Economic Community of West African States Ceasefire Monitoring Group (ECOMOG) in 2000 and 2003, respectively. The UN also took over the AU mission in Burundi and the Economic Community of West African States (ECOWAS) mission in Côte d'Ivoire in 2004, as well as the AU mission in Darfur in 2007. The UN Security Council has not done much to strengthen the capacity of regional organizations and to collaborate effectively with them in the field. I will address this important subject in the chapters on the Great Lakes region, West Africa, and the Horn of Africa.[18]

The UN missions in Sierra Leone, Liberia, Burundi, and the DRC could, however, signify an innovative approach to UN peacekeeping in Africa based on regional pillars supported by local hegemons like Nigeria and South Africa, whose political dominance of such missions is diluted by multinational peacekeepers from outside their regions. By placing regional forces under the UN flag, the hope is that the peacekeepers will enjoy the legitimacy and impartiality that the UN's universal 193 members often provide, while some of the financial and logistical problems of regional peacekeepers can be alleviated through greater burden sharing. These missions should also be more accountable, as the peacekeepers will have to report regularly to the UN Security Council. This might also force the Council to focus more effective attention on African conflicts.

The History and Dilemmas of UN Peacekeeping in Africa

Between 1948 and 1978, the UN deployed only thirteen peacekeeping missions around the globe. The first armed peacekeeping mission occurred during the Suez crisis in 1956. The UN Charter of 1945 had not mentioned peacekeeping, so Swedish UN Secretary-General Dag Hammarskjöld often referred to it as "chapter six and a half" because it fell between the UN Charter's chapter six (peaceful methods for resolving conflicts) and chapter seven (peace enforcement). The first peace-enforcement mission took place in the Congo between 1960 and 1964 (the actual enforcement was mandated in 1961). This "first generation" of traditional peacekeeping interpreted the rules in interstate wars to allow for deploying an interposing force based on the consent of warring parties to maintain an agreed peace, with the peace-keepers maintaining strict neutrality.[19] The phenomenon of peacekeeping triggered a financial crisis for the UN as the Soviet Union refused to pay for these missions during much of the Cold War era, and France also only selectively paid for peacekeeping missions. The UN General Assembly established a special committee on peacekeeping operations in February 1965 that tried to resolve some of these disputes.[20]

Between the end of the Cold War in 1990 and 2010, about fifty peace-keeping missions were deployed.[21] During the "second generation" of UN peacekeeping between 1988 and 1993, twenty UN peacekeeping missions were launched. Africa again innovated "multidimensional" peacekeeping in Namibia, in which tasks such as human rights monitoring; training police forces; disarmament, demobilization, and reintegration (DDR) of soldiers; and strengthening state institutions became part of the UN's mandate. The world body's rigid "first generation" peacekeeping approach of not combining peace enforcement with consent-based peacekeeping came under serious challenge after the Cold War due to the difficult intrastate environments in which missions were now being deployed. This recalled the Congo crisis of the 1960s, which the world body had vowed never to repeat. With a proliferation of warlords in Angola, Liberia, and Somalia attacking peacekeepers in a bid to wreck peace processes, the issue of consent became more complicated. As UN peacekeeping evolved within a conservative UN Security Council that was reluctant to use force under any circumstances, Africa again pioneered the first mission in which peacekeepers were given an explicit right to enforce peace. The consent granted to the UN mission was at best ambiguous during the US-led peacekeeping mission into Somalia (Unified Task Force, or UNITAF) in December 1992.[22]

UN Secretary-General Boutros Boutros-Ghali's *An Agenda for Peace* was a landmark document published in 1992 on the tools and techniques of peacemaking, peacekeeping, and peacebuilding for a post–Cold War era. The Security Council had asked the Egyptian scholar-diplomat to present it in January 1992. Boutros-Ghali's *Agenda* called for "preventive deployment," a rapid-reaction UN force to enable action without the need to seek new troops for each mission, heavily armed peace enforcers for dangerous missions, and the strengthening of regional peacekeeping bodies to lighten the burden on the United Nations.[23] In the same year, Boutros-Ghali established a Department of Peacekeeping Operations (DPKO) at the UN Secretariat in New York to oversee peacekeeping missions while the rival Department of Political Affairs (DPA) continued to focus on peacemaking and mediation efforts. At its peak in 1994, the UN deployed seventy-five thousand peacekeepers to seventeen trouble spots at an annual cost of $3.6 billion, reflecting the euphoria of this era. UN debacles in Bosnia, Angola, Somalia, and Rwanda quickly dampened this optimism and led to a retrenchment of peacekeeping missions between 1993 and 1998, so that by 1999, only nineteen thousand peacekeepers were deployed around the world.

Based on these disappointing peacekeeping failures, Boutros-Ghali released the more circumspect *Supplement to an Agenda for Peace* in January 1995.[24] This was followed several years later by the Brahimi Report on peacekeeping of August 2000, which sought to strengthen the UN's peacekeeping capacity and suggested innovations such as preapproving funds for peacekeeping missions; improving the rapid deployment of civilian personnel to UN missions; strengthening communication between UN headquarters in New York and the field; and increasing the size of the UN's Department of Peacekeeping Operations from four hundred to six hundred.[25] However, this report, named after the man who chaired it, Algeria's Lakhdar Brahimi,[26] was disappointingly short on details on how to improve relations between the UN and Africa's regional organizations—the continent's main peacekeeping preoccupation. The report's constant warnings that the UN should not undertake those missions where it could not guarantee success was seen by many in Africa as code for avoiding African conflicts, following UN debacles in Somalia (1993) and Rwanda (1994). A report named after one of Africa's most illustrious public servants had thus ironically ignored the continent's most urgent peacekeeping needs.

The "third generation" of UN peacekeeping emerged in 1999 with the deployment of peacekeepers to the DRC, Sierra Leone, Ethiopia-Eritrea, Kosovo, and East Timor, and later in Liberia, Burundi, and Sudan. The UN peacekeeping budget had grown to $5 billion in 2005 (equal to US expenditures in Iraq in one month in the same year).[27] Many of these missions, however, failed to heed the conditions set out in the Brahimi Report: the pace of deployment continued to be lethargic; peacekeepers brought poor equipment to missions; the DPKO struggled to cope with managing the missions; and the UN Secretariat often failed to stand up to the Security Council's sometimes quixotic demands. UN peacekeeping fell back into its usual pattern of "muddling through," being directed largely by the consensus that could be mustered among the great powers in the Security Council, but sometimes improvising successes and saving lives in the process in places like Burundi, the DRC, Liberia, and Sierra Leone.

The UN and Africa's Regional Organizations

In this book, I focus on relations between the UN and Africa's regional organizations, which remains the continent's most pressing peacekeeping challenge. The five cases of Liberia, Sierra Leone, Côte d'Ivoire, Burundi, and Sudan's Darfur region all represent examples of the UN's peacekeeping cooperation with ECOWAS and the AU. Unlike the Brahimi Report of August 2000, the December 2004 UN High-Level Panel report seemed at first to give priority to relations between the UN and Africa's regional organizations. This approach was championed by a prominent African on the panel, Salim Ahmed Salim, Tanzania's former OAU secretary-general, who had sat in Addis Ababa for twelve years (1989–2001) experiencing the frustrations of seeking assistance from the UN Security Council in many African conflicts in countries such as Burundi, Liberia, and Sierra Leone.[28] David Hannay, another panel member and former British permanent representative to the UN, was also a strong advocate of strengthening ties between the UN and Africa's regional organizations, having worked on these issues from 1994 to 1995 with Ibrahim Gambari, Nigeria's former permanent representative to the UN (1990–1999). The UN High-Level Panel held one of its meetings in Addis Ababa in April 2004 and met with senior AU officials and African civil society actors to gain their perspectives on relations with the UN. At the time, it was felt that this was a clear sign of the blue-ribbon commission's desire to focus on the UN's ties with African actors and institutions. But in the end, the panel's report devoted five paragraphs out of 302 to Africa's most important peacekeeping challenges. Like the Brahimi Report before it, another high-level group had failed to grasp the UN–regional cooperation nettle, despite assurances from representatives during their meetings—one of which I attended as a resource person—that this was a key area of high priority.

UN Secretary-General Kofi Annan's report to the General Assembly of March 2005, "In Larger Freedom," called on donors to devise a ten-year capacity-building plan with the AU, which is developing an African standby force for peacekeeping. The 15,000-strong pancontinental force is based on five subregional brigades built around members of the Southern African Development Community (SADC), the Economic Community of West African States, the Economic Community of Central African States (ECCAS), the Intergovernmental Authority on Development (IGAD), and the Arab Maghreb Union (AMU). Both Annan's 2005 report and the UN High-Level Panel report of December 2004 advocated UN financial support for Africa's regional organizations. Although there is still a lack of sufficient financial and political support for this plan, particularly among the P-5, the world body must learn lessons from the AU's difficult peacekeeping experience in Sudan's Darfur region between 2004 and 2007. These challenges effectively forced the AU to hand the mission over to the UN through the authorization of a AU/UN Hybrid Operation in Darfur (UNAMID) in July 2007. Africa must ensure that the UN assumes its proper peacekeeping responsibilities on the continent, supporting and then taking over regional peacekeeping missions to ensure sufficient legitimacy and resources.[29] The continent must also be vigilant to ensure that the proposed UN/AU ten-year capacity-building plan is implemented and expanded to subregional bodies, given the tendency since 2002 of donors such as the Group of Eight industrialized countries to make similar, yet unfulfilled promises.

Building on the ten-year capacity-building plan with the AU, in April 2008 the UN Security Council adopted a resolution on peace and security in Africa, in which it recognized "the importance of strengthening the capacity of regional and subregional organizations in conflict prevention and crisis management" and acknowledged "the need to enhance the predictability, sustainability and flexibility of financing regional organizations when they undertake peacekeeping under a United Nations mandate."[30] Nine months later, an AU/UN panel, led by former Italian prime minister and former president of the European Commission, Romano Prodi, submitted a report suggesting ways to enhance cooperation between both organizations. The Prodi report was brutally frank in defining the problem: "There is a growing anomalous and undesirable trend in which organizations lacking the necessary capabilities have been left to bear the brunt in terms of providing the international community's initial response, while others more capable have not engaged. This inversion of responsibility is generating a trend of benign neglect in which interests rather than capabilities prevail."[31] The panel criticized the deployment of peacekeeping missions into difficult environments without the means to keep peace, on the basis that "having something on the ground is better than doing nothing." It dismissed this approach as a "recipe for failure."[32] The report then made sensible proposals such as: enhancing the strategic relationship between the UN and the AU, particularly between the UN Security Council and the African Union Peace and Security Council; having the UN provide resources to AU peacekeeping in a sustainable way; funding UN-authorized AU missions for six months before the UN takes over such missions; and establishing a multidonor trust fund to finance such missions.

A major problem with this report, however, was that it focused almost exclusively on the African Union, to the detriment of African subregional bodies such as ECOWAS and SADC, which have often acted independently of the AU in undertaking peace initiatives. ECOWAS also has more peacekeeping experience than the AU and in some ways demonstrated more capacity than the continental body in missions in Liberia and Sierra Leone between 1990 and 2003. In suggesting technical solutions to some of the UN's peacekeeping challenges with regional bodies, the Prodi report also missed the politics behind peacekeeping decisions in which the P-5 seeks to retain as much flexibility in decisionmaking as possible and to determine on a case-by-case basis whether its interests are at stake before supporting interventions.

By the time South Korean UN Secretary-General Ban Ki-moon reported on progress on the ten-year capacity-building program in February 2011, it was clear that not much progress had been made in establishing sustainable support for regional peacekeeping in Africa. The UN had provided capacity-building support to the AU Commission in Addis Ababa to establish its African Standby Force, as well as furnished planning, operational, and logistical support to AU missions in Sudan's Darfur region and Somalia; the UN Office to the African Union (UNOAU) was coordinating activities between both bodies by July 2010; the world body supported AU mediation efforts in Guinea-Bissau, Kenya, Somalia, and Darfur; and four meetings had been held between the UN Security Council and the AU Peace and Security Council. But the funding to implement the ten-year capacity-building program of 2005 had not been approved, resulting in ad hoc support from existing projects, while no full-fledged program of activities had been developed to fulfill the objectives of the plan, nearly halfway through its ten-year life span.[33]

Another important document worthy of mention is the UN Departments of Peacekeeping Operations and Field Support's (the latter department was created in 2007) report of July 2009, *A New Partnership Agenda: Charting a New Horizon for UN Peacekeeping*,[34] a review of nearly a decade of the Brahimi report's implementation. This "New Horizon" report was explicit about the strain on the UN's resources made by the growing demands for peacekeeping missions with 116,000 personnel deployed across fifteen countries at the time (compared to 20,000 when the Brahimi report was published in 2000).[35] The report offered eight key practical recommendations: requiring peacekeeping to be part of an active political strategy aligning mandates, objectives, and resources; sustained dialogue between the UN Secretariat and member states, as well as between the field and headquarters to ensure impartiality in Secretariat planning and the integrity of UN command and control; improved rapid deployment; clarity on the requirements for "robust" peacekeeping and the protection of civilians, as well as on key peacebuilding tasks such as security sector reform; a new and comprehensive approach to resource generation for peacekeeping; more highly mobile military, police, and civilian capabilities for future UN peacekeeping missions; improved burden-sharing and interoperability with regional organizations; and a new field support strategy that stresses flexibility, accountability, and innovation, including sharing assets and creating regional service centres.

The "New Horizon" report, however, failed to define a strategic vision between the UN and regional organizations in Africa, due to the desire of powerful Security Council members to continue to retain flexibility in launching peacekeeping operations. The report echoed many of the Brahimi report's recommendations on the need for peacekeeping to be linked to a viable political strategy; for protecting civilians through robust action; for improving the UN's peacekeeping capacity at both headquarters and in the field; and for timely provision of resources to back up mandates. It also echoed the Prodi report's call for greater cooperation with regional organizations. At its February–March 2010 session, the UN Special Committee on Peacekeeping (chaired by Nigeria's permanent representative, Joy Ogwu) also took up this call, urging the UN Secretariat to improve interoperability and to enhance cooperation with regional bodies.[36] However, the failure of the powerful members of the UN Security Council to adopt many of these recommendations and to craft a strategic approach to engaging with Africa's regional organizations continues to stall progress on many of these sensible proposals.

Returning to the history of UN peacekeeping in Africa, in the first four and a half decades of the UN's existence, there was only one UN peacekeeping operation in Africa—the controversial Congo intervention (1960–1964). The UN only returned to Africa as a peacekeeper twenty-five years later in 1989, when it administered apartheid South Africa's military withdrawal from Namibia and supervised that country's first democratic election. During the next decade, seventeen peacekeeping operations were undertaken by the UN in Africa. The UN's peacekeeping efforts in Ethiopia-Eritrea and the critical support of Western governments for the UN operations in Mozambique, Sierra Leone, Liberia, Sudan, Côte d'Ivoire, and the DRC demonstrate the importance of powerful external actors to peacekeeping missions in Africa. The P-5 must, however, be more even handed in considering where the UN should deploy. The United States, France, and Britain successfully pushed for peacekeeping interventions in stabilizing their historical spheres of influence in Liberia, Côte d'Ivoire, and Sierra Leone, respectively, between 2000 and 2004. It is worth noting that Africa has played its part in UN peacekeeping missions; the continent's armies took part in 53 out of 63 UN peace missions between 1948 and 2008, while 40 percent of peacekeepers deployed globally during this period came from Africa.[37] Between 2000 and 2010, Nigeria, Ghana, and Kenya were among the top ten troop-contributing countries to UN peacekeeping missions around the globe. Many prominent Africans have also served as special representatives of the UN Secretary-General[38] in diverse peacekeeping theaters and have commanded UN peacekeeping missions,[39] with varying degrees of success. By 2008–2009, the UN peacekeeping budget had risen to $7.1 billion, with about $5.1 billion spent in African missions.[40] In July 2009, the UN's four largest and most complex missions—the DRC, Darfur, South Sudan, and Chad—were based in Africa, accounting for 63 percent of the organization's peacekeeping budget.[41] Between 2008 and 2009, an incredible $6.8 billion out of an annual $7.8 billion peacekeeping budget was spent on meeting the direct needs of UN missions (including $4.1 billion spent on military and civilian personnel costs), while only $10.8 million went toward "quick impact" projects to assist local communities.

The Responsibility to Protect and to Rebuild

Since the Somalia peacekeeping debacle in 1993, there have been frequent arguments that the UN should pursue "selective" rather than "collective" security, on the grounds that the world body does not have the resources to intervene everywhere. The Brahimi report of 2000 sought to entrench such an approach, arguing that the UN must learn to say no to unrealistic requests from the Security Council. I argue strongly throughout this book that such a dangerous approach in fact lets the powerful members of the Security Council off the hook instead of keeping their feet to the fire. Arguments for selective security, though clearly not intended to do so, could unwittingly lead to condoning mass killings, and even genocides, such as in Rwanda in 1994. Furthermore, this approach ignores the normative development of concepts such as "sovereignty as responsibility" and the "responsibility to protect," which insist that the Security Council has the primary responsibility—as the UN Charter clearly notes—for maintaining international security *everywhere* around the globe.

In similar guise to the Brahimi report, respected scholar Stephen Stedman argued in 2002 that "Without great or regional power interest, the United Nations should not implement the hard cases."[42] Two equally respected scholars of the UN, Adam Roberts and Dominik Zaum, though recognizing that selectivity has undermined the UN's legitimacy and reputation as an impartial body, note that "selectivity has been part of the UN framework, and has been an unavoidable feature of the actions of the UN Security Council and of all UN member states."[43] Accepting such selectivity as inevitable could, of course, result in UN interventions being based solely on cases in which powerful Security Council members have important interests to protect, rather than on the need to protect innocent civilians in violent conflicts. The regional interventions launched by ECOWAS in Liberia (1990) and Sierra Leone (1997) and by the AU in Burundi (2003) and Darfur (2004) demonstrated that even logistically and financially deficient missions can often help save lives and stabilize conflict situations until UN peacekeeping support can be attracted. Even the more limited British intervention in Sierra Leone (2000) and French-led European Union interventions in the DRC in (2003 and 2006) helped to strengthen already deployed, but deficient, UN peacekeeping missions.

Africans have contributed greatly to the normative case that the international community has a responsibility to protect civilians in cases of armed conflicts. Sudanese scholar-diplomat Francis Deng, the UN special representative of the Secretary-General for internally displaced persons between 1992 and 2004, in 2007 became the special adviser of the UN Secretary-General for the prevention of genocide. Along with other academic colleagues at the Washington, DC–based Brookings Institution, he developed the concept of "sovereignty as responsibility" in 1996. This approach sought ways to operationalize the idea and to convince African governments to adapt the continent's changing post–Cold War security architecture to protect populations in danger.[44] Deng also argued that, in situations of armed conflicts, countries are often so divided on fundamental issues of sovereignty and legitimacy—with some factions calling for external intervention—that the validity of sovereignty must be judged by the views of African populations rather than just national governments or powerful warlords.[45] He further observed that in domestic disputes in parts of Africa, relatives and elders have traditionally intervened even without being invited to do so.[46] Aside from scholars, African statesmen have also championed these ideas. South Africa's president and Nobel peace laureate, Nelson Mandela, told his fellow leaders at the OAU summit in Ouagadougou, Burkina Faso, in 1998: "Africa has a right and a duty to intervene to root out tyranny . . . we must all accept that we cannot abuse the concept of national sovereignty to deny the rest of the continent the right and duty to intervene when behind those sovereign boundaries, people are being slaughtered to protect tyranny."[47]

Both the 2001 International Commission on Intervention and State Sovereignty (ICISS) on the "responsibility to protect" (R2P) cochaired by former Australian foreign minister Gareth Evans and Algerian diplomat Mohamed Sahnoun, and the 2004 UN High-Level Panel built on Deng's ideas. The commission noted that, if governments are unwilling or unable to protect their citizens from serious harm, then the international community has a duty to protect them, ignoring the principle of nonintervention for a higher goal.[48] Five criteria were laid out to legitimize such interventions: (1) the seriousness of the threat must justify the use of force; (2) the purpose of the military action must be to avert the specific threat; (3) all nonmilitary options must have been exhausted; (4) the use of military force must be proportionate to the threat; and (5) the chances of the military action succeeding in averting the threat must be high.[49]

In his 1992 *An Agenda for Peace,* Boutros-Ghali had argued forcefully for humanitarian intervention in places like Somalia, Liberia, and Sierra Leone, advocating the use of regional security arrangements to lighten the UN's heavy peacekeeping burden. He saw the "responsibility to protect" in universal terms, castigating Western powers for focusing disproportionate attention on "rich men's wars" in the Balkans, while neglecting Africa's more numerous orphan conflicts. UN Secretary-General Kofi Annan was also a vociferous proponent of "humanitarian intervention." As Annan noted, "States are now widely understood to be instruments at the service of their peoples, and not vice-versa. Nothing in the UN Charter precludes recognition that there are rights beyond borders."[50] Annan's promotion of humanitarian intervention and his support of the idea of "sovereignty as responsibility,"[51] developed by his special representative for internally displaced persons, Francis Deng, met with strong opposition from many leaders, particularly in Africa and much of the Third World. These leaders feared that such interventions might be used by powerful states to threaten their own sovereignty. This was ironic, considering that the AU's Constitutive Act of 2000 has one of the most interventionist systems in the world in cases of genocide, egregious human rights violations, unconstitutional changes of government, and situations that have the potential to lead to regional instability. Though this mechanism has not been widely used, the AU has applied sanctions on military regimes in Côte d'Ivoire, Togo, Mauritania, and Guinea.

In a similar guise to Deng and Boutros-Ghali, Salim Ahmed Salim, Tanzania's former permanent representative at the UN (1970–1980), the secretary-general of the OAU (1989–2001), and the chief mediator for the AU in Sudan's Darfur region between 2005 and 2008, noted: "We should talk about the need for accountability of governments and of their national and international responsibilities. In the process, we shall be redefining sovereignty."[52] Salim regarded Africa's regional organizations as the "first line of defense" and called on them to promote democracy, human rights, and economic development.[53] He further argued that "every African is his brother's keeper" and called for the use of African culture and social relations to manage conflicts.[54] Salim was instrumental in the establishment of an OAU security mechanism in 1993, which subsequently sought to manage conflicts and to protect populations in Rwanda, Burundi, and the Comoros through deploying military observers. The mandate of the AU mission in Darfur (2004–2007) explicitly called for the protection of civilians even if this was often difficult to implement in practice. The mandates for UN missions in Ethiopia-Eritrea, Sierra Leone, the DRC, South Sudan, and Darfur also included clauses for the protection of civilians,[55] even if again this was often difficult to do in practice. The recognition of the need for peacekeepers to protect civilians is an important normative development after the shameful Rwandan genocide of 1994.

More recently, UN Secretary-General Ban Ki-moon, in his 2009 report *Implementing the Responsibility to Protect,* noted that "the evolution of thinking and practice in Africa [of R2P ideas] has been impressive."[56] Ban outlined three pillars in a bid to operationalize the idea of the responsibility to protect around the world: the protection responsibilities of the state, international assistance and capacity building, and timely and decisive response. Possible mechanisms to be used included: legal instruments, the UN Human Rights Council, the Hague-based International Criminal Court (ICC), carefully targeted sanctions, and the UN/AU ten-year capacity-building program. The emphasis is clearly on conflict prevention, but failing that, on early and flexible responses carefully tailored to specific situations.[57] Francis Deng, as the UN Secretary-General's adviser on genocide prevention, and US scholar Edward Luck, as his special adviser on R2P, both worked closely to develop and implement these ideas.

One of the key constraints on peacekeeping in Africa and elsewhere has been the failure to undertake effective and sustained peacebuilding after conflicts and to provide the necessary resources to try to ensure that countries do not slide back into conflict. Peacebuilding, if effectively undertaken, can help avoid further peacekeeping interventions through early prevention of conflicts. The concept is often associated with the "second generation" of post–Cold War UN missions in places like Angola, Mozambique, Namibia, and Somalia, where efforts have been made to adopt a holistic approach to peace. Not only are diplomatic and military tools employed in building peace; today's peacebuilders also focus on the political, social, and economic root causes of conflicts in societies emerging from civil war. Peacebuilding thus aims to promote not only political peace, but also social peace, and the redressing of economic inequalities that could lead to further conflict.[58] Both the UN High-Level Panel report of 2004 and Kofi Annan's 2005 report "In Larger Freedom" called for the establishment of a peacebuilding commission, as well as a peacebuilding support office within the UN Secretariat, which were both agreed in December 2005 and established in 2006.

The peacebuilding commission aims to improve UN postconflict planning, focusing particularly on establishing viable institutions; ensuring financing in the period between the end of hostilities and the convening of donor conferences; and improving the coordination of UN bodies and other key regional and global actors. This commission interacts both with the UN Security Council and its Economic and Social Council (ECOSOC) and involves the participation of international financial institutions such as the World Bank and the African Development Bank (AfDB). The peacebuilding commission is composed of thirty-one members from the Security Council, ECOSOC, and the most significant contributors of financial support and troops to the UN. The first chair of the commission was Angola's permanent representative to the UN, Ismael Gaspar Martins, while the first two countries to be reviewed were Burundi and Sierra Leone. A multiyear standing fund was established with voluntary contributions. Due to pressure from developing countries, the commission focuses largely on postconflict reconstruction and not on conflict prevention. However, based on UN experiences in Rwanda, Sierra Leone, Liberia, and Central African Republic, many Africans feel that this commission may represent yet another effort at political alchemy that does not make much difference in mobilizing the resources required for postconflict reconstruction efforts in Africa. The first five years of the commission's existence have proved disappointing and have so far failed to match the great expectations at its birth that it would promote more effective peacebuilding in Africa and improve UN coordination in countries such as Sierra Leone, Burundi, Guinea-Bissau, and the Central African Republic.[59]

Having provided a background of the approach of this book and the key issues involved in UN peacekeeping in Africa, the rest of the book will address the fifteen cases and offer some concluding reflections and recommendations flowing from the cases. Through a comparative examination of these cases of UN peacekeeping in five African subregions, from Suez to Sudan, over a period of five and a half decades, I seek to draw out the key domestic, regional, and external factors that have often contributed to the success or failure of peacekeeping missions. The concluding chapter summarizes these key factors and argues for the need to ensure greater burden sharing between the UN and Africa's fledgling regional organizations, as well as to establish an effective division of labor between these actors. Only through such efforts can what Kenyan scholar, Ali Mazrui, described as a Pax Africana be achieved on the African continent.[60]

Notes

The author would like to thank Devon Curtis, Page Fortna, Paul Williams, and Musifiky Mwanasali for their insightful comments, which greatly improved this introduction.

1. Boutros Boutros-Ghali, *Unvanquished: A US-UN Saga* (New York: Random House, 1999), p. 192.

2. See Adekeye Adebajo, ed., *From Global Apartheid to Global Village: Africa and the United Nations* (Scottsville: University of KwaZulu-Natal Press, 2009).

3. For this insight, I am grateful to Marrack Goulding, *Peacemonger* (London: John Murray, 2000), p. 26.

4. For this summary, I am indebted to Singapore's former permanent representative to the UN, Kishore Mahbubani, "The Permanent and Elected Council Members," in David M. Malone, ed., *The UN Security Council: From the Cold War to the 21st Century* (Boulder: Lynne Rienner, 2004), pp. 253–266.

5. See, for example, John Bolton, *Surrender Is Not an Option: Defending America at the United Nations and Abroad* (New York: Threshold, 2007); Jeremy Greenstock, "The Security Council in the Post–Cold War World," in Vaughan Lowe, Adam Roberts, Jennifer Welsh, and Dominik Zaum, eds., *The United Nations Security Council and War: The Evolution of Thought and Practice Since 1945* (Oxford: Oxford University Press, 2008), pp. 248–262; and David Hannay, *New World Disorder: The UN After the Cold War—An Insider's View* (London: Tauris, 2009).

6. See Alex J. Bellamy and Paul D. Williams, *Understanding Peacekeeping* (Cambridge: Polity Press, 2010); Mats Berdal, "The Security Council and Peacekeeping," in Lowe, Roberts, Welsh, and Zaum, eds., *The United Nations Security Council and War*, pp. 175–204; Paul F. Diehl, *International Peacekeeping* (Washington, DC: Johns Hopkins University Press, 1994); Michael W. Doyle and Nicholas Sambanis, "Peacekeeping Operations," in Thomas G. Weiss and Sam Daws, eds., *The Oxford Handbook on the United Nations* (Oxford: Oxford University Press, 2007), pp. 323–348; William Durch, ed., *The Evolution of UN Peacekeeping: Case Studies and Comparative Analysis* (New York: St. Martin's, 1993); Page Virginia Fortna, *Does Peacekeeping Work? Shaping Belligerents' Choices After Civil War* (Princeton: Princeton University Press, 2008); Lise Howard Morjé, *UN Peacekeeping in Civil Wars* (Cambridge: Cambridge University Press, 2008); Roland Paris, *At War's End: Building Peace After Civil Conflict* (Cambridge: Cambridge University Press,

2004). See also International Peace Institute, "Peace Operations," Task Force on Strengthening Multilateral Security Capacity, IPI Blue Papers, no. 9, New York, 2009.

7. For some African perspectives on UN peacekeeping, see the chapters by Christopher Saunders, Comfort Ero, Gilbert Khadiagala, Medhane Tadesse, and Hakima Abbas in Adebajo, *From Global Apartheid to Global Village.* See also Adekeye Adebajo, "From Congo to Congo: United Nations Peacekeeping in Africa After the Cold War," in Ian Taylor and Paul Williams, eds., *Africa in International Politics: External Involvement on the Continent* (London: Routledge, 2004), pp. 195–212; Ibrahim Gambari, "The United Nations," in Mwesiga Baregu and Christopher Landsberg, eds., *From Cape to Congo: Southern Africa's Evolving Security Challenges* (Boulder: Lynne Rienner, 2003), pp. 255–274; James O. C. Jonah, *What Price the Survival of the United Nations? Memoirs of a Veteran International Civil Servant* (Lagos: Evans Brothers, 2006); James O. C. Jonah, "The United Nations," in Adekeye Adebajo and Ismail Rashid, eds., *West Africa's Security Challenges: Building Peace in a Troubled Region* (Boulder: Lynne Rienner, 2004), pp. 251–268; Dumisani S. Kumalo, "The UN: A Personal Appreciation," in Garth le Pere and Nhamo Samasuwo, eds., *The UN at 60: A New Spin on an Old Hub* (Midrand, South Africa: Institute for Global Dialogue, 2006), pp. 29–50; Theo Neethling, "Whither Peacekeeping in Africa: Revisiting the Evolving Role of the United Nations," *African Security Review* 18, no. 1 (March 2009), pp. 2–20; Agostinho Zacarias, *The United Nations and International Peacekeeping* (London: Tauris, 1996).

8. See, for example, Edward W. Said, *Representations of the Intellectual* (New York: Vintage Books, 1994).

9. These ideas were first developed in Adekeye Adebajo, *Liberia's Civil War: Nigeria, ECOMOG and Regional Security in West Africa* (Boulder: Lynne Rienner, 2002).

10. See Barry Buzan, *People, States, and Fear: An Agenda for International Security Studies in the Post–Cold War Era,* 2nd ed. (Boulder: Lynne Rienner, 1991).

11. See, for example, Paul F. Diehl and Daniel Druckman, *Evaluating Peace Operations* (Boulder: Lynne Rienner, 2010). This book is a far cry from the useful and more readable Paul F. Diehl, *Peace Operations* (Cambridge: Polity, 2008).

12. See Virginia Page Fortna and Lise Morjé Howard, "Pitfalls and Prospects in the Peacekeeping Literature," *Annual Review of Political Science* 11 (2008): 283–301.

13. See, for example, Diehl and Druckman, *Evaluating Peace Operations.*

14. John Lewis Gaddis, "International Relations Theory and the End of the Cold War," *International Security* 17, no. 3 (Winter 1992–1993): 5–58.

15. See Bolton, *Surrender Is Not an Option;* Boutros-Ghali, *Unvanquished;* Rajeshwar Dayal, *Mission for Hammarskjöld: The Congo Crisis* (Princeton, NJ: Princeton University Press, 1976); Chinmaya R. Gharekhan, *The Horseshoe Table: An Inside View of the UN Security Council* (New Delhi: Longman, 2006); Goulding, *Peacemonger;* Jonah, *What Price the Survival of the United Nations?;* Hannay, *New World Disorder;* Mahbubani, "The Permanent and Elected Council Members"; Conor Cruise O'Brien, *The United Nations: Sacred Drama* (London: Simon and Schuster, 1968); Shashi Tharoor, "Should UN Peacekeeping Go 'Back to Basics'?" *Survival* 37, no. 4 (1995–1996): 52–64; Brian Urquhart, *A Life in Peace and War* (New York: W. W. Norton, 1987).

16. Adebajo, "From Congo to Congo," pp. 195–212.

17. See Christopher Clapham, "The United Nations and Peacekeeping in Africa," in Mark Malan, ed., *Whither Peacekeeping in Africa?* (Halfway House, South Africa: Institute for Security Studies, 1999), pp. 25–44; Oliver Furley and Roy May, eds., *Peacekeeping in Africa* (Brookfield, VT: Ashgate, 1998); Gambari,

"The United Nations"; Marrack Goulding, "The United Nations and Conflict in Africa Since the Cold War," *African Affairs* 98, no. 391 (April 1999): 155–166.

18. See, for example, Margaret Vogt, "The UN and Africa's Regional Organisations," in Adebajo, ed., *From Global Apartheid to Global Village,* pp. 251–268.

19. For a lucid introduction to the topic, see Alan James, *Peacekeeping in International Politics* (Basingstoke: Macmillan, 1990). For an entertaining review of the early years, see O'Brien, *The United Nations.*

20. Goulding, *Peacemonger,* pp. 13–14; Jonah, *What Price the Survival of the United Nations?* pp. 113–115.

21. Thomas G. Weiss and Sam Daws, "World Politics: Continuity and Change Since 1945," in Thomas G. Weiss and Sam Daws, eds., *The Oxford Handbook on the United Nations* (Oxford: Oxford University Press, 2007), p. 13.

22. Goulding, *Peacemonger,* p. 17.

23. United Nations, *An Agenda for Peace: Preventive Diplomacy, Peacemaking, and Peace-Keeping,* Report of the Secretary-General (pursuant to the statement adopted by the Summit Meeting of the Security Council on 31 January 1992), A/47/277-S/24111, 17 June 1992, www.un.org/docs/sg/agpeace.html.

24. Boutros Boutros-Ghali, *Supplement to an Agenda for Peace,* A/47/277-S/24111, 3 January 1995.

25. See *Report of the Panel on United Nations Peace Operations* (Brahimi Report), S/2000/809, 21 August 2000.

26. See Harriet Martin, "The Seasoned Powerbroker," in *Kings of Peace, Pawns of War* (London: Continuum, 2006), pp. 1–28.

27. Weiss and Daws, "World Politics: Continuity and Change Since 1945," p. 14.

28. Salim Ahmed Salim, "The OAU Role in Conflict Management," in Olara Otunnu and Michael Doyle, eds., *Peacemaking and Peacekeeping for the New Century* (Lanham, MD: Rowman and Littlefield, 1998), pp. 245–253.

29. See, for example, A. Sarjoh Bah and Bruce D. Jones, "Peace Operation Partnerships: Lessons and Issues from Coordination to Hybrid Arrangements," in Center on International Cooperation, *Annual Review of Global Peace Operations, 2008* (Boulder: Lynne Rienner, 2008); Jonah, "The United Nations"; Margaret Vogt, "The UN and Africa's Regional Organisations," pp. 251–268.

30. UN Security Council Resolution 1809, S/RES/1809, 16 April 2008.

31. UN General Assembly and Security Council, "Comprehensive Review of the Whole Question of Peacekeeping Operations," A/63/666-S/2008/813, 31 December 2008, p. 7.

32. Ibid., p. 8.

33. UN General Assembly and Security Council, "Cooperation Between the United Nations and Regional and Other Organizations: Cooperation Between the United Nations and the African Union," A/65/716-S/2011/54, 2 February 2011.

34. UN Department of Peacekeeping Operations and Department of Field Support, *A New Partnership Agenda: Charting a New Horizon for UN Peacekeeping* (New York: United Nations, July 2009).

35. Ibid., p. 4.

36. UN General Assembly, "Report of the Special Committee on Peacekeeping Operations," A/64/19, 22 February–19 March 2010.

37. UN General Assembly and Security Council, "Comprehensive Review of the Whole Question of Peacekeeping Operations," p. 9.

38. These UN special representatives include: Cameroon's Jacques-Roger Booh-Booh (Rwanda); Mali's Alouine Blondin Beye (Angola); Nigeria's Ibrahim Gambari

(Angola and Darfur); Algeria's Mohamed Sahnoun (Somalia); Mauritania's Ahmedou Ould-Abdallah (Burundi, the West Africa office, and Somalia); Senegal's Ibrahima Fall (the Great Lakes region); Nigeria's Olu Adeniji (Central African Republic and Sierra Leone); Senegal's Lamine Cissé (Central African Republic); Togo's Albert Tévoédjré (Côte d'Ivoire); Tunisia's Kamal Morjane and Cameroon's Namanga Ngoni (both served in the DRC); Botswana's Joseph Legwaila (Ethiopia-Eritrea); Ethiopia's Berhanu Dinka (the Great Lakes region); Uganda's Francis Okelo (Sierra Leone); Tunisia's Hédi Annabi (Haiti); Kenya's Yash Ghai (Cambodia); Guinea's François Lonseny Fall (Central African region); Tunisia's Azouz Ennifar (Ethiopia-Eritrea); Congo-Brazzaville's Rodolphe Adada (Sudan's Darfur region); Haile Menkerios (Sudan); Egypt's Hany Abdel-Aziz (Western Sahara); Chad's Abou Moussa (Central Africa office); Mozambique's João Honwana and Rwanda's Joseph Mutaboba (both Guinea-Bissau); Tanzania's Augustine Mahiga (Somalia); Ethiopia's Sahle-Work Zewde and Nigeria's Margaret Vogt (both Central African Republic).

39. These UN force commanders include: Ghana's Emmanuel Erskine (Lebanon); Nigeria's John Aguiyi-Ironsi (Congo); Zimbabwe's Philip Sibanda and Nigeria's Chis Alli (both served in Angola); Kenya's Daniel Opande (Liberia and Sierra Leone); Senegal's Abdoulaye Fall and Togo's Gnakoundé Béréna (both served in Côte d'Ivoire); Nigeria's Chikadibia Isaac Obiakor (Liberia); South Africa's Derrick Mbuyiselo Mgwebi (Burundi); Nigeria's Martin Agwai and Patrick Nyamvumba (both served in Darfur); Nigeria's Moses Bisong Obi (South Sudan).

40. UN General Assembly and Security Council, "Comprehensive Review of the Whole Question of Peacekeeping Operations," pp. 6 and 9.

41. UN Department of Peacekeeping Operations and Department of Field Support, *A New Partnership Agenda,* pp. 28–29.

42. Stephen John Stedman, "Policy Implications," in Stephen John Stedman, Donald Rothchild, and Elizabeth M. Cousens, eds., *Ending Civil Wars: The Implementation of Peace Agreements* (Boulder: Lynne Rienner, 2002), p. 667.

43. Adam Roberts and Dominik Zaum, *Selective Security: War and the United Nations Security Council Since 1945,* Adelphi Paper 395 (London: International Institute for Strategic Stidies, 2008), pp. 8–9.

44. Francis M. Deng et al., *Sovereignty as Responsibility: Conflict Management in Africa* (Washington, DC: Brookings Institution, 1996). See also Francis M. Deng, "The International Challenge of State Failure," in Adekeye Adebajo and Helen Scanlon, eds., *A Dialogue of the Deaf: Essays on Africa and the United Nations* (Johannesburg: Jacana, 2006), pp. 111–130; Francis M. Deng, "Africa's Internally Displaced Persons," in John Akokpari, Angela Ndinga-Muvumba, and Tim Murithi, eds., *The African Union and Its Institutions* (Johannesburg: Jacana, 2008), pp. 183–204; Francis M. Deng, "The Evolution of the Idea of 'Sovereignty as Responsibility,'" in Adebajo, *From Global Apartheid to Global Village,* pp. 191–213.

45. Francis M. Deng, *Protecting the Dispossessed: A Challenge for the International Community* (Washington, DC: Brookings Institution, 1993), p. 19. See also Francis M. Deng, "From 'Sovereignty as Responsibility' to the Responsibility to Protect," *Global Responsibility to Protect* 2, no. 4 (2010): pp. 353–370.

46. Deng, *Protecting the Dispossessed.*

47. Quoted in Eboe Hutchful, "Understanding the African Security Crisis," in Abdel-Fatau Musah and J. Kayode Fayemi, eds., *Mercenaries: An African Security Dilemma* (London: Pluto Press, 2000), p. 218.

48. See *The Responsibility to Protect: Report of the International Commission on Intervention and State Sovereignty* (Ottawa: International Development Research Center, 2001).

49. See Gareth Evans, "When Is It Right to Fight?" *Survival* 46, no. 3 (2004): 75.

50. Kofi Annan, "Two Concepts of Sovereignty," *The Economist,* 18–24 September 1999, p. 49.

51. See Deng et al., *Sovereignty as Responsibility.*

52. Quoted in Solomon Gomes, "The OAU, State Sovereignty, and Regional Security," in Edmond Keller and Donald Rothchild, eds., *Africa in the New International Order: Rethinking State Sovereignty* (Boulder: Lynne Rienner, 1996), p. 41.

53. Salim, "The OAU Role in Conflict Management."

54. Cited in Deng, *Protecting the Dispossessed,* p. 17.

55. Musifiky Mwanasali, "The African Union, the United Nations, and the Responsibility to Protect: Towards an African Intervention Doctrine," *Global Responsibility to Protect* 2, no. 4 (2010): 388–413.

56. Report of the UN Secretary-General, *Implementing the Responsibility to Protect,* A/63/677, 12 January 2009, p. 6.

57. Ibid. See also Adekeye Adebajo, Mark Paterson, and Jeremy Sarkin, eds., Special Issue: Africa's Responsibility to Protect, *Global Responsibility to Protect* 2, no. 4 (2010); and Edward C. Luck, "Sovereignty, Choice, and the Responsibility to Protect," *Global Responsibility to Protect* 1, no. 1 (2009): 10–21.

58. See Boutros-Ghali, *An Agenda for Peace;* Thomas M. Franck, "A Holistic Approach to Building Peace," in Otunnu and Doyle, *Peacemaking and Peacekeeping for the New Century;* World Bank, *Post-Conflict Reconstruction: The Role of the World Bank* (Washington, DC: World Bank, 1998).

59. See Mwanasali, "The African Union, the United Nations, and the Responsibility to Protect," pp. 388–413.

60. See Ali A. Mazrui, *Towards a Pax Africana: A Study of Ideology and Ambition* (Chicago: University of Chicago Press, 1967).

2

The Stealing of
Suez and the Sahara:
The UN in North Africa

How can I declare war against a nation, half of it backing Eden, and
the other half in the streets and Trafalgar Square objecting to him?
—*Gamal Abdel Nasser, Egyptian leader, 1954–1970*[1]

In this chapter I examine two cases of UN peacekeeping in North Africa.
The Suez crisis of 1956 was the first-ever armed UN peacekeeping mission
in the organization's history, and it set many of the rules that were followed
in the subsequent five and a half decades. This case demonstrates how the
five powerful veto-wielding members of the Security Council—the United
States, the Soviet Union, Britain, France, and China—often shape the outcome of UN peace initiatives in strategic parts of the world and how divisions between these powers can actually help reach solutions to difficult
issues. (Taiwan, which occupied the Chinese seat during this period until
1971, did not play a major role in this crisis.) Peacekeeping was, by its very
nature, an improvised and pragmatic response from the start: a face-saving
response to the invasion of Egypt by Britain, France, and Israel, with
Washington and Moscow opposing the intervention for their own strategic
interests. The second case, Western Sahara, saw the UN send peacekeepers
three and a half decades later to a territory that had been occupied by
Morocco since 1975. Despite being a classic case of self-determination,
much like Namibia (see Chapter 4), French and US support of the occupying power was enough to frustrate the UN's efforts to organize a referendum
for two decades. In the first case, the "stealing" of a canal was reversed as a
result of superpower pressure; in the second case, the "stealing" of a desert
territory was condoned by two permanent members of the Security Council.
My focus here is on the games that great powers play, as well as on the
domestic, regional, and external dynamics that shape the outcomes of UN
peacekeeping missions in Africa. Three questions are important to these two

cases. First, how did the interests of the veto-wielding permanent members of the UN Security Council determine the outcomes of these two cases? Second, what factors accounted for the belligerents cooperating with or frustrating UN peacemaking and peacekeeping efforts? And third, what role did regional actors play in determining the outcome in each case?

The Suez Crisis: Ending Imperial Delusions

The first armed UN peacekeeping mission in the world—the UN Emergency Force (UNEF)—was born in the North African country of Egypt in 1956. The mission was mandated to oversee the withdrawal of invading British, French, and Israeli troops from Egyptian territory, and it laid the basic ground rules of peacekeeping that have since been followed for the subsequent five and a half decades.

The roots of the "original sin" of the Suez crisis must be traced to the British occupation of Egypt in 1882, as the "scramble for Africa" got underway. Ironically, this occupation resulted in a continuing squabble between London and Paris that only the entente cordiale of 1904 resolved. This original colonial theft would breed animosity between Britain and Egypt, as a proud ancient pharaonic civilization built up resentment against an arrogant, rampaging empire. British indirect control of its Egyptian "protectorate" continued until 1936, but, as late as 1942, London installed a puppet regime in Cairo. The Suez crisis itself erupted when Colonel Gamal Abdel Nasser (the Egyptian leader and Africa's first military putschist with the Free Officers in 1952, an act of regicide against King Farouk) nationalized the Suez Canal in July 1956. Two years earlier, Nasser, as prime minister, had successfully negotiated a closing of the British base in the Suez Canal Zone, and eighty thousand of Her Majesty's soldiers were withdrawn from Egypt by June 1956. This withdrawal ended a seventy-two-year military occupation that many of the country's leaders had always regarded as a national humiliation. Nasser had assumed power in Egypt with the knowledge of the US Central Intelligence Agency (CIA) and had, ironically at first, been seen as pro-West before seizing power.[2]

The nationalization of the Suez Canal was a response to Washington, London, and the World Bank's reneging on an earlier promise to provide a $400 million loan for the building of the Aswan Dam (which the Soviet Union later agreed to build). This Anglo-American decision was made after Nasser's purchase of arms from the communist bloc. The British and French—the major shareholders in the Suez Canal Company—then launched an invasion with Israel three months after the nationalization of the canal, seeming to have forgotten that the old European world of "gunboat diplomacy" had been replaced by the bipolar world of the nuclear age in which two superpowers in Washington and Moscow now reigned supreme. Economic and political pressure on their Western allies by US president Dwight Eisenhower and his forceful secretary of state, John Foster Dulles, finally forced an end to the Anglo-French-Israeli theft of the canal.[3] Nasser had scored a famous political victory and added perhaps the sharpest nail to the imperial coffin.

Focusing on the domestic, regional, and external dynamics that shaped peacekeeping outcomes, this chapter examines four key aspects of the Suez crisis that shaped the course of the conflict and helped to determine the successful outcome of the UN peacekeeping mission: (1) the geostrategic interests of the three veto-wielding permanent members of the UN Security Council: Britain, France, and the United States, as well as Egypt; (2) the determination of the Anglo-French-Israeli invasion to defy the UN by toppling Nasser through the illegal use of force and the catastrophic miscalculation of the three governments about the American reaction to their aggression; (3) the decision of the Eisenhower administration and its secretary of state, John Foster Dulles, to reverse the invasion of Egypt through the threat of economic sanctions on its British ally (as well as diplomatic pressure on France and Israel), due to the need to protect wider geostrategic interests relating to the Soviet Union and the Third World; and (4) the cooperation of the United States and the Soviet Union—two veto-wielding permanent members of the UN Security Council—in using diplomatic pressure at the UN, through its General Assembly and Swedish Secretary-General Dag Hammarksjöld, to end the crisis.

The Conflicting Geostrategic Interests of Britain, France, and Egypt

The British loss of India in 1947 and the French loss of Vietnam in 1954 appeared to signal the decline of these two European great powers. Both were losing empires but were yet to find a role in a rapidly changing world. London and Paris had treacherously betrayed Arab nationalism for its help during World War I (1914–1918) by effectively carving up the Middle East among themselves. British policy in the region had since been guided for three decades by the need to preserve oil interests in Iraq, Saudi Arabia, and smaller Gulf sheikdoms. Ernest Bevin, British foreign minister between 1945 and 1951, regarded the Suez Canal as "the jugular vein" of the British Empire, linking the country to India, East Africa, and Australia: about 70 percent of the canal's ships flew British flags.[4] In 1945, the British Middle East Command (stretching to Greece, Turkey, Iran, Kenya, Malta, and India) was based in Cairo, while a Mediterranean Fleet resided in Alexandria. By 1955 Anthony Eden, Britain's prime minister since April of that year, had also negotiated the Baghdad Pact with Iraq (which London often tried to promote to rival Egypt as the leader of the Arab world), Pakistan, Turkey, and Iran. This was a strategy to maintain Britain's Middle Eastern sphere of influence and prevent Nasser and Moscow from extending their political influence into the Arab world.

Nasser denounced the Baghdad Pact as an effort to weaken pan-Arab solidarity, set out consistently to discredit it, convinced Jordan's Palestinian politicians to ensure the country did not join the grouping,[5] and dismissed members like Iraq as "imperialist lackeys."[6] Egypt stood at the intersection of the Non-Aligned Movement (NAM) as the gatekeeper of North Africa as well as the political and cultural leader of the Arabian peninsula.[7] As Nasser immodestly noted, "For some reason it seems to me that within the Arab circle there is a role wandering aimlessly in search of a hero. And I do not know why it seems to me that this role, exhausted by its wanderings, has at last settled down, tired and weary, near the borders of our country and is beckoning us to move, to take up its lines, to put on its costume since no one else is qualified to play it."[8]

Cairo also sought to act as a bridge between Africa and Asia, and Nasser was a strong supporter of the Algerian liberation movement against French colonial excesses and outrages in a savage war between 1954 and 1962 that resulted in about one million Algerian deaths.[9] The charismatic and impulsive Nasser was an Arab nationalist who was keen to overcome decades of humiliation at the hands of British imperialists. The vain and hot-tempered Eden, in contrast, remained a firm believer in the British Empire and was determined to achieve regime change in Cairo.[10] The time was thus fast approaching when an irresistible force would confront an immutable object.

But there were also differences between Paris and London. France was opposed to the Baghdad Pact, and Britain did not support French arms sales to Israel.[11] Paris had also historically vied for rivalry with London over North Africa and the Middle East. However, a new entente cordiale was struck between the two countries based on a mutual hatred of Nasser. Paris had similar interests to London's in preserving its historical political and economic interests in the Middle East, in addition to countering nationalist movements in North Africa, especially in Algeria after 1954.[12] French politicians (including Prime Minister Guy Mollet) and journalists jingoistically compared Nasser to Adolf Hitler. The Quai d'Orsay (French foreign ministry) was, however, concerned about the spread of Francophobia in the Arab world and was less keen than its defense ministry to foster close military ties with Israel.[13] Nasser had, in fact, assured French foreign minister Christian Pineau in Cairo that he would neither train Algerian cadres in Egypt nor back the Algerian rebellion.[14] But the anticolonial Egyptian leader had not been honest in this assurance and continued to back a struggle he truly believed was a just war of liberation. Paris was thus determined to take military action against Egypt even without American support or British cooperation.[15] Nasser was an enfant terrible and, like Guinea's Sékou Touré, who had defied his colonial masters in 1958 by calling on his people to vote for independence from France and suffered economic and administrative dislocation from a vengeful Mother Country, Nasser would also have to be given a bloody nose.

Having consistently but unsuccessfully requested arms from the United States and observed France continuing to arm Israel, Nasser arranged an arms deal with Czechoslovakia in September 1955 and gave diplomatic recognition to "red" China eight months later. He, however, was careful to note that the arms deal was a unique transaction and that no Soviet military technicians would be welcome in Cairo.[16] The Egyptian leader's stubborn efforts at practicing nonalignment were erroneously misread in London as Nasser having become a Soviet stooge. Washington adopted a more nuanced approach and wanted to leave Nasser a bridge back to better relations with the West if he so desired.[17] Anthony Eden also erroneously blamed Nasser for the sacking by Jordanian King Hussein of General John Glubb, the British commander of the king's Arab Legion in April 1956.

From this time on, Eden was determined to remove Nasser, who had become an obstacle to the declining Pax Britannica in the region. A blind hatred of Nasser (akin to the enraged reaction to an "uppity native" who had the temerity to tweak the tail of an imperial lion or an intemperate "kaffir" needing to be flogged by the colonial master) clouded Eden's judgment, and he even privately expressed a wish to have Nasser murdered.[18] A paranoid British premier saw Nasserite "plots" in Libya, Saudi Arabia, and Iraq.[19] As Albert Hourani noted, "In the tormented mind of Eden, there may have been some loss of judgment, due perhaps to ill health."[20] Eden clearly belonged to a different era in which a "heaven's breed" of white colonialists saw themselves as having a right to lord it over "darker" races who were still unable to stand on their own feet without the assistance of Western "civilization." He spoke in his self-justifying, unrepentant 1960 memoirs of "the vigorous tradition of our race"; described Saudi Arabia and Liberia as "more backward countries"; and talked of apartheid South Africa as a country that was "growing apace."[21]

The delusional Eden convinced himself that a declining Britain was still among the world's most powerful nations. He underestimated the strength of Arab nationalism even among the puppet regimes whose populations—the fabled "Arab street" or "Arab souk"—genuinely regarded Israel as an illegitimate aggressor in the region. Rather than preserving Britain's position in the Middle East, the Suez crisis destroyed it. The withdrawal of all British troops east of Suez by 1971 was the culmination of the decline of a British Empire on which the sun had finally set.

The Perfidious Anglo-French-Israeli Plot

Despite often publicly portraying himself as a strong supporter of the United Nations, Eden—like other members of the UN's veto-wielding permanent five—often showed himself to value the world body only when it served British interests. He noted privately in June 1956: "The United Nations becomes an increasing source of trouble. I wish we could glimpse any good it does."[22] British officials in the Colonial Office also often dismissed the UN as a "motley international assembly."[23] Charles de Gaulle, French president between 1958 and 1969, would later notoriously dismiss the UN as *le machin* (the thing), demonstrating another permanent member's instrumentalist approach to the world body. In stark contrast, the UN's Third World majority strongly condemned brutal and sanguinary Gallic tactics in Algeria (with widespread use of torture), which was absurdly considered to be part of France despite the geographical illogic of such a claim. Algeria had become the main flashpoint in French politics in 1956 and would lead to the death of the French Fourth Republic and election of De Gaulle to save French democracy in 1958.

The Suez Canal had, ironically, been built by a Frenchman, Ferdinand de Lesseps, between 1859 and 1869. The canal company was based in Paris, and Britain was its largest shareholder. But the company was Egyptian and subject to Egyptian law,[24] and Nasser was prepared to pay just compensation for his nationalization of the canal,[25] which he eventually did. Even as the British and French were seemingly seeking a settlement on the internationalization of the Suez Canal at the London conferences in August and September 1956, they were secretly planning a joint military invasion with Israel to take over the canal through a meeting in the Parisian suburb of Sèvres in October 1956. In the same month as the nationalization of the Suez Canal, London sought "regime change" in Egypt by overthrowing Nasser. Paris sought to eliminate the Egyptian leader's support for Algerian liberation fighters, while Tel Aviv sought a more secure southern frontier.[26] This perfidious plan was, however, too neat, based on flawed thinking and faulty assumptions, as well as an extraordinary *folie de grandeur* (delusion of grandeur) by Anglo-French neoimperialists. The plot unsurprisingly unraveled when exposed to the harsh realities of Cold War geopolitics.

On 29 October 1956, Israeli forces attacked Egypt's central Sinai, seventy kilometers from the Suez Canal. In accordance with the prior secret plan, the British and French issued an ultimatum to Egypt and Israel to retreat sixteen kilometers from the canal, threatening to send "peacekeepers" to the area if they did not. Nasser not unreasonably refused to withdraw from sovereign Egyptian territory under threats based on an illegal invasion. Even Gerald Fitzmaurice, the legal adviser to the British Foreign Office, had warned Eden that London was "on an extremely bad wicket legally" in using force over the Suez crisis.[27] An angry and betrayed Washington asked the UN Security Council to order an Israeli withdrawal from Egyptian territory.

On 31 October 1956, the Anglo-French air offensive was launched, with British troops landing at Port Said and French forces at Port Fouad a week later. Both pretended implausibly to be peacekeepers seeking to separate Egyptian and Israeli belligerents. This was an amateurish plot by two declining imperial powers acting like international gangsters and robber barons. The assumption was that, just as in colonial days, a compliant, puppet regime could be installed once Nasser had been overthrown.[28] Another flawed assumption of this operation was that the Egyptians would not be able to manage the flow of shipping into the canal once the British had deliberately tried to create congestion by diverting ships to the canal in the rather unsubtly named Operation Pile-Up. This scheme was meant to create another pretext for removing Nasser.[29] After the tripartite invasion, the Egyptians in fact managed to keep the canal running smoothly. They also disrupted oil shipments to the invaders. Brian Urquhart, the respected British former UN Undersecretary-General for Peacekeeping, described the invasion as "a fiasco from the start. Conceived in anger and deceit, foolishly planned, and hesitantly carried out . . . a doomed, dishonest, and contemptible aberration by the British and French governments."[30] The Suez crisis reinforced historical notions of perfidious Albion: the treachery and deception of British realpolitik. After this crisis, many Third World countries refused to take London at its word,[31] as decolonization battles were fought at the UN. Britain was a country on the brink of decline, in arrogant and prejudiced denial.

The United States Spoils the Imperial Party

During the Suez crisis, Washington tried hard to defuse the situation, while London and Paris worked hard to trigger a confrontation with Nasser. Eden arrogantly seemed to want to play at what his successor, Harold Macmillan, described as the guile of Athens to the power of America's Rome and was clearly hoping to trap Washington into backing the invasion, miscalculating catastrophically that a Soviet threat would force the United States back into the Western camp. Under serious pressure from Washington, Britain agreed to a ceasefire on 6 November 1956, leading to an inevitable crumbling of French resolve. Both London and Paris were dependent on US financial assistance to purchase oil supplies.[32] International speculation against sterling—"the run on the pound"—led to a precipitate fall in British currency reserves by $141 million in September and October 1956 and by $279 million in November 1956.[33] Arab countries and oil companies were the largest holders of sterling. This collapse of British currency reserves and lack of US support would prove decisive in ending the Suez crisis. Millions of Egyptians also rallied to Nasser's side after the Anglo-French-Israeli invasion,[34] and the predicted fall of his regime proved to be a catastrophic miscalculation.

Despite later attempts at revisionist history by some British politicians and sections of the press that they had been betrayed by the United States and particularly by Secretary of State John Foster Dulles, President Dwight Eisenhower and Dulles were both consistently unambiguous throughout the crisis that they opposed the use of force against Nasser. Both American statesmen accepted that it was Egypt's sovereign right to nationalize the canal (while they held sway in Cairo, the British had ironically always insisted that the canal was Egyptian and consistently opposed any form of international control[35]), and as long as free shipping continued on the canal and no foreign nationals were under threat, no military action was warranted.[36] Washington, unlike London and Paris, continued to pay shipping dues for use of the canal to Cairo throughout the crisis. Eisenhower, in fact, set the US policy during this crisis that Dulles was implementing, and both shared similar views on the Suez crisis and consulted closely with each other.[37]

Both Dulles and Eisenhower spoke out forcefully against a reversion to old-style European colonialism and kept urging European powers to decolonize. Dulles described Suez as an "old-fashioned variety of colonialism of the most obvious sort."[38] He felt that both the British and the Israelis had damaged the prospects for a comprehensive Middle East peace centered on the 1950 Tripartite Declaration involving the United States, Britain, and France, to regulate arms flows and secure the armistice frontiers of 1949. However, the fiery US secretary of state had little faith in the French and was less surprised by their deceit.[39] Both Dulles and Eisenhower particularly detested the French brand of imperialism, and Dulles was irritated by the extent of French military support for Israel.[40] Paris would become one of the largest suppliers of arms to Israel,[41] as it later would assist apartheid South Africa to develop its nuclear capability. French foreign minister Christian Pineau sought to paint an apocalyptic picture to Dulles of Arab dominoes falling in North Africa and spreading to black Africa, with the resultant loss of European influence on the continent.[42] Washington, however, remained skeptical, reasoning that it was actually Anglo-French actions—and not Nasser's—that could trigger such a scenario.

Though the US anticolonial approach was often presented as resulting from a lack of the country's imperial history (despite its colonialism in the Philippines and "gunboat diplomacy" and economic exploitation in the Caribbean and Latin America, which locals had appropriately dubbed "Yankee imperialism"), it was more likely that this pragmatic policy was driven by Soviet attempts to support leftist revolutions in much of the emerging Third World. Eisenhower and Dulles supported evolutionary decolonization in the Third World to prevent Moscow from capitalizing on anti-Western revolutionary change.[43] Britain and France thought *locally,* while the United States acted *globally.*

Both Eisenhower—a general who had fought in World War II (1939–1945)—and Dulles were anticommunist Republican Cold Warriors fighting the "evil" Soviet empire. But the fact that Eden was dealing mostly with Dulles rather than Eisenhower during this crisis was a clear sign of the declining British position from the first rank of great powers. Eisenhower believed that Britain and France no longer possessed the economic and military clout to dominate the Middle East, and he was privately contemptuous of British claims of "world power" status.[44] The US president felt that London and Paris were exaggerating the threat posed by Nasser and that it was the loss of prestige and influence in the Middle East and other spheres of influence that was the real driving force for the actions of the two European powers.[45]

Eisenhower and Dulles were, however, also both wary of Nasser and had, after all, canceled the Aswan Dam contract. But they feared even more being tainted by an illegal, neocolonial invasion that could push Nasser into the embrace of the Soviet bear and rally the Third World majority at the UN against Western interests. Washington felt that Nasser could be contained and did not buy into Eden's hyperbolic comparison of the Egyptian leader to Adolf Hitler and Benito Mussolini. The fear of Moscow expanding its influence into the Middle East is what effectively drove US policy during this crisis. Washington thus let Nasser know that it accepted Cairo's leadership of the Arab world, and Eisenhower regarded the Egyptian leader as a pragmatic nationalist who was seeking to end what he regarded as foreign domination over his country and to increase his political independence through whatever means he could.[46]

Eisenhower and Dulles worked hard to get into direct touch with the leaders of Britain, France, and Israel, pushing them to accept UN General Assembly resolutions calling for withdrawal and the deployment of a UN peacekeeping force as a way of digging themselves out of the dangerous hole they had got themselves into. Eisenhower and Dulles were also concerned not to let the Suez crisis overshadow the US presidential election of 1956.

Despite Washington's having been on the anticolonial side during the Suez crisis, the US removal of the democratically elected government of Muhammad Musaddiq in Iran in 1953, three years before Suez, through American and British intelligence services[47] (an incident acknowledged by President Barack Obama during a speech in Cairo in June 2009) was clear proof that, despite its anticolonial rhetoric during Suez, the Eisenhower administration was capable of rank hypocrisy in promoting principles of self-determination and noninterference. Ironically, Eden had been the British foreign secretary during this 1953 operation but failed as prime minister to heed the lesson of prior American agreement for neocolonial plots. The Iran incident had been as much a reversion to old colonial ways as Suez was, but the Iran intervention (unlike Suez) had been undertaken with the full acquiescence of Washington, which would soon become more comfortable with replacing Britain in a neocolonial role in the Middle East to ensure that the Soviet Union was kept out of an oil-rich strategic region of the world.

The Diplomatic Battles at the UN

At the time of the Suez crisis, anticommunist demonstrations in Hungary had resulted in Soviet tanks rolling into Budapest in November 1956 to quell the rebellion. The UN General Assembly condemned this invasion, as it would condemn the invasion of Egypt. John Foster Dulles described the Anglo-French bombing of Egypt as having been equally as brutal and barbaric as the simultaneous Soviet invasion of Hungary,[48] a comparison that both European powers found particularly irksome. Moscow tried to exploit the Suez crisis to sow discord among the Western powers by threatening Britain and France, and the Russians were providing military support to Egypt. At the UN, the Soviet Union and the United States found themselves in an unusual and unprecedented marriage of convenience against old-style Anglo-French imperialism as they competed for support and influence in the Middle East and the broader Third World. UN membership had expanded from fifty-one in 1945 to sixty-seven by 1956, and the large wave of African independence was about to increase the world body's Third World majority even more.

Amid fears of Anglo-French vetoes in the Security Council, the Suez issue was tabled at the UN General Assembly in September 1956, two months after the crisis had erupted. The British privately referred to one of the central figures in mediating an end to the Suez crisis—Swedish UN Secretary-General Dag Hammarskjöld—derisively as "the Pope on the East River."[49] The Swede was unhappy that the organization had been marginalized at the start of the conflict but did not want the UN to become too closely involved in the controversial issues over management of the Suez Canal.[50] Contrary to the widespread portrayal of Hammarskjöld as being consistently sympathetic to Third World nationalism, he actually sought to exploit divisions between Nasser and Arab countries and felt that maintaining the issue as an East-West conflict would unite the Arabs behind Nasser.[51] As the Swede reportedly put it to the British, "If the Suez crisis led to the disappearance of Nasser, so much the better."[52] Hammarskjöld, though, did eventually side with the view of the UN General Assembly majority, which regarded Egypt as the victim of aggression[53] and the Anglo-French-Israelis as the villains.

Even though Britain's seasoned permanent representative at the UN, Pierson Dixon, loyally defended his government's policy, he privately felt that it was misguided and eventually disastrous[54] and considered resigning over the issue.[55] Dixon later noted that defending this sticky diplomatic wicket before the UN General Assembly caused "the severest moral and physical strain I have ever experienced."[56] Incredibly, Britain's diplomatic representatives in New York, Washington, Cairo, and Tel Aviv had not been informed of the secret invasion plan drawn up at Sèvres.[57] Also interesting is the admission of Douglas Hurd, British foreign secretary between 1989 and 1995, who was serving as a young diplomat at the British mission to the UN during the Suez crisis: "In these few days our reputation at the UN was destroyed."[58] The British were treated as lepers by much of the UN community, with even the United States shunning them for months and excluding them from important meetings on Suez at the UN.[59]

In October 1956, six principles eventually emerged as a basis for resolving the Suez dispute: (1) free and open navigation through the Suez Canal; (2) respect for Egypt's sovereignty; (3) separation of the administration of the canal from the politics of any country; (4) agreement on tolls and charges between Cairo and canal users; (5) allotment of a fair share of dues from the canal to its development; and (6) settlement of outstanding issues between Egypt and the old Canal Company through arbitration.[60] These principles were, however, hard to reconcile as Cairo—supported strongly by Moscow and Belgrade—not unreasonably insisted on controlling the canal while showing flexibility in negotiating other issues. London and Paris, for their part, insisted on international administration of the canal. Nasser sought to rally his Third World allies at the UN and across the world and worked to cement the divisions between the Western allies, firmly and correctly believing that the United States wanted to supplant Britain and France in the Middle East.[61]

India, a leading member of the Non-Aligned Movement, at first tried to find a solution to the crisis. Nehru did not respect Nasser's intellect and privately felt that the nationalization of the Suez Canal was "intemperate and even warmongering." Nasser was disappointed with this even-handed approach, but once the invasion of Egypt had occurred New Delhi wholeheartedly backed Cairo, and Nehru noted: "I cannot imagine a worse case of aggression."[62] From this point on, India championed its Third World ally's position through the indefatigable eloquence of its legendary defense minister, Krishna Menon, who shuttled between Cairo, London, and New York in search of a diplomatic solution to the crisis. When Egypt refused to attend the London conference, India stepped in as its quasi representative, and Jawaharal Nehru himself personally conferred with Eden on the crisis. With the Soviets vetoing Anglo-French efforts to force Cairo to accept international control of the canal through the Users Association, the European neoimperalists moved from the diplomatic to the military battlefield, launching their premeditated invasion of Egypt, described above. Hammarskjöld, who had always thought that a diplomatic deal was there to be made, felt betrayed.[63] He would later reportedly break down in tears in the company of the British ambassador to the UN, as the physical strain of this tortuous crisis took its toll on the usually unflappable Swede.[64]

At the eleven-member UN Security Council meeting on 30 October 1956 (the Council's membership was increased to fifteen in 1965), Henry Cabot Lodge, the US permanent representative to the UN, called for an immediate Israeli withdrawal from Egypt. The United States and the Soviets then agreed on an unprecedented common course of action to support this decision. A clearly rattled Pierson Dixon halfheartedly read out Eden's earlier statement to the British House of Commons, explaining London's Suez policy, before casting his country's first-ever veto in the Security Council. France also cast a veto, and both permanent members continued to behave like wayward outlaws from the "wild West" telling Cabot Lodge that the Tripartite Declaration on the Middle East had been rendered a dead letter.[65] Among the Council's nonpermanent members, Australia and Belgium backed the Anglo-French position, while Yugoslavia—a founding member of NAM in 1955—strongly opposed the Suez invasion. It later turned out that London and Paris were negotiating in bad faith—it was during this period that they were also hatching the secret invasion with Israel at Sèvres.

Britain and France had launched their invasion of Egypt on 31 October 1956. At the General Assembly the next day, Pierson Dixon was implausibly seeking to persuade the UN to allow the Anglo-French force to fly the UN flag as peacemakers,[66] as the United States had done in Korea in 1950 due to a temporary Soviet boycott of the UN. Dulles entered the room to deliver an eloquent speech stating his commitment to the UN Charter and expressing regret at having to disagree so publicly with historic European allies. He then rejected a British suggestion to transfer authority from Anglo-French forces to a UN peacekeeping operation.[67]

On 2 November 1956, two days after the Anglo-French occupation of Egyptian territory, the UN General Assembly—under the Uniting for Peace resolution that had been crafted, ironically, by Western powers to bypass Soviet objections in the Security Council during the Korean war in 1950—adopted a US-drafted resolution calling for a ceasefire and the withdrawal of foreign troops, condemning the invasion of Egypt. Only five countries voted against: Britain, France, and Israel, as well as the two anglophile former "white dominions" of New Zealand and Australia. On 4 November 1956, another former "white dominion," Canada, acted more constructively through its foreign minister, Lester Pearson (assisted by the US State Department[68]), in asking Dag Hammarskjöld to establish a UN force to oversee a ceasefire and to provide a face-saving mechanism for the ill-conceived tripartite invasion. (Pearson won the Nobel Peace Prize for his efforts in 1957.) Hammarskjöld was at first skeptical about the idea of a UN peacekeeping force but was obliged by the General Assembly to explore the concept, with even London and Paris eventually supporting this face-saving climb down.[69] A day later, the General Assembly established the UN Emergency Force.

Amid this diplomatic flurry, Dwight Eisenhower found time to secure reelection as president of the United States on 6 November 1956. With a blustering Moscow threatening rocket attacks on London and Paris,[70] Eisenhower was careful to try to balance criticisms of the Anglo-French-Israeli actions with efforts not to antagonize European allies that he would need for future crises against the Soviet Union and radical Third World forces. The US president studiously avoided supporting any economic sanctions against London and Paris, and once Eden had agreed to withdraw from Egypt he arranged a $1 billion loan for Britain from the International Monetary Fund (IMF) and the US Export-Import Bank.[71] Eisenhower's behavior was as mature and measured as the Anglo-French action had been rash and reckless. A subsequent UN General Assembly resolution on 24 November 1956 called for the withdrawal of British and French troops from Egypt, which occurred by December 1956. Israel also withdrew from Egypt by March 1957, following strong US pressure and a threat by Eisenhower to support sanctions against Tel Aviv.

The UN Emergency Force's mandate gave the force four key responsibilities: to secure and supervise a ceasefire by creating a buffer zone between Anglo-French-Israeli and Egyptian forces; to oversee the withdrawal of foreign troops from Egypt; to patrol borders and deter military incursions; and to ensure implementation of the Egypt-Israel Armistice Agreements.[72] UNEF would also oversee exchange of prisoners, clear minefields, and investigate reported ceasefire violations. Hammarskjöld negotiated an agreement with Nasser in which Egypt's sovereignty would be respected, and Cairo agreed to maintain UNEF on its territory until it had fulfilled its mandate. The UN agreed not to function in Port Said or the Suez Canal areas, and its presence would be conditional on continued approval from the Egyptian government.[73] The UN Secretary-General was given forty-eight hours to submit a report for establishing UNEF, with no military planners or intelligence officers to guide him. For the first time in UN history, the soldiers would carry light arms.

The first peacekeepers arrived in Egypt in November 1956, and the six thousand–strong mission, with infantry, signals, and logistics units, consisted largely of troops from Brazil, Canada, Colombia, Denmark, Finland, India, Indonesia, Norway, Sweden, and Yugoslavia. The countries were carefully balanced to accommodate Egyptian and Israeli interests in a political trend that would continue throughout the history of UN peacekeeping. UNEF's 300-mile area of operation stretched from Gaza to Sharm el Sheikh. Israel did not allow any peacekeepers to deploy on its side of the border and destroyed roads and railway communications as it withdrew from Egypt.[74] In a trend that would affect the history of peacekeeping, with catastrophic consequences in Angola (1992) (see Chapter 4) and Rwanda (1994) (see Chapter 3), despite annual warnings from UNEF's Indian force commander Indar Rikhye, the mission's size continued to be reduced (at the urging of the main paymasters, the United States and Britain) by the Security Council to save costs. By the time of the force's withdrawal in May 1967, its troop strength stood at only 3,400.

Moscow supported the creation of UNEF but refused to pay assessed contributions to the mission (which was to be funded from the regular budget, with voluntary contributions expected to meet any shortfall). The Russians argued that Britain, France, and Israel—as the "aggressors"—should bear the costs of UNEF. By December 1960, $21.6 million—over 60 percent—of the UN's budget deficit of $34.6 million was due to UNEF.[75] After 1961, only Washington and London made voluntary contributions to the peacekeeping force to cover the deficit from the lack of payment by Moscow and its allies.[76] This marked the beginning of the financial crisis in UN peacekeeping that France would later exacerbate by refusing to contribute effectively to UNEF and the UN Operation in the Congo (see Chapter 3). UNEF expenses were $25 million in 1958 and declined to $14 million by 1967.[77]

The first armed UN mission effectively set the ground rules for future peacekeeping interventions: the UN Secretary-General selected participating countries and the force commander, while the five permanent members of the Security Council were excluded from the mission. This was done at the insistence of Eisenhower, who wanted to exclude not just the Anglo-French but also the Soviets.[78] The operation took into account geographical spread across regions, and the command center of the mission was based at the UN headquarters in New York, with a special representative reporting directly to the Secretary-General, guided by a force commander on the ground.[79]

Western Sahara: The Tragic Tale of a Referendum

The Sahara desert evokes images of the famed caravans traversing the great trade routes of one of Africa's wondrous geographical landmarks in ages past. The Western Sahara conflict, which has remained unresolved for over two and a half decades, must, however, qualify as one of the world's most neglected.[80] The referendum in the former Portuguese colony of East Timor in 1999,[81] which led to Indonesia's granting independence to the territory in 2002, failed to attract attention to the similar case of Western Sahara. East Timor and Western Sahara are, in fact, both cases of irresponsible Iberian decolonization. In the two cases, the territories were abandoned by colonial masters, Spain and Portugal, who did not bother to determine the wishes of the people before they left, leading to the military annexation of the territories by rampaging neighbors: Indonesia in East Timor and Morocco and Mauritania in Western Sahara. Independence movements waged guerrilla struggles in both territories to challenge what they saw as alien occupation. For decades, both Indonesia and Morocco were considered too important as allies of the West to trouble them with issues as "trivial" as self-determination. The fall of the autocratic Suharto regime in Indonesia resulted in a referendum and the granting of independence to East Timor in 2002. The death of King Hassan II of Morocco in

July 1999 and the coming to power of his son, Mohammed VI, has failed to produce a similar result in Western Sahara as of 2011.

I argue in this chapter that the failure to implement the UN-negotiated peace agreement to hold a referendum in Western Sahara has been due to four main factors. First, both belligerents, Morocco and the Frente Popular para la Liberación de Saguia el-Hamra y de Rio de Oro (POLISARIO Front), have transferred the military conflict that was waged for sixteen years between 1975 and 1991 to the diplomatic battlefield, and efforts at identifying voters for the referendum effectively became a proxy for waging war by other means. Second, the main external implementing agents of the peace agreement, the UN and the Organization of African Unity, were distrusted by both parties: POLISARIO regarded the UN as sympathetic to Morocco, while Rabat considered the OAU to be partial to POLISARIO. Third, the most powerful members of the UN Security Council did not show much interest in efforts to resolve this dispute. This situation was exacerbated by the fact that two of the five permanent members of the Security Council, the United States and France, were traditional allies of Morocco, protecting the kingdom and easing pressure on Rabat for fear of triggering domestic instability. Finally, the success of the two-decade ceasefire in Western Sahara has combined with these three other factors to reduce the urgency of finding a solution to the conflict.

Morocco, with the military advantage by the time of the peace plan, was content to drag out the process as long as it took to secure a referendum that would work to its advantage and legitimize its rule in the territory. Rabat also knew that the Western-dominated post–Cold War international order was more advantageous to it than to POLISARIO, whose main backer, Algeria, had experienced a civil war since military brass hats annulled elections that Islamists were poised to win in 1991 (at the subsequent cost of over one hundred thousand deaths) even as the voices of its mostly African allies were increasingly marginalized as the continent lost its strategic value to the West after the Cold War. This realization and the lack of Western pressure on Morocco emboldened the kingdom in its frustration of the UN's efforts.

POLISARIO became increasingly frustrated at efforts to stall the referendum process, but also contributed to delays due to its concerns about the UN's impartiality and its nervousness about a referendum process that it felt had been stacked in Morocco's favor. Thus, the failure to implement the peace plan in Western Sahara for two decades has been due to the frustrations resulting from the decision of both parties to opt for "jaw-jaw" over "war-war," their distrust of external implementers, the neglect of Western Sahara by potentially influential powers, and the lack of urgency resulting from military peace and slow progress in the referendum process.

The peace plan in Western Sahara contributed to some of the problems of implementation. Morocco's frequent refusal to negotiate directly with POLISARIO meant that the peace proposals on which the plan was based were negotiated separately with both sides by the UN, leaving the implementation of key points open to manipulation and differing interpretations. The vagueness of the plan's voting criteria led to predictable delays, since the interpretation of these criteria by the UN would determine the outcome of the referendum. This raised the stakes enormously for both sides to secure advantage in the interpretation of the voting criteria.

That the implementation of the plan became wholly dependent on the cooperation of the dominant Moroccan military and administrative presence in Western Sahara was also problematic for the UN, since such cooperation was not always forthcoming. Morocco quickly realized the strength of its position and the weakness of the UN's. It used this strength to delay the process at will. Rabat was confident in the knowledge that its Western allies would not threaten it with economic or military sanctions and was effectively still in charge of Western Sahara. This left the UN with few instruments to secure compliance from Morocco other than through diplomatic persuasion, a blunt instrument at the best of times. Thus, key parts of the peace plan were vague and imprecise, while the strategic environment in which it was to be implemented was far from conducive.

After providing a brief background on the roots of this conflict, which examines its domestic, regional, and external dimensions, I will discuss the peace plan that preceded the arrival of UN peacekeepers to Western Sahara in 1991. I then examine the difficulties faced by the UN in putting the plan into action due to differing interpretations by both sides. I analyze the effect of an increased US diplomatic presence on the implementation of the peace process from 1996 and assess the Baker plan of May 2001, which sought to avoid a lengthy appeals process, offering a detailed explanation for the failure to implement the peace plan between 2002 and 2010.

The Roots of a Desert Conflict

Western Sahara, a barren, desolate territory of unending sand in northwest Africa, was declared a Spanish protectorate in 1884.[82] Nomadic Saharan groups, who migrated long distances with their camels and goats in search of water and pasture, inhabited the territory. Being at the mercy of the gods of thunder and rain, they became known as "the sons of the clouds." The body that claims to speak for their descendants is the POLISARIO Front, a liberation movement founded by Saharan students in May 1973 to fight for independence against Spanish colonial rule. POLISARIO has today become something of an anachronism: a liberation movement seeking the political kingdom in a world that has largely assumed the end of decolonization, a political dinosaur in search of a giant Jurassic Park of rocky plains and golden sand dunes.[83]

The roots of this desert conflict lie in ancient claims by Morocco and Mauritania that their sultans and emirs had historically controlled Saharan groups who owed them sovereign allegiance. An International Court of Justice (ICJ) advisory opinion on 16 October 1975 challenged this view, noting that though there were legal ties of allegiance between their monarchs and some, but not all, Saharan groups in the past, these were not determinant in the issue of self-determination and did not constitute ties of territorial sovereignty since there was no administrative presence in the territory until Spanish conquistadors appeared. The ICJ supported the view of the UN General Assembly that the people of Western Sahara be allowed to determine their own future through a referendum.[84]

On 6 November 1975, King Hassan II, a shrewd politician who sat on the Moroccan throne from 1961 until his death in 1999, launched the Green March, named after the holy color of Islam, to pressure Spain to abandon the territory. He ordered 350,000 of his Koran-wielding and flag-waving subjects into the territory, claiming they were *mujahidin* fighting a *jihad* against Spanish infidels. Having unleashed these nationalist demons, Hassan II could not simply put a lid on them without serious political repercussions at home. Socioeconomic grievances had led to two narrowly failed military coups d'état in Morocco in 1971 and 1972 as the international price of phosphates fell and Morocco suffered severe droughts. The palace was especially keen not to be outflanked by nationalist opposition parties, particularly the Istiqlal party, on the issue of "Greater Morocco," a concept which, for a while, involved irredentist claims on western Algeria, northern Mali, and all of Mauritania and Western Sahara.

Having organized a census in Western Sahara on 1 December 1974 to prepare for a UN-supervised referendum in order to determine the wishes of the people of the territory, fascist Spain made a stunning volte-face. With Generalissimo Francisco Franco on his death bed, the territory was carved up between Morocco and Mauritania in the November 1975 Madrid Agreement. Under the accord, Morocco obtained the northern Saguia el-Hamra and Mauritania the southern Rio de Oro, while Spain maintained a 35 percent interest in the territory's rich phosphate deposits in Bou Craa and was granted fishing rights.

At the end of November 1975, Moroccan and Mauritanian troops entered the territory, and Spain beat a speedy retreat. The invasion led to a massive exodus of Saharans, with nearly half of the population embarking on a trek across the desert into the southwestern Algerian town of Tindouf. Over one hundred thousand Saharan refugees still eke out a destitute existence in refugee camps in this barren desert terrain, where POLISARIO has organized a mass of dedicated supporters. That Morocco was prepared to cede to Mauritania a third of the territory it had claimed in its entirety on historical grounds exposed the political expediency and moral bankruptcy involved in what Rabat had consistently presented as strictly legal claims.[85]

In February 1976, POLISARIO declared the Saharan Arab Democratic Republic (SADR) as a government-in-exile and sought diplomatic recognition. The Front avoided being placed in an ideological pigeonhole, despite Morocco's attempts to portray it as a stooge of Moscow in an era of Cold War. Though POLISARIO obtained some support from Soviet-allied states like Algeria and Libya, Moscow never recognized the SADR and refused POLISARIO's requests to open a bureau in the Soviet Union.

Following the annexation of the territory, POLISARIO's Saharawi People's Liberation Army (SPLA) embarked on a guerrilla war, concentrating on targets in Mauritania, the weaker of the two occupying states. French Jaguar jets intervened against POLISARIO on four occasions between December 1977 and May 1978, bombing and strafing POLISARIO targets. A military coup d'état in Mauritania in 1978 forced Nouakchott to sue for peace and withdraw from the conflict in August 1979, leaving Morocco and POLISARIO as the two combatants.

For the next two years, the fifteen thousand–strong SPLA's desert warriors roamed unchallenged across 80 percent of the territory, launching raids on the one hundred thousand Moroccan soldiers confined to two coastal enclaves, representing 16 percent of the territory. By 1980, Morocco decided on a military strategy of protecting the "useful triangle" from Tan Tan in the north to Smara in the east and the capital of Laayoune in the west, where much of the population was concentrated. Rabat started building six interlocking 2,700 kilometer–long fortified sand walls, known as the *berm,* with mines, barbed wire, and electronic warning devices. The tactic was effective enough that by April 1987, 80 percent of the territory and the main population centers were largely shielded from SPLA attacks. Though far from impregnable and still vulnerable to occasional POLISARIO military attacks, the berm altered the military balance in Morocco's favor. POLISARIO was reduced to controlling a sliver of barren desert territory in the south and east of the territory, establishing a headquarters in Bir Lahlou.

A political settlement to the conflict is complicated by the consensus that has emerged in Morocco on the "moroccanity" of the former Spanish Sahara between crown and citizens and political parties and press. Rabat has also invested much economic capital in the territory, building roads, ports, schools, and hospitals. Between 1976 and 1989, Morocco spent an estimated $430 million annually on military and civilian costs in the territory: an annual 3 percent of its gross domestic product (GDP).[86] There have been sporadic protests and opposition to its rule by POLISARIO supporters, for example in Laayoune and Smara in October 1992, which have been harshly suppressed.

Though Morocco managed to reverse the military tide, it was being outflanked on the diplomatic battlefield by POLISARIO. King Hassan II accepted an OAU "committee of wise men"[87] plan for a ceasefire, UN peacekeepers, and a UN-OAU referendum in June 1981 for the largely tactical reasons of warding off recognition of the SADR. By 1983, fifty states, within and outside Africa, had recognized the SADR, and the OAU was calling for direct talks. The UN General Assembly passed a resolution in December 1985 calling for direct talks and a referendum. Rabat increasingly employed stalling tactics to stretch out the process, to avoid censure from the OAU and the UN, and to prevent increased support for, or recognition of, the SADR. Morocco left the OAU in 1984 after twenty-six of its fifty-one members saw through this game and recognized the SADR as a member.[88] Despite Morocco's insistence that it would never negotiate directly with POLISARIO, direct talks have taken place between the two. King Hassan II received a high-level POLISARIO delegation in Marrakesh in January 1989, and details of the referendum, ceasefire arrangements, and exchange of prisoners were discussed.[89] There were also unsuccessful secret talks in 1978 (Bamako), 1983 (Algiers), 1985 (Lisbon), and 1988 (Taif). Fighting resumed in Western Sahara in early 1987 and continued sporadically until UN peacekeepers arrived in 1991.

External Friends and Foes

The Maghreb region has sometimes been compared to a bird, with Algeria, Mauritania, and Tunisia constituting the body and Morocco and Libya the necessary wings for the bird to fly.[90] But this is a bird that has been so incapacitated by conflict between its various body parts that it has had difficulty lifting off. Algeria seemed, at first, to have acquiesced to Moroccan and Mauritanian claims to the Sahara. After 1975, however, POLISARIO moved its base to Algeria from the Mauritanian town of Zouerate and found its strongest backer in a country keen to curtail Morocco's regional ambitions. As Algerian leader, from 1965 to 1978, Colonel Houari Boumedienne put it: "I am not like Christ. I will not turn the other cheek."[91] Algerian troops entered Western Sahara to help evacuate Saharan refugees in November 1975. Algeria and Morocco had fought a brief border war—the "War of the Sands"—in October 1963, and Algeria's military brass hats, particularly under Boumedienne, felt that any weakness shown to Morocco could revive irredentist claims on parts of Algerian Sahara.[92]

During the Cold War, the relationship also involved a clash of systems with a "radical," pro-Soviet Algerian military regime pursuing a socialist economic system pitted against a "moderate," pro-Western Moroccan monarchy pursuing a liberal economy.[93] Both countries harbored each other's dissidents. The Western Sahara effectively became a stage on which the rivalry for the leadership of the Maghreb was played out.[94] Algiers wanted an independent but subordinate Western Sahara that would block Morocco's path to the south.[95] Algeria provided a sanctuary for Saharan refugees, a base for POLISARIO raids, and military training, fuel, and supplies. One of the most respected states in Third World diplomacy, Algiers energetically championed the POLISARIO cause at the UN, OAU, and NAM, encouraging member states to recognize the SADR. After French aerial attacks on POLISARIO guerillas in 1977, Boumedienne nationalized French holdings and withheld state contracts from French firms.

The main external actors in the Sahara dispute were France, Spain, and the United States. France provided much military and diplomatic support to Morocco, a country of strategic value to Gallic efforts to maintain a neo-colonial sphere of influence in Africa. Paris supplied Rabat with Mirage and Alpha jets and other arms and strongly supported Morocco's Sahara policies in the UN Security Council. Under President Giscard d'Estaing (1974–1981), Paris also provided military arms and training to Mauritania. But the socialist regime of François Mitterrand (1981–1995) attempted to balance its relations with Rabat and Algiers better by refusing to sell Morocco advanced Mirage jets in 1985, while still supplying it with other military equipment. France had lucrative commercial relations with Algeria in its oil and gas sectors, but commercial relations suffered under Giscard. Under Mitterrand, POLISARIO was allowed to open an office in Paris.

With Portugal withdrawing from Africa in 1974, Spanish colonialism was looking increasingly anachronistic. Under intense pressure from the UN General Assembly, Madrid had announced a self-determination referendum in Western Sahara for early 1975. A residual feeling of national guilt in post-Franco Spain over its irresponsible decolonization in Western Sahara perhaps explains the sympathy that POLISARIO enjoys among large sections of Spanish public opinion, though government policy has tended to tilt toward Rabat. When Felipe Gonzales's socialists swept to power in 1982, it seemed a more pro-POLISARIO policy might be adopted. In opposition, Gonzales had sharply condemned the Madrid agreement of 1975, visited the Tindouf refugee camps, and expressed support for the self-determination of Western Sahara.

Once in power, Gonzales continued to provide Morocco with much of its arms, signed a fishing agreement with Rabat in 1983 that covered the waters of Western Sahara, and concluded a bilateral trade agreement with Morocco in 1988. POLISARIO's frequent attacks on Spanish fishing vessels in Saharan waters from 1977 led to friction with Spain, which expelled POLISARIO representatives from Madrid in September 1985 after its guerrillas killed a Spanish sailor. The office was only reopened in 1989. Madrid continues rhetorically to support Saharan self-determination at the UN and has striven to improve its relations with Algeria, a major gas supplier to Spain. Madrid, like Paris and Washington, had to balance close diplomatic ties with Morocco with lucrative commercial ties with Algeria.[96]

The United States has maintained an official policy of neutrality in Western Sahara, recognizing neither Moroccan sovereignty nor the SADR.

Washington has rhetorically supported a self-determination referendum. But in practice, US policy has tended to favor Morocco, a strategic ally in the region. King Hassan II had strongly and covertly backed Egyptian leader Anwar Sadat's peace efforts toward Israel and sent troops to Zaire (now the Democratic Republic of Congo) in 1977 and 1978 to rescue the pro-Western regime of Mobutu Sese Seko. Though President Jimmy Carter withdrew arms sales to Morocco in 1976 to protest its use of US-supplied fighter planes in Western Sahara, this trade was resumed within three years. Washington provided Morocco with armored vehicles, and American companies supplied electronic detection devices for the construction of the berm in Western Sahara.

Under Ronald Reagan's presidency, American military aid to Morocco was tripled to $100 million a year. Rabat reciprocated by granting transit facilities for the US Rapid Deployment Force for Middle East emergencies in a Cold War era of holy crusades in search of communist infidels. Between 1980 and 1987, Morocco received 20 percent of all American aid to Africa, totaling over $1 billion in military assistance alone.[97] Moroccan and US defense ministers met regularly under a joint military consultative commission set up in 1984. Washington, like Paris, has, however, tried to balance its interests with Algiers and Rabat, while isolating its Libyan bête noire: Muammar Qaddafi. By 1977, the United States replaced France as Algeria's main trading partner, receiving 56 percent of Algeria's oil exports. By 1988, bilateral trade with Algeria was $2.6 billion compared to $391 million with Morocco.[98] Algerian leader Chadli Benjedid helped negotiate an end to the hostage crisis in Iran in 1980. Less radical than Boumedienne, he strove for better relations with Washington and its Western allies. Having assessed the regional and external dimensions of the conflict, I next turn our attention back to the peace plan for Western Sahara.

The Settlement Plan, August 1988–September 1991

A détente occurred in August 1988 following the efforts of Peruvian UN Secretary-General Javier Pérez de Cuéllar, who used his "good offices" to secure an agreement between Morocco and POLISARIO for a referendum to "enable the people of Western Sahara in the exercise of their right to self-determination, to choose between independence and integration with Morocco."[99] The UN would organize the referendum in cooperation with the OAU, and all Saharans in the 1974 Spanish census and those aged eighteen or over would constitute the electorate. De Cuéllar outlined a settlement plan in two reports to the Security Council in June 1990 and April 1991.

The main points of the plan involved a six-month transitional period encompassing: a ceasefire and declaration of D-Day; an exchange of prisoners supervised by the International Committee of the Red Cross (ICRC) and release of Saharan political prisoners within one week; UN control of key aspects of administration in the territory within two months; a reduction of Moroccan troops in the territory from one hundred thousand to sixty-five thousand within eleven weeks; disarmament and the confinement of the soldiers of both sides to designated locations within eleven weeks; the return, within six weeks, of about 120,000 Saharan refugees from Algeria and Mauritania starting eleven weeks after D-Day under the supervision of the Office of the UN High Commissioner for Refugees (UNHCR); the identification and registration of voters; the organization of a referendum involving a three-week campaign, seventeen weeks after the declaration of the ceasefire; and, finally, the withdrawal, within six weeks of the referendum, of Moroccan soldiers or the demobilization of POLISARIO troops, depending on the outcome of the vote.[100]

A military unit, of 1,850 soldiers at full strength, had the five-fold tasks of monitoring the ceasefire; overseeing the confinement of troops and arms to designated locations; verifying the reduction of troops; providing security for returning Saharan refugees; and monitoring the withdrawal or disarming of soldiers after the referendum.[101] They were also expected to be involved in mine clearing, basic infrastructure repair, and the operation of water points.[102] Before the referendum, the military unit of the UN Mission for the Referendum in Western Sahara (MINURSO) was also expected to oversee the neutralization of the paramilitary units of the Moroccan police force in the territory and to monitor the deposit of their weapons, ammunition, and military equipment in UN-protected armories.[103]

Who Is a Saharan? September 1991–August 1994

MINURSO was, for most of its first decade, a $60 million a year effort consisting of about six hundred peacekeepers from nearly seventy countries. Despite a promising start with the commencement of a ceasefire and the arrival of two hundred UN military observers on 6 September 1991, an impasse ensued that rendered impossible the expected January 1992 referendum, as both parties embarked on an arcane dispute over the criteria for identifying voters. This delayed the transitional process that was meant to follow automatically, deprived the UN of its powers to administer the territory during the transitional period, and halted implementation of the settlement plan for the next three years.

Controversy erupted in December 1991 when Pérez de Cuéllar expanded the criteria in a way that was widely believed, at the time, to favor Morocco. This was done in his last report to the Security Council on the eve of his departure as UN Secretary-General. From an electorate that was based entirely on the Spanish census of 1974, potential voters would now be able to claim other ties to the territory. King Hassan had sent De Cuéllar a proposal asking for the expansion.[104] Press reports of the UN Secretary-General's business interests in Morocco did not help allay suspicions of his lack of impartiality:

after his retirement, De Cuéllar was appointed to the board of Omnium Nord Africain, a Moroccan-owned holding company.[105] Some of the UN Secretary-General's aides later noted that the Secretary-General felt the vote would be in favor of integration, that Morocco needed to be appeased as the stronger party, and that the dispute was really between Morocco and Algeria.[106]

The two primary requirements for inclusion in the referendum are an age barrier of at least eighteen years old by 31 December 1993 and membership in one of the eighty-eight subfactions of the ten groups listed in the 1 December 1974 census conducted by colonial Spain.[107] POLISARIO objected vehemently to the expansion of the criteria beyond the revised 1974 census list and considered this to be a ploy by Rabat to flood the referendum with non-Saharans. The Moroccans, on the other hand, urged the widening of the criteria, arguing that Saharan migrants resident in Morocco, as well as the great-grandchildren of people born in the territory, be included in the referendum.[108] Rabat also wanted descendants of Saharans who had fled the territory after a Franco-Spanish raid in 1960 and settled around Goulimine to be included in the polling.[109] In the end, the fourth criterion regarding descendants of Saharans born outside the territory was limited to just one generation.

POLISARIO objected strongly to the extension of Moroccan municipal elections to Western Sahara in October 1992. These resulted in public demonstrations, and POLISARIO accused Morocco of heavy-handedness in arresting some demonstrators. The influx of forty thousand Moroccans into the territory after 1991 was described by some as a "second green march." It was felt that whatever the outcome of the referendum, Morocco was creating demographic facts on the ground that would make its departure from the territory difficult to imagine. By 1993, an estimated one hundred thousand Moroccan settlers had entered the territory.[110] The aristocratic former Pakistani foreign minister Sahabzada Yaqub-Khan was appointed UN special representative in 1992. This proved to be a controversial appointment, since Yaqub-Khan was known to be a friend of King Hassan II. Not surprisingly, POLISARIO never trusted him and eventually refused to do business with him, accusing him of doing the bidding of the Moroccan crown. The new UN Secretary-General, Boutros Boutros-Ghali, was himself close to the Moroccan ruling elite and had campaigned forcefully against the OAU's recognition of SADR in 1984 while serving as Egypt's minister of state for foreign affairs. As POLISARIO's representative in New York, Ahmed Boukhari confirmed: "We never felt Boutros-Ghali would be neutral because he was close to Morocco."[111]

After a visit to the region in June 1993, Boutros-Ghali presented compromise proposals to both parties on the voting criteria. The first direct talks between Morocco and POLISARIO were held in the Western Saharan capital of Laayoune under UN auspices from 17 to 19 July 1993. Boutros-Ghali suggested "compromise proposals" that would keep the five criteria, with three conditions: eligible subfactions would be included in the census; oral testimony would be taken into account where no documentation existed; and both sides would be allowed to send representatives to observe the process. Washington had been involved behind the scenes in pushing both sides to meet directly,[112] showing clearly the influence it could bring to bear, particularly on Morocco. The identification commission and civilian police unit started arriving in Western Sahara in May 1993 to begin their work. In November 1993, the identification commission published the revised list of the 1974 census.

In March 1994, Erik Jensen, a Malaysian of Danish origin, replaced the controversial Yaqub-Khan as chief of mission. Jensen had the advantage of having served as the chairman of the identification commission since May 1993 and was thus conversant with the key players and the process. An Oxford-trained anthropologist, he also had an extraordinary grasp of the intricacies of the arcane system of groups and subfactions that many before him had failed to master. Jensen met with both parties in Tindouf and Rabat in April and May 1994 and deserves credit for devising many of the innovative rules to guide the identification process. Following two days of mammoth negotiating sessions in Tindouf, POLISARIO agreed to start identifying and registering voters. Both sides submitted application forms to the UN in May 1994.

There was a slight delay in the identification process after Morocco refused to accept the presence of OAU observers. Rabat accused the continental body of having prejudged the outcome of the referendum by recognizing the SADR and demanded that the organization suspend the participation of the SADR in its activities until after the referendum. As Ahmed Snoussi, Morocco's former permanent representative at the UN, put it: "We consider that the OAU has been creating an illegal, illegitimate situation. Recognizing a people that have no flag or territory is a clear violation of the OAU Charter."[113] While POLISARIO regarded the OAU presence as a necessary balance to the UN, whose leadership it distrusted, Rabat insisted on a preponderant UN role and distrusted the OAU. In the end, a compromise was agreed in July 1994 by which OAU chairman, former Tunisian leader Ben Ali, designated four OAU officials, naming two as his "personal representatives." Morocco eventually submitted 176,533 application forms for potential voters in Western Sahara and southern Morocco (of which about one hundred thousand lived in Morocco), POLISARIO supplied 42,468 forms for potential electors in Algeria, and 14,468 applications were received for applicants in Mauritania. The total number of applicants thus came to 233,487.[114]

Searching for Saharans, September 1994–May 1996

The identification process finally got underway on 28 August 1994. The identification commissioners reviewed the evidence and testimony before making a final decision within twenty-four hours of interviews. The identification of voters took place in the Western Saharan towns of Laayoune, Smara, Dakhla, and Boujdour; in refugee camps in the Algerian town of Tindouf, namely *wilayas* Awsard, El-Aiun, Dakhla, and Smara; and in the Mauritanian towns of Atar, Nouadhibou, and Zouerate. In 1998, identification was extended to the Moroccan towns of Casablanca, Rabat, Marrakesh, El Kelaa Des Sraghna, Sidi Kalem, Tan Tan, and Goulimine. Both parties manipulated the indispensability of the sheiks to the process (to verify the identity of members of their clans) to stall progress. They sometimes refused to accept replacements for deceased sheikhs or announced to incredulous UN officials that sheikhs had mysteriously vanished to Las Palmas, Bilbao, Havana, or Nouakchott without leaving forwarding addresses. Sheiks sometimes genuinely fell ill, and severe sandstorms also delayed their transportation to identification centers. The sad case of the missing sheikhs became an almost farcical part of MINURSO folklore.[115]

During a visit by the UN Secretary-General to the region in November 1994, POLISARIO secretary-general, Mohammed Abdelaziz, urged Boutros-Ghali to arrange direct talks with Morocco, as well as a conference involving members of the UN Security Council and other interested parties, in order to resolve sensitive issues including the postreferendum settlement. He also complained about the large number of application forms submitted by Morocco at the last minute.[116] Amid frequent interruptions in identification over acceptance of substitute sheiks and contentious subfactions, a UN Security Council team of six ambassadors visited the region in June 1995 to observe the situation for themselves. The Security Council seemed to be growing increasingly frustrated with the endless breakdowns in the identification process in a journey without maps that seemed to drift precariously between tragedy and farce. In a replay of the South West African People's Organization (SWAPO) actions in attempting to keep troops in northern Namibia (see Chapter 4), POLISARIO's deputy secretary-general, Bachir Mustapha Sayed, insisted to the UN delegation that POLISARIO would maintain its troops in the "liberated territories" east of the berm.[117]

Human Rights Watch reported that Morocco had arrested and detained hundreds of Saharans in the territory, some of whom were released days or months later. There were allegations of torture during detentions. In June 1991, Morocco had released over two hundred Saharans who had "disappeared" for challenging Rabat's claims to the territory, some reportedly for almost two decades. There are continuing reports of unresolved cases of "disappearances" in the Sahara.[118] In a sign that some of the inhabitants of Western Sahara were unhappy with continued Moroccan rule, demonstrations took place in Smara on 17 November 2001 during which several dozen Saharans were arrested.[119] POLISARIO continued in the same period to detain 1,362 Moroccan prisoners of war despite calls by the UN for their release.

Two incidents further eroded POLISARIO's confidence in the UN's impartiality. First, following South African president Nelson Mandela's sending of a letter to Mohammed Abdelaziz pledging recognition of the SADR, Boutros-Ghali intervened to convince Tshwane (Pretoria) not to extend such recognition, which he considered detrimental to the referendum. Second, addressing the Security Council in October 1995, Boutros-Ghali made the curious statement that the identification process was only a means to encourage negotiations and suggested that it was never intended to be completed.[120] The Egyptian UN Secretary-General had in fact never envisaged a referendum in Western Sahara.[121]

With the identification process effectively stalled, a desperate Boutros-Ghali began to call on powerful members of the UN Security Council to consider holding secret talks with the parties to resolve the obstacles to the implementation of the settlement plan. In January 1996, he dispatched senior Indian UN official, Chinmaya Gharekhan, to the region in a bid to narrow the differences between both sides. During the visit, Morocco appeared to soften its stance on direct talks with POLISARIO, expressing doubts about their efficacy but not totally rejecting them. POLISARIO secretary-general Mohammed Abdelaziz again suggested the creation of a "contact group" for Western Sahara with the involvement of influential regional and nonregional states.[122] POLISARIO was clearly hoping that external pressure from powerful Security Council members like France and the United States could help force Morocco to the negotiating table and lead to discussions on a postreferendum phase.

Secret talks held in Rabat and Geneva in 1996 became caught up in Boutros-Ghali's tussle with Washington in an unsuccessful bid to retain his post as UN Secretary-General.[123] The talks failed despite the presence of high-powered delegations sent by Morocco and POLISARIO. By the time identification was halted in December 1995, only 60,112 out of 233,487 persons had been identified. In May 1996, Boutros-Ghali suggested that identification be suspended until both parties mustered the political will to overcome the obstacles. Most of the UN civilian staff and civilian police were withdrawn from the territory, leaving a small political office to continue consultations with the parties and leaving behind 223 military observers to monitor the ceasefire.

Pax Americana? June 1996–January 2000
On 10 February 1997, the UN General Assembly adopted a resolution calling for direct talks between the parties, which POLISARIO accepted but Morocco rejected. A month later James Baker III, the respected former US secretary of state, was appointed the UN special envoy for Western Sahara by new UN Secretary-General, Ghana's Kofi Annan. From 23 to 28 April 1997, Baker traveled to Algiers, Nouakchott, Rabat, and Tindouf, and heard both sides reiterate their commitment to the settlement plan.

During the UN envoy's visit to the refugee camps in Tindouf, POLIS-ARIO and its supporters constantly drew the analogy between their case and that of Kuwait in 1990, knowing that Baker had played an important role in the international effort to liberate Kuwait following an invasion by Iraqi autocrat Saddam Hussein. Both Iraq and Morocco's irredentist claims were based on historical grounds that no other country recognized. In one case, a US-led coalition acted swiftly to reverse the Iraqi annexation and restore an absolutist monarchy to power; in the other case, Washington and its allies condoned the annexation of another absolutist monarch and supplied it with arms. As critics of Western policy noted, Kuwait had oil, while Western Sahara had phosphates.

The first round of direct talks between both parties was held in Lisbon in June 1997. At the end of the meeting, Baker presented "bridging proposals" on identification to both sides, which they accepted. A second round of talks was held in London in July 1997, during which both sides accepted a compromise on the identification of potential voters for a referendum.[124] A third round of direct talks was held in Lisbon in August 1997, during which the parties agreed on issues related to the confinement of troops and release of Saharan political prisoners and exchange of prisoners of war. No more than two thousand POLISARIO troops were to be confined in the territory east of the berm and no more than three hundred in Mauritania, with the rest confined in Algeria. Both sides also agreed that all political prisoners and prisoners of war would be released in accordance with the settlement plan. In September 1997, a fourth round of talks was held in Houston, Texas, again brokered by a blunt-talking Baker, who warned both sides that he did not need success in the Sahara to add to his historical legacy. Both sides agreed on a code of conduct for the referendum campaign over which they had wrangled for the previous two years.[125]

The participation of such a prominent American envoy, with strong backing from the Bill Clinton administration, was considered crucial in wringing concessions from both sides, neither of which wanted to be fingered by Washington for stalling agreement. The United States was a strong ally of Morocco's, which therefore felt obliged to cooperate with its diplomatic efforts. POLISARIO had consistently demanded the attention of powerful states as a way of pressuring Morocco to hold a referendum. In February 1998, former US ambassador to Algeria, Charles Dunbar, replaced Erik Jensen as chief of MINURSO and UN special representative in Western Sahara. Even with Baker as special envoy, it was felt within the UN Secretariat that an American presence on the ground would also be helpful in securing the cooperation of both parties.

With the commitment of Morocco and POLISARIO to completing identification and fulfilling their other commitments under the settlement plan, MINURSO optimistically proposed a referendum for 7 December

1997. Identification, however, resumed only in December 1997 after a two-year hiatus.[126] The release of the results of eligible voters identified by the UN to both sides increased Morocco's nervousness. It was becoming clear that as many as 40 percent of applicants, many presented by Rabat, were being rejected for not meeting the voting criteria. The Moroccan press launched a vitriolic press campaign against MINURSO, and public demonstrations and protests were staged against the negative testimony of sheiks from the POLISARIO side.[127] The resignation of Charles Dunbar in March 1999, in apparent frustration at the difficult mandate and slow progress, was a stark reminder of the arduous road that the UN would still have to travel before arriving at a referendum. Dunbar was replaced by another American diplomat, William Eagleton.

The release of the results of eligible voters identified by MINURSO to both sides by January 2000 showed that as many as 109,177 applicants, many presented by Rabat, were rejected for not meeting the voting criteria. Only 86,412 out of 195,589 applicants were found eligible by the UN.[128] This bolstered POLISARIO's confidence. The roughly seventy-two thousand persons in the revised 1974 Spanish census formed the core of this electoral roll, as POLISARIO had consistently demanded. Nearly forty thousand of these successful applicants were thought to be POLISARIO supporters based mostly in the refugee camps and in Mauritania, while Morocco was less certain about the allegiances of the other successful applicants based largely in Western Sahara. Rabat would almost certainly have lost a referendum based on these figures. Morocco thus effectively spent the next decade stalling implementation of the "settlement plan."

The Baker Plan, February 2001–February 2002

In May 2001, James Baker announced that Morocco was prepared to offer some devolution of authority to Western Sahara. Baker traveled to Algiers on 5 May 2001 to present what he described as a draft "framework agreement on the status of Western Sahara." The special envoy also reviewed the draft agreement with the POLISARIO leadership in Tindouf. The proposed agreement offered the people of the Western Sahara a five-year transitional government in which the 86,412 people on the UN voter list would elect an executive to run the territory for four years, while a legislature would be elected by people who were eighteen and older and had been resident in the territory since October 1998 or listed on the repatriation list in October 2000. This legislature would then elect the executive for the last year of the five-year transition. The executive would be responsible for administration of the territory but leave foreign relations and defense under Moroccan sovereignty, while using Morocco's flag and currency. After five years, a referendum would determine the final status of Western Sahara, in which all full-time residents of the territory in the preceding year could vote.[129]

POLISARIO predictably rejected the proposal as a deviation from the settlement plan.[130] Algeria's rejection of the Baker plan was total. Algiers accused the plan of being biased in favor of Morocco's integration vision, of ignoring progress made in the referendum process, of abandoning the settlement plan, and of ignoring the UN's own basic principles of decolonization and self-determination.[131] Several critics of the plan described it as based largely on a devolution plan hatched in Rabat.[132] Unsurprisingly, only Morocco welcomed the proposal and was prepared to discuss its modalities. At a meeting with James Baker in Wyoming in August 2001, Algeria and POLISARIO reiterated their rejection of his plan. The decision not to invite Morocco to Wyoming was seen by Algeria as further proof that the Baker plan had originated from Rabat.[133] POLISARIO, for its part, saw an invisible French hand pushing Baker to support this plan, while the American diplomat had overestimated Paris's leverage in pushing it through the UN Security Council. As Ahmed Boukhari, POLISARIO's representative in New York put it: "The main obstacle to peace in our region is not Morocco but France. Morocco is a tool."[134] POLISARIO's depiction of Morocco as a French puppet echoed Rabat's continued reference to an Algerian puppeteer controlling POLISARIO.

The Baker proposal would effectively have legitimized Morocco's population transfers to the territory since 1991 and allowed non-Saharan voters to participate in the referendum, contrary to the UN's decade-long efforts to identify authentic Saharan voters. The UN Security Council reacted in a lukewarm manner to the Baker plan, though it did urge the UN special envoy to continue pursuing all options with both sides.[135] Baker's previous image as an "honest broker" was badly damaged by this proposal. Despite the arrival in Western Sahara in December 2001 of the third US diplomat in a row, William Swing, as the UN special representative, Washington was increasingly perceived, particularly since Baker was close to the George W. Bush administration, to be moving away from the settlement plan and closer to France's more openly partisan approach.

France remained Morocco's staunchest supporter. During a visit to Morocco in early December 2001, President Jacques Chirac described Western Sahara as "the southern provinces of Morocco"[136] contrary to international law. A permanent member of the UN Security Council, France, thus appeared to have prejudged the outcome of any future referendum organized by the world body. Equally alarming for POLISARIO, TotalFina Elf and Kerr McGee, a French and a US oil company respectively, signed unprecedented agreements with Morocco in November 2001 to prospect for oil in the waters of Western Sahara.[137] The UN legal department ruled in 2002 that a Moroccan oil exploration contract in Western Sahara was illegal.[138] Ghanaian UN Secretary-General Kofi Annan, always susceptible to pressure from Paris and Washington, lent his full support to the Baker plan.

POLISARIO criticized him for abdicating what it saw as his responsibility to be a guarantor of the UN's commitment to Western Sahara.[139] Like his predecessor had done with Mandela, Annan, for a while, managed to convince South African president Thabo Mbeki to delay recognition of the SADR, further ruffling POLISARIO feathers. Rabat had talked to Annan as well as French president Jacques Chirac and the Bill Clinton administration to persuade Mbeki to postpone a decision that Mandela had promised the POLISARIO leadership as early as 1994. Only in 2004, did South Africa finally recognize the SADR.[140]

The Baker plan was fraught with other dangers for POLISARIO. Once the international community had recognized Moroccan sovereignty over Western Sahara, any military action undertaken by Rabat in the territory could be considered by external powers like France and the United States, who had scarcely questioned Morocco's continued military occupation of the territory, as a purely internal affair. POLISARIO would then have to rely on strictly moral pressure without the benefit of legal remedies: recent lessons from the initially lethargic international response to East Timor, Kosovo, and Chechnya could not have been too encouraging for POLISARIO in this regard. The Baker plan also left the impression that the UN was transforming itself from impartial referee to putting on the jersey of one side and playing on its team. It was almost as if the UN, having spent ten years organizing a referendum that some of its senior members now thought Morocco might lose, wanted to change the rules that it was instrumental in setting until an outcome guaranteeing Morocco's victory could be assured.

Algerian president, Abdelaziz Bouteflika (who had followed this issue since his time as his country's foreign minister between 1962 and 1978), visited Baker in Houston in November 2001 and expressed his willingness to discuss or negotiate a possible partition of the territory.[141] It was unclear the extent to which POLISARIO had been consulted before this Algerian proposal was made. This suggestion also diluted the previous insistence by Algiers and POLISARIO on strictly applying the UN's principles of self-determination to the whole territory of Western Sahara. If both sides were eventually to accept the idea of partition, negotiations would be complicated by difficulties over how much territory each side would obtain and how to share phosphate and fishing resources as well as potentially oil-rich waters. Such negotiations would be protracted and could drag on for years. The promise of the plan, however, lay in the fact that its success would allow both sides to have both physical territory and diplomatic recognition and enable them to claim magnanimous victory.

At a closed-door briefing to the UN Security Council in February 2002, a clearly frustrated James Baker urged the Council to stop dragging its feet on the Sahara issue. The special envoy compared the Council's actions to continuing to supply drugs to an addict without penalizing him for a failure to kick his habit. Baker noted that the Sahara issue would never be resolved without requiring one party to do what it was unwilling to do. Each side would have to settle for some, but not all, of what it wanted. In a stunning admission, Baker conceded that there were valid objections to the draft framework plan he had presented in May 2001. He also challenged a British suggestion that an independent Western Sahara may not be a viable state. During the Council session, France predictably supported the continuation of the status quo in Western Sahara, which favored its Moroccan ally. The French representative compared the Sahara case to Lebanon and Cyprus, dismissed the viability of the settlement plan that the UN had supposedly been attempting to implement over the last decade, and poured cold water on any proposed partition plan.[142]

The Sad Case of the Somnolent Security Council, March 2002–December 2010

This dispute has dragged on for another decade with little prospect of a settlement in sight. The stalemate was exacerbated when Morocco rejected the peace plan in April 2004 on the basis that it would not accept a referendum with independence as an option. Experienced Peruvian diplomat Alvaro de Soto served as the UN special representative in Western Sahara between October 2003 and May 2005. Like his predecessors, he was, however, unable to achieve a diplomatic breakthrough as the Moroccans continued to insist on recognition of their sovereignty over the territory and POLISARIO continued to push for a self-determination referendum. Demonstrations by Saharans in the territory, which also continued between 2005 and 2010, were often harshly suppressed by Moroccan security forces. In one incident in October 2005, a young Saharan demonstrator died from injuries sustained during a protest in Laayoune, following which the Moroccan military presence was increased in all the major towns of the territory.[143] By October 2005, POLISARIO had released 404 Moroccan prisoners, some of whom had been held for two decades. Rabat also periodically released jailed Saharan political activists. Italian diplomat Francesco Bastagli replaced de Soto as special representative in August 2005, serving until September 2006.

Plain-speaking Dutchman Peter van Walsum was appointed as the UN Secretary-General's personal envoy for Western Sahara (a roving position different from the Laayoune-based special representative) in July 2005, serving until August 2008. He traveled tirelessly to the region and consulted influential Western governments as well as the African Union commission in Addis Ababa. He often offered incisive and blunt analysis of the issues. Briefing the UN Security Council in January 2006, van Walsum noted that none of the Council members had used their influence to try to convince Morocco to hold a referendum that would allow for self-determination, a principle the UN itself had consistently insisted on applying to the territory.

The special envoy regarded self-determination as applicable to the case of Western Sahara but called for a compromise between "international legality" and "political reality." He argued that since the Council had acquiesced in Morocco's rejection of the Baker Plan and was unprepared to impose a solution on Rabat, only two options remained: continuing the stalemate indefinitely or arranging direct negotiations between the two parties. The Dutchman dismissed the first option as unsustainable and called on Rabat's friends on the Council to push for negotiations as well as for Algeria to be invited to take part in direct negotiations.

Exposing its partisan irresponsibility and failure to uphold international legality, the somnolent UN Security Council had, by 2006, even given up calling for a referendum in Western Sahara in its resolutions.[144] Even new UN Secretary-General, South Korea's Ban Ki-moon, was forced to concede in October 2007 that a Security Council resolution that year was "more elaborate about the Moroccan proposal than about the Frente Polisario."[145] During his frank January 2006 briefing to the UN Security Council, van Walsum had exposed the cynicism of external powers who continued to attempt to remain on good terms with both Algiers and Rabat by selectively telling both sides what they thought they wanted to hear regarding the Western Sahara. The Dutch diplomat went on to note that this case was not high on the agenda of many countries, hinting that many states seemed content with the stalemate.[146] The European Union's signing of a fisheries agreement with Rabat in July 2006 that covered the waters of Western Sahara again illustrated the cynicism of external actors. POLISARIO reacted strongly against any attempts to negotiate a settlement on the basis of a referendum that excluded independence and was unhappy with van Walsum's elevating Algiers as a party to the conflict, a consistent approach by Rabat to downplay POLISARIO's role and portray it as an Algerian puppet.

British diplomat Julian Harston was appointed UN special representative in February 2007 and served until February 2009. He was replaced by Egyptian technocrat Hany Abdel-Aziz in November 2009. The first direct talks between Rabat and the POLISARIO Front since 2000 were held at the Greentree Estate in New York in June 2007, but they failed to achieve any substantive progress. A second meeting in the same venue two months later also ended in a similar stalemate. Morocco again provocatively held parliamentary elections in Western Sahara in September 2007. A third and fourth round of direct talks were held in New York in January and March 2008, again chaired by Peter van Walsum. The meetings confirmed the gulf between the two parties: the most that could be agreed upon at these sessions was an extension of family visits between Western Sahara and POLISARIO camps in Algeria.

Van Walsum was replaced (after apparently having incurred the wrath of the Algerians)[147] as the UN Secretary-General's personal envoy by

Christopher Ross, the former US ambassador to Algeria. Washington's increasingly close cooperation with Algeria in combating terrorism appeared to offer opportunities to apply pressure on POLISARIO. Ross, however, was unsuccessful in convincing Algiers to become directly involved in negotiations as a party to the dispute.[148] He convened informal talks between the two parties in Dürnstein, Austria, in August 2009, and in New York in February and November 2010. The November 2010 talks were held just after a Moroccan raid on a tent city outside Laayoune of about twelve thousand Saharans protesting against discrimination and lack of employment opportunities, in which fatalities were reported.[149] Ross, however, continued the same futile routine as his predecessors in a game that was beginning to resemble the 1993 movie *Ground Hog Day,* in which an egocentric weatherman—played by Bill Murray—gets caught in a blizzard and keeps reliving the same day over and over again. Albert Einstein's famous expression that insanity is doing the same thing over and over again and hoping for a different result also came readily to mind. The Western Sahara case had now become a farcical charade in which the parties pretended to negotiate, the mediators pretended to mediate, and the Security Council pretended to show concern at the continuing stalemate.

Two decades have now passed since the UN arrived on a four-month mission in September 1991 to organize a referendum to determine the territory's future. The world body still had 233 peacekeepers in Western Sahara in April 2010 (working alongside a small AU observer delegation) in a mission costing $53.5 million annually. Another generation of Saharan refugees has tragically been born, and grown up, in the harsh conditions of Algerian refugee camps. In December 2010, only 20 percent of Laayoune's population consisted of Saharans, as Morocco continued to create demographic facts on the ground.[150] The Moroccan/Algerian border also remained closed in December 2010. As the UN Security Council fell deeper into its slumber, the people of Western Sahara continued to be denied the right to determine their own future, and Morocco's stealing of the Sahara continued to go unpunished.

Concluding Reflections

The UN's priority in Western Sahara remained to complete the identification process as a way of locking both sides into a process from which neither could easily retreat without heavy diplomatic costs. The world body would then attempt to organize the referendum and simultaneously implement other aspects of the settlement plan. In the end, the UN played a weak hand in this period by convincing both sides to start the process of identification, which each party initially felt would work in its favor. Having made enough progress in the identification process, the UN then managed to obtain the participation of senior US officials—particularly James Baker—in order to apply the necessary pressure on both sides and to increase the interest of the UN's most powerful members in the implementation of the peace plan. But the plan then stalled, and neither Washington nor Paris was prepared to pressure Morocco to implement an agreement it had signed.

POLISARIO's position reflects both triumphs and disappointments. It was accorded diplomatic recognition by 76 countries (though, significantly, no major Western power) in 1995 but, by January 2010, this figure had dropped to 49, and only 17 out of 53 AU states supported the SADR. However, no country has yet recognized Morocco's sovereignty over the territory, and POLISARIO still has sympathizers in the European parliament and in European capitals. But in a post–Cold War era in which the West has shifted its strategic gaze from the Soviet bear to Islamic fundamentalists, particularly after the destruction of the World Trade Center towers on 11 September 2001 and the subsequent US occupation of Afghanistan and Iraq, Moroccan King Mohammed VI is still considered too valuable an ally as the "moderate" gatekeeper of the Mediterranean at a time when POLISARIO's mainly African backers have the least leverage to influence events in the international system. Unlike Morocco, which has firm allies in France and the United States on the Security Council that can help block unpalatable suggestions, POLISARIO lacks a similar veto-wielding ally on the UN's most powerful decisionmaking body on the Saharan issue. POLISARIO's main backer, Algeria, became increasingly focused on its own domestic civil war that erupted after annulled elections in 1991 and eventually resulted in over one hundred thousand deaths. Equally worrying for POLISARIO, several African states like Benin, Burkina Faso, Cape Verde, Congo-Brazzaville, Chad, Equatorial Guinea, Liberia, Malawi, São Tomé and Príncipe, Seychelles, Swaziland, and Togo reversed their previous recognition of the SADR.

Paradoxically, though MINURSO is the first UN mission that all five permanent members of the Security Council have contributed peacekeepers to, it is also probably the most neglected dossier on the Security Council agenda. It has been relegated to the background of the world's concerns. During the October 1996 meeting of the UN Fourth Committee on Special Political and Decolonization Issues, Tanzania and Zimbabwe accused the Security Council of having abandoned the Western Sahara issue. For the first time in this three and a half decade conflict that represents Africa's last act of decolonization, there was a real possibility, with the completion of the UN's tortuous identification process by the end of 1999, that a successful referendum would finally answer the perennial Western Sahara question. After spending over $500 million, the UN is, however, no closer to implementing its own settlement plan, and some powerful members of the Security Council such as France and the United States even seem prepared to abandon the world body's commitment to the principle of self-determination.

Turning to the Suez crisis, the first-ever armed UN peacekeeping mission's main achievement was that its presence would help to maintain peace between Egypt and Israel by patrolling the Sinai and Gaza strip for a decade, until it was withdrawn just before the May 1967 war, following Nasser's request to Burmese UN Secretary-General U Thant. There are interesting parallels between the Anglo-French invasion of Nasser's Egypt in 1956 and the US-led invasion of Saddam Hussein's Iraq in 2003 (with strong support from British troops). In both cases, Western powers arrogated to themselves the right to launch an invasion without the necessary UN authorization, based on flawed assumptions. They argued that if the Security Council failed to uphold a subjectively defined international "rule of law," then they would have to take this law into their own hands. The Anglo-French believed in 1956 that Nasser's regime would fall; the Anglo-Americans believed in 2003 that the invading soldiers would be welcomed by Iraqis as liberators. Neither happened, and both invasions were widely viewed as illegitimate and illegal.

While Britain was made to withdraw from Egypt under pressure from Washington in 1956, the US invasion of Iraq in 2003 was based on the false pretext of the existence of weapons of mass destruction, and the United States became embroiled in an insurgency that led to a catastrophic situation before Washington announced its intention to withdraw from the country under its new president, Barack Obama, in 2009. Both Suez and Iraq entailed London and Washington presenting the UN with a fait accompli after the decision of military action had already been made elsewhere. Both interventions confronted the huge constraint of keeping troops in a region at a high level of alert for too long.

In stark contrast to the Iraq invasion of 2003, the earlier US-led intervention in Kuwait in 1991 to free the oil-rich sheikdom from the "thief of Baghdad"—Saddam Hussein—enjoyed widespread international support at the UN and was a truly multilateral coalition, composed even of Arab contingents. Anthony Eden had also tried to portray Nasser as a "thief of Cairo" but was on very weak grounds since the Egyptian leader was nationalizing a canal in his own country. Eden also lacked the critical support of the United States and the UN.

Contrary to the Anglo-French motives for launching the invasion, Nasser actually emerged stronger from the Suez crisis as the indisputable leader of the Arab world, forming a political union with Syria between 1958 and 1961. He had suffered a crushing military victory but emerged politically victorious. By the time of his death in 1970, the Egyptian leader had become the undisputed political leader of the Arabs. His biographer, Saïd K. Aburish, described Nasser as "the most charismatic [Arab] leader since the Prophet Mohamed,"[151] while late Palestinian American intellectual Edward Said noted that: "Nasser was the first modern Egyptian leader to make claims for himself on the basis of caste or blood, and the first to transform Egypt into the major Arab and third world country."[152]

France and Britain drew different conclusions from the Suez debacle. London decided it would never again launch a military intervention in strategically important parts of the world without the knowledge and support of the United States and largely avoided deploying interventionist troops to the African continent after Suez, until the Sierra Leone intervention to support a crumbling UN mission in 2000 (see Chapter 5). Paris continued a *politique de grandeur* (pretence at great power) status, drawing the opposite conclusion that it needed to increase its independence of action from Washington. The Gallic power developed an independent nuclear capability (*force de frappe*); led efforts, with Germany, to create the European Economic Community (EEC) a year after Suez; and launched countless military interventions into its former African colonies, though it remained careful to avoid intervening in strategically important areas of the Middle East that the United States would come to dominate. Both the Suez crisis and Western Sahara case brilliantly captured the games that the powerful members of the Security Council play, which often determine the success or failure of UN peacekeeping missions.

Notes

The author would like to thank Hamid Abdeljaber, Erik Jensen, George Joffé, and David M. Malone for their invaluable comments on an earlier draft of the Western Sahara section of this chapter.

1. Amin Hewedy, "Nasser and the Crisis of 1956," in William Roger Louis and Roger Owen, eds., *Suez 1956: The Crisis and Its Consequences* (Oxford: Oxford University Press, 1989), p. 167.

2. Saïd K. Aburish, *Nasser: The Last Arab* (London: Gerald Duckworth, 2005), p. 1.

3. See, for example, J. D. Hargreaves, *Decolonization in Africa* (London: Longman, 1988), pp. 156–158; Louis and Owen, *Suez 1956;* William Roger Louis, *Ends of British Imperialism: The Scramble For Empire, Suez and Decolonization* (London: I. B. Tauris, 2006).

4. J. C. Hurewitz, "The Historical Context," in Louis and Owen, *Suez 1956,* p. 22.

5. Keith Kyle, "Britain and the Crisis, 1955–1956," in Louis and Owen, *Suez 1956,* p. 109.

6. Mona Ghali, "United Nations Emergency Force I: 1956–1967," in William Durch, ed., *The Evolution of UN Peacekeeping: Case Studies and Comparative Analysis* (New York: St. Martin's, 1993), p. 106.

7. Ali Mazrui, "Africa and Egypt's Four Circles," in Ali A. Mazrui, *On Heroes and Uhuru-Worship: Essays on Independent Africa* (London: Longman, 1967), p. 99.

8. Quoted in Stanley Meisler, *United Nations: The First Fifty Years* (New York: The Atlantic Monthly Press, 1995), p. 96.

9. See, for example, Alistair Horne, *A Savage War of Peace: Algeria 1954–1962* (New York: New York Review of Books, 2006).

10. See William Roger Louis, "A Prima Donna with Honour: Eden and Suez," in Louis, *Ends of British Imperialism,* pp. 627–638.

11. Maurice Vaisse, "France and the Suez Crisis," in Louis and Owen, *Suez 1956*, p. 140.

12. Ghali, "United Nations Emergency Force I," p. 105.

13. Vaisse, "France and the Suez Crisis," pp. 134–135.

14. Ibid., p. 137.

15. Ibid., p. 140.

16. Kyle, "Britain and the Crisis," p. 107.

17. Robert R. Bowie, "Eisenhower, Dulles, and the Suez Crisis," in Louis and Owen, *Suez 1956*, p. 191.

18. Cited in William Roger Louis, "An American Volcano in the Middle East: John Foster Dulles and the Suez Crisis," in Louis, *Ends of British Imperialism*, p. 649.

19. Anthony Eden, *Full Circle* (London: Cassell, 1960), p. 498.

20. Albert Hourani, "Conclusion," in Louis and Owen, *Suez 1956*, p. 396.

21. Eden, *Full Circle*, pp. 495, 500, 501.

22. Quoted in Louis, "An American Volcano in the Middle East," p. 648.

23. Cited in William Roger Louis, "Public Enemy Number One: Britain and the United Nations in the Aftermath of Suez," in Louis, *Ends of British Imperialism*, p. 710.

24. Kyle, "Britain and the Crisis," p. 112.

25. Hewedy, "Nasser and the Crisis of 1956," p. 162.

26. Ghali, "United Nations Emergency Force I," p. 108.

27. Kyle, "Britain and the Crisis," p. 114.

28. Ibid., p. 120.

29. Ibid., pp. 122–123.

30. Brian Urquhart, *A Life in Peace and War* (New York: W. W. Norton, 1987), pp. 132 and 134.

31. Louis, "Suez and Decolonization: Scrambling Out of Africa and Asia," in Louis, *Ends of British Imperialism*, p. 24.

32. Ghali, "United Nations Emergency Force I," p. 111.

33. Ibid., p. 112.

34. Hewedy, "Nasser and the Crisis of 1956," p. 170.

35. Kyle, "Britain and the Crisis," p. 111.

36. Louis, "An American Volcano in the Middle East," pp. 652–653.

37. Bowie, "Eisenhower, Dulles, and the Suez Crisis," p. 189; Louis, "An American Volcano in the Middle East," pp. 640–641.

38. Quoted in Louis, "An American Volcano in the Middle East," p. 641.

39. Louis, "An American Volcano in the Middle East," p. 642.

40. Ibid., pp. 658–659.

41. See Vaisse, "France and the Suez Crisis," pp. 131–143.

42. Ibid., p. 137.

43. Louis, "An American Volcano in the Middle East," p. 656.

44. Ibid., p. 641.

45. Bowie, "Eisenhower, Dulles, and the Suez Crisis," p. 200.

46. Ibid., pp.195–196.

47. Louis, "Suez and Decolonization," p. 29.

48. William Roger Louis, "The United Nations and the Suez Crisis: British Ambivalence Towards the Pope on the East River," in Louis, *Ends of British Imperialism*, p. 686; Louis, "Public Enemy Number One," p. 696.

49. Louis, "The United Nations and the Suez Crisis," p. 666.

50. Ibid., p. 667.

51. Ibid., p. 668.

52. Quoted in ibid., p. 668.

53. Louis, "The United Nations and the Suez Crisis," p. 688.

54. Cited in ibid., p. 668.

55. Louis, "The United Nations and the Suez Crisis," p. 686; Douglas Hurd, *Memoirs* (London: Abacus, 2004, first published in 2003), p.155.

56. Quoted in Louis, "The United Nations and the Suez Crisis," p. 687.

57. Louis, "The United Nations and the Suez Crisis," p. 680.

58. Hurd, *Memoirs,* p. 154.

59. Ibid., p. 156.

60. Louis, "The United Nations and the Suez Crisis," p. 675.

61. Hewedy, "Nasser and the Crisis of 1956," p. 171.

62. William Roger Louis and Roger Owen, "Introduction," in Louis and Owen, *Suez 1956,* p. 6.

63. Louis, "The United Nations and the Suez Crisis," p. 678.

64. Ibid., p. 688.

65. Bowie, "Eisenhower, Dulles, and the Suez Crisis," p. 208.

66. Louis, "The United Nations and the Suez Crisis," p. 683.

67. Ibid., pp. 683–684.

68. Louis and Owen, "Introduction," p. 10.

69. Urquhart, *A Life in Peace and War,* p. 133.

70. Louis, "The United Nations and the Suez Crisis," p. 683.

71. Niall Ferguson, *Empire: How Britain Made the Modern World* (London: Penguin, 2004, first published in 2003), p. 156.

72. Ghali, "United Nations Emergency Force I," pp. 112–113.

73. Ibid., p. 110.

74. Urquhart, *A Life in Peace and War,* p. 136.

75. Ghali, "United Nations Emergency Force I," p. 114.

76. Ibid.

77. Ibid., p. 115.

78. Bowie, "Eisenhower, Dulles, and the Suez Crisis," p. 212.

79. Ghali, "United Nations Emergency Force I," p. 118.

80. This section is based on Adekeye Adebajo, "Selling Out the Sahara? The Tragic Tale of the UN Referendum," Occasional Paper Series, Institute for African Development, Cornell University, spring 2002.

81. See Ian Martin, *Self-Determination in East Timor* (Boulder: Lynne Rienner, 2001).

82. For historical background of the conflict, see John Damis, *Conflict in Northwest Africa: The Western Sahara Dispute* (Stanford, CA: Hoover Institution Press, 1983); Tony Hodges, *Western Sahara: The Roots of a Desert War* (Westport, CT: Lawrence Hill, 1983); I. William Zartman, *Ripe for Resolution: Conflict and Intervention in Africa* (Oxford: Oxford University Press, 1989).

83. See Adekeye Adebajo, "Sheikhs, Soldiers, and Sand," *The World Today* 56, no. 1 (January 2000): 19–21.

84. See International Court of Justice, "Western Sahara Case: Advisory Opinion of 16 October 1975" (The Hague: International Court of Justice, 1975); Thomas Franck, "The Theory and Practice of Decolonization: The Western Sahara Case," and George Joffé, "The International Court of Justice and the Western Sahara Dispute," both in Richard Lawless and Laila Monahan, eds., *War and Refugees* (London: Pinter, 1987).

85. S. C. Saxena, *Western Sahara: No Alternative to Armed Struggle* (New Delhi: Kaliya, 1995), p. 48.

86. John Damis, "Morocco and the Western Sahara," *Current History* 89, no. 546 (April 1990): 167.

87. Members included Côte d'Ivoire, Guinea, Mali, Nigeria, Tanzania, and Sudan.

88. For an insider's account, see Ibrahim Gambari, *Theory and Reality in Foreign Policy Making: Nigeria After the Second Republic* (Atlantic Highlands, NJ: Humanities Press International, 1989).

89. Jarat Chopra, "A Chance for Peace in Western Sahara," *Survival* 39, no. 3 (Autumn 1997): 56.

90. I thank Hamid Abdeljaber for this observation.

91. Quoted in Anthony Pazzanita and Tony Hodges, *Historical Dictionary of Western Sahara*, 2nd ed. (Metuchen, NJ: Scarecrow, 1994), p. 83.

92. Hodges, *Western Sahara*, p. 332.

93. John Damis, "Western Sahara Conflict: Myths and Realities," *Middle East Journal* 37, no. 2 (Spring 1983): 170.

94. See, for example, George Joffé, "The Conflict in the Western Sahara," in Oliver Furley, ed., *Conflict in Africa* (New York: Tauris Academic Studies, 1995), p. 113; Anthony G. Pazzanita, "Morocco Versus POLISARIO: A Political Interpretation," *Journal of Modern African Studies* 32, no. 3 (1994): 278.

95. Zartman, *Ripe For Resolution*, p. 20.

96. See Phillip Naylor, "Spain, France, and the Western Sahara: A Historical Narrative and Study of National Transformation," in Yahia Zoubir and Daniel Volman, eds., *International Dimensions of the Western Sahara Conflict* (Westport, CT: Praeger, 1993).

97. Stephen Zunes, "The United States in the Saharan War: A Case of Low-Intensity Intervention," in Zoubir and Volman, *International Dimensions*, p. 54.

98. Richard Parker, "US Strategic Interests and the War in Western Sahara," in Zoubir and Volman, *International Dimensions*, p. 94.

99. "The Situation Concerning Western Sahara: Report by the Secretary-General," S/21360, 18 June 1990, p. 4.

100. See "The Situation Concerning Western Sahara: Report by the Secretary-General," S/21360, 18 June 1990, and S/22464, 19 April 1991.

101. See Adekeye Adebajo, "The UN's Unknown Effort," *Africa Report* (March–April 1995): 60–63.

102. "The Situation Concerning Western Sahara: Report by the Secretary-General," S/1997/882, 13 November 1997, p. 11.

103. William Durch, "The United Nations Mission for the Referendum in Western Sahara," in Durch, *The Evolution of UN Peacekeeping*, pp. 406–434.

104. Pazzanita and Hodges, *Historical Dictionary of Western Sahara*, p. 346.

105. Chopra, *A Chance for Peace in Western Sahara*, p. 54.

106. Confidential interviews.

107. See "The Situation Concerning Western Sahara: Report by the Secretary-General," S/23299, 19 December 1991, and S/26185, 28 July 1993.

108. John Damis, "The UN Settlement Plan for the Western Sahara: Problems and Prospects," *Middle East Policy* 1, no. 2 (Summer 1992): 39.

109. I thank George Joffé for this insight.

110. Durch, "The United Nations Mission for the Referendum in Western Sahara," p. 418.

111. Personal interview with Ahmed Boukhari, POLISARIO representative in New York, 11 August 1998.

112. Chopra, "A Chance for Peace in Western Sahara," p. 57.

113. Personal interview with Ambassador Ahmed Snoussi, former permanent representative of Morocco to the UN, New York, April 1999.

114. "The Situation Concerning Western Sahara: Report by the Secretary-General," S/1995/986, 24 November 1995, p. 3.

115. See Adekeye Adebajo, "The Sad Case of the Missing Sheikh," *West Africa,* 29 April–5 May 1996, p. 668.

116. "The Situation Concerning Western Sahara: Report by the Secretary-General," S/1994/1420, 14 December 1994, p. 2.

117. Ibid., pp. 5–7.

118. Fatemeh Ziai, "Keeping It Secret: The United Nations Operation in Western Sahara," *Human Rights Watch Middle East* 7, no. 7 (October 1995).

119. "Interim Report of the Secretary-General on the Situation Concerning Western Sahara," S/2002/41, 10 January 2002, p. 5.

120. Chopra, "A Chance for Peace in Western Sahara," p. 54.

121. Personal interview with Erik Jensen, former acting special representative of the UN Secretary-General in Western Sahara, Boston, 31 October 2000.

122. "The Situation Concerning Western Sahara: Report by the Secretary-General," S/1996/43, 19 January 1996, pp. 2–3.

123. See Boutros Boutros-Ghali, *Unvanquished: A US-UN Saga* (New York: Random House, 1999).

124. For details of these agreements, see "The Situation Concerning Western Sahara: Report by the Secretary-General," S/1997/742, 24 September 1997.

125. Ibid., pp. 10–13.

126. "The Situation Concerning Western Sahara: Report by the Secretary-General," S/1998/316, 13 April 1998, p. 2.

127. Letter dated 19 February 1998 from the Secretary-General addressed to the president of the Security Council, S/1998/142, p. 2.

128. "The Situation Concerning Western Sahara: Report by the Secretary-General," S/2001/148, 20 February 2001, p. 2.

129. "The Situation Concerning Western Sahara: Report by the Secretary-General," S/2001/613, 20 June 2001, pp. 11–12.

130. Ibid., pp. 22–26.

131. Ibid., pp. 15–17; "Government of Algeria Memorandum on the Question of Western Sahara," Permanent Mission of Algeria to the UN, New York, October 2001, p. 2.

132. Confidential interview.

133. Cherif Oazani, "Pari Perdu pour Baker," *Jeune Afrique,* 11–17 September 2001, p. 25.

134. Personal interview with Ahmed Boukhari, New York, 12 March 2002.

135. Oazani, "Pari Perdu pour Baker," p. 25.

136. Quoted in "Polisario's Sinking Hopes," *The Economist* 361, no. 825, 18–14 December 2001, p. 44.

137. Ibid.

138. George Joffé, "Sovereignty and the Western Sahara," *Journal of North African Studies* 15, no. 3 (September 2010): 378.

139. Personal interview with Ahmed Boukhari, New York, 12 March 2002.

140. Iqbal Jhazbay, "South Africa's Relations with North Africa and the Horn: Bridging a Continent," in Adekeye Adebajo, Adebayo Adedeji, and Chris Landsberg, eds., *South Africa in Africa: The Post-Apartheid Era* (Scottsville, South Africa: University of KwaZulu-Natal Press, 2007), p. 281.

141. "The Situation Concerning Western Sahara: Report by the Secretary-General," S/2002/178, 19 February 2002, p. 1.

142. My summary of this Security Council meeting is based on confidential correspondence.

143. "The Situation Concerning Western Sahara: Report by the Secretary-General," S/2006/249, 19 April 2006, p. 1.

144. "The Situation Concerning Western Sahara: Report by the Secretary-General," S/2006/817, 16 October 2006, p. 4.

145. "The Situation Concerning Western Sahara: Report by the Secretary-General," S/2007/619, 19 October 2007, p. 4.

146. "The Situation Concerning Western Sahara: Report by the Secretary-General," S/2006/249, 19 April 2006, pp. 9–10.

147. I thank George Joffé for this insight.

148. "Morocco v. Algeria," *The Economist,* 6 November 2010, p. 48.

149. See "Report of the UN Secretary-General on the Situation Concerning Western Sahara," S/2011/249, 1 April 2011.

150. "Morocco v. Algeria," *The Economist,* 6 November 2010, p. 48.

151. Aburish, *Nasser,* p. 4.

152. Edward W. Said, *Reflections on Exile and Other Essays* (Cambridge, MA: Harvard University Press, 2002), p. 161.

3

"No More Congos!"
The UN in the Great Lakes Region

> How can a beret colored blue erase, just like that, the prejudices
> of conservative officers from Sweden, Canada, or Britain?
> How does a blue armband vaccinate against the racism and
> paternalism of people whose only vision of Africa is lion hunting,
> slave markets, and colonial conquest; people for whom the history
> of civilization is built on the possession of colonies? Naturally
> they would understand the Belgians. They have the same past,
> the same history, the same lust for our wealth.
> —*Patrice Lumumba, Prime Minister of the DRC, 1960–1961*[1]

"No more Congos!" The forlorn cry rang out unmistakably across the African continent in 1964. The United Nations was struggling with one of its earliest peacekeeping challenges in the former Belgian Congo. The world body was expressing its deep frustration at a protracted four-year intervention: it had lost its Swedish Secretary-General, Dag Hammarskjöld, in a mysterious plane crash, and it became bogged down in a protracted civil war in the shadow of an ideological Cold War in an emerging Africa. The UN's credibility on the continent was badly damaged by its intervention in the turbulent civil war. Five decades later, it has struggled to keep peace in another protracted civil war in the same country. A large country at the heart of Africa, the Democratic Republic of Congo is a symbol of the difficulties that the UN has experienced in its peacekeeping efforts in Africa.[2]

In this chapter, I examine four cases of UN peacekeeping in Africa's Great Lakes region: the Congo between 1960 and 1964; Rwanda between 1993 and 1994; Burundi between 2004 and 2006; and the mission in the Democratic Republic of Congo between 2000 and 2010. I conclude with a brief discussion of three International Conferences on the Great Lakes and offer final reflections on the UN's role in this region.

The Great Lakes region, encompassing Burundi, Rwanda, Tanzania, and Uganda—and surrounded by the four Great Lakes of Tanganyika, Kivu, Edward, and Victoria—contains some of Africa's most spectacular landscape: rolling hills, dense forests, rising mountains, and lush valleys. But events over the past five decades have turned a natural paradise into a human-made disaster. The Great Lakes have become infested with ethnic crocodiles of the genocidal species. Rwanda and Burundi are tragic twins seemingly fated to repeat cycles of bloody massacres in a struggle between a Hutu majority and a Tutsi minority with deep roots in a pernicious process of highly divisive Belgian colonial social engineering. The conflict in the DRC has involved seven foreign armies and a myriad of militias and mercenaries in a country the size of Western Europe that was devastated by the thirty-one-year autocratic misrule of Western-backed Mobutu Sese Seko.[3] Military clashes between former allies Uganda and Rwanda, and their looting of the Congo's mineral resources, further exacerbated the conflict.

As I have argued throughout the book, UN Security Council support or neglect, the cooperation of domestic belligerents, and regional consensus were often the critical factors in determining the outcome of each of these four missions. The UN mission in the Congo in the early 1960s succeeded in reuniting a fractious country in spite of regional divisions and external meddling. America's client, Colonel Joseph Mobutu, eventually won power, and the Congolese parties agreed to cooperate in a political system led by Mobutu, an outcome that was also accepted by regional states. The UN mission in Burundi in 2004 to 2006 also eventually succeeded in its peacekeeping tasks through determined regional mediation and peacekeeping and belated UN and external support. The mission in Rwanda, in contrast, was tarred with the Somali brush of failure (see Chapter 6). The UN missions in Rwanda and Somalia were, in a sense, contrasts in failure, for Somalia was a well-funded mission in which some of the best-equipped soldiers in the world participated, while Rwanda was, from the start, a mission based largely on ill-equipped armies from developing countries that lacked strong political and financial backing from the UN Security Council. This weakness encouraged Rwanda's extremist factions to force the withdrawal of the UN by killing its peacekeepers. France, one of the veto-wielding permanent members of the UN Security Council, had trained and provided military support to the genocidal regime and was thus considered a partisan and compromised intervener, while the UN special representative, Cameroon's former foreign minister Jacques-Roger Booh-Booh, did not inspire much confidence.[4]

Furthermore, many of the domestic parties in Rwanda were unwilling to implement peace agreements that would force them to share power. They adopted a zero-sum approach to the conflict and signed accords that they had no intention of implementing. The regional spillover of the Rwandan genocide destabilized neighboring states, some of which sought unsuccessfully to mediate an end to the conflict. These regional actors were too weak to impose peace on the belligerents, and their roles were sometimes compromised by past and continuing support for individual factions. The UN special representative in Rwanda was widely considered to be a political liability, while the UN Security Council lacked the political will and interest to end the genocide in 1994 by strengthening the mandate and powers of its peacekeepers. The most powerful domestic parties in Burundi eventually cooperated in a government of national unity by 2004, facilitating efforts of South African–led regional actors and African Union peacekeepers who were then eventually able to convince the UN Security Council to take over the peacekeeping mission, increasing its logistics, legitimacy, and funding.

Regarding the UN mission in the DRC between 2000 and 2010, the existence of mineral resources was exploited by the warring factions, as well as by Rwanda, Uganda, and Zimbabwe, according to various UN panel reports. Regional actors involved in the DRC remained deeply divided. Rwanda and Uganda sent troops to support a rebellion against the government in Kinshasa in 1998, which in turn was provided with military support by troops from Zimbabwe, Angola, and Namibia. Kigali and Kampala soon fell out, clashing militarily in the Congolese town of Kisangani three times, resulting in hundreds of civilian casualties. Relations between the DRC and Angola became antagonistic, after earlier military collaboration. Only when regional states cooperated against "negative forces" was a modicum of stability restored to the country, though the provinces of Kivu and Orientale remained fragile in 2011.

Cold War Follies:
The UN Mission in the Congo, 1960–1964

The twenty thousand–strong United Nations Operation in the Congo (ONUC) was dispatched to Central Africa in July 1960.[5] Although it soon became embroiled in civil war, the new leaders of Congo had invited the UN with the original purpose of preserving its sovereignty from foreign intervention. Belgium had forgotten that the world had changed and that its brand of colonialism had become an anachronism in postindependence Africa. Having hastily abandoned its former colony, Belgian paratroopers returned to their former stomping ground within days. The Congolese army mutinied and, amid the chaos, Moise Tshombe, with Belgian connivance, declared the Congo's richest province, Katanga, independent.

A bitter power struggle erupted between the conservative president Joseph Kasavubu and his "radical," nationalist premier Patrice Lumumba. The United States and the Soviet Union—the two most powerful members of the UN Security Council—considered the Congo, a mineral-rich, strategically located state, a vital prize in the early Cold War stakes.[6] Moscow provided transport aircraft for pro-Lumumba troops, while Washington's Central Intelligence Agency was involved in assassination attempts against Lumumba.[7] Following Lumumba's death in January 1961, members of the "Casablanca group" of "radical" African states like Egypt, Guinea, and Morocco—but not Ghana—withdrew their peacekeepers from the Congo.

The UN's reputation suffered tremendous damage as a result of this mission. Western powers accused the Indian UN special representative in Congo, Rajeshwar Dayal, of Lumumbist leanings, while London accused the UN's Irish representative in Katanga, Conor Cruise O'Brien, of leftist sympathies. Secretary-General Dag Hammarskjöld replaced both envoys. The Soviets and many African states strongly criticized the UN's failure to protect Lumumba, who was killed under the noses of UN peacekeepers. Hammarskjöld was sympathetic to the Western view that the Congo was threatened by Soviet expansionism and felt that Lumumba should be undercut.[8] Many Africans were so enraged by Lumumba's death that the All-African People's Conference in Cairo in 1961 called for Hammarskjöld to be replaced as UN Secretary-General,[9] though many other African and Third World governments still regarded the Swede as a protector of the interests of the "global South."

Having achieved its strategic goals of eliminating Lumumba and helping Colonel Joseph Mobutu (later Mobutu Sese Seko) to power, Washington eventually devised the military plan to end the secession in Katanga.[10] For the first time in its history, the UN embarked on peace enforcement, using force to incorporate Katanga back into the Congo by January 1963. The control of the central government in Léopoldville (now Kinshasa) had become a game of musical chairs. Governmental authority was fully restored only after Mobutu staged a US-backed coup d'état, and by 1965 he was in control of the country. He remained in power for the next three decades, with strong support from Washington, Paris, and Brussels.

After the controversies of the Congo crisis, the UN Security Council refused to intervene in major civil wars in Africa, citing the difficulties of keeping peace in the shadow of a Cold War in which two ideological superpowers waged proxy wars, the French gendarme intervened in its *chasse gardée* (private hunting ground), and obstinate Portuguese colonialists and white minority regimes in Southern Africa clung desperately to power. Following the political shenanigans in the DRC that had led to the popular Lumumba's death, the Africans were also wary of UN peacekeeping interventions on their continent, creating the Organization of African Unity (OAU) in 1963 in part to resolve regional conflicts without external meddling.[11] For the next twenty-five years, no major UN peacekeeping mission took place in Africa, even as conflicts proliferated, often fueled by Cold War patrons.

Fiddling While Rwanda Burns:
The UN Mission in Rwanda, 1993–1994

With the end of the Cold War by 1990 and the emergence of unprecedented cooperation among the five permanent members of the UN Security Council, new peacekeeping missions were established in Namibia, Western Sahara, Mozambique, and Angola (see Chapters 2 and 4). But the disastrous peacekeeping missions in Somalia (1993) and Rwanda (1994) dashed the initial hopes that the UN would play a major role in ending African conflicts. The failure of the UN mission in Rwanda between 1993 and 1994 cannot be understood without reference to its retreat from Somalia six months earlier. Somalia and Rwanda had been orphans of the Cold War in an era of intervention by external powers in Africa. Somalia was fought over by the superpowers, while Rwanda was entangled in French efforts to maintain a sphere of influence in Africa. The UN Security Council erroneously treated both conflicts as humanitarian disasters, and the political will for stronger military action disappeared after Western peacekeepers had been killed in the two countries. Political support for the UN missions in Somalia and Rwanda simply crumbled in the Security Council, and, rather than bolstering the UN presence, its peacekeepers were withdrawn. After the death of eighteen US soldiers and about one thousand Somalis in October 1993, the UN withdrew all its peacekeepers from Somalia (see Chapter 6). Six months after this fiasco, Washington led the opposition to a UN response to the genocide in Rwanda in a situation that was tragically viewed through a tainted Somali prism.

Before analyzing the UN mission in Rwanda, it is important to provide a brief background to the conflict. The Rwandese Patriotic Front (RPF) had invaded Rwanda from Uganda in October 1990. These refugee warriors came from Rwanda's Tutsi minority who had been forced out of their homeland and denied the right to return by the Hutu-dominated government of Juvénal Habyarimana. Uganda's leader, Yoweri Museveni, whose successful guerrilla army had included Tutsi exiles, backed the RPF, while France, which had trained and armed Habyarimana's militias and sent a military contingent to Rwanda as late as 1993, along with Mobutu's Zaire, supported Habyarimana. The UN Observer Mission for Uganda-Rwanda (UNOMUR) was established in June 1993 to monitor the common border between both countries. The OAU also arranged peace talks in Arusha, Tanzania, that resulted in a comprehensive peace settlement by August 1993. Arusha called for a transitional government involving the country's political groups, a power-sharing arrangement, and the establishment of a new army composed equally of Hutus and Tutsis, as well as the demobilization of the remaining fighters.[12]

The 2,500-strong and \$120 million a year UN Assistance Mission in Rwanda (UNAMIR) was mandated to implement the Arusha agreement.

The Security Council resolution establishing UNAMIR, however, made two crucial changes that weakened the peacekeeping force before its deployment. Arusha had called for the peacekeepers to guarantee the overall security of Rwanda and to confiscate illegal arms. The UN resolution mandated the force only to contribute to security in Kigali and its environs and did not sanction a seizure of arms. The UN peacekeepers arrived in Rwanda two months behind schedule and without the armored unit and helicopters that had been authorized by the Security Council.

General Roméo Dallaire, the Canadian UN force commander, had also initially called for a contingent that was twice the size of the one deployed.[13] The force, consisting largely of soldiers from Belgium, Bangladesh, Ghana, and Tunisia, lacked an intelligence unit and had a small civilian police unit with no human rights cell, further limiting its ability to monitor abuses.[14] To make matters worse, the situation in Kigali was scarcely conducive to peacekeeping: the transitional government was not installed, Rwanda's soldiers were not demobilized, and arms were flooding illegally into the capital. Jaques-Roger Booh-Booh, the UN special representative in Rwanda, was widely regarded to be out of his depth.[15] He annoyed the RPF by calling for the inclusion of the extremist Coalition pour la Défense de la République (CDR) in the future government and raised further suspicion by accepting an invitation to visit Habyarimana's village.[16] His criticisms of Habyarimana's delay in establishing the transitional government infuriated Hutu parties. The personal relationship between Booh-Booh and Dallaire was also marked by conflict, with General Henry Anyidoho, the Ghanaian UN deputy force commander, often having to act as an intermediary between the two men.[17]

On 6 April 1994, Habyarimana's plane was shot down over Kigali, signaling the start of the genocide against the Tutsi minority and moderate Hutus. The genocide had been planned by a group of extremists within the Habyarimana regime, including members of the ruling party, officers of the Presidential Guard, the *interahamwe* and *impuzamugambi* militias, and members of the CDR. These groups regarded power sharing as not only a betrayal but a threat to their own positions and privileges. They also feared that the RPF's presence in a new national army would facilitate the launching of a Tutsi military coup, fears heightened by the assassination of neighboring Burundi's first Hutu president, Melchior Ndadaye, by Tutsi military extremists in October 1993.

Within twenty-four hours of the start of the genocide, 250,000 Rwandan refugees flooded into Burundi, Uganda, Tanzania, and Zaire (now DRC). Over the next three months, the *génocidaires* eliminated approximately eight hundred thousand mostly Tutsi citizens as well as Hutu "moderates."[18] The killing of ten Belgian UN peacekeepers led to the withdrawal of its entire contingent, the backbone of the UN force, from Rwanda in April 1994. Brussels then lobbied for the withdrawal of all UN peacekeepers from its former colony. The slaughter ended only with an RPF military victory in July 1994. The genocidal militias and the Rwandan army retreated into eastern Zaire with a hostage Hutu population of about one million people. This retreat was facilitated by the controversial UN-sanctioned French intervention, Opération Turquoise,[19] which had ostensibly been launched to save lives. However, revelations that France had trained and continued to allow arms to flow to Rwanda's death squads raised troubling questions.[20] As French scholar René Lemarchand put it: "No amount of retrospective guilt can diminish its [France's] place in history as the principal villain in the Rwandan apocalypse."[21] The fact that the Security Council granted the French-led mission a "robust" chapter VII peace-enforcement mandate in contrast to the feeble chapter VI peacekeeping mandate granted to UNAMIR in 1993, again demonstrated how powerful P-5 countries manipulated the Council to serve their parochial interests and underlined the fact that some countries within the Security Council were more equal than others.

At the start of the genocide, African governments and their allies at the UN urged the Security Council to strengthen and reinforce UNAMIR to be able to protect civilians. Nonpermanent member Nigeria's permanent representative to the UN, Ibrahim Gambari (the UN special representative in Sudan's Darfur region in 2011), wondered aloud whether Africa had fallen off the map of the world's concerns,[22] while the OAU condemned the UN's "indifference or lack of sufficient concern" for Africans.[23] But led by strong British and American demands, the Security Council withdrew most of its peacekeepers from Rwanda, leaving a token force of 270 by the end of April 1994.[24] The Ghanaian contingent stayed behind, bravely protecting civilians in Kigali with 450 troops in breach of the authorized Security Council figure of 270.[25] The Security Council was led by the Bill Clinton administration, determined to prove that it could "shut down" a UN mission.[26] Washington therefore pursued an inappropriate diplomatic posture in search of an elusive ceasefire. The Clinton administration refused for weeks to call genocide by its proper name for fear of being pressured to act. Susan Rice, the US permanent representative to the UN in 2011, was at the time on the National Security Council, and reportedly argued against using the word *genocide* due to upcoming Congressional elections, though she later claimed not to have remembered making such an argument, noting that it would have been inappropriate if she had.[27] The representative of the genocidal Rwandan regime, Jean-Damascène Bizimana, sat on the Security Council throughout the genocide as a nonpermanent member, reporting back on the unwillingness of the Council to take action and effectively encouraging Rwanda's génocidaires to complete their macabre operation. The UN Secretariat provided inadequate information and often made poor recommendations to the Security Council, forcing some of its members, like Colin Keating, New Zealand's permanent representative to the UN, to rely on information provided by nongovernmental organizations.[28]

Egyptian UN Secretary-General Boutros Boutros-Ghali also dithered before belatedly calling for a stronger UN force. He, however, desisted from criticizing the dubious French role in Rwanda (and in fact vigorously supported Opération Turquoise), in stark contrast to his criticisms of the US role in both Rwanda and Somalia. Boutros-Ghali's imperious leadership style and his distaste for Council members "micromanaging" him led to his refusal to allow Kofi Annan, the Ghanaian Undersecretary-General for Peacekeeping, to brief Council members regularly. This may also have contributed to the caution of bureaucrats under Boutros-Ghali's authority.[29] Many observers, including General Dallaire and his deputy, General Anyidoho, have since argued that a strengthened UN force could have prevented many of the civilian deaths, most of which were carried out by gangs using machetes, clubs, knives, and spears. Dallaire wrote several distressed cables calling for this option but never found support for such an approach within the UN Secretariat. Much controversy still remains over the failure of the UN's Department of Peacekeeping—led at the time by Kofi Annan,—to report the contents of a January 1994 cable from Dallaire warning of the impending genocide and asking for authorization to take military action to forestall it. A subsequent UN inquiry report published in December 1999 criticized Annan and his deputy, Iqbal Riza, for this shortcoming.[30] Boutros-Ghali must also accept some responsibility as UN Secretary-General.

About two weeks after the start of the genocide, Annan and Riza had argued that, since a ceasefire was a dim prospect in Rwanda, the UN Secretariat must advise the Council to plan UNAMIR's withdrawal from Rwanda.[31] The safety of UN personnel and Western civilians in Kigali seemed to matter more to many in New York than the slaughter of eight hundred thousand innocent civilians in Africa. The urgent need for the UN Security Council to act to prevent genocide was abandoned. In May 1994, the Council belatedly reversed its decision and authorized the dispatch of 5,500 peacekeepers (UNAMIR II) to Rwanda. The troops were fully deployed only in October 1994, far too late to save victims of genocide. Nine African countries that had volunteered troops for a UN mission to Rwanda four months earlier had failed to receive the promised logistics from foot-dragging Western countries. The international community had fiddled while Rwanda burned.[32] The crisis had been dismissed as another bout of primordial bloodletting on "the dark continent" where ignorant armies clash by night in a tiny country that much of the West knew little about and about which it cared even less.[33] The UN's lethargic response to the Rwandan genocide seriously damaged its reputation around the globe as well as its relations with the new RPF-led Rwandan government and others across the continent. UN calls for the investigation of massacres in eastern Congo after the Rwandan-backed ousting of Mobutu's regime in 1997 further strained relations with the RPF government and its strongman, Paul Kagame. The relationship reached its nadir during Kofi Annan's visit to Kigali as UN Secretary-General in May 1998 when the country's most senior government officials boycotted a state banquet in his honor. During the commemoration of a decade of Rwanda's genocide in April 2004, Annan decided not to risk an embarrassing repeat of this incident, sending instead Ibrahim Gambari, his special adviser on Africa at the time, to represent him in Kigali.

An Improvised Success:
The UN Mission in Burundi, 2004–2006

The peace process in Burundi began in 1995 and by early 1996, former Tanzanian president, Julius "Mwalimu" (Teacher) Nyerere, had become the chief mediator in this process. The Tanzanian town of Mwanza hosted peace talks in April and May 1996 under Nyerere's chairmanship, with the Hutu-dominated Front pour la Démocratie au Burundi (FRODEBU) party and the Tutsi-dominated Union pour le Progrès National (UPRONA) as the main parties. At a regional summit a month later, Nyerere, Tanzania's Benjamin Mkapa, and Uganda's Yoweri Museveni insisted that the Burundian parties request a regional military intervention force. A Tutsi-led military coup in July 1996 followed, deposing the Hutu president Sylvestre Ntibantunganya, who had been in office since his predecessor, Cyprien Ntaryamira, had died in the plane crash that killed the Rwandan leader Juvénal Habyarimana in April 1994. A former Tutsi military leader, Pierre Buyoya, who had handed power to Hutu president Melchior Ndadaye after democratic elections in June 1993, was put in charge of the junta. At a regional meeting in Arusha in July 1996, Nyerere insisted on a trade and arms embargo being imposed on Burundi, leading to two years of diplomatic stalemate.

Another round of talks was launched in Arusha in June 1998 that made little progress, though the trade embargo was lifted in January 1999. Nyerere remained as chief mediator until his death in October 1999. South Africa's retired president and Nobel Peace Prize laureate Nelson Mandela was named as Nyerere's replacement. The contrast between the two titanic African leaders was stark: where Nyerere was regarded as a good listener and patient and methodical negotiator, the impatient Mandela often acted like a hectoring headmaster, scolding the Burundian parties as if they were disobedient schoolchildren.[34] More broadly, there were tensions throughout the mediation process, with the Tanzanians feeling that the South Africans did not understand the intricacies of regional diplomacy and were sometimes arrogant.

Over twenty-five summits on Burundi provided a roadmap for ending this conflict. The Arusha agreement of August 2000, signed by most Hutu and Tutsi political parties under Nelson Mandela's facilitation and in the presence of US president Bill Clinton, outlined a three-year power-sharing agreement in which the parties pledged to combat genocide and political exclusion through an international commission of inquiry; to promote national reconciliation through a truth and reconciliation process; to reform the judicial sector; to improve access to political participation, economic development, and land reform; to ensure the safe return of refugees and internally displaced persons to their homes; to implement security sector reform in both the military and police; and to organize national elections.[35] But the accord did not include a ceasefire and had been hastily signed before full agreement had been reached with all parties and on the key issues. A three-year power-sharing deal was eventually reached in which Buyoya would remain president for eighteen months from November 2001 to May 2003, after which he would hand power to a FRODEBU Hutu candidate.

In order to ensure effective implementation of Arusha, a cash-strapped African Union mission in Burundi (AMIB) involving 2,645 South African, Mozambican, and Ethiopian peacekeepers and forty-three military observers from Benin, Burkina Faso, Gabon, Mali, and Tunisia was deployed to the small Central African country in February 2003. P-5 Security Council members the United States and Britain helped the deployment of Ethiopian and Mozambican troops. AMIB, however, struggled to keep peace in a decade-long civil war that had killed an estimated 250,000–300,000 people, due to the lack of financial and logistical support.[36] AMIB had to help repel the shelling of the capital of Bujumbura in April and July 2003 by Pierre Nkurunziza's Conseil National pour la Défense de la Démocratie (CNDD-FDD) and Agathon Rwasa's PALIPEHUTU-Forces Nationales de Libération (FNL) rebels. By September 2003, the two rebel groups were also fighting each other in Bujumbura Rural and Bubanza provinces.[37]

By May 2003, President Pierre Buyoya handed power to his deputy, Domitien Ndayizeye. The Arusha accord was later bolstered by the Pretoria Protocols on political, defense, and security power sharing signed by the transitional government and the CNDD-FDD in November 2003. South Africa (through the facilitator, Deputy President Jacob Zuma) and Tanzania were the most active peacemakers, with Uganda also chairing the Regional Peace Initiative on Burundi to ensure effective monitoring of the peace accords. Uganda's Yoweri Museveni pushed for the deployment of Tanzanian peacekeepers to reassure CNDD-FDD, which regarded the South Africans as pro-Tutsi and too close to the transitional government. Jacob Zuma insisted on a neutral, reinforced AMIB and argued that a Tanzanian force could inflame the volatile situation. Rwanda supported the South African position.[38] South African president Thabo Mbeki and Jacob Zuma had brought the two main Hutu players—Domitien Ndayizeye and Pierre Nkurunziza—to the "gambler's paradise" casino of Sun City in August 2003 and to Tshwane (Pretoria) in October 2003, pressuring them to sign the Pretoria protocols. With Pierre Nkurunziza becoming minister of state for good governance and state inspection in March 2004, fighting continued sporadically between the joint Burundian Armed Forces (FAB) and the CNDD-FDD against the FNL.

UN Secretary-General Kofi Annan had appointed Ethiopian diplomat Berhanu Dinka as his special representative for Burundi in July 2002. The UN office in Burundi had been established in 1993 under Mauritanian diplomat Ahmedou Ould-Abdallah (who occupied the post until 1995)[39] to support peace efforts in the country, working closely with national and regional actors. Dinka chaired the implementation monitoring committee, which sought to ensure effective compliance with the Arusha agreement. Kofi Annan also appointed Senegalese general El Hadji Alioune Samba in February 2003 to chair the joint ceasefire commission established two months previously as part of the implementation of the Arusha agreement.

In further support of regional actors, the UN Security Council finally heeded African calls to take over AMIB. In May 2004, the UN Security Council established the UN Operation in Burundi (ONUB), with an authorized strength of 5,650 peacekeepers and a chapter VII peace enforcement mandate. The mission, headed by Canadian UN special representative Carolyn McAskie, was mandated to monitor and provide security for disarming troops (Burundi had about seventy thousand armed combatants), to collect and destroy weapons, and to monitor the cantonment of troops and the disarmament of militias. The peacekeepers were also expected to protect the civilian population in areas in which they were deployed; to report on ceasefire violations; and to monitor, in cooperation with the UN mission in the Congo, illegal arms shipments and cross-border movements by armed groups.[40]

By August 2004, the $292 million a year, eventually 5,650-strong ONUB was in place. The troops had deployed to Burundi after the integration of former AMIB peacekeepers and the addition of significant contingents from Kenya, Nepal, and Pakistan. The mission's force commander was South African general Derrick Mbuyiselo Mgwebi, in recognition of the country's large role under AMIB. ONUB experienced delays in obtaining troops, deployment was slow, and even the mission's South African backbone expressed an unwillingness to continue providing many of its specialized units to the mission.[41] One of the UN's earliest tasks was to provide security to refugees after a massacre of 160 Congolese Banyamulenge refugees at a transit camp in the Burundian town of Gatumba, near the Congolese border, in August 2004. The transitional government and CNDD-FDD were also fingered for committing human rights abuses against civilians.[42] Despite the UN's presence in Burundi, armed skirmishes continued, particularly in the three western provinces of Cibitoké, Bujumbura Rurale, and Bubanza. ONUB established a maritime unit to patrol Lake Tanganyika and observe the Congolese border. By November 2004, the UN had 5,526 peacekeepers, assisted by the "rehatting" of AMIB troops. ONUB also escorted humanitarian convoys and deployed close to refugee camps in a bid to protect civilians.

Though 7,329 Burundian combatants were demobilized between December 2004 and April 2005, internal political divisions among the fractious transitional government continued. Carolyn McAskie sought to engage the transitional government and FNL, while working with the key regional states of South Africa, Tanzania, and Uganda in mediation efforts. Regular meetings were held between the UN missions in Burundi and the DRC to discuss cross-border issues and share peacekeeping lessons. The UN also supported the improvement in relations between Bujumbura and Kinshasa. The UN Security Council embarked on its sixth visit to the Great Lakes region since 2000 in November 2005, noting that Burundi could benefit greatly from the UN Peacebuilding Commission, which was agreed to as part of UN reform efforts in December 2005. Seizing on this suggestion, the government in Bujumbura told the visiting plenipotentiaries that the world body should focus on reconstruction and development assistance and withdraw its peacekeepers from the country by December 2006. In response, Council members cautioned against the negative impact on Burundi's stability that might follow from a precipitate withdrawal of ONUB.[43]

Burundi's constitution was finally endorsed by 90 percent of voters in February 2005 following a referendum. In legislative elections five months later, the CNDD-FDD won 57.8 percent of the votes to FRODEBU's 21.6 percent. In August 2005, CNDD-FDD's Pierre Nkurunziza was elected president of Burundi by a Joint Parliamentary Congress.[44] Four months later, in response to a request by Bujumbura, ONUB began to reduce its troops in the country, though it continued to focus much of its peacekeeping efforts on the three volatile western provinces of Cibitoké, Bujumbura Rurale, and Bubanza.

The United States sought to support the peace process in the Great Lakes region through the tripartite joint commission, which it facilitated, involving the DRC, Rwanda, and Uganda, with Burundi invited to join the body in September 2005. The group called for punitive measures (travel bans and financial restrictions) against armed rebels in eastern Congo and neighboring states such as Rwanda's Forces Démocratiques pour la Libération du Rwanda (FDLR)—former Forces Armées Rwandaises (FAR)/Interahamwe—and the Congolese Mayi-Mayi, as well as Burundi's FLN.[45] Washington also took part in the nineteen-member, UN-chaired Burundi Partners' Forum, established in October 2005 and involving regional and donor countries. The body discussed issues such as the FNL, security sector reform, transitional justice, and human rights.

South Africa—under its facilitator, Minister of Safety and Security Charles Nqakula—and Tanzania continued their efforts to convince the FNL to bid farewell to arms and enter the peace process. They finally succeeded in September 2006 when a comprehensive ceasefire was signed by the government and rebels, though continued clashes were reported in Burundi's

"Wild West" as the FNL continued to push for provisional immunity from prosecution and the release of its prisoners. Sudanese diplomat Nureldin Satti, who had served as Berhanu Dinka and Carolyn McAskie's deputy since September 2002, took over from McAskie in an acting capacity in April 2006, continuing to support national and regional peace efforts. The early termination of the UN peacekeeping mission in December 2006 resulted in continued instability in Burundi,[46] despite the establishment of a small UN Integrated Office in the country. Among ONUB's main achievements were the disarming and demobilization of 21,769 fighters, supporting the country's electoral process, protecting returning refugees and humanitarian convoys, and providing training to Burundi's integrated National Police.

Peacekeepers, Plunderers, and Politicians: The UN Mission in the DRC, 2000–2011

Let us now return to the DRC. Three decades of bad governance under the Western-backed Mobutu dictatorship eventually resulted in civil war in the Congo, triggered in October 1996, with Mobutu ousted in the next year. During peace negotiations, various factions often failed to demonstrate genuine commitment to implementing peace agreements that they had signed and used their access to economic resources to fund their military campaigns. Despite the destabilizing regional consequences of this conflict, key regional actors provided military support to the warring parties. While energetic regional diplomacy helped seal peace agreements, the permanent members of the UN Security Council did not always demonstrate the necessary political commitment to help end this conflict, though France contributed to peacekeeping efforts through the European Union, and Council members eventually mandated a more robust force to focus on establishing stability in the volatile eastern Congo.

A brief background to the conflict is helpful in understanding this UN mission, effectively established in February 2000. In October 1996, Laurent Kabila's Alliance of Democratic Forces for the Liberation of Congo-Zaire (AFDL) launched a devastating rebellion against Mobutu's dictatorship. With help from Rwanda, Uganda, and Angola, the revolt succeeded in toppling the autocrat in May 1997. Despite hopes that the Congolese would finally be liberated from tyranny, Kabila's rule continued in the autocratic traditions of Mobutu. In August 1998, the Congolese leader's former allies, Uganda and Rwanda, invaded the country in support of antigovernment rebels.[47] Burundi also sent in troops on the side of Kigali and Kampala. In response to the invasion by Uganda and Rwanda, a pro-Kabila alliance of Zimbabwe, Angola, Namibia, and Chad sent troops to the DRC to prop up his regime. Foreign armies sought financial rewards from the country's rich mineral wealth and backed assorted rebels. Though most Western countries strongly criticized Zimbabwe for its role in the DRC, they were more muted in their criticism of the flagrant violation of Congolese sovereignty by Rwanda and Uganda. Not until 2000 (two years after the breach of Congolese sovereignty) did the UN Security Council find its voice. It then criticized Kigali and Kampala's invasion of one of its member states, requesting them to withdraw their troops from the Congo.[48] Washington, particularly under the Bill Clinton administration between 1993 and 2000, was an ally of Kigali and Kampala, providing them with military training and advice as part of an anti-Sudan strategy (see Chapter 6).

From Lusaka to Sun City, 1999–2003

Differences between South Africa and its interventionist neighbors— Zimbabwe, Angola, and Namibia—paralyzed the Southern African Development Community (SADC), an organization that the DRC had joined in 1997 with strong South African support, and the OAU took over mediation efforts. At a meeting in Lusaka in July 1999, Angola, the DRC, Namibia, Rwanda, Uganda, and Zimbabwe signed a peace accord. The agreement called for a ceasefire and the redeployment of troops to specified positions; the release of prisoners of war; the withdrawal of all foreign troops from the DRC; a national dialogue between Kabila, the armed opposition groups—the Rally for a Democratic Congo (RCD) and the Movement for the Liberation of Congo (MLC)—and the unarmed civilian opposition; the disarming of all militias and "armed groups";[49] the reestablishment of state administration throughout the DRC; and the creation of a new national army. The UN was asked to deploy a peacekeeping force to the Congo, in collaboration with the OAU. Lusaka also called on the OAU to nominate a chair for a joint military commission (JMC) and to designate a neutral facilitator for an inter-Congolese dialogue. The JMC was mandated to verify the disengagement of forces and the quartering and disarmament of armed groups, as well as to monitor the withdrawal of foreign troops. To facilitate implementation of the accord, a political committee, consisting of the foreign and defense ministers of the parties, was established to assist the JMC.[50] Ketumile Masire, the former president of Botswana, was nominated to be the facilitator of the inter-Congolese dialogue.

Not until April 1999, eight months after the outbreak of hostilities in the DRC, did the UN Security Council adopt its first resolution on the conflict, with its powerful members insisting on a ceasefire before the UN could become actively involved in the crisis.[51] In February 2000, the Council finally established the UN Organization Mission in the DRC (MONUC) under the leadership of Tunisian diplomat Kamel Morjane. Amos Namanga Ngongi, a Cameroonian agronomist and UN bureaucrat, replaced Morjane in October 2001. Former Senegalese foreign minister Moustapha Niasse and former Nigerian heads of state Generals Abdulsaalam Abubakar and Olusegun

Obasanjo have also served as roving UN envoys in the DRC. After deploying ninety military liaison officers by the end of 1999, only 4,386 out of an initially authorized strength of 5,537 MONUC peacekeepers had been deployed by February 2003.

In May 2000, a UN Security Council team visited Kinshasa, Kigali, Kampala, Lusaka, and Harare on a peace mission led by the late Richard Holbrooke, the forceful US ambassador to the UN at the time. The mission called for the withdrawal of Rwandan and Ugandan troops from the Congo and urged Kabila to cooperate with MONUC's deployment.[52] SADC ambassadors in New York also continually lobbied the UN Secretary-General, Kofi Annan, and the Security Council, accusing the Council of neglect and overcautiousness in expecting more stable conditions in the DRC than required elsewhere before deploying a substantial UN force.[53] An intricate series of diplomatic games continued as Luanda, Windhoek, and Harare sought to pressure Kabila to cooperate with the UN, while Tshwane (Pretoria), which had earlier supplied military material to Rwanda and Uganda, urged Kigali and Kampala to withdraw their troops from the DRC.

In January 2001, Laurent Kabila was assassinated by one of his presidential bodyguards. Kabila's son, Joseph, assumed power in Kinshasa. Four months later, another UN Security Council mission visited the Great Lakes region to consult with regional leaders on implementing the Lusaka accord. By October 2001, sporadic fighting continued, particularly in Orientale province and the volatile Kivu region. Laurent Kabila had refused to cooperate with former president Masire, accusing him of bias and a lack of fluency in French. Joseph Kabila extended better cooperation to the facilitator, and the inter-Congolese dialogue was finally launched with a meeting in Addis Ababa, Ethiopia—seat of the OAU—in October 2001, before reconvening in South Africa's Sun City between 25 February and 18 April 2002. A power-sharing agreement was thereafter negotiated between some of the key parties, which the Rwandan-backed RCD at first declined to sign.

Energetic South African diplomacy had finally produced some political results, with Tshwane also sending 1,400 troops to a strengthened MONUC. In July 2002, South African president Thabo Mbeki, in close collaboration with UN Secretary-General Kofi Annan, brokered the Pretoria accord between Kinshasa and Kigali by which Rwanda agreed to withdraw from the DRC in exchange for Kabila's promise to track down and disarm interahamwe and ex-FAR militias that had launched attacks into Rwanda from the DRC. Most Rwandan troops had withdrawn by the end of 2002 in fulfillment of the accord, with US pressure through Secretary of State Colin Powell also playing an important part in Kigali's withdrawal. (Rwandan troops, though, periodically reentered the DRC, as their presence in North Kivu in 2005 attested.[54]) The George W. Bush administration started reversing the Clinton administration's policy by creating some distance from

Kigali, though it still remained close to Kampala.[55] Despite the Pretoria agreement, the UN, however, received reports that Rwandan forces may have reentered areas in the DRC—particularly around Bukavu—and that withdrawing Rwandan troops had left significant quantities of arms and some personnel with its RCD-Goma allies.[56] Namibia had already withdrawn its troops from Congo. Zimbabwe, Angola, and Burundi also started bringing the rest of their own contingents home in 2002.

A month after South Africa's diplomatic triumph, Angola brokered the Luanda accord between Kinshasa and Kampala by which Uganda agreed to withdraw from the DRC and to restore full diplomatic relations between both countries. In December 2002, Congolese parties meeting in Tshwane signed the Global and All-Inclusive Agreement on the Transition in the DRC. The accord called for a two-year transition period during which Joseph Kabila would remain president and run the country with four vice presidents nominated by the government, RCD-Goma, the MLC, and the unarmed opposition. The agreement also aimed for the reunification of the country, adoption of a new constitution, holding of national elections, promoting transitional justice and national reconciliation, and disarming armed groups.

Many Congolese, however, expressed concerns that this government of warlords lacked popular support and consisted largely of self-serving political figures that had held office under Mobutu's discredited dictatorship.[57] This agreement was confirmed in Sun City, South Africa, in April 2003—attended by over three hundred delegates with external funding provided by donors—with the signing of the Final Act of the inter-Congolese political negotiation. A week after the signing of the accord, UN special representative Namanga Ngongi convened the first meeting of the International Committee in Support of the Transition in Kinshasa, comprising ambassadors of permanent members of the UN Security Council; representatives of the African Union troika—South Africa, Mozambique, and Zambia—as well as diplomats from Angola, Belgium, Canada, Gabon, the African Union, and the European Union.

From Bullets to Ballots, 2003–2006

In May 2003, UN Secretary-General Kofi Annan called for an increase in MONUC's forces to 10,800 and urged a strengthening of the UN's mandate to enable the mission to contribute more effectively to peacemaking efforts and to provide greater political support to the transitional government in Kinshasa.[58] By November 2003, MONUC had 10,415 troops and an annual budget of $641 million. But despite progress on the political front, instability continued in the Kivu region, while the security situation in Bunia (Orientale province) deteriorated sharply following the withdrawal of Ugandan troops from the northeastern town in May 2003. The departure of

Ugandan soldiers left a security vacuum that ethnic-based militias rushed in to fill, slaughtering hundreds of civilians and threatening the beleaguered UN compound. Bunia had been the battleground of conflicts between Lendu and Hema militias for several years, and Kampala had been accused of supporting both sides at different periods.

With increasing concern about genocide, and following the killing of two UN military observers, Kofi Annan called on the Security Council to deploy a well-equipped peace-enforcement force to Bunia to protect the town's twenty thousand civilians, UN staff, and key installations. In June 2003, France led the one thousand–strong Interim Emergency Multinational Force (IEMF) to conduct Operation Artemis, which was mandated to protect civilians in Bunia until 2,400 Bangladeshi, Indian, Indonesian, Pakistani, and Uruguayan UN peacekeepers took over from the force in September 2003. MONUC thereafter conducted cordon-and-search operations in Bunia and its environs. Though helpful in stabilizing the situation and leading to a strengthened military mandate for MONUC, this force had as much to do with the European Union's attempts to find a testing ground for its evolving rapid-reaction force. With unilateral French military interventions having become discredited after the Rwandan debacle in 1994, widespread suspicion remained in many parts of Africa that France was using the EU as political cover to continue its interventionist policies in francophone Africa. More positively, the United States and Britain had put pressure on Rwanda and Uganda to allow the French-led EU force to deploy to Bunia.[59]

In July 2003, the UN Security Council mandated MONUC to use force to implement its mandate in Orientale and Kivu and imposed an arms embargo on the two provinces. This latter action was more symbolic than real since there was no effective mechanism to monitor the embargo along a 2,500-kilometer border between the Congo and its neighbors (Uganda, Rwanda, and Burundi). In August 2003, William Swing, a veteran, avuncular US diplomat, was appointed as the UN special representative in Kinshasa, raising hopes that the presence of a high-profile American in the post would encourage Washington to lend greater support to MONUC. Swing had been his country's ambassador in Kinshasa between 1998 and 2001 and so knew many of the key players. The Congolese politicians tended to act deferentially toward him, and some even feared him. He thus acquired the reputation of being a viceroy in the country. Within the UN, he was regarded as a good manager who consulted his staff well, but there were sometimes concerns that he took orders from Washington as well as New York: US secretary of state Colin Powell had pushed his appointment strongly with Kofi Annan.[60]

Though there was some optimism that the inauguration of the transitional government in Kinshasa in July 2003 might finally end five years of conflict in the DRC, fighting still continued in parts of Orientale and Kivu provinces. Despite the establishment of a strengthened MONUC Ituri brigade, the area saw a continued splintering of armed factions and attacks on UN peacekeepers.[61] The transitional government also struggled—amid widespread allegations of corruption against its members and the military top brass as well as a lack of financial and logistical support—to implement a national disarmament, demobilization, and reintegration program, making it difficult to deal with fighters who were ready to surrender their arms throughout the Congo. In 2005, it was reported that over $3 million was stolen from the army payroll, which had countless "ghost soldiers."[62]

South Africa continued to be the main driving force behind the UN's Third Verification Mechanism for implementing the Pretoria agreement. In November 2003, President Thabo Mbeki continued diplomatic efforts to bring the leaders of Congo and Rwanda to South Africa to discuss the implementation of their earlier accord.[63]

At a meeting in Paris in December 2003, donors pledged $3.9 billion for the reconstruction of the DRC between 2004 and 2006. Drawing lessons from its difficult experiences in Ituri, the UN announced the creation of a 3,500-strong South African–led Kivu brigade in March 2004. With increasing factionalism within the transitional government, such plans failed to stop the brief capture of Bukavu by rebels two months later, before Congolese government troops retook the town. MONUC had only 450 troops in Bukavu, a number it soon increased to 1,004. But the UN's overstretched peacekeepers were unable to intervene effectively to bring peace to a town of 550,000 residents, though MONUC did protect four thousand internally displaced persons who had sought shelter at the UN's office in the town. MONUC was often dismissed as a toothless body by several senior officials of the transitional government for failing to use its peace-enforcement powers to prevent the fall of Bukavu.[64]

These tensions lit the fuse of anti-UN sentiments that extremists had earlier stoked by calling for attacks on MONUC personnel. There were also increasingly negative media reports about the role of the UN in the DRC.[65] These criticisms revived unpleasant memories of the UN's days in the Congo four decades earlier. The UN was accused of failing to prevent Bukavu from falling to rebels; its vehicles were burned; and there were violent demonstrations outside its offices in Kinshasa, Lubumbashi, Kalemie, Mbandaka, Beni, Kindu, and Kisangani that led to the destruction of equipment and property estimated to be worth $1 million. UN staff were also harassed and assaulted, and their homes were looted. MONUC soldiers killed three demonstrators who had infiltrated the UN compound in Kinshasa.[66] This incident, along with allegations of sexual exploitation and rape of women by MONUC staff in Bunia, further damaged the UN's increasingly tarnished image in the Congo.[67]

The crisis in Bukavu led to the deterioration in relations between Kinshasa and Kigali, with the Congolese accusing Rwanda of involvement in the capture of Bukavu, and the Rwandans accusing Kinshasa of failing to prevent attacks on its territory from the DRC. In June 2004, the government of Joseph Kabila announced the foiling of a coup attempt by about forty members of the presidential guard who briefly took over the national television station in Kinshasa, again underlining the unpredictable and unstable nature of this conflict. This was further underlined by the announcement, in August 2004, by the representative of RCD-Goma on the transitional government executive, Vice President Azarias Ruberwa, that his party was leaving the interim government. Thabo Mbeki had to fly to Kinshasa a few days later to stitch things back together.

Many committees and mechanisms were established, with UN assistance, to implement the Lusaka accord. But many of these bodies often floundered due to a lack of commitment, adequate resources, and political attention by domestic and regional actors. In April 2003, the UN convened the International Committee in Support of the Transition to coordinate diplomatic efforts for the Congo's peace process in order to exert joint political pressure on the domestic parties. With the continuing presence of Uganda's Allied Democratic Forces/National Army for the Liberation of Uganda (ADF/NALU) rebels in northeastern Congo, MONUC helped to establish the Joint Uganda/DRC Bilateral Security Intelligence Commission in December 2003. At the African Union summit in Addis Ababa in July 2004, Kofi Annan convened a meeting with key African leaders to pressure Kigali and Kinshasa to establish the Joint Verification Mechanism agreed to by Joseph Kabila and Rwandan leader Paul Kagame during an earlier meeting in Abuja with Nigerian president Olusegun Obasanjo, the AU chair. MONUC drew up the draft terms of reference for this mechanism.

The conflict in Bukavu underlined the UN's folly in deploying an inadequate number of logistically deficient peacekeepers with an ambiguous mandate to help disarm over three hundred thousand combatants in a country the size of Western Europe. Critical guidelines of the Brahimi Report on peacekeeping of August 2000—urging the UN Security Council to send in sufficient troops into conflict zones, to have clear mandates, and to ensure the capacity to respond decisively to threats—had simply been ignored (see Chapter 1).[68] As Kofi Annan candidly admitted in a report to the UN Security Council in August 2004, "The establishment of MONUC's peacekeeping mandate under Chapter VII of the United Nations charter has raised expectations that the Mission will 'enforce' the peace throughout the country. However, there is a wide gap between such expectations and MONUC's capacity to deliver on them."[69]

In the same report, Annan proposed new roles for a strengthened MONUC, calling for the mission to establish three joint commissions with the transitional government on legislation (including a new constitution), on security sector reform, and on elections, in order to help coordinate efforts and to mobilize international support in these important areas. Significantly, the UN Secretary-General also called for an increase in MONUC's strength from 10,800 to 23,900, with the addition of 13,100 military personnel to the UN force. He outlined a revised concept of military operations, with strengthened UN brigades in Ituri, North and South Kivu, and Katanga/Kasai mandated to preempt conflicts, assist disarmament efforts, and help the government to extend its authority throughout the country. A brigade-sized force was proposed for Kinshasa. Annan also called for MONUC to establish two rapid reaction forces—reserve battalions—to respond to emergencies.[70] In October 2004, the Security Council again demonstrated its frugality in the face of an urgent need to strengthen the peacekeeping mission, increasing MONUC's authorized strength to 16,700: 7,200 fewer troops than the UN Secretary-General had requested.

Rwanda and the DRC had agreed to the terms of the Joint Verification Mechanism in September 2004, while both countries and Uganda signed a US-brokered tripartite agreement a month later. In the latter accord, all three countries vowed to stop "negative forces" from destabilizing the region by expelling them from their own territories. But the reality of the situation on the ground was very different from these diplomatic niceties. Between September and December 2004, forty incidents of direct fire were reported against MONUC's Ituri brigade.[71] The UN attempted to play its more robust "peace enforcement" role in Ituri, with infantry troops from Pakistan, Nepal, and South Africa conducting cordon-and-search operations and arresting militia leaders in February and March 2005. These tactics, however, carried risks: during the operations in February 2005, nine UN peacekeepers were killed, while MONUC also killed about sixty militia members.[72]

Twenty-eight million Congolese voters were registered to take part in the country's first polls in forty years, which cost an estimated $422 million. The EU was the largest funder of the elections, and Aldo Ajello, its blunt-speaking Italian special envoy for the Great Lakes between 1995 to 2007 and former UN special representative in Mozambique between 1992 and 1994 (see Chapter 4), played an important role in mobilizing support for peacebuilding efforts in the DRC.[73] The *brassage* process of the disarmament, demobilization, and reintegration of soldiers into civilian life was grossly underresourced despite the efforts of the EU, Belgium, the Netherlands, South Africa, and Angola. For example, in July 2005, two-thirds of excombatants in Ituri remained unemployed.[74] Strong suspicion and accusations continued that Rwanda and Uganda were still supporting militias in Kivu and Ituri respectively, and the Congolese army and the myriad of militias were accused of continued killings and abuses of civilians.

In May 2005, Kofi Annan proposed that the UN Security Council increase MONUC's peacekeepers to 19,290 in order to help augment security before national elections. Astonishingly, eleven thousand of MONUC's

16,700 troops were deployed in Orientale and Kivu provinces, leaving the other 5,700 thinly and dangerously spread across a massive country with dilapidated infrastructure and communication.

The DRC held historic elections in 2006, overseen by the dynamic president of its electoral commission, Apollinaire Malu-Malu, and supported by MONUC. The EU deployed a small force of 800 soldiers in Kinshasa, which helped provide security to the capital during and after elections. The incumbent president, Joseph Kabila, won the election after a runoff in October 2006 with 58 percent of the vote to Jean-Pierre Bemba's 42 percent. The Swahili-speaking Kabila carried much of the East (the Kivus and Orientale)—the most populated and richest part of the Congo—and his home province of Katanga as well as Maniema, while Bemba won the West, particularly his home province of Equateur, Bas-Congo, and the capital of Kinshasa.[75] However, fighting between Kabila's troops and those of his closest rival, Jean-Pierre Bemba, in Kinshasa in August 2006 killed at least twenty-three people and rendered the security situation unstable. Even as Kabila was inaugurated as president in December 2006, the enormity of the challenges faced by the government was illustrated by the fact that his country's budget for 2007–2011 was $14 billion, half of which he hoped to receive from external donors. By 2008, the Congo's rich mineral resources contributed only $40 million a year to government coffers amid widespread illegal mining.[76]

Waging War to Keep Peace, 2007–2011

Even after the first elections in the DRC in forty years, instability continued in many areas of the country: the Kivus, the Kasais, Katanga, Equateur, Ituri, Bas-Congo, and the capital of Kinshasa. It was clear that a premature withdrawal of the $1 billion a year UN mission could result in full-scale fighting. In North Kivu, indictee of the Hague-based International Criminal Court Laurent Nkunda's Rwandan-backed (he had fought with Kagame's Rwandese Patriotic Front in Rwanda before going to the DRC and received substantial military support from Kigali)[77] Congrès National pour la Défense du Peuple (CNDP) clashed with the Armed Forces of the DRC (FARDC), claiming to be protecting the rights of the Tutsi minority. Cross-border incidents continued between the Rwandan Defence Forces (RDF) and the FDLR—former FAR/Interahamwe—rebels based in the Congo. FDLR and Mayi-Mayi elements also worked together in South Kivu. In Bas-Congo, the Bundu Dia Kongo (BDK) clashed frequently with the Congolese security forces, resulting, for example, in over one hundred deaths in January and February 2007.[78] A month later, fighting again erupted between government forces and supporters of Jean-Pierre Bemba in Kinshasa, which resulted in at least three hundred deaths.[79] Bemba took refuge in the South African embassy in Kinshasa, before fleeing into exile in Portugal. He was subsequently arrested for war crimes allegedly committed by his troops in the Central African Republic, and his trial at the International Criminal Court started in 2010.

Clashes involving FARDC, the FDLR, CNDP, and Mayi-Mayi groups in North Kivu displaced 150,000 people between August and November 2007.[80] In the Orientale province city of Ituri, FARDC was struggling to contain the Front Nationaliste Intégrationiste (FNI) and Forces de Résistance Patriotique d'Ituri (FPRI) militias. In Maniema and Katanga provinces, the FARDC battled Mayi-Mayi militias. Uganda's rebel Lord's Resistance Army (LRA) also operated in the Garamba Park border region of northeastern DRC, pillaging, raping, abducting, and killing civilians there and in border areas in South Sudan and the Central African Republic.

By 2007, the UN had 17,342 peacekeepers (with India, Pakistan, Uruguay, Bangladesh, and South Africa providing the largest contingents) in the Congo. British diplomat Alan Doss (the former UN special representative in Liberia) replaced William Swing as the UN special representative in the DRC in October 2007. MONUC launched operations alongside FARDC in North Kivu, South Kivu, and Ituri, as the peacekeepers started paradoxically waging war to keep peace. Most of the UN's efforts focused on Ituri, the Kivus, and northern Katanga. The danger of such close cooperation with the Congolese army was that MONUC's reputation could be damaged by the human rights abuses perpetrated by elements of the country's often ill-trained, ill-disciplined, and irregularly paid army. The UN's postelection mandate as an integrated mission was primarily to build a stable security environment in the DRC, help to consolidate democratic rule, plan security sector reform, protect human rights, and conduct local elections. Other tasks included protecting civilians in areas in which MONUC was deployed, securing national borders, monitoring illegal arms flows, and protecting humanitarian personnel.[81]

In January 2008, a Conference on Peace, Security, and Development in the Kivus was held in Goma, attended by Congolese political, civil society, and armed groups. All parties pledged their commitment to a MONUC-monitored ceasefire, to militias entering the brassage process, and to the safe return of refugees and internally displaced persons. In the same month, clashes occurred in Bas-Congo between Congolese police and the Bundu Dia Kongo. MONUC continued to conduct joint operations with, and provide support for, FARDC, particularly in Ituri, Haut Uélé, and North Kivu. UN peacekeepers also trained FARDC units, while regional states (Angola and South Africa) and external actors (the United States and Belgium) helped to train the Congolese army; the African Development Bank and the World Bank supported DDR efforts; and the EU played an important role in security sector reform. Based on UN Security Council direction, particularly from 2007, and a "robust" chapter VII mandate to use force for enforcement activities in December 2008, 90 percent of the UN's peacekeepers (fifteen out of seventeen battalions) were deployed in eastern Congo by 2008, with 60 percent based in the two volatile Kivu provinces and others in Ituri and Katanga.[82] Fighting between FARDC and Laurent Nkunda's forces in August 2008 led to 250,000 people being displaced.[83] It was only after MONUC's Pakistani battalion had killed about three hundred of Nkunda's men that he agreed to enter into the disarmament process.[84]

The enormity of the task of building peace in the DRC was further underlined by the fact that, in July 2008, 130,207 combatants still had to pass through the brassage process.[85] By January 2009, there were 1.4 million internally displaced people in the DRC, mostly in the Kivus and Orientale provinces.[86] Putting the Congolese Humpty Dumpty back together again was an enormous task, and the UN Security Council had not yet invested the requisite financial resources and political will to match the huge challenges.

Former Nigerian president Olusegun Obasanjo was appointed as the UN Secretary-General's special envoy for the Great Lakes region in November 2008. Along with former Tanzanian president Benjamin Mkapa he traveled tirelessly across the region meeting with regional leaders and Congolese domestic actors. The two men helped to facilitate a peace deal between Kinshasa and the CNDP in March 2009 and to strengthen cooperation between Kinshasa and Kigali. The special envoy's office was finally closed by June 2010.

Armed attacks were launched against rebels in North and South Kivu by government forces in September 2009. A month later, intercommunal clashes in Equateur province resulted in the displacement of nearly two hundred thousand people in four months. The security situation in the DRC was still fragile in 2010, as the FDLR and the LRA continued to attack civilians in the Kivus and Orientale province respectively. MONUC's efforts to support the Congolese army militarily to dislodge rebels in eastern Congo proved to be controversial, as elements of the FARDC were accused of committing major human rights violations and were also involved in mutinies and desertions.[87] By November 2009, UN peacekeepers suspended their logistical support to FARDC units accused of human rights abuses. Though the world body was trying to avoid being tarred with the same brush as FARDC's bad eggs, its close collaboration with a force that was regarded by many rebels and civilians as one among many armed factions undoubtedly raised serious questions about MONUC's own impartiality.

Despite this insecure environment, noting that it was time for the country to "fly with its own wings,"[88] President Joseph Kabila asked the UN to start withdrawing its 19,800 troops (reinforcements had arrived from Bangladesh, Egypt, and Jordan) from June 2010 when the DRC celebrated its fiftieth anniversary as an independent nation. The idea of having UN peacekeepers in the Congo both for its golden jubilee celebrations and during its painful birth in the 1960s appeared to be damaging to national pride. The UN would thereafter focus on military, rule of law, and stabilization and peace consolidation issues, with the peacekeepers expected to leave the country in stages by December 2013. Kinshasa was now insisting on asserting its "sovereignty" after the 2006 elections, against what many Congolese regarded as the overbearing arrogance of UN officials. It rejected the MONUC plan to train FARDC, saying that it preferred mainly to work through bilateral partners, and outlined its own future priorities to be security sector reform, socioeconomic development, and rebuilding state institutions. Kinshasa had earlier requested that MONUC leave the country by June 2011, two years earlier than the UN itself wanted.[89] Alan Doss finally resigned as UN special representative in May 2010 after having lost the confidence of the government, several of whose members had called on him to leave. In contrast to Swing, Doss was seen to have distanced himself from the Congolese population. Several UN staff members saw him as aloof and secretive, relying on a small cabal to make decisions but not enjoying the confidence of several members of his senior staff.[90] He was replaced by another US diplomat, Roger Meece.

This premature reduction of UN peacekeepers being pushed by Kinshasa was a replay of the ill-conceived UN withdrawal from Burundi in 2006, which had also been orchestrated by the country's leaders on the false belief they would receive vastly increased UN development assistance once the peacekeepers had left.[91] In July 2010, MONUC was renamed the UN Organization Stabilization Mission in the DRC (MONUSCO) in recognition of its changing mandate. Even as instability continued in Kivu and Orientale provinces, three UN peacekeepers were killed by armed factions in North Kivu in October 2010. Progress in the area of security sector reform continued to be very slow in January 2011. FARDC still battled FDLR, ADF/NALU, and other Congolese armed groups in North Kivu, with MONUSCO assisting efforts to deter the FDLR and Mayi-Mayi in the province. In neighboring South Kivu, UN peacekeepers were seeking to deter the FDLR and armed groups such as the Burundian Forces Nationales de Libération in order to protect civilians. In Orientale province, MONUSCO worked with FARDC and the Uganda People's Defense Forces against the LRA. The human toll of this conflict was underlined by the fact that 1.7 million people had been internally displaced by January 2011, 1.3 million of them in the Kivus. Amid these continuing difficulties, presidential and parliamentary polls were scheduled for November 2011.[92]

Regional dynamics at first complicated the resolution of the Congo conflict until national governments decided to cooperate to battle "negative forces" on their territories. Rwandan troops were massed on the DRC border, and Kinshasa accused Kigali of supporting Nkunda's CNDP and periodically reentering Congolese territory, charges which Rwanda denied. FARDC and the Ugandan army clashed on Lake Albert, and Ugandan troops were also massed on the Congolese border. The DRC and Angola had an unsettled Kahemba border dispute amid disputes over oil-rich areas. Kinshasa and Luanda thus expelled each other's citizens: between December 2008 and December 2009, Angola expelled more than 160,000 Congolese from its territory; in October 2009, the DRC expelled nearly two thousand Angolans from its territory.[93] Between September 2010 and January 2011, over 12,000 more Congolese nationals were expelled from Angola.[94]

SADC, the African Union, and the International Conference on the Great Lakes all sought to play supportive roles in efforts to manage the Congolese conflict and convened regular meetings with key actors. Kinshasa chaired SADC and the Economic Community of Central African States in 2009, seeking to use the two regional platforms to focus greater attention on its need for stability and reconstruction assistance. At the bilateral level, the DRC and Rwanda had finally set up a joint verification body in September 2007 and, two months later, agreed in Nairobi to eliminate the threat posed by armed groups in eastern Congo, particularly the roughly six thousand ex-FAR/Interahamwe. A task force was set up, chaired by MONUC, for joint monitoring of the common border. But cross-border exchanges of fire between both armies in 2008 suggested that mutual suspicions had not yet fully dissipated. Having earlier looted the Congo's resources, Rwanda continued to benefit from resources extracted by local Congolese militias from the country's mines, which were then exported to Rwanda on light planes.[95] There was a widespread feeling, after a while, that Kigali was exaggerating the threat posed by the FDLR and that the continued access to the Congo's riches, which sustained its impressive growth rates, was more at issue.[96]

In December 2008, Kinshasa and Kigali put aside their differences and devised a joint military plan by which Rwandan forces would enter the eastern Congo and fight alongside FARDC to eliminate the threat of the FDLR. In exchange, Kigali effectively cut off support for the CNDP (elements of which were incorporated into FARDC) and arrested Laurent Nkunda in Rwanda. The implausible month-long operation began in January 2009 and managed to flush out the FDLR from most of its Congolese strongholds, though the rebels visited brutal reprisals on local populations. MONUC sought to reinforce its presence along Lake Tanganyika in order to stop the FDLR from retreating into and destabilizing Burundi. Eight months after this operation, Kinshasa and Kigali had established full diplomatic relations with the exchange of ambassadors.

The DRC and Uganda also improved their bilateral relationship by pledging in May 2008 to work together against the ADF/NALU, which were destabilizing North Kivu. This cooperation was extended to the Central African Republic, with all three countries coordinating military actions against the LRA. Joint military operations were also conducted against the LRA by the armies of Uganda, the DRC, and the Sudan People's Liberation Army, particularly in 2008 and 2009, resulting in brutal reprisals by the rebels against local populations. But these military attacks reduced LRA fighters in the DRC to no more than one hundred by December 2009.[97] It is worth briefly considering here French scholar Séverine Autesserre's interesting 2010 critique of peacebuilding efforts in the DRC. Her main argument was that these efforts failed to achieve durable peace in the Congo due to the peacebuilding "culture" and "ideology" of African and Western diplomats, UN peacekeepers, and staff of nongovernmental organizations (NGOs) who did not prioritize "grassroots peacebuilding" but instead focused on macrointerventions.[98] The fundamental problem with Autesserre's approach, however, is the fact that in order for the UN to undertake the sort of local peacebuilding initiatives she proposes, the world body would surely have required far greater resources as well as a mandate as a quasi government that neither international nor domestic actors were prepared to provide. The peacebuilders, therefore, necessarily had to use tools and techniques built up over two decades of multidimensional peacebuilding, which many of the more knowledgeable of them knew were not perfect, but represented the degree of political will and support that powerful actors within the UN Security Council were prepared to provide to the DRC. It is certainly not the "socialization" of these actors that made them act in the ways they did, as the author claims, and applying so broad a brush to actors from such diverse backgrounds seems a bit naive. While Autesserre's observations about the importance of local initiatives are useful, such an approach would clearly struggle to affect larger regional and external processes.

Autesserre fails to give sufficient weight to the crucial deficiencies in the number and resources of the thinly dispersed twenty-thousand-strong UN peacekeepers that were eventually sent to an infrastructure-starved country the size of Western Europe. She refers several times to the fact that the mission is the largest UN peacekeeping mission in the world, but fails to recognize that the peacekeepers were dangerously vulnerable to attacks in the huge country and were barely able to protect themselves let alone large populations. After all, sixty thousand North Atlantic Treaty Organization (NATO) peacekeepers were sent to the much smaller territory of Kosovo in 1999. Autesserre's reference to MONUC as the "only effective military force in the country"[99] is a claim that will surely not go unchallenged, as the three million Congolese who were murdered, the 2.4 million who were displaced from their homes, and the tens of thousands who were raped will certainly not be convinced that they had the protection of the most "effective" force in the country. Though the UN's peacekeepers often tried their best under very difficult circumstances and took more robust military action from 2007 onward, for the most part, MONUC observed the decade-long slaughter in the Congo rather than intervened decisively to stop it. It is also unclear how Autesserre proposes undertaking "grassroots peacebuilding" given the enormous difficulties in even convincing the UN Security Council to agree to the clearly inadequate deployment of twenty thousand peacekeepers; the unwillingness of donors to provide sufficient resources for disarmament, demobilization, and reintegration tasks, as well as crucial security sector reform; and the increasing assertiveness of domestic political actors in the DRC—particularly after democratic elections in 2006—who, in their desire to run their own affairs, would not tolerate the overbearing international presence that would surely have been required for grassroots peacebuilding.

Another analysis of the Congo that needs to be critiqued is British economist Paul Collier's prescriptions for resolving the postelection crises by 2008.[100] Collier stated: "What is needed is a massive contracting-out approach to health and education, using whatever agencies work: NGOs, churches, private firms." However, fledgling civil society groups—while they are often courageous—cannot be a panacea for providing security in postconflict situations. As the continuing instability in the Kivus and Orientale provinces demonstrate, the Congolese government urgently needs to be strengthened to enable it to provide security and promote development for its people.

Civil society actors are therefore no substitute for a strong state. Collier also overlooks the fact that many local NGOs lack the capacity to absorb large funds as well as the security to undertake the work that governments usually perform. His dismissal of the need for an effective Congolese state, claiming that "donors and government share an attachment to the chimera of 'building an effective state,'" repeats the dangerous proselytizing of his former employer, the World Bank, which for decades called for less government involvement. This approach did much damage to health, education, and social services across Africa.

Equally dangerous is Collier's disregard for the sovereignty of African states: "The international community has been frightened to infringe on sovereignty . . . post-conflict governments must accept limits on their behaviour." This sentiment represents an increasing neocolonial Western discourse in which unaccountable outsiders are urged to make decisions for elected African governments. By strengthening their states, many African governments would, in fact, gradually develop the ability to tackle corruption and provide services to their citizens. Collier's proposal for the UN Peacebuilding Commission to step into the breach in the Congo ignores the spectacular failure of this ineffectual body in the smaller cases of Burundi and Sierra Leone.[101]

Before concluding this section, it is worth noting the increasing role in the Congo of a permanent member of the UN Security Council. During the country's 1998–2002 civil war, some Chinese companies were implicated in the illicit export of coltan, a business which also involved invading Rwandan and Ugandan armies. Many Western and South African companies were also fingered for involvement in similar activities. Until 2007, the DRC was not among China's top ten African trading partners. In September of that year, however, came news that China had agreed to an $8 billion deal with the Congo, in which $5 billion would go toward infrastructural development (including a 3,200-kilometer railway and a 3,200-kilometer road, as well as several hospitals). China also pledged to invest $3 billion in the country's mining sector: a direct challenge in an area of large South African investment.[102] These developments could provide Kinshasa with the leverage to assert even more independence from the UN and its Western donors.

Despite the enormity of the problems in the Congo and the improved stability following the 2006 elections, the international community still continued its frugal ways. By September 2009, only 53 per cent of assessed requirements of the Humanitarian Action Plan for the DRC of $946 had been met.[103] MONUSCO also lacked adequate military helicopters a decade after the UN's deployment.[104] The UN Security Council clearly had not fully learned the lessons of Rwanda and was still failing to provide the resources required to help sustain efforts to end a thirteen-year war that had claimed an estimated 2.5 million lives, internally displaced 3.4 million people, involved seven foreign armies, and spanned three of Africa's subregions.

Concluding Reflections

It is important to note that the UN sought to promote a regional approach to the conflicts in the Great Lakes after Kofi Annan appointed Ibrahima Fall, the Senegalese UN Assistant Secretary-General for political affairs, as his special representative to the Great Lakes region in July 2002. Fall organized an international conference on the Great Lakes in November 2004, in partnership with the AU, involving regional governments, civil society actors, and foreign donors. This idea had first been proposed in the UN Security Council in October 1994, but, partly because it was strongly backed by France, enjoyed little support in Kigali and Kampala. Rwanda and Uganda also opposed the inclusion of Angola and Congo-Brazzaville as full participants in the conference.

The conference aimed to address the root causes of the Great Lakes region's interlocking conflicts, to craft a regional settlement to the crises, and to muster donor support for the economic reconstruction of the region. Conferees were requested to forge a Stability, Security, and Development Plan for the region and to undertake regional integration projects in the energy, transport, infrastructure, and information sectors. The core countries that were involved in the conference included: Burundi, the DRC, Kenya, Rwanda, Uganda, Tanzania, and Zambia, with other countries invited as contiguous states. The meeting had four main areas of focus: peace and security, democracy and "good governance," economic development and regional integration, and humanitarian and social issues.[105] On 19 and 20 November 2004, the first heads of state summit of the International Conference of the Great Lakes took place in Dar es Salaam and was attended by eleven African leaders. The Dar es Salaam Declaration of Principles on Peace, Security, Democracy, and Development in the Great Lakes Region was signed at the meeting, committing regional states to principles, plans of action, and draft protocols for promoting peace and security.

Four days after the meeting, officials in Kigali threatened to launch a "surgical strike" into the DRC to flush out Rwandan rebels operating there. It was clear that the "spirit of Dar" had not spilled over into the treacherous political waters of the Great Lakes. In December 2006, regional states signed the Pact on Security, Stability, and Development in the Great Lakes Region, committing them to nonaggression, democracy, regional integration, cooperation on human rights and humanitarian issues, disarmament and the extradition of foreign armed groups, and creating joint mechanisms to manage their common borders.[106]

In August 2009, an International Conference on the Great Lakes Region was held in Lusaka, Zambia, attended by several heads of state to discuss security issues, especially in eastern DRC. The summit agreed to convene every two years. In December 2010, a second high-level International Conference on the Great Lakes Region was held in Lusaka, focusing on mineral resources management and certification, underlining the importance of curbing illegal exploitation of mineral resources in an effort to end the region's conflicts. Between 1994 and 2010, Security Council ambassadors made 13 visits to the region.

In contrast to its cowardly retreat from Rwanda and hesitant entry into Burundi, the UN attempted to enforce peace in the Congo in both the 1960s and the 2000s, underlining the difficulty of entering a war zone in which there was no peace to keep. Most of the armed factions eventually cooperated with UN peacekeepers in Burundi, resulting in successful elections in 2005 and 2010, though the country remains fragile. Despite the Congolese election in 2006, fighting continued in Kivu and Orientale provinces until key regional states such as Rwanda and Uganda, which had previously been destabilizing and looting the country, cooperated with the Congolese government in a bid to rid the DRC of rebels from their own territories. This again underlined the importance of regional cooperation to the success of UN peacekeeping missions. In order to create a somewhat more robust MONUC, the UN Security Council eventually offered some strategic direction to the peacekeepers, strengthening their mandate and focusing their attention on the volatile east from 2007, while key external actors such as France, the United States, and the EU supported peacekeeping efforts.

However, the military and financial resources and political attention devoted to the Congo by the Council were clearly inadequate to meet the country's enormous needs.

The international community must finally recognize that it cannot succeed in the DRC unless it provides massive and sustained support and continues to adopt a regional approach to the conflicts in Central Africa that prioritizes peace in Burundi and Rwanda as well as the DRC. Only then can the troubled waters of the Great Lakes be calmed.

Notes

This chapter builds on Adekeye Adebajo, "The United Nations," in Gilbert Khadiagala, ed., *Security Dynamics in Africa's Great Lakes Region* (Boulder: Lynne Rienner, 2006), pp. 141–161. The author would like to thank Devon Curtis, Gilbert Khadiagala, and Chris Saunders for comments on an earlier version of this chapter.

1. Quoted in Ludo De Witte, *The Assassination of Lumumba* (London: Verso, 2001), p. v.

2. See Adekeye Adebajo and Chris Landsberg, "Back to the Future: UN Peacekeeping in Africa," in Adekeye Adebajo and Chandra Lekha Sriram, eds., *Managing Armed Conflicts in the 21st Century* (London: Frank Cass, 2001), pp. 161–188; Christopher Clapham, "The United Nations and Peacekeeping in Africa," in Mark Malan, ed., *Whither Peacekeeping in Africa?* (Halfway House, South Africa: Institute for Security Studies, 1999), pp. 25–44; Oliver Furley and Roy May, eds., *Peacekeeping in Africa* (Brookfield, VT: Ashgate, 1998); Ibrahim Gambari, "The United Nations," in Mwesiga Baregu and Christopher Landsberg, eds., *From Cape to Congo: Southern Africa's Evolving Security Challenges* (Boulder: Lynne Rienner, 2003), pp. 255–274; Marrack Goulding, "The United Nations and Conflict in Africa Since the Cold War," *African Affairs* 98, no. 391 (April 1999): 155–166; Agostinho Zacarias, *The United Nations and International Peacekeeping* (London: I. B. Tauris, 1996).

3. See René Lemarchand, *The Dynamics of Violence in Central Africa* (Philadelphia: University of Pennsylvania Press, 2009); Kankwenda Mbaya, ed., *Zaire: What Destiny?* (Dakar: Council for the Development of Social Science Research in Africa, 1993); Georges Nzongola-Ntalaja, *The Congo: From Leopold to Kabila* (London: Zed, 2002); Gérard Prunier, *From Genocide to Continental War: The "Congolese" Conflict and the Crisis of Contemporary Africa* (London: Hurst, 2009); Peter Uvin, *Life After Violence: A People's Story of Burundi* (London: Zed Books, 2009); Crawford Young and Thomas Turner, *The Rise and Decline of the Zairian State* (Madison: University of Wisconsin Press, 1985).

4. See Agnes Callamard, "French Policy in Rwanda," in Howard Adelman and Astri Suhrke, eds., *The Path of a Genocide: The Rwanda Crisis from Uganda to Zaire* (New Brunswick, NJ: Transaction, 1999), pp. 157–183; Jared Cohen, *One Hundred Days of Silence: America and the Rwanda Genocide* (Lanham, MD: Rowman and Littlefield, 2007); René Lemarchand, "Foreign Policy Making in the Great Lakes Region," in Gilbert Khadiagala and Terrence Lyons, eds., *African Foreign Policies: Power and Process* (Boulder: Lynne Rienner, 2001), pp. 87–106; Gérard Prunier, *The Rwandan Crisis: History of a Genocide* (New York: Columbia University Press, 1995); Paul Williams, "The Peacekeeping System, Britain and the 1994 Rwandan Genocide," in Phil Clark and Zachary D. Kaufman, eds., *After*

Genocide: Transitional Justice, Post-Conflict Reconstruction and Reconciliation in Rwanda and Beyond (London: Hurst, 2009), pp. 71–91.

5. See Georges Abi-Saab, *The United Nations Operation in the Congo 1960–1964* (Oxford: Oxford University Press, 1978); Catherine Hoskyns, *The Congo Since Independence, January 1960–December 1961* (London: Oxford University Press, 1965); Conor Cruise O'Brien, *To Katanga and Back: A UN Case History* (London: Hutchinson, 1962); Indar Jit Rikhye, *Military Adviser to the Secretary-General: UN Peacekeeping and the Congo Crisis* (London: Hurst, 1993).

6. See Brian Urquhart, *A Life in Peace and War* (New York: W. W. Norton, 1987), pp. 145–170.

7. See Larry Devlin, *Chief of Station, Congo* (New York: Public Affairs, 2007).

8. Alan James, "The Congo Controversies," *International Peacekeeping* 1, no. 1 (Spring 1994): 44–58.

9. Kwame Nkrumah, *Africa Must Unite* (London: Panaf, 1963), p. 139.

10. James, "The Congo Controversies," p. 53.

11. James Jonah, "The Security Council, the General Assembly, the Economic and Social Council, and the Secretariat," in Adekeye Adebajo, ed., *From Global Apartheid to Global Village: Africa and the United Nations* (Scottsville, South Africa: University of KwaZulu Natal Press, 2009), pp. 67–68.

12. See Gilbert M. Khadiagala, "Implementing the Arusha Peace Agreement on Rwanda," in Stephen John Stedman, Donald Rothchild, and Elizabeth M. Cousens, eds., *Ending Civil Wars: The Implementation of Peace Agreements* (Boulder: Lynne Rienner, 2002), pp. 463–498; Turid Laegreid, "UN Peacekeeping in Rwanda," in Adelman and Suhrke, *The Path of a Genocide*, pp. 231–251; Ami Mpunge, "Crisis and Response in Rwanda," in Malan, *Whither Peacekeeping in Africa?* pp. 14–24.

13. Laegreid, "UN Peacekeeping in Rwanda," p. 232. See also Roméo Dallaire, *Shake Hands with the Devil: The Failure of Humanity in Rwanda* (London: Arrow Books, 2004).

14. Astri Suhrke, "UN Peacekeeping in Rwanda," in Gunnar Sørbø and Peter Vale, eds., *Out of Conflict: From War to Peace in Africa* (Uppsala: Nordiska Afrikainstitutet, 1997), pp. 107–108.

15. See, for example, Ibrahim A. Gambari, "Rwanda: An African Perspective," in David M. Malone, ed., *The UN Security Council: From the Cold War to the 21st Century* (Boulder: Lynne Rienner, 2004), p. 514.

16. Henry Kwami Anyidoho, *Guns over Kigali* (Accra: Woeli, 1999), p. 11.

17. Henry Anyidoho, "Remembering Rwanda," paper presented at a policy seminar on the UN, regional organizations, and future security threats, organized by the Centre for Conflict Resolution in Cape Town, South Africa, 21–23 May 2004.

18. For an eyewitness account by UNAMIR's deputy force commander, see Anyidoho, *Guns over Kigali*, pp. 20–38.

19. See, for example, Lemarchand, "Foreign Policy Making in the Great Lakes Region," p. 91.

20. Prunier, *The Rwandan Crisis*, p. 287.

21. Quoted in Callamard, "French Policy in Rwanda," p. 174.

22. Linda Melvern, *A People Betrayed: The Role of the West in Rwanda's Genocide* (London: Zed Books, 2000), p. 159.

23. Cited in Laegreid, "UN Peacekeeping in Rwanda," p. 243.

24. Boutros Boutros-Ghali, *Unvanquished: A US-UN Saga* (New York: Random House, 1999), p. 138.

25. Anyidoho, "Remembering Rwanda."

26. Colin Keating, "Rwanda: An Insider's Account," in Malone, *The UN Security Council*, p. 504.

27. Samantha Power, *A Problem from Hell* (New York: Basic Books, 2002), p. 359.

28. Keating, "Rwanda," p. 506.

29. Ibid., p. 503.

30. Melvern, *A People Betrayed,* p. 93.

31. See "Report of the Independent Inquiry into the Actions of the United Nations During the 1994 Genocide in Rwanda," S/1999/1257, 16 December 1999.

32. See Michael Barnett, *Eyewitness to a Genocide: The United Nations and Rwanda* (Ithaca: Cornell University Press, 2002); Melvern, *A People Betrayed;* Organization of African Unity, *The International Panel of Eminent Persons to Investigate the 1994 Genocide in Rwanda and the Surrounding Events,* July 2000; "Report of the Independent Inquiry into the Actions of the United Nations During the 1994 Genocide in Rwanda."

33. The line "where ignorant armies clash by night" is from the 1867 poem by English poet Matthew Arnold. See Dwight Culler, ed., *Poetry and Criticism of Matthew Arnold* (Boston: Houghton Mifflin, 1961).

34. See Kristina Bentley and Roger Southall, *An African Peace Process: Mandela, South Africa, and Burundi* (Cape Town: Human Sciences Research Council, 2005).

35. "Report of the UN Secretary-General on Burundi," S/2003/1146, 4 December 2003, pp. 7–12.

36. Ibid., p. 10.

37. Ibid., p. 8.

38. Bentley and Southall, *An African Peace Process,* p. 103.

39. See Ahmedou Ould-Abdallah, *Burundi on the Brink, 1993–95: A UN Special Envoy Reflects on Preventive Diplomacy* (Washington, DC: US Insitute of Peace Press, 2000).

40. See "Report of the UN Secretary-General on Burundi," S/2004/210, 16 March 2004.

41. See "First Report of the Secretary-General on the United Nations Operation in Burundi," S/2004/682, 23 August 2004, p. 8.

42. "Report of the UN Secretary-General on Burundi," S/2005/149, 8 March 2005, p. 4.

43. "Report of the UN Secretary-General on Burundi," S/2005/728, 21 November 2005, p. 4.

44. See Devon Curtis, "South Africa: 'Exporting Peace' to the Great Lakes Region?" in Adekeye Adebajo, Adebayo Adedeji, and Chris Landsberg, eds., *South Africa in Africa: The Post-Apartheid Era* (Scottsville, South Africa: University of KwaZulu-Natal Press, 2007), pp. 253–273; "Report of the Chairperson of the African Union Commission on Conflict Situations in Africa," Executive Council, Seventh Ordinary Session, 28 June–2 July 2005, pp. 12–14.

45. "Report of the UN Secretary-General on Burundi," S/2005/728, 21 November 2005, p. 4.

46. "Report of the Chairperson of the African Union Commission on Conflict Situations in Africa," Executive Council, Seventh Ordinary Session, 28 June–2 July 2005, pp. 12–14.

47. See Lemarchand, "Foreign Policy Making in the Great Lakes Region," pp. 87–106; Nzongola-Ntalaja, *The Congo,* pp. 227–240.

48. Nzongola-Ntalaja, *The Congo,* p. 232.

49. These groups included: the interahamwe, the ex-FAR, the Allied Democratic Front, the Lord's Resistance Army, the Forces for the Defence of Democracy, the former Ugandan National Army, the Uganda National Rescue Front II, the West Nile Bank Front, and UNITA.

50. On the Lusaka accord, see Musifiky Mwanasali, "From the Organization of African Unity to the African Union," in Mwesiga Baregu and Christopher Landsberg, eds., *From Cape to Congo: Southern Africa's Evolving Security Challenges* (Boulder: Lynne Rienner, 2003), pp. 213–215; "Report of the Secretary-General on the United Nations Preliminary Deployment in the Democratic Republic of the Congo," S/1999/790, 15 July 1999, pp. 1–3.

51. Virgil Hawkins, "History Repeating Itself: The DRC and the UN Security Council," *African Security Review* 12, no. 4 (2003): 49. See also, Mark Malan and Joao Gomes Porto, eds., *Challenges of Implementation: The UN Mission in the Democratic Republic of the Congo* (Tshwane: Institute for Security Studies, 2004).

52. See "Third Report of the Secretary-General on the United Nations Organization Mission in the Democratic Republic of the Congo," S/2000/566, 12 June 2000, pp. 1–2.

53. "Fifth Report of the Secretary-General on the United Nations Organization Mission in the Democratic Republic of the Congo," S/2000/1156, 6 December 2000, pp. 2–3.

54. Lemarchand, *The Dynamics of Violence in Central Africa*, p. 274.

55. Peter J. Schraeder, "Belgium, France, and the United States," in Gilbert Khadiagala, ed., *Security Dynamics in Africa's Great Lakes Region* (Boulder: Lynne Rienner, 2006), p. 174.

56. "Twelfth Report of the Secretary-General on the United Nations Organization Mission in the Democratic Republic of the Congo," S/2002/1180, 18 October 2002, p. 3.

57. Emeric Rogier, "MONUC and the Challenges of Peace Implementation in the Democratic Republic of Congo," Report on the Institute for Security Studies International Expert Workshop, Tshwane, 17–19 September 2003, p. 3.

58. "Second Special Report of the Secretary-General on the United Nations Organization Mission in the Democratic Republic of the Congo," S/2003/556, 27 May 2003, pp. 9 and 28.

59. Schraeder, "Belgium, France, and the United States," p. 177.

60. Confidential interviews.

61. "Fifteenth Report of the Secretary-General on the United Nations Organization Mission in the Democratic Republic of the Congo," S/2004/251, 25 March 2004, pp. 7–8.

62. Lemarchand, *The Dynamics of Violence in Central Africa*, p. 274.

63. See Jean-Jacques Cornish, "In Praise of Peace in the DRC," *Mail and Guardian* 19, no. 48 (28 November–4 December 2003): 16.

64. On the Bukavu crisis, see "Third Special Report of the Secretary-General on the United Nations Organization Mission in the Democratic Republic of the Congo," S/2004/650, 13 August 2004, pp. 10–14.

65. "Fifteenth Report of the Secretary-General on the United Nations Organization Mission in the Democratic Republic of the Congo," S/2004/251, 25 March 2004, p. 10.

66. See "Third Special Report of the Secretary-General on the United Nations Organization Mission in the Democratic Republic of the Congo," S/2004/650, 13 August 2004, p. 12.

67. Ibid., p. 9.

68. See "Report of the Panel on United Nations Peace Operations," S/2000/809, 21 August 2000.

69. See "Third Special Report of the Secretary-General on the United Nations Organization Mission in the Democratic Republic of the Congo," S/2004/650, 13 August 2004, p. 21.

70. Ibid., pp. 27–33.

71. "Sixteenth Report of the Secretary-General on the UN Organization Mission in the Democratic Republic of the Congo," S/2004/1034, 31 December 2004, p. 3.

72. "Seventeenth Report of the Secretary-General on the UN Organization Mission in the Democratic Republic of the Congo," S/2005/167, 15 March 2005, pp. 4–5.

73. See Aldo Ajello, *Brasiers d'Afrique: Mémoires d'un Émissaire pour la Paix* (Paris: L'Harmattan, 2010). See also *International Peacekeeping* 16, no. 2 (April 2009), articles on the UN and EU in the DRC by Denis M. Tull, Catherine Gegout, Gorm Rye Olsen, Claudia Morsut, and Eirin Mobekk.

74. "Eighteenth Report of the Secretary-General on the UN Organization Mission in the Democratic Republic of the Congo," S/2005/506, 2 August 2005, p. 5.

75. Lemarchand, *The Dynamics of Violence in Central Africa,* pp. 262–266.

76. Prunier, *From Genocide to Continental War,* p. 319.

77. Lemarchand, *The Dynamics of Violence in Central Africa,* p. 277.

78. "Twenty-Third Report of the Secretary-General on the UN Organization Mission in the Democratic Republic of the Congo," S/2007/156, 20 March 2007, p. 4.

79. "Twenty-Fourth Report of the Secretary-General on the UN Organization Mission in the Democratic Republic of the Congo," S/2007/671, 14 November 2007, p. 6.

80. Ibid., p. 1.

81. "Twenty-Third Report of the Secretary-General on the UN Organization Mission in the Democratic Republic of the Congo," S/2007/156, 20 March 2007, p. 10.

82. "Twenty-Fifth Report of the Secretary-General on the UN Organization Mission in the Democratic Republic of the Congo," S/2008/218, 2 April 2008, p. 18; "Fourth Special Report of the Secretary-General on the UN Organization Mission in the Democratic Republic of the Congo," S/2008/728, 21 November 2008, p. 13.

83. "Fourth Special Report of the Secretary-General on the UN Organization Mission in the Democratic Republic of the Congo," S/2008/728, 21 November 2008, p. 1.

84. Prunier, *From Genocide to Continental War,* p. 323.

85. "Twenty-Sixth Report of the Secretary-General on the UN Organization Mission in the Democratic Republic of the Congo," S/2008/433, 3 July 2008, p. 11.

86. "Twenty-Seventh Report of the Secretary-General on the UN Organization Mission in the Democratic Republic of the Congo," S/2009/160, 27 March 2009, p. 5.

87. "Twenty-Eighth Report of the Secretary-General on the UN Organization Mission in the Democratic Republic of the Congo," S/2009/335, 30 June 2009, p. 15

88. Quoted in "Thirty-First Report of the Secretary-General on the UN Organization Mission in the Democratic Republic of the Congo," S/2010/164, 20 March 2010, p. 23.

89. "Thirty-First Report of the Secretary-General on the UN Organization Mission in the Democratic Republic of the Congo," S/2010/164, 20 March 2010, p. 23.

90. Confidential interviews.

91. The summary in this paragraph relies on the "Twenty-Ninth Report of the Secretary-General on the UN Organization Mission in the Democratic Republic of the Congo," S/2009/472, 18 September 2009; "Thirtieth Report of the Secretary-General on the UN Organization Mission in the Democratic Republic of the Congo," S/2009/623, 4 December 2009.

92. "Report of the Secretary-General on the United Nations Organization Stabilization Mission in the Democratic Republic of the Congo," S/2011/20, 17 January 2011.

93. "Thirtieth Report of the Secretary-General on the UN Organization Mission in the Democratic Republic of the Congo," S/2009/623, 4 December 2009, p. 7.

94. "Report of the Secretary-General on the United Nations Organization Stabilization Mission in the Democratic Republic of the Congo," S/2011/20, 17 January 2011, p. 7.

95. Prunier, *From Genocide to Continental War,* p. 326.

96. Lemarchand, *The Dynamics of Violence in Central Africa,* p. 276.

97. "Thirtieth Report of the Secretary-General on the UN Organization Mission in the Democratic Republic of the Congo," S/2009/623, 4 December 2009, p. 20.

98. Séverine Autesserre, *The Trouble with the Congo: Local Violence and the Failure of International Peacebuilding* (Cambridge: Cambridge University Press, 2010), pp. 1–14.

99. Ibid., p. 12.

100. Paul Collier, "Naive Faith in the Ballot Box," *The Guardian* (London), 3 November 2008, p. 30.

101. For the full version of this critique, see Adekeye Adebajo, "The Last Thing Congo Needs Is These Neo-Colonial Remedies," *The Guardian* (London), 12 November 2008, p. 33.

102. Devon Curtis, "Partner or Predator in the Heart of Africa? Chinese Engagement with the DRC," in Kweku Ampiah and Sanusha Naidu, eds., *Crouching Tiger, Hidden Dragon? Africa and China* (Scottsville, South Africa: University of KwaZulu-Natal Press, 2008), pp. 86–107.

103. "Twenty-Ninth Report of the Secretary-General on the UN Organization Mission in the Democratic Republic of the Congo," S/2009/472, 18 September 2009, p. 7.

104. "Report of the Secretary-General on the United Nations Organization Stabilization Mission in the Democratic Republic of the Congo," S/2011/20, 17 January 2011, p. 17.

105. See "Report of the Secretary-General on Preparations for an International Conference on the Great Lakes Region," S/2003/1099, 17 November 2003.

106. "Twenty-Third Report of the Secretary-General on the UN Organization Mission in the Democratic Republic of the Congo," S/2007/156, 20 March 2007, p. 5.

4

Orphans of the Cold War:
The UN in Southern Africa

Savimbi . . . personifies a lesson that powerful governments need
to learn: do not arm and pay and flatter local proxies to fight
for your interests in their countries, for those proxies may well
become malevolent genies whom you will not be able to put
back into the bottle when you no longer need them.
—*Marrack Goulding, UN Undersecretary-General, 1986–1993*[1]

After the traumatic events of the Congo crisis of 1960–1964 (see Chapter
3), it took UN peacekeepers three decades to return to Africa. The world
body launched a long-delayed mission to end South Africa's seventy-five-
year colonial occupation of Namibia in 1989 and helped organize the elections that led to the country's independence a year later. Two further UN
peacekeeping missions were deployed into Angola and Mozambique, with
all three interventions possible only due to the changed international environment as a result of the ending of the Cold War. Liberation movements in
Namibia, Angola, and Mozambique were abandoned by their former Soviet
patrons, and all three were orphans of the Cold War. This paradoxically
turned out to be a blessing in disguise for Namibia and Mozambique and a
tragic curse for Angola.

The three cases[2] examined in this chapter demonstrate the importance
of one of the key themes of this book: the crucial role of great powers in
supporting or obstructing UN peacekeeping missions in Africa. Despite a
UN Security Council resolution in 1978 calling for Namibia's independence
from apartheid South Africa, the US administration of Ronald Reagan cynically linked the country's independence to the withdrawal of Cuban troops
from Angola, delaying, with its apartheid South African allies, the country's
independence for twelve years. Despite some difficulties in implementation,

the UN eventually achieved its first peacekeeping success in Africa for three decades, steering Namibia to independent statehood in March 1990.

In April 1974, a military coup in Lisbon—the Carnation Revolution—had led Portugal to abandon its former African colonies of Angola and Mozambique. Democratic transitions collapsed in both countries, leading to civil wars in which Washington and Moscow backed ideologically compatible clients. The ending of the Cold War made it possible for the installation of UN peacekeeping missions in both countries. The role of two veto-wielding permanent members of the UN Security Council was thus critical to the outcomes of these conflicts.

In this chapter I assess the domestic, regional, and external factors that obstructed and eventually contributed to UN peacekeepers achieving their goals in Namibia and Mozambique while failing spectacularly in Angola. Five key questions emerge from this analysis that are addressed here. First, why were some belligerents in the three countries prepared to cooperate with the UN, while others remained recalcitrant? Second, what role did the United States, Russia, Britain, Portugal, and Italy play in first obstructing and then ensuring the success of peace efforts in Namibia and Mozambique? Third, why did the UN manage to develop an effective strategy to deal with the "spoiler" Afonso Dhlakama in Mozambique but not the warlord Jonas Savimbi in Angola? Fourth, how important were regional actors in obstructing and then contributing to peace efforts in all three cases? Finally, what role did UN special representatives play in seeking to steer peace processes to success in Namibia, Mozambique, and Angola?

Namibia

Of Regional Allies and External Patrons

Namibia's independence became possible only after major developments at the domestic (South African), regional, and external levels. By the late 1980s, apartheid South Africa was straining under international sanctions that were having a devastating effect on its economy. By the end of 1989, the government of the hard-line president P. W. Botha had built up an external debt of $20 billion, and the South African currency—the rand—was in several years of free-fall.[3] The bloody nose suffered by the South African Defence Force (SADF)—with at least two dozen deaths—at the hands of Cuban/Angolan government troops at the battle of Cuito Cuanavale in 1988 had also shattered the myth of the SADF's military invincibility and increased the anticonscription backlash within South Africa's white minority population. The six Frontline States (Angola, Botswana, Mozambique, Tanzania, Zambia, and Zimbabwe; also referred to as the FLS) were instrumental in coaxing the South West African People's Organization (SWAPO) to accept a peace settlement. The increasing cooperation of the superpowers—the United States and the Soviet Union—following the end of the Cold War also rendered irrelevant Pretoria's hysterical rhetoric about a communist "encirclement" of, and "total onslaught" against, South Africa, even as its army continued to wreak death and destruction on its neighbors.[4] In the 1980s alone, South Africa's rampaging army caused an estimated one million deaths and $60 billion in destruction in Southern Africa.[5]

Namibia represented a struggle of national self-determination by a liberation movement, SWAPO, to reclaim a territory that had been forcibly annexed by a rampaging neighbor. South Africa had seized South West Africa in 1915. The territory became a mandate of the Western-dominated League of Nations in 1920 after Germany's defeat in World War I (1914–1918). In the territory of South West Africa, as in South Africa, whites were coopted and compromised by the system and granted privileges based on skin color that then gave them a stake in the survival of the system. Apartheid policies were effectively transplanted from South Africa after 1948, creating two racial groups that were doomed to be in perpetual conflict with each other. Pretoria sought to create facts on the ground through creeping annexation of land and incorporation of the territory into South Africa's political, economic, and legal system. The apartheid regime hoarded the black majority in its "colony" into labor reserves while providing political representation only to white inhabitants. This perverse albinocracy was supported by an Afrikaner-dominated civil service, with generous financing and farmland being provided to white German and South African farmers.[6]

The UN refused to recognize South Africa's claims on the territory after 1945 and insisted instead that a vote be held in which the people of Namibia would have the right to determine their own future in accordance with the usual practice of decolonization. After South Africa extended its racist apartheid laws to South West Africa, the UN General Assembly—through a sizable majority of members of the Group of 77 (G-77) developing countries—revoked Pretoria's mandate over the territory in 1966, a decision later endorsed by the fifteen-member UN Security Council.[7] The General Assembly created the UN Council for Namibia in 1967 as a legal authority to administer the territory until its independence. Four years later, the International Court of Justice declared South Africa's rule in South West Africa to be illegal and called for its withdrawal from the territory.[8] From 1966 on, SWAPO's People's Liberation Army of Namibia (PLAN) had also started to launch guerrilla attacks against South Africa's occupation of the territory.

The Western members on the UN Security Council (United States, France, Britain, West Germany, and Canada) created a Contact Group on Namibia in March 1977 and in April 1978 proposed a peace settlement. This body was established to blunt persistent accusations from the global

South that the West was more interested in supporting apartheid and protecting its commercial interests in the country and in South West Africa than in promoting the liberation of Africa from colonial rule. In 1976, Britain, France, and the United States had vetoed draft Security Council resolutions pushed by developing countries that had tried to impose sanctions on apartheid South Africa for its refusal to disgorge the territory it had illegally swallowed.

The "settlement plan" devised by the Western Contact Group in April 1978 called for the establishment of a UN Transition Assistance Group (UNTAG). The body was mandated to supervise the election of a constituent assembly that would write a constitution for an independent Namibia in a process expected to take one year. Under the plan, South Africa would administer elections under UN supervision and control. Pretoria was, however, determined to prevent the election of a SWAPO government in Namibia and pretended to cooperate with the UN while consistently placing obstacles in its way.[9] It is important to note that the Contact Group was strongly pushed by the US administration of Jimmy Carter (1977–1980), which sought to promote human rights around the world, though it sometimes contradicted these policies by continuing to support autocrats whom Washington considered useful to promoting its parochial strategic goals, such as Zaire's Mobutu Sese Seko and Sudan's Gaafar Numeiri. The Carter administration also tied recognition of the Marxist regime in Luanda to the withdrawal of Cuban troops from the country. Donald McHenry, the African American permanent representative at the UN at the time, played a particularly important leadership role in driving the work of the US-inspired Contact Group. Brian Urquhart, the long-serving British UN Undersecretary-General for Peacekeeping, described McHenry as a "tough and realistic professional with great experience and intelligence."[10]

However, a new US administration came to power under Ronald Reagan in January 1981 determined to "roll back" communism around the world. This crusade would be waged regardless of whether its rabid anticommunism contradicted such principles as self-determination and ending apartheid. New US secretary of state Alexander Haig trenchantly told UN officials that Washington would not allow "the Hammer and Sickle to fly over Windhoek" and categorically ruled out the possibility of a SWAPO-led government in Namibia,[11] an identical policy to that of apartheid South Africa. Despite the appointment by Austrian UN Secretary-General Kurt Waldheim of Finnish diplomat Martti Ahtisaari as his special representative to Namibia, the settlement plan remained unimplemented for a decade, as Pretoria—which had earlier agreed to the plan under Western pressure—frustrated its implementation. South Africa's intransigence was greatly encouraged by Chester Crocker, the prejudiced US assistant secretary of state for Africa, whose misguided policy of "constructive engagement" gave apartheid a fresh lease on life and a license to kill and destroy during the bloody destabilization of its neighbors in the 1980s. Crocker's "linkage" of the withdrawal of Cuban troops from Angola to a settlement of the South West Africa case—a policy that had consistently been advocated by Pretoria—delayed Namibia's independence by a decade and destroyed the US-inspired Contact Group.

After 1982, the Peruvian UN Secretary-General Javier Pérez de Cuéllar, and most of the other members of the Contact Group, did not support Crocker's egregious linkage strategy, noting that this idea fell outside the world body's settlement plan. As former US ambassador to the UN Donald McHenry sardonically noted: "No mention of Cuban forces was made at the time of South Africa's agreement."[12] Britain's right-wing prime minister Margaret Thatcher was widely seen as a strong supporter of "constructive engagement," though she stopped short of officially backing the US "linkage" policy. As early as February 1981, Thatcher was pushing for the Cubans to leave Angola before any Namibian settlement, and she complained that, if this case were ever settled, the Africans would turn all their attention on apartheid South Africa.[13] The British premier was close to the apartheid regime, opposed economic sanctions against it, and regarded the African National Congress (ANC) leadership—including Nelson Mandela—as "terrorists." Brian Urquhart observed that the Iron Lady "seemed to believe that the UN was, or should be, primarily the instrument for asserting Western values in the world."[14] This again confirms a major theme of this book: the efforts of the permanent five members of the Security Council to manipulate the organization for their own parochial interests.

The Soviet Union for its part was unhappy—as a permanent member of the UN Security Council—at having been excluded from the Contact Group. Moscow strongly supported the implementation of the settlement plan and condemned Crocker's linkage strategy. The Russians at first refused to talk to Washington and instead focused on Luanda and Havana, with Soviet military advisers assisting the Popular Movement for the Liberation of Angola (MPLA) in its battles against the National Union for the Total Independence of Angola (UNITA) and the South African army. Soviet leader Mikhail Gorbachev's explicit support, from January 1986, for "political solutions" to regional problems, as well as his quest for détente with the West—pursued energetically by his foreign minister Eduard Shevardnadze—was designed to ease his country's economic problems. This approach eventually led Moscow to cooperate closely with Washington on mediation efforts in Southern Africa, especially after 1988.[15]

Washington mediated meetings between Angola, Cuba, and South Africa in London, Cairo, Geneva, and Brazzaville in 1988. Crocker sought to convince the Angolans that they need not fear South African aggression once the Cubans had departed and Namibia was free, since Pretoria would automatically stop backing UNITA. Luanda often appeared to be prepared to sacrifice SWAPO for the sake of a deal (as Maputo had sacrificed the ANC during the 1984 Nkomati accord with Pretoria, described below). The Angolans disliked the presence of SWAPO rebels on their territory—despite repeated rhetoric of solidarity—because that presence meant continued South African destabilization. Pretoria still wanted to replace the MPLA government in Luanda—which it saw as part of a Soviet-backed communist onslaught—with UNITA.[16]

Since the United States did not have formal diplomatic relations with Angola, Britain acted as an intermediary between Washington and Luanda. Angola's leaders—like SWAPO and most African liberation movements and governments—despised Crocker's linkage policy. The US assistant secretary of state simply saw African actors as pawns to be moved around a global geostrategic chessboard. He failed to understand the depth of resentment against the odious apartheid regime and its invasion of Angola in 1975 that had pushed African states to recognize the MPLA regime in Angola despite strong American pleas not to do so. Crocker would later disingenuously claim that Washington resumed military support to UNITA in 1986 to increase the brutal rebel movement's independence from South Africa.[17] In reality, most of Africa regarded the United States, South Africa, and UNITA as part of an "axis of evil" in Southern Africa. Ronald Reagan's welcome of UNITA rebel leader Jonas Savimbi to the White House in January 1986 further reinforced this perception.

Angolan leader José Eduardo Dos Santos treated Washington with both respect and fear[18] and was pragmatic in cooperating with Crocker's process if it could achieve an end to South African occupation and termination of support to UNITA. The Angolan government held secret talks with Pretoria as early as 1980 in a desperate bid to secure direct talks between South Africa and SWAPO.[19] Washington's resumption of military support to UNITA, however, poisoned relations with Luanda and negatively affected the negotiation of a settlement. Angola complained that the United States had forfeited any pretense at playing an "honest broker" role and refused to take part in negotiations for nearly a year between 1986 and 1987. In November 1987, the Soviet-backed government Forces of the Angolan People's Liberation (FAPLA) suffered heavy casualties as well as the capture of Russian military hardware in battles against the South African–backed UNITA. The Cubans sent fifteen thousand additional troops to Angola and, in the historic battle of Cuito Cuanavale in 1988, the reckless South African gendarme finally got its comeuppance, as Cuban troops inflicted casualties on the SADF. This incident probably did more than any other to hasten the negotiations that resulted in the withdrawal of foreign troops from Angola, the independence of Namibia, and the end of apartheid in South Africa. As Cuban leader Fidel Castro noted: "From now on the history of Africa will have to be written before and after Cuito Cuanavale."[20]

South Africa's first postapartheid president, Nelson Mandela, similarly described the battle as "a turning point for the liberation of our continent and my people."[21]

Despite efforts to portray Cuba as a Soviet stooge, military commanders from both countries based in Angola often argued about military strategy,[22] and Havana largely pursued an independent policy while regularly consulting Moscow. Cuban leader Fidel Castro, however, later admitted that there was strong Soviet pressure for Cuba to withdraw from Angola due to Moscow's fears of Washington's adverse reaction to its continued intervention in the country.[23]

Discussions in New York eventually resulted in the signing of the Principles for a Peaceful Settlement in South-Western Africa in July 1988. The document called for the implementation of Namibia's settlement plan once Cuban and South African troops had withdrawn from Angola. Further meetings in November 1988 in Geneva, and in Brazzaville a month later, agreed respectively to a timetable for withdrawal of Cuban troops and an implementation mechanism. SWAPO forces would be redeployed to Angola 150 kilometers north of the Angola/Namibia border. A tripartite joint commission was established between the three countries, on which Washington and Moscow both sat as "observers." Angola, Cuba, and South Africa signed the agreement at the UN Secretariat in New York in December 1988, and a de facto ceasefire was established in Namibia. While Pretoria distrusted the UN, with the General Assembly having suspended the apartheid regime from its deliberations in September 1974, SWAPO looked to G-77 members in the UN General Assembly to defend its interests.

Aside from the G-77's role at the UN, African states played an important role in the negotiations over Namibia. The Frontline States met frequently (often with Nigeria present as a de facto member), and their interventions were sometimes needed to keep SWAPO on board during negotiations. Mozambique, Tanzania, and Zambia often provided advice and venues for meetings. Congo-Brazzaville, a neighbor and friend of Luanda, also provided support for a settlement and a venue for negotiations, hosting five tripartite meetings in 1988.[24]

There has been much debate about the efficacy of Crocker's controversial policy of "constructive engagement." Though he later tried to rationalize this policy as a well thought-out strategy, Crocker's main obsession was to get the Cubans out of Angola. He did not anticipate that two-thirds of the US Congress would override Ronald Reagan's reactionary veto to impose economic sanctions on South Africa through the Comprehensive Anti-Apartheid Act in October 1986 (after which Crocker stopped using the term *constructive engagement*). Crocker had also overlooked the fact that most black African states and liberation movements would not support his approach of supping with the apartheid devil while seeking to achieve a regional settlement. The US assistant secretary of state tried to justify his policy as one that was trying to gain independence for Namibia and end apartheid in South Africa, but few in Africa were convinced by this American werewolf in sheepskin.

Constructive engagement and *linkage* were terms based on patronizing, prejudiced, and flawed logic. One of the main factors behind Crocker's strategy appeared to be the US Congress's cessation of support for antigovernment rebel groups in Angola in 1976, which right-wing conservatives saw as a defeat they were determined to avenge. Crocker later admitted that Namibian independence was not his first priority and that he was wary of a SWAPO victory.[25] Namibia's independence occurred *despite* Crocker and not *because of* him. Soviet leader Mikhail Gorbachev's policy of cooperation with Washington and support for ending regional wars was undoubtedly a more influential factor in moving this process forward. These developments led to a reduction in the high levels of Cold War support by the superpowers to Cuba, Angola, and liberation movements like SWAPO and the ANC and removed South Africa's main casus belli of a communist "onslaught" threatening the apartheid state. On leaving office in 1988, Crocker in fact thought that apartheid would continue for many years,[26] which raises serious doubts about both the integrity of his policies and his powers of prophecy. One of the most incredible silences in recent Western scholarship on the region is the failure to raise pertinent questions about the attempts by policymakers like Crocker to portray themselves as objective analysts rather than interested parties in the cases they describe.

The UN Mission in Namibia

As with Suez (1956) and the Congo (1960–1964) (see Chapters 2 and 3), Africa again proved to be an innovative laboratory for UN peacekeeping as the Cold War was coming to an end. The UN mission in Namibia was the world body's first "multidimensional" initiative, one that involved armed peacekeepers, civilian and police units, supervision of demobilization and disarmament, assisting the return of refugees, and overseeing a political transition through a UN-monitored election. UNTAG's main tasks involved monitoring the ceasefire, supervising the encampment and disarming of troops, demobilizing the South West African Territorial Force (SWATF), monitoring the reduction of South African troops in the territory from about thirty-five thousand (though some estimates put the actual number at eighty thousand)[27] to 1,500 within twelve weeks, disarming SWAPO guerrillas before their repatriation, monitoring the activities of South West African Police (SWAPOL) forces—particularly the notorious Koevoet (crowbar) counterinsurgency unit, notorious for its brutality against civilians—overseeing the organization of democratic elections, and monitoring the withdrawal of South African troops from the territory.

For the first time in the UN's history, a 1,500-strong civilian police unit was sent to the field, which monitored the activities of local police forces and provided security to returning refugees and voters at polling stations. The UN Secretary-General's special representative Martti Athisaari was charged with repealing discriminatory laws, ensuring the release of political prisoners, and overseeing the repatriation of about forty-five thousand Namibian refugees from neighboring countries. The elections were to be conducted by South Africa's administrator-general in the territory, Louis Pienaar, under the UN's supervision and control,[28] with the UN special representative being responsible for ensuring the conditions for a free and fair election.

In January 1989, the first group of fifty thousand Cuban troops started their withdrawal from Angola, which was completed thirty months later. As the UN started arriving in Namibia in March 1989, problems soon developed with the implementation of the peace accord that nearly led to UNTAG's death immediately following its painful, prolonged birth. Led by the United States, the five penny-pinching permanent members of the Security Council, who pay about half of the total UN peacekeeping expenses, called for the slashing of UNTAG's budget from $650 million to $450 million and a reduction by half of UNTAG's proposed 7,500 troops. Supported by apartheid South Africa, the five permanent members argued that the security situation in Southern Africa had vastly improved since UNTAG was devised in 1978.[29] G-77 members expressed their outrage and argued that UNTAG needed sufficient troops to counter any South African attempts to avoid withdrawing from the territory it had controlled for seven and a half decades. UN Secretary-General Javier Pérez de Cuéllar eventually crafted a compromise deal through which 4,650 troops were deployed and another 3,100 were held in reserve, thus reducing UNTAG's budget to $416 million.

Predictably, the cantankerous budget dispute delayed the deployment of UN peacekeepers. The insistence of the G-77 that the UN not buy supplies from apartheid South Africa resulted in further delays. There were divisions within the UN Secretariat itself regarding the size of the contingent. Martti Ahtisaari—who had no prior peacekeeping experience—was influenced by his principal assistant, Irish lawyer Cedric Thornberry, into supporting the reduction of troops, which the two Indians—General Prem Chand, UN force commander-designate, and Virendra Dayal, De Cuéllar's chef de cabinet—as well as the Ghanaian military adviser, General Timothy Dibuama, and the British Undersecretary-General for Special Political Affairs, Marack Goulding, all opposed. This division almost mirrored the North/South split in the UN General Assembly, reinforcing the UN's system of "global apartheid."[30]

UNTAG's principal contingents—under the leadership of India's Prem Chand—were contributed by Finland, Kenya, and Malaysia. Only the Finns, however, brought their own equipment, and many of the other battalions from developing countries were poorly equipped. UNTAG's deputy force commander was Kenya's Daniel Opande, who went on to lead UN missions in Liberia and Sierra Leone (see Chapter 5). The UN Angola Verification Mission's force commander, General Péricles Ferreira Gomes, had earlier ruffled feathers with an interview to the *New York Times* that seemed to echo Pretoria's doubts about the UN's ability to monitor the withdrawal of Cuban troops from Angola:[31] a sine qua non for the implementation of the settlement plan for Namibia.

In what might have appeared at first as a macabre April fool's joke, South Africa announced on 1 April 1989—the start date of the implementation of the peace plan—that PLAN guerrillas were crossing into northern Namibia from Angola to establish bases there, which Pretoria described as a contravention of the peace accord. The peace plan had, in fact, largely been silent about the demobilization of SWAPO fighters, only noting that they should be confined to their bases at the start of implementation of the settlement plan, while those outside the country were to return peacefully through designated entry points that the UN would monitor. SWAPO insisted that it already had bases inside Namibia before the ceasefire. South Africa disputed this, noting that raids on the territory were usually carried out from Angola.[32]

The government in Luanda was reluctant for the UN to monitor the confinement of bases inside Angola and, as I will discuss in greater detail later, was wary of a UN presence on its territory as well as a continuing SWAPO presence through setting up cantonment sites. The Angolans felt that SWAPO did not always respect their sovereignty and attracted South African attack, and they wanted to avoid blame if any SWAPO fighters arrived unannounced in Namibia.[33] SWAPO for its part continued to insist that it had camps inside Namibia and that it had never agreed to its fighters, being cantoned in Angola. The fact that SWAPO had been excluded from the US-brokered talks that secured the withdrawal of Cuban troops from Angola created problems throughout implementation of the peace plan. SWAPO leader Sam Nujoma—a prickly, short-tempered, and difficult character[34]—resented having to be briefed by Luanda on issues that directly affected Namibia's independence settlement, while the Angolans were clearly impatient to finalize a deal that would see SWAPO leave their territory.

Martti Ahtisaari had only left New York on 29 March 1989 to take up his post in Windhoek. He had thus been in the country for barely two days without any solid UN peacekeeping presence when the infiltration of SWAPO fighters into Namibia occurred. This was perhaps an attempt by Nujoma to strengthen his electoral hand by showing that his movement had "liberated" part of the country. The troops infiltrated through Ovamboland in northern Namibia, the heartland of SWAPO support.[35] British prime minister Margaret Thatcher happened to be visiting Windhoek as events unfolded and told the long-serving, whiskey-drinking South African foreign minister "Pik" Botha to seek UN permission before taking any action: advice that Pérez de Cuéllar also offered to Botha. The Peruvian UN Secretary-General—acutely aware of the strong anti–South African feelings among the Third World majority in the organization that he led—urged his special representative to stand firm and to keep the South African army on a tight leash. Pretoria, however, pressured Ahtisaari to allow the SADF to expel PLAN fighters from the territory. SWAPO continued to insist that its fighters were simply looking for UN officials to hand over their weapons to. With only 300 military observers on the ground at the time of the incursion,[36] UNTAG was clearly not in a position to deter fighting between the two sides.

South African forces engaged the SWAPO guerrillas in April 1989, resulting in three hundred SWAPO fatalities and thirteen SADF deaths. The Frontline States met in Luanda on 6 April 1989 and pressured SWAPO to canton its troops in UN-monitored camps in Angola, from where they could return to Namibia after their leaders had arrived in Windhoek. Angolan leader Eduardo Dos Santos played an important role in pushing SWAPO to agree to this plan, though he insisted on a small UN observer force of only twenty-eight monitors. The Angola-Cuba–South Africa joint commission—with Washington and Moscow present, but again excluding SWAPO—met at Mount Etjo near Windhoek two days later and recommitted all parties to the peace process.

Ahtisaari's decision to allow some cantoned South African troops to join the battle against SWAPO forces incurred the wrath of African members at the UN. They took out their anger on Pérez de Cuéllar, who, in turn, was increasingly wary of his special representative's inability to muzzle South Africa's rampaging "mad dogs."[37] The Secretary-General established and chaired a Namibia Task Force in the UN Secretariat that met every day and effectively micromanaged Ahtisaari, who had to report to New York every evening and whom a majority of task force members distrusted. In order further to assuage the anger of African diplomats at the UN, De Cuéllar agreed to their demand to dispatch a strong African, Botswana's permanent representative to the UN since 1980, Legwaila Joseph Legwaila (later UN special representative to Ethiopia-Eritrea; see Chapter 6), to Windhoek as Ahtisaari's deputy. De Cuéllar had not consulted his special representative before the appointment, and the Finn considered resigning, but stayed put in his position.[38] Ahtisaari had also not reported sufficiently strongly on South Africa's failure to dismantle its command structure in the territory, in violation of the settlement plan. He felt that the UN should stand up to the G-77 and often dismissed their criticisms as ill-informed and ill-intentioned.[39] In one incident, the Finn threatened to mobilize member states against the UN Secretary-General after De Cuéllar insisted—in accordance with UN regulations—that Cedric Thornberry return to New York following death threats against him.[40] (Ahtisaari was awarded the Nobel Peace Prize in 2008, following later peacemaking efforts in Aceh and Kosovo.)

Other troubling incidents during the UNTAG mission included: the continued operation of South African murder squads in the territory, the continued terrorization of civilians by Koevoet platoons (an issue on which De Cuéllar himself privately pressured the South Africans[41]), the firing on unarmed crowds by the local police, and the funding by South Africa of anti-SWAPO political parties. The UN Security Council actually passed a resolution in August 1989 calling for the disbandment of the notorious Koevoet unit, which Pretoria never fully complied with.[42] Members of the murderous unit were transferred to the police force, while South African army personnel violated the peace plan by remaining in the territory to perform "civilian" tasks as air traffic controllers.[43] In September 1989, a South African hit squad is believed to have assassinated SWAPO member Anton Lubowski under the noses of UN peacekeepers.

But despite these problems, UNTAG managed, within eight months, to organize successful elections in November 1989. As expected, SWAPO won a majority of the seventy-two parliamentary seats (57.4 percent), while the South African–sponsored Democratic Turnhalle Alliance (DTA) won twenty-one seats (28.5 percent). Five parties shared the remaining ten seats. Two nonpermanent African members of the Security Council—Zambia and Zimbabwe—sought to block Ahtisaari from declaring the election to be "free and fair" until they were sure that due process had been followed.[44] The constituent assembly convened in November 1989 to draw up a new constitution, and SWAPO leader Sam Nujoma became Namibia's first democratically elected president in March 1990. A request from Zambia for UNTAG to remain in Namibia for another three months was given short shrift by the UN Security Council.[45] PLAN and SWATF forces were integrated into a new national army; South African troops left the territory; and UNTAG members helped in the creation of a new Namibian police force (NAMPOL).

In retrospect, Namibia was a test case for South Africa in transferring power through a constitutional process from a white minority to a black majority, with built-in guarantees for white capitalists and civil servants. South Africa's transition between 1990 and 1994 followed the Namibian model in many ways: establishing a constitutional conference to draft a new constitution that protected white minority rights, safeguarding white economic privileges in industry and land ownership, guaranteeing the jobs of white civil servants, and inviting the UN to legitimize the settlement.[46] An incoming new black government under the revered Nelson Mandela attended Namibia's independence celebrations in March 1990, and, in an act of poetic justice, South Africa handed back Walvis Bay and contingent islands to Namibia in February 1994 to end a sordid, destructive seventy-five-year albinocratic colonial rule over its smaller neighbor.

Angola

Domestic and External Friends and Foes

Turning our attention from Namibia to the related case of Angola,[47] it is again important to employ the framework of the dynamics at the domestic, regional, and external levels that also complicated peace efforts in Angola. At the domestic level, the Soviet-educated Angolan president, José Eduardo Dos Santos, was a quiet but calculating politician who kept a tight grip on state and party. He was the perfect foil to the flamboyant, urbane, but ruthless Savimbi, who had obtained a doctorate in political science from Switzerland's University of Lausanne in 1965. The level of distrust between the two parties was deep, not helped by Savimbi's megalomaniacal tendencies. Though masquerading as a democrat, the ruthless US-backed warlord was prepared to use any means—foul or fair—to secure absolute power in Angola. Having run a corrupt, one-party state for a decade and a half, Dos Santos insisted—as the Front for the Liberation of Mozambique (FRELIMO) tried to do with the Mozambique National Resistance (RENAMO)—that UNITA be incorporated into the MPLA and that Savimbi be exiled.[48] Like rebel leader Afonso Dhlakama, in Mozambique, Savimbi dismissed the government in Luanda as a communist dictatorship and sought to portray himself as a democratic advocate of multiparty politics.

At the regional level, after suffering defeat by the MPLA and the Cubans in 1975–1976, the South Africans (and Americans) helped to rebuild Jonas Savimbi's UNITA rebel movement.[49] Pretoria had occupied southern Angola between 1981 and 1988 in support of UNITA and was accused of using chemical weapons in prosecuting this war.[50] A pair of unsavory African autocrats also attempted to promote peacemaking in Angola. Gabonese leader Omar Bongo convened meetings with regional leaders to try to secure Dos Santos's agreement for negotiations. Zaire's Mobutu Sese Seko, despite being Savimbi's closest collaborator and leader of the main transit country for supplying American arms and fuel to UNITA, also sought to play a role as a mediator. In June 1989, Mobutu convened a summit in his ancestral village of Gbadolite at which Dos Santos and Savimbi shook hands in front of eighteen African leaders. But there were no direct talks and no written accord of the summit, besides a communiqué calling for a ceasefire and a joint MPLA/UNITA commission to negotiate the country's future under Mobutu's stewardship. The Zairian autocrat then went to Washington on a state visit, during which he called on the United States to halt its military support for Savimbi. Four more negotiation sessions occurred in Kinshasa between June and August 1989, though the MPLA churlishly refused to sit in the same room with UNITA.

With Zimbabwe and Zambia continuing to call for Savimbi's exile, the UNITA leader distrusted the regional process that Mobutu, the United States, and apartheid South Africa were insisting he engage in. After

Washington issued a statement calling for "free and fair" elections (following heavy lobbying by UNITA), Mobutu correctly regarded this as an attempt to sabotage his mediation efforts and suspended arms shipments to UNITA through his territory in September 1989. With the United States unable to find an alternative transit route, President George H. Bush invited Mobutu and Savimbi to Washington a month later, where a rapprochement was engineered and arms supplies resumed by November 1989.[51] Despite Nigeria's role in providing financial and military assistance to Southern African liberation movements and the country's being a de facto member of the Frontline States, Angolan leader Eduardo Dos Santos was unhappy with the UN's appointment of a Nigerian general—Edward Unimna—to lead UNAVEM II as chief military observer. Luanda had sometimes found the Nigerian approach to be brash and arrogant, if not overbearing.[52]

Turning to the external level, after the 1988 accords that eventually secured Namibian independence, the United States had cynically reassured Jonas Savimbi that he was not a signatory to the agreement and was thus not bound by its terms.[53] US secretary of state James Baker told the UN in 1991 that Washington would continue to fund Savimbi so that he could campaign effectively,[54] and the State Department was in regular touch with UNITA through its office in the US capital. This unflinching support for UNITA continued even as US oil companies and banks operated profitably in Angola through the Luanda government. UNITA had many friends among right-wing conservative Cold Warriors in the United States. Despite lending support to mediation efforts, Washington was clearly a dishonest broker in Angola, since it was working toward a UNITA victory and was even strategizing with Savimbi on how he could win national elections.[55] However, opinion in the US Congress was changing with the democratic transition in South Africa. The Solarz amendment of October 1990—named after Congressman Stephen Solarz—called for an end to lethal aid for UNITA. Despite American officials like Assistant Secretary of State for African Affairs Herman Cohen retrospectively seeking to express shock at Savimbi's horrific killing of opposition figures and their families in areas that the warlord controlled,[56] these events had been widely reported for years. It was clear to many that Washington was in bed with a ruthless psychopath who would stop at nothing to achieve his political ambitions. Support for Savimbi continued despite these killings, and Uncle Sam continued to speak out of both sides of his mouth.

It is also important to note that the desire of the United States and the Soviet Union—two veto-wielding permanent members of the UN Security Council—for greater cooperation had a major impact on peacemaking. Just as Washington delivered UNITA to the peace table, Moscow pushed the MPLA to keep negotiating. By 1983, many senior Angolan officials were already critical of Moscow, while praising the reliability of the Cubans.[57] The superpowers were still moving African pawns around a global geostrategic chessboard. It was in fact the fear of superpower collusion that would later push the MPLA regime to accept Portuguese mediation in 1990.[58] During a meeting in Houston, Texas, in December 1990, James Baker and Soviet foreign minister Eduard Shevardnadze agreed to craft an accord between the two Angolan parties that would put some political muscle behind Portuguese mediation efforts.[59] By September 1991, Dos Santos visited Washington in a further sign of the shifting dynamics of this conflict. As in Mozambique, the end of the Cold War and transition to majority rule in South Africa were forcing the MPLA government to negotiate a peace deal.

Keeping Peace Where There Is None
As earlier noted, in August 1988, US-brokered peace talks had been held in Geneva involving South Africa, Cuba, and Angola. South Africa agreed to withdraw its troops from Angola and to stop its military support to UNITA. With the involvement of the UN, two peace agreements were signed in New York in December 1988, calling for Namibian independence and the withdrawal of fifty thousand Cuban troops from Angola in thirty-one months. The first UN Angola Verification Mission (UNAVEM I), involving about seventy unarmed military observers, was created in December 1988 to verify the withdrawal of Cuban troops by 1 July 1991. The mission cost $18.8 million and completed its tasks early, with Cuban troops withdrawing by 25 May 1991, over a month ahead of schedule.[60] Though the mission was a success, there were some hiccups, with UNITA's killing of ten Cuban troops in January 1990 leading to the suspension of the withdrawal for a month.[61]

The success of UNAVEM I provided the impetus for US secretary of state James Baker to alert UN Secretary-General Javier Pérez de Cuéllar, during Namibia's independence celebrations in March 1990, that Washington wanted to work with Moscow to bring peace to Angola. Baker thus urged the world body to enlarge UNAVEM in order to monitor a ceasefire that the United States had proposed to both sides.[62] The ruling MPLA and UNITA rebels signed the Bicesse peace accords in May 1991, after a year of arduous negotiations in Portugal. The main sticking point had been the refusal of the MPLA government to recognize UNITA as a political party until an effective ceasefire was in place, while UNITA refused to agree a ceasefire until other political and military issues had been settled.[63] There was also disagreement on the length of the transitional period before elections (the MPLA wanted a three- to five-year transition, while UNITA wanted a much shorter period) as well as the role of the MPLA-controlled national police in a transition, with UNITA fearing that the force would be used to intimidate its supporters.[64] The agreement was negotiated with the help of the troika of former colonial power, Portugal (chair and host), the United States, and the Soviet Union, without UN participation. Bicesse called for a ceasefire, the demobilization of two hundred thousand MPLA and UNITA troops, the creation of a new unified fifty thousand–strong army, the extension of central administration to the entire country, the development of a neutral police force, and the holding of national elections within eighteen months.

The accord consisted of four key documents. First, the Joint Political-Military Commission, consisting of MPLA and UNITA representatives, and troika observers, was mandated to oversee the political supervision of the ceasefire. Angola's parties took turns in chairing this commission, and the UN played only a marginal role on it. The second document related to "fundamental principles" for establishing peace. Under its terms, UNITA would recognize the MPLA as the legitimate government until elections, the rebel movement would participate in political activities, both sides would discuss amending the constitution, internationally supervised elections would occur, and the joint army would be set up before elections. The third document noted how the principles in the second document would be implemented, while the final document noted the areas of agreement in the second and third documents.[65]

The second UN mission to Angola (UNAVEM II) was established by the Security Council in May 1991, and had only a limited observation and verification role. The parties would unusually be responsible for monitoring their own compliance with the accord, with the UN's role being to verify this compliance.[66] Jonas Savimbi arrived in Luanda in September 1991 and was trailed by large crowds. Not until December 1991 was a civilian mission added to the UN mission to oversee the electoral process. Margaret Joan Anstee, the British special representative of the UN Secretary-General, arrived in Luanda only in March 1992, six months before the elections. UNAVEM II had 350 unarmed military observers, 126 civilian police, and 400 electoral observers to monitor a country the combined size of Germany, France, and Spain. Its seventeen-month budget was about $150 million. As with most UN missions, there were shortages of vehicles and other logistical equipment due to the UN's bureaucratic authorization procedures: the General Assembly approved the budget for the mission two and a half months after the Security Council had created UNAVEM II.[67] This was "peacekeeping on a shoestring" and yet another attempt, like Namibia, by frugal Security Council members to achieve peace on the cheap. UNAVEM II clearly lacked the human and financial resources to execute its mandate effectively. Its peacekeepers proved to be too few for their demobilization tasks, and the parties did not cooperate with its security sector reform mandate.[68]

The Namibia case above had demonstrated the reluctance of the MPLA government to allow a large UN role on its territory. The same concerns about UN infringement on the government's sovereignty were demonstrated by the FRELIMO regime in Mozambique (see below). As former Nigerian leader Olusegun Obasanjo (1976–1979 and 1999–2007) noted, many left-leaning regimes in Africa had held the UN responsible for Patrice Lumumba's assassination in 1961 (see Chapter 3).[69] Such regimes were thus wary of a large UN role in their countries. It was the MPLA that had insisted during peace negotiations on limiting UNAVEM II to a few hundred monitors (UNITA had argued in contrast for thousands of monitors),[70] an approach that suited a cost-saving Security Council as well as the United States, which shared UNITA's analysis that an early election could help Savimbi win power.[71] Luanda seemed to trust former colonial power Portugal (which led the process to craft the peace accord) more than it did the UN; while Maputo similarly appeared to prefer to put its fate more in the hands of Italy (which led the country's peace process) than in those of the UN.

By September 1991, UNAVEM II was struggling to implement Bicesse. Barely half of the troops to be demobilized were in the assembly areas, many disappeared in acts of "spontaneous demobilization," and almost no heavy weapons were brought into the assembly areas. No recruitment into a joint army, let alone training, had started. The two joint commissions that were mandated to oversee the peace process were dysfunctional, with UNITA withdrawing from them for a while. The rebel group was also refusing to let the government reestablish authority in areas under its control. The UN peacekeepers further lacked decent accommodation. There were even problems within UNAVEM itself, with Margaret Anstee not getting along with Nigerian general Edward Unimna. She seemed isolated and lonely, lacking a confidant to support her in a difficult mission.[72] Some Africans also accused Anstee and representatives of several observer countries of racism, while Western UN staff expressed prejudice about senior African personnel on the mission.[73] It must be noted that these sorts of disturbing charges have been fairly widespread in many UN missions, as well as within the UN Secretariat and its agencies. In June 1992, new UN Secretary-General, Egyptian scholar-diplomat Boutros Boutros-Ghali, expressed "cautious optimism" to the Security Council about UNAVEM II, while noting that many tasks would not be completed before elections took place in Angola.[74] The Council responded with its usual haughty Olympian proclamations, urging the parties to take "urgent steps" to complete the tasks. In Angola and elsewhere, the Security Council in New York often acted like fifteen ineffective sorcerers waving magic wands that frequently failed to have any practical effect on warring parties on the ground.

In a bizarre redefinition of the democratic process, Jonas Savimbi, acting more like a warlord than a statesman, started telling the media that if he lost the election, it would mean that the polls had been rigged. It seemed that Savimbi would only accept one outcome—a UNITA victory—and his strategy appeared to be to capitalize on popular discontent with a corrupt ruling elite in Luanda, while mobilizing his Ovimbundu ethnic base to carry him to victory. Failing that, the warlord would take up arms again to achieve his presidential ambitions. Savimbi incredibly confided to Herman

Cohen, US assistant secretary of state for African affairs, in September 1992, that his UNITA military chiefs were telling him that he did not need an election to win power,[75] suggesting that he could take power through the barrel of a gun rather than through the ballot box. The Angolan warlord's decision to enter the process was thus a tactical one rather than one born out of a commitment to democratic principles. The UN's tasks were soon complicated by Savimbi's refusal to conclude the electoral process and to disarm his fighters. Acting as a classic spoiler, he openly defied the peacekeepers and instead continued to rebuild his army. The Angolan warlord refused to bid a final farewell to arms and would soon return to war, funded by the sale of diamonds. Only 41 percent of both armies had been demobilized by the time of elections in September 1992, and voting barely took place in the province of Cabinda—a volatile area in the geographic belly of the DRC that has historically had two secessionist movements, from which the Angolan government obtains much of its oil.

On the hustings, Savimbi ran a vituperative campaign against Angolan elites of mixed parentage who dominated the MPLA, dismissing them as "evil foreigners," while some ethnic groups disproportionately represented in the ruling party were also disparaged.[76] The quiet, reserved president, Eduardo Dos Santos, was persuaded by his aides to be more of a "man of the people" on the campaign trail and to contrast presidential statesmanship with Savimbi's belligerent warlordism. Voting took place in about six thousand polling stations in September 1992. The presidential election was won narrowly by incumbent president Dos Santos, with 49.57 percent of the vote (Savimbi won 40.07 percent), and thus required a runoff. In legislative elections, the government won 53.7 percent of the vote to UNITA's 34.1 percent. Predictably, Savimbi alleged fraud and despite the UN's investigations failing to confirm these claims and in spite of pleas from Boutros-Ghali not to abandon the process, the truculent warlord left his villa in Luanda and secretly returned to Huambo in central Angola. Savimbi then withdrew all his fighters from the national army in October 1992. UNITA radio launched a poisonous campaign against Margaret Anstee and the UN, while its fighters seized territory across the country. Fighting broke out in Luanda, with Anstee fleeing to the British embassy, and several UNITA officials were killed in the capital. By November 1992, the rebel movement controlled fifty-seven of the country's 164 municipalities.[77] A clearly rattled Dos Santos called for the UN to play a leading role in organizing new elections,[78] even as Savimbi continued the fire-spitting hubris of a power-drunk warlord, capturing or denying the government access to 70 percent of Angolan territory.

Three UN efforts to mediate an end to the conflict took place in Namibe (Angola), Addis Ababa (Ethiopia), and Abidjan (Côte d'Ivoire) between November 1992 and May 1993. All ended in abject failure. UNITA captured the capital of the northern province of Uige in November 1992. Two months later, the government in Luanda launched its own offensive to recapture towns from UNITA. In the two years after the collapse of Bicesse, Angola suffered more death and destruction than in the previous decade and a half of fighting, with estimates of more than a thousand people a day perishing from war-related causes.[79] In March 1993, the UN Security Council finally recognized what had been blatantly obvious to many observers for two decades: UNITA was designated a spoiler of the peace process in Angola. Six months later, the Council imposed sanctions on the sale of arms and oil to the rebel movement, threatening further sanctions if UNITA did not comply with UN resolutions calling for an end to the fighting. Savimbi had become Uncle Sam's Frankenstein. Having seen the monster it had fed and nurtured for a decade spin out of control and descend into rampaging madness, Washington finally offered diplomatic recognition to the MPLA government under the new administration of Bill Clinton in May 1993. (Dos Santos would later visit the White House in December 1995.) With the loss of his former dedicated patron, accumulated external military hardware and the seizure of diamond fields in northeastern Angola would help Savimbi continue to sustain his war for another decade. A UN panel of inquiry fingered Zaire (now the Democratic Republic of Congo), Congo-Brazzaville, Togo, and possibly Burkina Faso as the main facilitators of continued military support to UNITA during this period.[80]

From Lusaka to Luanda: Further Peacekeeping Travails

Fighting continued in Angola for another two years after the 1992 election debacle. The MPLA government was able to recapture some of the territory it had lost to UNITA, assisted by the South African group of mercenaries Executive Outcomes, some of whose members had ironically fought alongside UNITA against the government between 1975 and 1988. In November 1993, the Lusaka peace process was launched under the dynamic former Malian foreign minister and jurist Alioune Blondin Beye, who had replaced Anstee after the failed Abidjan talks of April–May 1993. Talks in the Zambian capital lasted one year and began as relations between Washington and UN Secretary-General Boutros Boutros-Ghali soured following the Somali peacekeeping debacle in which eighteen US soldiers had been killed (see Chapter 6). UNITA regarded Beye's style as undiplomatic and brusque, but the Malian ensured that the troika (the United States, Russia, and Portugal) became an integral part of his mediation team, and they in turn supported him whenever the MPLA or UNITA criticized the UN special representative.[81] During negotiations, Lisbon and Moscow tended to be supportive of Luanda, while Washington was viewed, at times, as being pro-UNITA.[82] There was unsurprisingly deep distrust between the parties, exacerbated by continued fighting even as negotiations were conducted.

In November 1994, the Lusaka Protocol was signed in the Zambian capital, establishing the third UN mission in Angola (UNAVEM III). It is noteworthy that Lusaka, unlike Bicesse, had been directly facilitated by the UN.[83] Just before the accord was signed, the government in Luanda had recaptured the key provinces of Uige and Huambo from UNITA, forcing Savimbi to the peacemaking table. UNAVEM III was a deliberate effort to correct the flaws of Bicesse by giving the UN a central role in its implementation and by providing seven thousand peacekeepers: twenty times the size of UNAVEM II. Having seen the negative impact of a small UN force in 1992, the MPLA government now shed its prior fears about the world body's infringement on its sovereignty and supported UNITA's push for a sizeable peacekeeping force. Under Lusaka, UNITA troops would be demobilized at designated assembly points supervised by the UN, while government forces were to adopt defensive positions and be withdrawn to their barracks. The rebel army was to be disbanded, with some troops and officers joining a new national army, and the group becoming a legal political party. UNITA representatives would be brought into a transitional government in Luanda, with its parliamentarians elected in the 1992 polls finally taking their seats. The position of second vice president was also to be offered to Savimbi. Unlike Bicesse, Lusaka prioritized the establishment of a Government of National Unity and Reconciliation rather than the holding of national elections. Unlike Bicesse also, but like the Rome accord for Mozambique (see below), the new joint commission would be chaired by the UN special representative.[84]

Two key issues dominated discussions in Lusaka: disarming UNITA's troops, and the rebel group's role in government. UNITA accepted the quartering of its fighters in UN-supervised assembly points but was reluctant to surrender its weapons to international peacekeepers. As Savimbi memorably put it: "What leader has ever given up his army and survived?"[85] In the end, it was agreed that the rebel fighters would surrender their weapons to their commanding officers at the assembly points, with these officers then turning them over to UN peacekeepers. The second issue of UNITA's participation in government took six months of discussion. Beye and the troika offered UNITA two deputy governorships and several municipal and communal posts. The government objected but was told that if it accepted this approach, Luanda would not have to make concessions in any other areas. Dos Santos finally relented in May 1994. Savimbi continued to insist unsuccessfully on being given the governorship of Huambo, which he had won in the 1992 elections—this province was the heartland of his Ovimbundu ethnic group.

More than seven thousand UN troops deployed throughout Angola in 1995, and the ceasefire at first largely held. Nine UNITA generals were incorporated into the army. Bridges were repaired and roads demined. Peace efforts were, however, complicated by Savimbi's visit to South Africa in January

1997, which had not been coordinated with the UN. Luanda took great umbrage at the visit and often accused Nelson Mandela's government of continuing to support UNITA.[86] The situation would also poison relations between Dos Santos and South Africa's Thabo Mbeki throughout the latter's presidency between 1999 and 2008. However, the government of national unity came into existence in April 1997 and included four UNITA ministers and seven deputy ministers. Rebel parliamentarians also joined the National Assembly. But Savimbi had never been serious about implementing the Lusaka agreement, which suggests that it was not just the lack of sufficient UN peacekeepers or a strong special representative that had scuttled Bicesse. The Angolan warlord refused to let the government extend state administration into UNITA-held territory and attacked government administrators and police. As the security situation deteriorated, UN peacekeepers were withdrawn. In June 1997, the weaker UN Observer Mission in Angola (MONUA) was established with 1,500 troops under Guinean Special Representative Issa Diallo. Four months later, the UN Security Council imposed sanctions on UNITA's diamond exports. But Savimbi continued to rearm, and sanctions continued to be breached. The tragic situation was further compounded when Beye—like the martyred Swedish UN Secretary-General Dag Hammarskjöld, who died in a plane crash while pursuing peace efforts in the Congo in 1961 (see Chapter 3)—perished in a tragic plane crash over Abidjan in June 1998 in pursuit of peace efforts with regional governments. By 1998, full-scale war had returned to Angola. Paul Hare, US special envoy for the Angolan peace process, paid the Malian UN envoy a moving tribute: "Beye's diplomatic experience, intelligence, unflagging energy, and tenacity made him an outstanding choice. His African antecedents were also important for providing a better understanding of the motivations and sensitivities of the two parties to the conflict."[87]

After fighting intensified and two UN planes were shot down by UNITA in December 1998 and January 1999, MONUA was closed down in March 1999 and UN peacekeepers left Angola for good. A small, unobtrusive UN office was created in October 1999. In the end, it was a deus ex machina event rather than the world body that would prove decisive in securing peace in Angola. The killing of Savimbi by government troops in February 2002 led to the signing of a Memorandum of Understanding between the government and UNITA. Both sides then undertook to implement the Lusaka Protocol with the assistance of the UN mission in Angola (UNMA), created in August 2002 under the leadership of Nigerian scholar-diplomat Ibrahim Gambari. The UN chaired the joint commission, which was mandated to deal with the outstanding issues from Lusaka. A government of national unity was created, and some UNITA elements were reintegrated into the national army and police. But problems still remained, as by February 2003, 105,000 excombatants and their family members still required reintegration assistance, about 20 percent of excombatants remained outside the government's payroll,[88] uncertainty remained about the government's commitment to democracy (particularly after the scrapping of direct presidential elections in January 2010), and concerns continued to be raised by foreign donors and multilateral lending institutions about the lack of transparency in government oil receipts.

Mozambique

Domestic, Regional, and External Friends and Foes

Turning to the third Southern African "orphan" of the Cold War, between 1975 and 1990, after the departure of the colonial Portuguese administration from Mozambique in 1974, the FRELIMO government and RENAMO rebels were locked in a brutal civil war.[89] FRELIMO supported black liberation groups fighting Ian Smith's illegitimate regime in Rhodesia, while Salisbury (now Harare) recruited Mozambican expatriate soldiers to create RENAMO. The rebel group was known as the "locust people" for destroying everything in its path. Its nihilistic brutality was rivaled, in recent times in Africa, perhaps only by the Revolutionary United Front (RUF) in Sierra Leone (see Chapter 5) and Uganda's Lord's Resistance Army (see Chapter 6). In 1986–1987, RENAMO was said to have committed six massacres, including the July 1987 Homoine killings in which over four hundred civilians were murdered.[90] While Moscow supported FRELIMO, South Africa and the United States (as well as former Portuguese residents in Mozambique largely based in South Africa, Brazil, and Portugal) propped up the brutal RENAMO rebels following Robert Mugabe's victory as the first democratically elected prime minister (later president) in a liberated Zimbabwe in 1980.

It is important again, as with the previous two cases, to assess dynamics at the national, regional, and external levels that first obstructed and then facilitated the move from war to peace in Mozambique. At the national level, FRELIMO often described RENAMO as "armed bandits" terrorizing local populations. Mozambican president Joaquim Chissano dismissed RENAMO leader Afonso Dhlakama as an incompetent former low-ranking sergeant in the Mozambican army and was shocked that such a person could aspire to high office.[91] Dhlakama, for his part, regarded Chissano as part of Africa's Marxist club of "atheistic corrupt dictators."[92] When discussions began in the late 1980s to find a solution to this conflict, FRELIMO's main goal was to incorporate RENAMO into its one-party state.

At the regional level, Harare was a key supporter of the FRELIMO government, since Maputo had supported Zimbabwe's liberation movement against Ian Smith's obdurate albinocracy in Rhodesia between 1965 and 1980. Land-locked Zimbabwe deployed seven thousand troops to

Mozambique's Beira corridor in order to protect road and railway lines to the port (the first contingent was deployed in 1982), which was vulnerable to RENAMO attacks. RENAMO crossed the Zimbabwean border to kill civilians, to steal food and cattle, and to terrorize local populations, while Harare also hosted an estimated one hundred thousand Mozambican refuges,[93] giving it a further motive for seeking an end to the conflict through RENAMO's defeat. Zimbabwe thus provided air and ground support for the Mozambican military in battles to recapture towns from RENAMO in 1987 and 1988.[94] In January 1992, Mugabe met with Dhlakama and urged negotiations between the two sides. Tanzania also deployed one thousand troops to Mozambique in 1983 in support of FRELIMO. By 1987, about six thousand Tanzanian troops were helping the FRELIMO government in offensives to recapture towns from RENAMO before most of these troops were withdrawn by December 1988. As in Zimbabwe and Malawi, RENAMO was a regional menace whose brutal and ill-disciplined forces abducted people and plundered villages in Tanzania and Zambia, forcing the Zambian army to launch cross-border raids into Mozambique in 1988.[95]

Relations between Mozambique and Malawi had long been tense, with Hastings Banda—one of the few African leaders to maintain open relations with apartheid South Africa—harboring anti-FRELIMO dissidents as well as RENAMO elements, until a security pact between the two countries in December 1986. Land-locked Malawi continued to suffer from RENAMO rebels fleeing into its territory, attacking local populations, and creating a population of one million Mozambican refugees in Malawi.[96] Another regional leader, Kenya's Daniel arap Moi, and the permanent secretary in his foreign ministry, Bethuel Kiplagat, provided much advice and logistical support to RENAMO. Moi acted as a political mentor to Dhlakama in a relationship cemented by their active involvement in Protestant networks to which Kiplagat also belonged.[97] As Moi—himself not above acts of autocratic excesses despite the pretense of sanctity—noted in March 1990: "How can people say Dhlakama is so evil when he goes around his territory giving out Bibles?"[98] Kenya provided shelter, passports, and reportedly military support to RENAMO in the 1980s, even as Moi sought to act as a co-mediator with Robert Mugabe to resolve the conflict in Mozambique.[99] During peace negotiations in Rome between 1990 and 1992, Kiplagat served as a key adviser to the RENAMO delegation.[100]

Further afield, South Africa took over support of RENAMO from Ian Smith's Rhodesia in 1979. The March 1984 Agreement on Non-Aggression and Good Neighborliness (also known as the Nkomati Accord) between Mozambique and South Africa was clearly a pact with the apartheid devil without the requisite long spoon. This humiliating agreement with a regime that only a handful of African countries even admitted to talking to, graphically illustrated the government's military weakness. Under this accord,

Pretoria agreed to stop supporting RENAMO in exchange for Maputo's desisting support to the African National Congress. FRELIMO kept its side of the bargain, but South Africa did not and continued supporting REN-AMO.[101] From 1985, FRELIMO had already started to abandon its Marxist-Leninist ideology and to embrace the political liberalization and market economics that was crucial to gaining loans from the World Bank and the International Monetary Fund (IMF). By 1990, South Africa had withdrawn from Namibia, and its last white ruler, F. W. De Klerk, was starting the democratic transition to black majority rule. Washington pushed Pretoria to end military support to RENAMO, though reports of South African military support continued, as well as support from Malawi.[102]

At the external level, conservative Cold Warriors in the United States were particularly supportive of RENAMO. Within the US government, the Department of Defense (DOD) and the Central Intelligence Agency were enthusiastic backers of the rebel movement, while the State Department urged caution due to RENAMO's links to apartheid South Africa. American diplomats argued that unlike UNITA in Angola, RENAMO had no political constituency in Mozambique.[103] In contrast to its approach in Angola, Washington provided diplomatic recognition to the FRELIMO government and opened an embassy in Maputo. Mozambican president Joaquim Chissano paid a state visit to Washington in October 1987 and, prompted by Chester Crocker, pledged to President Ronald Reagan his willingness to open dialogue with RENAMO. The Mozambican leader visited Washington again in March 1990, where President George H. Bush urged him to open negotiations with RENAMO without any preconditions.[104]

Turning to the Soviet Union—the other Cold War superpower—FRE-LIMO was not keen to sign a formal military cooperation accord with Moscow despite having declared itself a Marxist party in 1977. Maputo wanted guarantees of Soviet protection in the event of South African military action, which Moscow was not prepared to provide. South Africa was launching military attacks against Mozambique (which was itself sheltering ANC fighters) in the 1980s. This was thus not a theoretical request. The Russians did, however, provide $600 million a year in arms and military training to the Mozambican army and by 1984 had four hundred military advisers in the country. Mozambican president Samora Machel, though, remained pragmatic, visiting Washington in 1983. On a visit to Moscow in 1986 by Machel and his foreign minister, Joaquim Chissano, the Mozambicans realized that Mikhail Gorbachev was largely interested in a deal with the United States and would not provide further substantial military or economic support to Maputo.[105] Such support did indeed cease in 1988.[106]

Mozambique was, however, fortunate to have been able to gain the attention of not only the United States and Russia but also the other three permanent members of the UN Security Council. Britain provided training to the country's army from 1987. France had become the country's second largest creditor and trading partner after Italy by 1985, while China provided arms to FRELIMO,[107] though others accused Beijing of backing RENAMO as part of its global struggle with Moscow.

From Rome to Maputo: Peacemaking and Peacekeeping

For two years, from July 1990, direct meetings were hosted in Rome between FRELIMO and RENAMO by the Italian government and the Community of Sant' Egidio, a Catholic lay organization.[108] Significantly, these sessions were assisted by four important Western countries: the United States, France, Britain, and Portugal, gaining early donor interest and potential support for an eventual peace settlement. The early involvement of three veto-wielding permanent members of the UN Security Council in the peace process was also significant. In terms of regional actors, Botswana played an important role in supporting peace efforts.[109] In October 1992, President Joaquim Chissano and RENAMO leader Afonso Dhlakama signed a General Peace Agreement (GPA). The accord called for the deployment of UN peacekeepers within a few weeks, the demobilization of eighty thousand FRELIMO and RENAMO troops within a few months, and the organization of elections within a year. This unrealistic timetable was unsurprisingly not met and reflected the "euphoric planning" of the mediators.

In December 1992, the Security Council approved the UN Operation in Mozambique (ONUMOZ), which had political, military, humanitarian, electoral, and civilian police units. The mission's military and civilian staff totaled seven thousand, and ONUMOZ cost nearly $1 million a day, totaling nearly $1 billion for the two years. The mission's most important body was the Supervision and Monitoring Commission (CSC), which took over some of the FRELIMO government's sovereign powers in areas relevant to implementing the peace accord. Members of the UN-chaired commission included the two warring parties, the OAU, Britain, France, Germany, Italy, Portugal, and the United States. The fact that the world body was chosen to drive this powerful commission was an important lesson from the mission in Angola, where the UN had merely been an "observer" in implementing the peace process. Other commissions were established to oversee the ceasefire, the reintegration and demobilization of soldiers, the creation of a new thirty thousand–strong army, and the conducting of elections. Three other commissions dealt with issues related to police, intelligence, and administration.

ONUMOZ had five military battalions of about six thousand troops and 350 military observers who were tasked to supervise the assembly and demobilization of FRELIMO and RENAMO troops, to investigate ceasefire violations, and to provide security to humanitarian relief convoys and returning refugees. The main peacekeeping contingents were provided by

Bangladesh, Italy, India, Zambia, Uruguay, Botswana, and Portugal. The mission was also mandated to repatriate two million refugees from neighboring countries (over four million Mozambicans actually returned home), to oversee the coordination of humanitarian assistance, and to verify the conduct of national elections.[110]

Despite its common reputation for being a flawless success—while failures proliferated in Angola, Somalia, and Rwanda (see Chapters 3 and 6)— ONUMOZ experienced several difficulties. Most of the UN's contingents started arriving only in March 1993, and their deployment took seven months. The Italian and Uruguyan contingents were accused of the sexual exploitation of young girls,[111] charges that would reappear against peacekeepers in UN missions in Sierra Leone and the DRC. Other problems were also encountered by the UN: the thirty thousand–strong Mozambican army that was mandated to be created by the mission was only twelve thousand strong by the time ONUMOZ left in 1994. The UN's 1,095-strong civilian police component was also fully deployed only in May 1994, the last five months of the mission. Despite these difficulties, however, this was one of the UN's genuine peacekeeping successes.

Demobilization of Mozambican fighters took place between March and August 1994, and the UN had to set up a trust fund to provide soldiers with an additional eighteen months of wages. Rioting by government and rebel troops in assembly points in June and July 1994 forced the acceleration of the pace of demobilization. The UN's experts had patronizingly decided to make combatants traveling long distances build their own "farm huts" rather than providing military tents in assembly areas, causing great resentment and damaging the organization's reputation in the eyes of many of the fighters.[112] Only 180,000 weapons were collected, and even UN special representative Aldo Ajello later conceded that the world body had fallen short in this area,[113] as millions of AK-47s still proliferated throughout the country. There was also no comprehensive demining program in a nation blighted by the scourge of land mines. The elections themselves took two years to organize. Disagreements between the parties about postelection powersharing and monitoring the impartiality of the media were also never fully resolved and dogged the process throughout the two years of the UN presence.[114] As Ajello later admitted: "The timetable was unrealistic and unprofessional and should never have been accepted by UN officials in Rome."[115]

Afonso Dhlakama acted as a classic spoiler, refusing at first to relocate to Maputo from his central Mozambican base in Meringue. Shortly after the first twenty-five UN peacekeepers arrived in October 1992, the Mozambican warlord launched an attack that captured four towns, in clear violation of the ceasefire. The government would recapture all the towns a month later. Ajello immediately convened a meeting with the ambassadors of the United States, Britain, France, Portugal, and Italy to issue a strong statement, which led to Dhlakama's pledging to avoid such attacks in future.[116] In January 1993, the Mozambican warlord refused to demobilize his troops until the UN had fully deployed its troops and demanded that 65 percent of the peacekeepers be dispatched to RENAMO-controlled territory.[117] Two months later, Dhlakama recalled his officials from Maputo and refused to cooperate with the UN's commissions. He announced a halt to the demobilization of his troops unless more funds were provided for transforming his guerrilla movement into a political party. RENAMO eventually received $17.5 million for this purpose, much of it from the Italian government, with other contributions from the United States, Britain, Portugal, South Africa, and the Nordic countries. The warlord also received $3.9 million during the last thirteen months of the mission.[118]

Part of the problem with RENAMO was that it lacked sufficient skilled officials to cover the complex institutions established by the peace accord.[119] There was also a strong sense of insecurity and distrust bred by sixteen years of conflict. Dhlakama refused to move to Maputo until enough UN peacekeepers had been deployed to the capital and until Zimbabwean and Malawian troops had withdrawn from the Beira and Nacala corridors and been replaced by UN troops (which occurred by June 1993).[120] At the Frontline States summit in Harare in October 1994, Dhlakama's suspicion of regional leaders was further heightened when Zimbabwe's Robert Mugabe acceded to Chissano's petty request not to allow the warlord to address the summit. A humiliated Dhlakama was kept waiting in his hotel room and was later briefed by Mugabe on the ultimatum that emerged from the summit: RENAMO must accept the election results or face "appropriate measures."[121] Whereas FRELIMO distrusted the UN, which it felt was constraining its sovereignty, and banked on African diplomatic support, RENAMO welcomed the UN as its best hope for providing the legitimacy and security to transform itself into a political party.

On the government side, President Joaquim Chissano was not as powerful or as charismatic as his martyred predecessor, Samora Machel (who died in a plane crash in October 1986), had been within FRELIMO. He thus had to negotiate with his military to convince them to demobilize rather than simply ordering them to do so.[122] Chissano had earlier used US pressure on his government to move FRELIMO "hawks" to embrace negotiations with RENAMO.[123] Mozambique's president, a former foreign minister before becoming head of state in 1986, was a primus inter pares within his national system rather than an all-powerful "imperial" president. But the fact that the government was so dependent on aid donors and had lost its main sponsor by the time the Soviet Union collapsed in 1991 was also important leverage for the international community.

UN Secretary-General Boutros Boutros-Ghali visited Maputo in October 1993. During the visit, the "Pharaoh" warned the parties that they must avoid a repeat of Angola's debacle and strive for an African peace-keeping success story.[124] Less diplomatically, he privately warned FRE-LIMO and RENAMO leaders that unless they implemented the peace accord expeditiously, they would be abandoned by the international community, which had other pressing priorities across the globe.[125] The Egyptian Secretary-General's visit helped to accelerate demobilization and facilitated the establishment of the country's long-delayed electoral commission.[126] As tensions ran high in August 1994, a UN Security Council mission visited Mozambique to pressure both sides to live up to their commitments on demobilizing their troops. The Council was determined to avoid a repeat of the debacle in Angola when both sides had kept soldiers in reserve for the postelection phase. On the eve of elections in October 1994 (monitored by 2,300 international observers), Dhlakama threatened a boycott of the polls, citing evidence of government-organized fraud. He intriguingly noted: "I am not going back to the bush. I am not Savimbi. I am sure the international community will understand my decision."[127] In the end, a declaration promising to investigate electoral fraud signed by Ajello and international members of the CSC proved sufficient to keep Dhlakama urinating in the peace tent rather than taking his grievance outside it.

The mediation role played by the UN special representative Aldo Ajello, combined with external pressure, was crucial in convincing the RENAMO leader to implement the peace agreement. The Italian diplomat had been an official at the UN Development Programme (UNDP) and joked that, since his country had hosted the mediation, his name had been plucked out of the UN telephone directory in alphabetical order in a desperate search for an Italian UN employee![128] Ajello interpreted his mandate with flexible dexterity; he effectively used the Supervision and Control Commission to resolve military issues and tirelessly lobbied donors to provide funds for implementing the accord, even agreeing to draft UN Secretary-General reports to the Security Council with them before sending them on to New York.[129] He was one of the most effective UN special representatives in the organization's history.

Some, however, criticized Ajello for exceeding his powers, and his critics within the Mozambican government found him brusque and imperious.[130] Others noted Ajello's poor coordination of the UN bureaucracy.[131] His unorthodox methods were seen by some as effectively "buying" peace by "bribing" Dhlakama with monetary inducements. Such critics noted that future warlords could hold external players hostage to similar financial rewards. Ajello was also much closer to the Western ambassadors in Maputo than to their African counterparts, particularly at the beginning of his mission when he was said to have forged an alliance with these Western plenipotentiaries. The Italian envoy later consulted regularly with the group of African ambassadors in Maputo; Tunisia's diplomat, Ahcene Fzeri, joined the CSC as the OAU Representative; and representatives from Botswana, Egypt, Kenya, Nigeria, and Zimbabwe were members of the Ceasefire Commission (CCF). Another criticism of the special representative was that Ajello was not a strong manager and could be rough and hot tempered with his staff.[132] The former Italian senator acted more like a pragmatic "big picture" politician than a detail-oriented bureaucrat. His unorthodox methods, however, succeeded in cutting through the often Byzantine workings of the UN bureaucracy and finding pragmatic solutions to difficult problems as they arose.

One thousand two hundred UN electoral observers oversaw Mozambique's parliamentary and presidential elections in October 1994. In the presidential election, Chissano won 53.3 percent of the vote to Dhlakama's 33.7 percent. FRELIMO won 44.3 percent of parliamentary seats to RENAMO's 37.8 percent: a surprisingly strong showing from the former brutal rebel movement. RENAMO had lost the support of its South African patron and, unlike the belligerents in Angola, had no access to domestic natural resources—oil and diamonds—with which to fund continued war, even if it wanted to. The European Union and the United States were particularly important donors in supporting the success of this mission. Of the individual European nations, Britain managed to recruit Mozambique into the Commonwealth in 1995, while former colonial power, Portugal, and chief mediator, Italy, sought to bolster their influence as middle powers in the international system through supporting peace efforts in the country.

Though this mission has often been considered one of the UN's unblemished peacekeeping success stories, British analyst Richard Synge noted that the international presence had a detrimental rather than reinforcing effect on Mozambique's state structures and authority and increased the government's dependence on international financial and humanitarian support. As in Angola with the MPLA, the FRELIMO government in Mozambique complained about the infringement of its sovereignty by the UN. The General Peace Agreement, for example, took precedence over the Mozambican constitution. Synge went on to criticize the lack of focus in the coordination of the UN mission as well as an overambitious mandate. He further noted that the UN ran a parallel administration that was sometimes quasi colonial in its emphasis on a foreign rather than a domestic agenda. In effect, he argued, Mozambique's long-term socioeconomic needs were sacrificed to the short-term goals of an international community desperate for a peacekeeping success story. ONUMOZ also left a plethora of tasks uncompleted: collection of arms, creation of a new army, reintegrating demobilized soldiers into local communities, and demining.[133] Perhaps seeking to learn from this case, the UN subsequently established peacebuilding offices in Liberia, the Central African Republic, Sierra Leone, Guinea-Bissau, and Burundi. But these offices have often been too small and underfunded to have a real impact on postconflict reconstruction efforts. Aldo Ajello strongly disagreed with Synge's analysis and provided a staunch defense of the UN mission. In his view, the government of Mozambique's dependence on international financial and humanitarian resources was not increased by the UN presence; it was not the resources used by the UN and the international donor community for implementing a peace accord—limited in time and scope—that created such external dependence. For Ajello, such dependence occurs when donors provide funds for development cooperation and humanitarian assistance on a long-term basis. He also felt that concerns about the infringement of Mozambique's sovereignty were exaggerated, as this issue was raised once by the country's parliament, but dropped once UN peacekeepers had been deployed. Ajello also rejected the charge that the UN was running a parallel quasi-colonial administration, as the ONU-MOZ mandate was limited to implementing the peace accord, and the government in Maputo still exercised much political and administrative powers.

Ajello further challenged the idea that Mozambique's long-term socioeconomic needs were sacrificed for short-term goals by an international community desperate for success, noting that Maputo needed such peacekeeping success even more than the international community did. He saw no contradiction between short-term success and long-term development. Furthermore, the special representative argued that disarmament, demobilization, and reintegration of soldiers was, in fact, successfully completed in Mozambique and often seen as the most successful part of the UN mission. He further noted that the failure to create a new national army was due to the unwillingness of soldiers on both sides to join the army and that sections of the Mozambican government were in fact glad for the lower cost of a smaller army. Finally, Ajello noted that demining had always been considered a long-term task that exceeded the ONUMOZ mandate. In his view, the only task left unfinished by the UN mission was the disarmament of civilians, which he admitted was a low priority on the list of goals crafted to ensure durable peace.[134] Without a doubt, the UN mission in Mozambique remains one of the UN's most successful peacekeeping missions, and the country has remained stable for two decades following the peacekeepers' departure.

Concluding Reflections

All three countries in this chapter were "orphans of the Cold War," demonstrating the importance of external actors (particularly the five permanent members of the UN Security Council) in fueling conflicts and obstructing peaceful solutions to conflicts. More positively, the cases also show the important role that powerful states can play in ensuring the success of UN peacekeeping missions in Africa and beyond. The case of Namibia is illustrative in this regard. The United States was able to delay the implementation of a peace plan for the territory due to Cold War calculations of curbing Cuban and Soviet military support for Angola. Only after US-Russian rapprochement with the advent of the reformist administration of Mikhail Gorbachev in Moscow in 1985 did Washington pressure its South African client to withdraw from the territory and allow the 1978 peace plan to be implemented. Namibia's independence in March 1990 was delayed for twelve years due largely to Chester Crocker's machinations, with the cynical linking of the withdrawal of Cuban troops from Angola. Only after Havana and Moscow agreed to withdraw Cuban troops from Angola could UN peacekeepers be deployed to Namibia. The improved post–Cold War security environment also made deployment of UN peacekeepers in Mozambique possible in 1992.

The peace talks in Mozambique took seventeen months longer than the negotiations in Angola. Unlike the peace process in Angola, where the warring parties chaired the key commissions, the process in Mozambique put the UN firmly in charge of implementation and provided the world body with more peacekeepers to get the job done. Learning further lessons from Angola, the UN also insisted that demobilization and disarmament of troops must occur before elections could take place in Mozambique. Both Angola and Mozambique had spoiler warlords—Jonas Savimbi and Afonso Dhlakama respectively—who often seemed determined to wreck peace processes. Both were brutal and committed atrocities against civilian populations. But where Savimbi could be charming and urbane; Dhlakama was unsophisticated and lacked charisma. The presence of economic resources in Angola and the greater cooperation of the warring parties in Mozambique were crucial in explaining the different outcomes in the two cases.

The sustained interest and cooperation of the powerful members of the UN Security Council and their contribution of financial, diplomatic, and logistical support to UN missions was important to success in Namibia and Mozambique and mostly lacking in the first peacekeeping mission in Angola. The better-resourced second UN mission in Angola, however, revealed Savimbi to be the main obstacle to peace, and international sanctions were imposed on his rebel movement. Only the Angolan warlord's assassination by government forces in 2002 eventually ended the country's twenty-seven-year war, suggesting that even an increased UN presence could be deterred by a determined well-resourced warlord. In Mozambique, the UN had a dynamic special representative—Aldo Ajello—who was able to take advantage of more auspicious circumstances for peacekeeping to craft innovative solutions to political challenges. The equally able Alioune Blondin Beye was the special representative for the second Angola mission, but even his diplomatic skills could not overcome the obstructionist efforts of the megalomaniac Jonas Savimbi.

Notes

The title of this chapter is borrowed from Margaret Joan Anstee, *Orphan of the Cold War: The Inside Story of the Collapse of the Angolan Peace Process, 1992–1993* (New York: St. Martin's, 1996). The author would like to thank Chris Saunders and Gwinyayi Dzinesa for extremely useful comments on an earlier version of this chapter.

1. Marrack Goulding, *Peacemonger* (London: John Murray, 2000), p. 197.

2. For comparative analyses of these cases, see Gwinyayi A. Dzinesa, "A Comparative Perspective of UN Peacekeeping in Angola and Namibia," *International Peacekeeping* 11, no. 4 (2004): 644–663; Gwinyayi A. Dzinesa, "Postconflict Disarmament, Demobilization, and the Reintegration of Former Combatants in Southern Africa," *International Studies Perspectives* 8 (2007): 73–89; Assis Malaquias, "The UN in Mozambique and Angola: Lessons Learned," *International Peacekeeping* 3, no. 2 (summer 1996): 87–103; Chris Saunders, "UN Peacekeeping in Southern Africa: Namibia, Angola and Mozambique," in Adekeye Adebajo, ed., *From Global Apartheid to Global Village: Africa and the United Nations* (Scottsville, South Africa: University of KwaZulu-Natal Press, 2009), pp. 269–281.

3. Rodney Davenport and Christopher Saunders, *South Africa: A Modern History,* 5th ed. (London: Macmillan, 2000), p. 538.

4. See, for example, James Barber, and John Barratt, *South Africa's Foreign Policy 1948–88: The Search for Status and Security* (Cambridge: Cambridge University Press, 1990); William Minter, *Apartheid's Contras: An Inquiry into the Roots of War in Angola and Mozambique* (London: Zed Books, 1994).

5. Adebayo Adedeji, "Within or Apart?" in Adebayo Adedeji, ed., *South Africa in Africa: Within or Apart?* (London: Zed, 1996), p. 9.

6. See, for example, Ruth First, *South West Africa* (Baltimore: Penguin, 1963); Peter H. Katjavivi, *A History of Resistance in Namibia* (Paris: UN Educational, Scientific and Cultural Organization Press, 1988).

7. See, for example, Davenport and Saunders, *South Africa;* Katjavivi, *A History of Resistance in Namibia;* Cedric Thornberry, *A Nation Is Born: The Inside Story of Namibia's Independence* (Windhoek: Gamsberg Macmillan, 2004). For insider accounts by the Nigerian and Ghanaian permanent representatives to the UN respectively, see also Simeon Ola Adebo, *Our International Years* (Ibadan: Spectrum, 1988); Alex Quaison-Sackey, *Africa Unbound: Reflections of an African Statesman* (London: André Deutsch, 1963).

8. See Tor Sellström, "The Trusteeship Council: Decolonisation and Liberation," and Muna Ndulo, "The International Court of Justice," both in Adebajo, *From Global Apartheid to Global Village,* pp. 107–137 and 139–166.

9. Brian Urquhart, *A Life in Peace and War* (New York: W. W. Norton, 1987), p. 309.

10. Ibid., p. 308.

11. Ibid., p. 321.

12. Donald F. McHenry, "The United Nations: Its Role in Decolonization," in Gwendolen M. Carter and Patrick O'Meara, eds., *African Independence: The First Twenty-Five Years* (Bloomington: Indiana University Press, 1986), p. 41.

13. Urquhart, *A Life in Peace and War,* p. 320.

14. Ibid., p. 306.

15. Chester A. Crocker, "Peacemaking in Southern Africa: The Namibia-Angola Settlement of 1988," in Chester Crocker, Fen Osler Hampson, and Pamela Aall, eds., *Herding Cats: Multiparty Mediation in a Complex World* (Washington, DC: US Institute of Peace, 1999), pp. 234–239.

16. I am grateful for this analysis to former British ambassador to Angola and later UN Undersecretary-General for Peacekeeping, Marrack Goulding. See Goulding, *Peacemonger,* p. 142.

17. Crocker, "Peacemaking in Southern Africa," p. 226.

18. Ibid., p. 217.

19. Urquhart, *A Life in Peace and War,* p. 312.

20. Quoted in Vladimir Shubin, *The Hot "Cold War": The USSR in Southern Africa* (London: Pluto, 2008), p. 105.

21. Quoted in Ronnie Kasrils, "Turning Points at Cuito Cuanavale," in *The Sunday Independent* (South Africa), 23 March 2008.

22. Shubin, *The Hot "Cold War,"* p. 107.

23. Cited in ibid., p. 108.

24. Crocker, "Peacemaking in Southern Africa," pp. 231–232.

25. J. E. Davies, *Constructive Engagement? Chester Crocker and American Policy in South Africa, Namibia and Angola, 1981–1988* (Oxford: James Currey, 2007), p. 199.

26. Ibid., p. 204.

27. Lise Morjé Howard, "UN Peace Implementation in Namibia: The Causes of Success," in *International Peacekeeping* 9, no. 1 (Spring 2002): 101.

28. See Virginia Page Fortna, "United Nations Transition Assistance Group in Namibia," in William Durch, ed., *The Evolution of UN Peacekeeping: Case Studies and Comparative Analysis* (New York: St. Martin's, 1993), pp. 353–375; Howard, "UN Peace Implementation in Namibia," pp. 99–132; Cedric Thornberry, "Namibia," in David M. Malone, ed., *The UN Security Council: From the Cold War to the 21st Century* (Boulder: Lynne Rienner, 2004), pp. 407–422.

29. Goulding, *Peacemonger,* p. 145.

30. See Adebajo, *From Global Apartheid to Global Village.*

31. Goulding, *Peacemonger,* p. 144.

32. Ibid., p. 149

33. Ibid., p. 150.

34. See, for example, ibid., pp. 150–161; Urquhart, *A Life in Peace and War,* p. 310. For his own interpretation of events, see Sam Nujoma, *Where Others Wavered: The Autobiography of Sam Nujoma* (London: Panaf, 2001).

35. Goulding, *Peacemonger,* p. 153; James O. C. Jonah, *What Price the Survival of the United Nations? Memoirs of a Veteran International Civil Servant* (Lagos: Evans Brothers, 2006), p. 287.

36. Figure cited in Lise Morjé Howard, *UN Peacekeeping in Civil Wars* (Cambridge: Cambridge University Press, 2008), p. 63.

37. Goulding, *Peacemonger,* p. 161.

38. Ibid., pp. 166–167.

39. Ibid., p. 168.

40. Ibid., p. 170.

41. Ibid., p. 168.

42. Ibid., p. 169.

43. Ibid., p. 171.

44. Ibid., p. 172.

45. Ibid., p. 173.

46. See Ibrahim A. Gambari, "Apartheid and Current Developments Inside South Africa: The Role of the United Nations," lecture presented to the African Studies Group, Fletcher School of Law and Diplomacy, Massachusetts, 30 April

1993; Chris Landsberg, "Exporting Peace? The UN and South Africa," Center for Policy Studies, *Policy: Issues and Actors* 7, no. 2 (April 1994).

47. For background, see Virginia Page Fortna, "United Nations Angola Verification Mission II," in Durch, ed., *The Evolution of UN Peacekeeping,* pp. 388–405; Tony Hodges, *Angola: From Afro-Stalinism to Petro-Diamond Capitalism* (Oxford: James Currey, 2001); Lise Morjé Howard, *UN Peacekeeping in Civil Wars* (Cambridge: Cambridge University Press, 2008), pp. 35–42.

48. Herman J. Cohen, *Intervening in Africa: Superpower Peacemaking in a Troubled Continent* (New York: St. Martin's, 2000), p. 90.

49. Goulding, *Peacemonger,* p. 164.

50. Shubin, *The Hot "Cold War,"* p. 144.

51. For this narrative, I am grateful to Cohen, *Intervening in Africa,* pp. 91–97 and 101.

52. Goulding, *Peacemonger,* p. 181.

53. Cohen, *Intervening in Africa,* p. 88.

54. Goulding, *Peacemonger,* p. 181.

55. Cohen, *Intervening in Africa,* p. 112.

56. Ibid., p. 113.

57. Jonah, *What Price the Survival of the United Nations?* pp. 303–304.

58. Cohen, *Intervening in Africa,* p. 102.

59. Ibid., pp. 105–108.

60. See Virginia Page Fortna, "United Nations Angola Verification Mission I," in Durch, *The Evolution of UN Peacekeeping,* pp. 376–387.

61. Goulding, *Peacemonger,* p. 145.

62. Ibid., pp. 176–177.

63. Cohen, *Intervening in Africa,* pp. 103 and 105.

64. Ibid., p. 109.

65. Goulding, *Peacemonger,* p. 178.

66. Ibid., p. 178.

67. Ibid., p. 181.

68. See Margaret J. Anstee, "The United Nations in Angola: Post Bicesse Implementation," in Crocker, Hampson, and Aall, *Herding Cats,* pp. 587–613; Philip Sibanda, "Lessons from UN Peacekeeping in Africa: From UNAVEM to MONUA," in Jakkie Cilliers and Greg Mills, eds., *From Peacekeeping to Complex Emergencies: Peace Support Missions in Africa* (Johannesburg: South African Institute of International Affairs, 1999), pp. 119–125.

69. Cited in Goulding, *Peacemonger,* p. 178.

70. Cohen, *Intervening in Africa,* pp. 111 and 123.

71. Ibid., p. 124.

72. Goulding, *Peacemonger,* pp. 190 and 194.

73. Ibid., p. 194.

74. Ibid., pp. 182–187.

75. Cohen, *Intervening in Africa,* p. 116.

76. Ibid., p. 115.

77. Goulding, *Peacemonger,* p. 190.

78. Ibid., p. 191.

79. Paul J. Hare, "Angola: The Lusaka Peace Process," in Crocker, Hampson, and Aall, *Herding Cats,* p. 645.

80. "Report of the UN Panel of Experts on Violations of Security Council Sanctions Against UNITA," S/2000/203, 10 March 2000, paragraphs 18–35.

81. Hare, "Angola," pp. 647–648.

82. Ibid., p. 647.

83. I thank Gwinyayi Dzinesa for this important insight.

84. For the information on Lusaka, I am grateful to Hare, "Angola," pp. 645–661.

85. Quoted in Hare, "Angola," p. 653.

86. Hare, "Angola," p. 659.

87. Ibid., p. 658.

88. See Ibrahim Gambari, "Peacebuilding in Post-Conflict Angola," address at the IPA Policy Forum, New York, 3 June 2003; "Report of the Secretary-General on the United Nations Mission in Angola," S/2003/158, 7 February 2003.

89. See, for example, William Finnegan, *A Complicated War: The Harrowing of Mozambique* (Berkeley: University of California Press, 1992); Alex Vines, *RENAMO: Terrorism in Mozambique* (Bloomington: Indiana University Press, 1991).

90. Howard, *UN Peacekeeping in Civil Wars*, p. 189.

91. Cited in Cohen, *Intervening in Africa*, p. 190.

92. Cohen, *Intervening in Africa*, p. 190.

93. Ibid., p. 191; Vines, *RENAMO*, p. 62–64.

94. Vines, *RENAMO*, p. 61.

95. Ibid., pp. 66–67.

96. Ibid., pp. 55–58.

97. Cohen, *Intervening in Africa*, pp. 186 and 191.

98. Quoted in Cohen, *Intervening in Africa*, p. 191.

99. Vines, *RENAMO*, pp. 59–60.

100. Cohen, *Intervening in Africa*, p. 188.

101. Shubin, *The Hot "Cold War,"* p. 145.

102. Cohen, *Intervening in Africa*, pp. 193–194.

103. Ibid., pp. 181–184.

104. Ibid., p. 187.

105. Shubin, *The Hot "Cold War,"* pp. 137–147.

106. Howard, *UN Peacekeeping in Civil Wars*, p. 190.

107. Ibid., pp. 190–191.

108. See Andrea Bartoli, "Mediating Peace in Mozambique: The Role of the Community of Sant' Egidio," in Crocker, Hampson, and Aall, *Herding Cats*, pp. 245–273.

109. I thank Gwinyayi Dzinesa for this insight.

110. Sibanda, "Lessons from UN Peacekeeping in Africa," p. 123.

111. Richard Synge, *Mozambique: UN Peacekeeping in Action 1992–1994* (Washington, DC: US Institute of Peace Press, 1997), p. 158.

112. Aldo Ajello, "Mozambique: Implementation of the 1992 Agreement," in Crocker, Hampson, and Aall, *Herding Cats*, p. 629.

113. Ibid., p. 639.

114. Ibid., p. 624.

115. Ibid.

116. Aldo Ajello and Patrick Wittmann, "Mozambique," in Malone, *The UN Security Council*, p. 441.

117. Cameron Hume, *Ending Mozambique's War: The Role of Mediation and Good Offices* (Washington, DC: US Institute of Peace Press, 1994), p. 142.

118. Ajello, "Mozambique," p. 637.

119. Ibid., p. 624.

120. Ibid., p. 626.

121. Ajello and Wittmann, "Mozambique," p. 447.

122. Ajello, "Mozambique," p. 633.

123. Cohen, *Intervening in Africa,* p. 187.
124. Ajello and Wittmann, "Mozambique," p. 450, fn. 3.
125. Jonah, *What Price the Survival of the United Nations?,* p. 357.
126. Hume, *Ending Mozambique's War,* p. 143.
127. See Ajello, "Mozambique," p. 620.
128. See ibid.
129. Ibid., p. 628.
130. Jonah, *What Price the Survival of the United Nations?* p. 354.
131. Synge, *Mozambique,* pp. 46–47.
132. Ibid., p. 153.
133. Ibid., pp. 145–167.
134. Personal correspondence with Aldo Ajello, 2 March 2011.

5

The Tragic Triplets:
The UN in West Africa

The case was made by senior UN officials to replace ECOMOG with a
UN force. Even though the majority of Sierra Leoneans appreciated
and supported ECOMOG, there was a clear preference, particularly
in the local press, for the creation of a UN force. Sierra Leoneans,
like Somalis and Rwandans, later turned against the UN when it
refused to fight on the grounds that it had no mandate to do so.
—*James Jonah, UN Undersecretary-General
for Political Affairs, 1992–1994*[1]

Since the end of the Cold War in 1990, West Africa has been among the
most volatile regions in the world. Local brushfires have raged from
Liberia to Sierra Leone to Guinea to Guinea-Bissau to Senegal to Côte
d'Ivoire in an interconnected web of instability.[2] Due in large part to neglect by the UN Security Council, West Africa has gone further than any
other African subregion in efforts to establish a security mechanism to
manage its own conflicts.[3] The Economic Community of West African
States Ceasefire Monitoring Group (ECOMOG) intervention in Liberia
between 1990 and 1998 was the first such action by a subregional organization in Africa relying principally on its own men, money, and military
matériel. It was also the first time the UN had sent military observers to
support an already established subregional force. The ECOMOG intervention in Sierra Leone to restore the democratically elected government of
Ahmed Tejan Kabbah to power in 1998 was equally unprecedented, and
the UN took over ECOMOG's peacekeeping responsibilities between 1999
and 2000.[4]

Building on experiences in Liberia and Sierra Leone, as well as the
ECOWAS interventions in Côte d'Ivoire and Liberia, both in 2003—three
of four missions were eventually taken over by the UN—West Africa's

leaders are currently attempting to institutionalize a security mechanism to manage future subregional conflicts. This mechanism could eventually become a system of subsidiarity directed by a Nigerian-led ECOWAS in which West Africans make decisions over security issues in their own sub-region without prior UN Security Council authorization: an issue that does not seem yet to trouble the Council much. In crafting the ECOWAS security mechanism of 1999, West African leaders feared that the UN Security Council could delay approval for necessary action in cases of subregional stability. They have thus interpreted Chapter VIII of the UN Charter—dealing with regional arrangements—to allow military interventions in cases of regional instability and unconstitutional changes of government, with the flexibility of informing the Council *after* troops have already been deployed. (The African Union has also adopted similar principles.) This approach is controversial and not universally recognized under international law, with many arguing that the UN Security Council is the only legitimate body that can sanction the use of force.[5] In seeking to establish a Pax West Africana, ECOWAS leaders may be trying to define their own subsystem of international law that does not necessitate prior UN authorization but rather legitimation by ECOWAS.

Despite the lofty aspirations of West African leaders, however, hopes of a self-run security system currently confront the harsh reality of a lack of unity, capacity, and resources, as the three cases of Liberia, Sierra Leone, and Côte d'Ivoire will clearly demonstrate. The UN Security Council was forced eventually to take over three of the four missions from ECOWAS's logistically ill-equipped and underresourced peacekeepers. A division of labor was then worked out between the Council and ECOWAS in which the West Africans contributed the core of UN peacekeepers (and usually the political or military heads of the missions), while the Security Council contributed additional troops, financing, and political oversight.

In this chapter I examine peacemaking and peacekeeping cooperation between the UN and ECOWAS in Liberia, Sierra Leone, and Côte d'Ivoire.[6] I conclude by drawing policy lessons from all three missions, which can guide future cooperation in the area of conflict management between the UN and ECOWAS.[7] I discuss four important questions related to the role of the UN in West Africa. First, what impact did the UN have on the management of the conflicts in Liberia, Sierra Leone, and Côte d'Ivoire, and can its role be considered a success or a failure in each case? Second, did the UN's role change during the course of the three conflicts? Third, what was the reaction of regional actors in West Africa to the UN's role in these three cases? Finally, what lessons can the world body learn from these three conflicts in order to act more effectively in future cases in West Africa and beyond? The first three questions will be addressed in examining the three cases, as well as in a short analytical section on the significance of the cases in relation to these questions. The final question about the policy lessons for the UN will be tackled briefly in a concluding section. As with other chapters in this book, the framework of the three interdependent levels of domestic, regional, and external will be used to assess the outcomes of UN peacekeeping in these three West African cases.

West Africa's Tragic Triplets

Liberia and Sierra Leone both endured a decade of civil wars that resulted in nearly three hundred thousand deaths and the spilling across borders of over one million refugees. Liberia's civil war lasted from December 1989 until early 1997 and was fought mainly by eight factions.[8] Elections in July 1997 were won by the most powerful warlord, Charles Taylor. The conflict erupted again in 1999 and ended only with Taylor's enforced exile to Nigeria in 2003. ECOMOG's involvement in Sierra Leone's civil war was inextricably linked to its peacekeeping efforts in neighboring Liberia's civil war. The Revolutionary United Front (RUF) had invaded Sierra Leone from Liberia in March 1991 with the assistance of Taylor's National Patriotic Front of Liberia (NPFL), resulting in several hundred Nigerian, Ghanaian, and Guinean troops being deployed to assist Sierra Leone, a fellow ECOMOG member, to defend its capital of Freetown. ECOMOG's role in Sierra Leone increased tremendously after Nigerian autocrat General Sani Abacha diverted peacekeepers from the concluding Liberia mission to Sierra Leone in an attempt to crush a military coup by the Sierra Leone Army (SLA) in Freetown in May 1997. After the putsch, the military junta invited the RUF to join its administration. They thus cemented a marriage of convenience between soldiers and rebels, giving birth to the "sobel"[9] phenomenon in West Africa. A Nigerian-led ECOMOG force reversed the coup in February 1998 and restored the elected president, Ahmed Tejan Kabbah, to power. However, the unsuccessful but devastating rebel invasion of Freetown in January 1999 demonstrated that ECOMOG was unable to eliminate the rebels as a military threat. In both Liberia and Sierra Leone, logistically ill-equipped and poorly funded peacekeeping missions[10] were unable to defeat recalcitrant rebels who refused to implement peace accords, and a military stalemate forced political accommodation and the appeasement of local warlords. The UN Security Council eventually stepped in to authorize a more international peacekeeping force under its control in both countries.[11]

The conflicts in Liberia and Sierra Leone highlight the interdependence of security in West Africa and the importance of adopting a regional approach to conflict management, a point that the Security Council recognized by establishing a UN Office for West Africa (UNOWA) in Senegal in

2001.[12] The civil war in Liberia had led to deep political splits within ECOWAS, with several francophone states opposing the Nigerian-led intervention, which had also largely involved Ghana, Guinea, Sierra Leone, Senegal, Mali, and Gambia. The Liberian civil war had been triggered from Côte d'Ivoire, and the rebels received military support from Burkina Faso and Libya. The subsequent instability on the Guinea-Liberia border, and the invasion of Liberia's northern Lofa County by Liberians United for Reconciliation and Democracy (LURD) rebels in 1999 saw governments in Conakry and Monrovia supporting rival movements against each other's regime.

The descent of Côte d'Ivoire—formerly an oasis of calm amid West Africa's troubled waters—into conflict took many observers by surprise. Though operating an autocratic, patrimonial political system between 1960 and 1993, Ivorian leader Félix Houphouet-Boigny had managed the political system with dexterity and adopted an enlightened policy toward the country's large Burkinabè and Malian immigrant population—estimated at a quarter of the population.[13] But he had also stored up problems for the future as his cocoa-based economy declined from the 1980s, even as he built one of the largest churches in the world—the infamous "Basilica in the bush"—in his hometown of Yamoussoukro. The Ivorian leader died in December 1993. Houphouet's heirs—Henri Konan Bédié, General Robert Guei, and Laurent Gbagbo—showed less skill and foresight than *le vieux* (the old man) in managing the political system.[14] They instituted a xenophobic policy of Ivoirité, which discriminated against Ivorians of mixed parentage and "foreigners," many of whom had been born in Côte d'Ivoire or lived in the country for a long time. The exclusion of former Ivorian premier Alassane Ouattara (who reportedly had one parent born in Burkina Faso) from contesting presidential elections alienated many of his northern Muslim constituents, while Gbagbo—whose flawed election under the Ivorian Patriotic Front (FPI) in November 2000 was boycotted by most of the North—dismissed about two hundred mostly northern soldiers from the army. These tensions eventually culminated in a coup attempt by largely northern officers in September 2002 and the eventual emergence of three rebel factions: the Mouvement pour la Justice et la Paix (MJP), the Mouvement Populaire Ivoirien du Grand Ouest (MPIGO), and the Mouvement Patriotique de la Côte d'Ivoire—which all later became known as the Forces Nouvelles (and later as the Republican Forces). Gbagbo accused Burkina Faso and Liberia of fomenting the rebellion, while Charles Taylor accused Côte d'Ivoire of backing Movement for Democracy in Liberia (MODEL) rebels. Liberian and Sierra Leonean fighters were reported to be fighting on the side of both the government and rebels in the Ivorian conflict. The war spilled over 125,000 Ivorian refugees into Liberia, Ghana, Guinea, Mali, and Burkina Faso.

Having provided the context for understanding the UN's role in West Africa's wars, I next turn to the three individual cases of Liberia, Sierra Leone, and Côte d'Ivoire.

The UN and ECOWAS in Liberia

The UN's involvement in Liberia's civil war was slow and tentative, underlining its historical reluctance to undertake peacekeeping missions alongside regional organizations.[15] ECOWAS requested technical assistance from the UN Security Council in 1990 to establish a peacekeeping force. The UN Secretariat in New York did not respond positively, though James Jonah, the Sierra Leonean UN Undersecretary-General for special political questions, was dispatched to regional peace meetings and became a trusted adviser for ECOWAS leaders and a strong advocate for ECOMOG within the Secretariat.[16] When the Liberian civil war erupted, UN Security Council action was blocked at first by the three African members—Côte d'Ivoire, Zaire (now the Democratic Republic of Congo), and Ethiopia—who reflexively opposed interference in the internal affairs of an OAU—now the AU—member state. While African countries could not veto any Security Council action, Council members traditionally deferred to their African colleagues when discussing action on continental issues. Côte d'Ivoire was also supporting Charles Taylor's NPFL faction. Only after political consensus had emerged within ECOWAS, and ECOMOG had intervened in the conflict, did the Security Council issue a statement, at Abidjan's request, commending ECOMOG's efforts in January 1991.[17] Many ECOWAS states strongly opposed a UN presence in Liberia in these early stages, as they did in Sierra Leone, out of fear that the Blue Helmets would steal the glory for ECOWAS's sacrifices.[18]

West African governments, however, strongly lobbied the UN Security Council to impose an arms embargo against Liberia's warlords in November 1992 after nine ECOWAS foreign ministers had participated in a Council debate in New York.[19] This marked the start of increasing UN involvement in peacemaking efforts in the same year that new Egyptian UN Secretary-General Boutros Boutros-Ghali had just published his landmark 1992 *An Agenda for Peace* report calling for increased collaboration between the UN and regional organizations.[20] The Cotonou accord of July 1993 saw the UN Secretary-General dispatch Special Representative Trevor Gordon-Somers to take the lead from ECOWAS in peace negotiations. The agreement also called for the involvement of UN and OAU peacekeepers in Liberia. A joint ceasefire monitoring committee was mandated to investigate and resolve ceasefire violations. The body was overseen by a UN Observer Mission in Liberia (UNOMIL) and involved ECOMOG as well as representatives of all of Liberia's armed factions. ECOMOG's sixteen thousand peacekeepers had an explicit right of self-defense under Cotonou that mandated them to exercise "peace enforcement powers" with the approval of a UN-chaired ceasefire violations committee. The UN was effectively being sent to "police" ECOMOG's peacekeepers: a role that was to fuel tensions between the two forces.

Demonstrating the increasing but still insufficient international attention that Liberia was attracting, the Security Council established the $5,650,000 a month UN Observer Mission in Liberia in September 1993, dispatching 368 unarmed military observers to Liberia by early 1994 under Kenyan general Daniel Opande.[21] Under the Cotonou agreement, UNOMIL was responsible for monitoring the cantonment, disarmament, and demobilization of Liberian combatants, as well as overseeing the UN-imposed arms embargo of 1992. UNOMIL was also mandated to work with ECOMOG, which had primary responsibility for disarming the factions. The UN's mandate further obliged it to report on human rights violations and to coordinate humanitarian assistance. ECOMOG would be responsible for ensuring the security of UNOMIL's civilian and unarmed military personnel.

Sharp disagreements soon arose between ECOMOG and UNOMIL. Initial friction was already evident after the arrival of the UN military observers in 1993. ECOMOG's logistically ill-equipped peacekeepers were often heard complaining that the UN did not make its vehicles and helicopters available for their use and felt that the better-paid UN staff flaunted their status while leaving most of the difficult military tasks to ECOMOG. These problems were further exacerbated by Boutros-Ghali's allegations in an October 1994 report to the Security Council that ECOMOG had collaborated with anti-NPFL combatants during fighting in Gbarnga in September 1994.[22] ECOMOG officers felt that these accusations detracted from other praiseworthy activities by their peacekeepers like escorting humanitarian relief convoys to the countryside and providing security to displaced persons in Monrovia and Tubmanburg. But ECOMOG's cooperation with anti-NPFL factions, dating back to the beginning of its mission in Liberia, was not in dispute.

There were five other key areas of disagreement between ECOMOG and UNOMIL. First, ECOMOG soldiers, who earned $5 a day and were often irregularly paid, were irritated that UNOMIL observers were earning $100 per day for performing far less strenuous and risky activities. Second, ECOMOG wanted UNOMIL strictly to "observe" rather than "supervise" disarmament. Third, ECOMOG's officials were irritated by what they regarded as UN special representative Gordon-Somers's unilateral disarmament negotiations with the parties without proper consultation with ECOMOG staff. The fourth area of disagreement involved UNOMIL's chief military observer, General Opande, and ECOMOG's Nigerian field commander between 1993 and 1996, General Mark Inienger, who each held different views about disarmament strategy. Opande asked that Charles Taylor be given the benefit of the doubt in his offer to disarm his combatants unilaterally and talked of the NPFL's "good faith."

Inienger and his officers considered this view naive and regarded Taylor's offer as an attempt to avoid close scrutiny of his arms and military positions. The final area of disagreement involved ECOMOG's criticism of UNOMIL for deploying some of its military observers without consultation with the West Africans who were mandated to protect them.[23] UNOMIL argued that it had obtained the consent of the factions to deploy and that it could not fulfill its mandate by remaining in the capital of Monrovia. The UN also accused ECO-MOG of violating its mandate by not protecting UNOMIL personnel and by restricting their freedom of movement.[24]

It is important to note how regional and Liberian actors viewed the UN's role in Liberia. Gordon-Somers resigned his post in December 1994. During his two-year stint, the Jamaican technocrat had become deeply unpopular among Liberian political actors for what they considered to be a reckless push for the premature installation of an interim government before the completion of the disarmament process and for his apparent willingness to accommodate warlords like Charles Taylor and Alhaji Kromah. After the debacle over the stillborn Akosombo accord in September 1994, which awarded Liberia's powerful warlords seats on a ruling council and was strongly opposed by Liberia's civil society groups as well as the Nigerian government, Gordon-Somers wrote to Boutros-Ghali and requested that he be withdrawn from his post, saying that he had achieved as much as he could in Liberia.[25]

With ECOMOG struggling to overcome its financial difficulties and political divisions, Boutros-Ghali suggested in February 1995 that the Security Council establish a large UN peacekeeping force under which ECOMOG would be subsumed.[26] But with the most powerful members of the Council—particularly the United States—increasingly wary of prolifer-ating peacekeeping missions amid debacles in Somalia in 1993 (see Chapter 6) and Rwanda in 1994 (see Chapter 3), the proposal met with an eloquent silence. After Boutros-Ghali's threat in June 1995 to withdraw the UN's sixty-three observers from Liberia, nervous ECOWAS states reacted by warning that any UN withdrawal would compromise ECOMOG's efforts and could lead to the further destabilization of the West African subregion.[27] This again underlined the importance, for reasons of international legitima-cy and attention, of the largely symbolic UN presence to ECOMOG's efforts. But it also underlined the complex relationship between the UN and ECOWAS. While ECOWAS leaders welcomed the UN's political legitima-cy and greater military and economic resources, they were concerned about the UN coming in late in the day to steal ECOMOG's thunder after several years of lonely peacekeeping. Military cooperation between the UN and ECOMOG after the start of the disarmament and demobilization process in 1996 saw continued joint investigations of ceasefire violations and UNOMIL's verification of the arms and ammunition secured during

ECOMOG's cordon-and-search operations. Two weeks before elections in July 1997, the UN deployed two hundred observers to Liberia to monitor the poll. The four-year UNOMIL presence in Liberia eventually cost the international community no more than $115 million.[28] This mission was, however, more effective in providing ECOMOG with political legitimacy than in bolstering military efforts on the ground.

Despite ECOMOG's peacekeeping presence in Liberia between 1990 and 1998, the lack of security sector reform and reintegration of excombatants into local communities, as well as Charles Taylor's autocratic rule and the transformation of his NPFL rebel movement into a private security force to protect his regime, eventually triggered the second civil war in a decade when LURD rebels attacked Liberia from Guinea in 1999. The volcanic situation in Liberia threatened to spread its deadly lava across the subregion. After fighting between Taylor's government and rebels in June and July 2003 that killed an estimated one thousand civilians in Monrovia, the warlord-turned-president was pressured by regional leaders and the United States to go into exile in Nigeria in August 2003. In the same month, a Comprehensive Peace Agreement (CPA) was signed by all of Liberia's parties in Accra, Ghana, that called for the establishment of the National Transitional Government of Liberia (NTGL) under businessman Charles Gyude Bryant.

A Nigerian battalion deployed in Liberia shortly after Taylor's departure. These were the advanced units of a 3,600-strong ECOWAS mission in Liberia (ECOMIL), which became part of a UN peacekeeping mission to which Ghana, Senegal, Mali, Benin, Gambia, Guinea-Bissau, and Togo also contributed troops. The United States sent a small force of two hundred soldiers—who remained off the Monrovian coast—to provide limited logistical support to ECOMIL, while the UN took over the peacekeeping mission by November 2003.[29] Burned by its earlier experiences in Liberia and Sierra Leone, the Nigerians agreed to deploy troops to Liberia in August 2003 only on the condition that the UN take over the force three months later. Scarred by its own experiences in Somalia when eighteen US troops had been killed in October 1993 during a botched military mission (see Chapters 6), Washington was only too willing to support a Nigerian-led mission in order to avoid pressure to intervene itself in Liberia—a country set up by freed American slaves in 1847 with long historical ties to the United States.

The Security Council mandated the UN Mission in Liberia (UNMIL) to support the implementation of the ceasefire agreement and peace process, to provide assistance for security sector reform, and to facilitate humanitarian and human rights assistance.[30] No doubt to maintain Washington's interest in the mission, American diplomat Jacques Paul Klein was named special representative of the UN Secretary-General. UNMIL's largest contingents came from Bangladesh, Ethiopia, Nigeria, and Pakistan (Ghana and China also contributed sizeable contingents by 2010). By May 2004, 14,131 troops had arrived in Liberia.[31] While UN peacekeepers were able to avert the imminent bloodshed in Monrovia and to increase stability in the country, sporadic incidents continued throughout UNMIL's stay: interfactional fighting within LURD; fighting in Nimba, Grand Bassa, and Bong counties; churches, mosques, and property being burned in acts of communal violence; and excombatants embarking on violent demonstrations. Rampant corruption within the interim government was also a frequent source of concern.

The joint monitoring committee, chaired by UNMIL—and former UNOMIL—force commander General Daniel Opande, and consisting of all the factions and government forces, met regularly to try to resolve security disputes. Disarmament of the factions began in December 2003 and was completed in October 2004. Combatants numbering 101,449 were disarmed and demobilized, as well as 612 "mercenaries" from Côte d'Ivoire, Ghana, Guinea, Mali, Nigeria, and Sierra Leone. An implementation monitoring committee also started meeting in November 2003 chaired by UNMIL and ECOWAS and involving representatives of the AU, the European Union, and the UN-led International Contact Group on Liberia, which extended its work to the Mano River basin in September 2004. An International Reconstruction Conference for Liberia in New York in February 2004 pledged $522 million toward the country's rebuilding, $244 million of which had arrived six months later.

Liberia held elections on schedule in October and November 2005. UN peacekeepers provided security in the election, which Ellen Johnson-Sirleaf, a former Liberian finance minister and former head of the UNDP's Africa Bureau, won to become Africa's first elected female head of state.[32] Despite these polls, the security situation in Liberia remained fragile. Plans for restructuring a new Liberian army proceeded slowly as the international community once more failed to provide sufficient funding for both this exercise and for reintegrating excombatants into local communities. There was a $3 million shortfall for security sector reform in December 2005[33] and a $5 million deficit in the reintegration of excombatants in March 2006,[34] raising fears of future insecurity. Since the failure to undertake security sector reform in 1997 and to provide jobs for excombatants had contributed greatly to a return to war after only two years, the UN Security Council was unwise not to prioritize these two key areas to ensure that its annual peacekeeping investment in Liberia of about $700 million between 2004 and 2006 was not wasted. The Council wisely decided to maintain the UN peacekeeping mission in Liberia so as to ensure a gradual drawdown of its troops.

As the UN prepared to reduce the number of peacekeepers in Liberia in 2011, the situation in the country remained fragile, and the trial of Charles Taylor in The Hague on war crimes charges cast a long shadow over the country. There were tensions in 2009 between members of the Armed Forces of Liberia and the national police, as well as a riot in Maryland

County, which UNMIL troops were sent to quell. A year earlier, the UN mission had also had to calm violent protests by former combatants in Nimba, Grand Cape Mount, and Grand Gedeh counties. In July 2009, the country's demobilization program of 101,000 excombatants was declared completed, but with widespread youth unemployment across Liberia, it was clear that this would remain a source of future instability despite external efforts (led by the United States) to train a new two thousand–strong Liberian army and a national police force. But the government struggled to receive concrete donor assistance to complete its critical security sector reform efforts amid charges of continuing corruption.[35] In February 2010, widespread violence again erupted in Lofa County between Muslim Mandingos and largely Christian Lormas. Four fatalities resulted from the clashes, and churches, mosques, and homes were burned down. UNMIL's military and police contingents again helped to quell the fighting.[36]

Regional instability was also an issue in this case, as 1,500 to 2,000 Liberian combatants were thought to be involved with Ivorian militias.[37] More positively, 169, 072 people returned to their homes in Liberia between 2004 and 2010.[38] In May 2010, the Liberian government requested that the country be placed on the agenda of the UN Peacebuilding Commission, but it was clear that the struggling body did not have the resources to match the country's enormous postconflict challenges. The UN mission was steered to completion by Denmark's tough but respected former permanent representative to the UN, Ellen Margrethe Løj, one of the few female UN special representatives, despite the world body's lip service to promoting gender equality.[39] Accusations of sexual exploitation and abuse, however, continued against UN peacekeepers in Liberia in 2010, to which Løj adopted a "no-nonsense" approach.[40] By December 2010, about 8,000 UN troops remained in Liberia, a strength that was to be maintained until after the country's November 2011 elections. By February 2011, only limited progress had been made toward the recommendations of the country's Truth and Reconciliation Commission. Liberia's security remained fragile, with intercommunal clashes reported in Lofa County in December 2010, and riots and demonstrations from labor disputes occurring in Grand Bassa and Maryland counties in September 2010. Most of the 100,000 refugees fleeing instability following Côte d'Ivoire's postelection crisis in March and April 2011 were entering Liberia along with reports of Liberian mercenaries fighting in Côte d'Ivoire.[41]

The UN and ECOWAS in Sierra Leone

Significant cooperation between the UN and ECOWAS in Sierra Leone started in March 1995 with the appointment of Ethiopian UN special representative Berhanu Dinka, who was involved in negotiations between the government of Ahmed Tejan Kabbah and RUF rebels in Abidjan in 1996. The

Abidjan accord was soon declared a dead letter due to the profound distrust between Dinka and Côte d'Ivoire—the host—as well as the pernicious role played by Akyaaba Addai-Sebo, a friend of Charles Taylor and reportedly of Ivorian foreign minister Amara Essy.[42] Addai-Sebo was the representative of International Alert, a London-based nongovernmental organization (NGO), and is said to have encouraged RUF intransigence during negotiations. Five months after a military coup toppled Kabbah in May 1997, the Security Council imposed an arms and oil embargo on Sierra Leone.[43]

The Security Council established the UN Observer Mission in Sierra Leone (UNOMSIL) in July 1998 under Indian general Subhash Joshi.[44] UNOMSIL was tasked with monitoring the military and economic situation in Sierra Leone, observing respect of international humanitarian law, and monitoring the disarmament and demobilization of excombatants. But with only about fifty observers, the UN played a very limited role alongside ECOMOG's thirteen thousand troops. As in Liberia, there was strong resentment among ECOMOG soldiers against the better-paid and better-resourced UN military observers. As one ECOMOG officer wryly put it: "They [UN observers] are here on picnic and holiday. I wish we could open the beaches for them to suntan and enjoy their dollars."[45] Another issue that caused friction between ECOWAS and the UN was the intervention by a largely Nigerian force in Freetown to reverse a military coup in February 1998. An ECOWAS committee of five foreign ministers was consulting with UN Security Council members in New York at the time, and diplomats on the Council felt that they should have been informed about the intervention. The foreign ministers were, however, themselves unaware of the timing of the intervention.[46]

The Lomé agreement was signed in July 1999 between Kabbah's government and the RUF. The accord provided for cabinet posts for the RUF in a Government of National Unity and gave its leader, Foday Sankoh, a ceremonial vice presidency as well as the chairmanship of a commission for the management of strategic resources. The RUF had committed many atrocities during the conflict—including the amputation of limbs and countless massacres—and many people were uncomfortable with its presence in the government. As with earlier accords in Abidjan (1996) and Conakry (1997), a controversial amnesty was offered for war crimes, though Ugandan UN special representative Francis Okelo entered a reservation for the world body in cases of crimes against humanity. The UN was asked to contribute troops to help oversee disarmament and to provide staff to help conduct elections, while an ECOWAS-chaired joint implementation committee was established to meet every three months to oversee the agreement's implementation. This committee was also charged with monitoring the repatriation and resettlement of five hundred thousand Sierra Leonean refugees from Guinea and Liberia.[47]

On 19 August 1999, Nigeria's new president, Olusegun Obasanjo,[48] wrote to Ghanaian UN Secretary-General Kofi Annan, informing him of Nigeria's intention to withdraw two thousand of its peacekeepers from Sierra Leone every month. The Nigerian president, however, offered to subsume some of his twelve thousand troops under a new UN mission.[49] Obasanjo began the phased withdrawal on 31 August 1999 and suspended the process only after a plea by Sierra Leonean president Ahmed Tejan Kabbah and Annan not to leave a security vacuum in Sierra Leone. But with the UN's realization that Obasanjo was not bluffing when he announced the withdrawal of Nigerian troops from Sierra Leone, the Secretary-General was forced to recommend to the Security Council that a UN peacekeeping mission in Sierra Leone (UNAMSIL) take over from ECOMOG. The mission was established in October 1999 under an Indian force commander, General Vijay Jetley.[50]

Obasanjo rejected a UN Security Council proposal that ECOMOG continue to protect Freetown and undertake enforcement actions against rogue rebel elements. Nigeria's president realized that ECOMOG, in being saddled with these dangerous tasks, would remain a useful scapegoat if things went wrong in Sierra Leone. As the UN was widely criticized for failing to protect "safe havens" in Bosnia and civilians in Rwanda (see Chapter 3), critics would have been able to blame any failings in Sierra Leone on ECOMOG rather than on the UN. Nigeria thus refused to remain in Sierra Leone in a situation in which there would be two peacekeeping missions with different mandates, commands, and conditions of service.[51] The UN Secretariat turned down ECOMOG's request for the Security Council to finance the entire ECOMOG force, though about four thousand of the West African body's peacekeepers were subsumed under the new UN force.[52] ECOWAS and other subregional organizations continue to question why their peacekeepers should be accountable to a UN Security Council that refuses to finance their missions.[53] There was also much hostility directed against the presence of Nigerian peacekeepers within the UN's Department of Peacekeeping Operations. Many UN officials insisted on a reduced Nigerian role while overselling a new UN mission to Sierra Leoneans who were misled into believing that the Blue Helmets would be prepared to fight the country's rebels.[54]

In order to fill the vacuum left by the departure of Nigerian peacekeepers, UNAMSIL was expanded to eleven thousand troops in February 2000,[55] and eventually to twenty thousand peacekeepers. Oluyemi Adeniji, a Nigerian diplomat who had served as the UN special representative in the Central African Republic, was appointed as the UN special representative in Sierra Leone. This appointment compensated Nigeria for not gaining the force commander position that Obasanjo had wanted but which had been strongly resisted within the UN Secretariat and Security Council.[56] UNAMSIL's core contingents consisted of Nigerian, Indian, Jordanian, Kenyan, Bangladeshi, Guinean, Ghanaian, and Zambian battalions. But the logistically ill-equipped UN force soon ran into difficulties. The RUF prevented the deployment of UNAMSIL to the diamond-rich eastern provinces and, from May 2000, attacked UN peacekeepers, killing some of them, holding five hundred of them hostage, and seizing their heavy weapons and vehicles.[57] The rebels were seeking to exploit the vacuum created by the departure of Nigerian peacekeepers from Sierra Leone. A brief British military intervention with about eight hundred troops helped to stabilize the situation in Freetown and its environs between May and June 2000.

UNAMSIL also experienced its own internal problems. A UN assessment mission sent to Sierra Leone in June 2000 found serious management problems in the mission and a lack of common understanding of the mandate and rules of engagement. The assessment mission noted that some of UNAMSIL's military units lacked proper training and equipment.[58] There were constant reports of tension between the UN's political and military leadership[59] even before a confidential report written by General Jetley was inadvertently leaked to the international media in September 2000. In the report, the Indian force commander accused senior Nigerian military and political officials of attempting to sabotage the UN mission in Sierra Leone by colluding with RUF rebels to prolong the conflict in order to benefit from the country's illicit diamond trade. No evidence was provided for the allegations. Tremendous political damage was, however, done to UNAMSIL by this incident: Nigeria refused to place its peacekeepers under Jetley's command, and India subsequently announced the withdrawal of its entire three thousand–strong contingent from Sierra Leone in September 2000. New Delhi was followed by Jordan, which cited the refusal of Britain to put its own forces under UN command as a reason for its departure.[60] Following the difficulties with the RUF, ECOWAS also agreed, as the Nigerians were withdrawing their troops, to send a three thousand–strong rapid reaction force, consisting largely of US-trained Nigerian, Ghanaian, and Senegalese troops, to bolster UNAMSIL.

After the events of May 2000, an International Contact Group for Sierra Leone was established by the UN Security Council involving the United States, Britain, and key donor and ECOWAS governments. The group held periodic meetings to mobilize funds for Sierra Leone's peace process. In recognition of the role of the illicit diamond trade in fueling this conflict, the Security Council prohibited the global importation of rough diamonds from Sierra Leone in July 2000 until a certification scheme was put in place for official diamond exports three months later.[61] At a UN hearing in the same month, Washington and London strongly criticized Liberia and Burkina Faso for their alleged role in diamond smuggling and gun running in support of RUF rebels in Sierra Leone. The Council thus imposed sanctions on Liberia's diamond exports and slapped a travel ban on its officials in March 2001,[62] even in the face of opposition from several ECOWAS leaders who argued that Taylor's help had been vital in securing the Lomé accord.

The UN's disarmament program for seventy-two thousand Sierra Leonean combatants was completed in January 2002. UN-monitored elections in May 2002 saw President Kabbah reelected in a landslide victory and the RUF Party (RUFP) failing to win a single seat. The decade-long war in Sierra Leone was finally over. In September 2004, UNAMSIL completed the transfer of primary responsibility for maintaining peace and security to the government of Sierra Leone. By the end of December 2004, the UN had about four thousand peacekeepers in Sierra Leone.[63] After five years of sometimes tortuous peacekeeping, the world body finally withdrew its remaining troops from Sierra Leone in December 2005. Though the country remained largely peaceful, many peacebuilding challenges remained unresolved. The UN had spent an estimated $5 billion in Sierra Leone in five years,[64] but much of this had gone toward its peacekeeping mission rather than to reintegrate excombatants into society, to reverse massive youth unemployment, to restructure a new national army, and to help restore state institutions.

The UN Security Council established an Integrated Office in Sierra Leone (UNIOSIL) in January 2006 to coordinate international peace consolidation efforts and to support the government with the organization of elections in 2007. However, similar to past experiences in Liberia, Angola, and the Central African Republic, this office lacked sufficient resources and staff to assist the Sierra Leonean government effectively in its postconflict peacebuilding and reconstruction tasks. The government in Freetown collected revenues from its diamond industry of only $82 million in the first half of 2005, and more than half of its diamond mining still involved unlicensed operators.[65] Violent student and labor protests increased amid widespread youth unemployment and weak government capacity. Instability in Côte d'Ivoire, the fragile situation in Liberia, and reports of encroachment into Sierra Leonean territory by Guinean troops occupying disputed border areas in April 2006 further threatened the country's new-found peace.[66]

The UN and ECOWAS in Côte D'Ivoire

I now turn to the role of the UN in Côte d'Ivoire. Several mediation efforts by ECOWAS in Ghana and Togo eventually led to the brokering of the Linas-Marcoussis accord in France in January 2003. The accord established a transitional government with a neutral prime minister, Seydou Diarra, a respected Northern former diplomat, who was mandated to oversee the disarmament of the rebels and to organize elections. Ivorian president Laurent Gbagbo and his supporters, however, complained that they had been railroaded into this accord and resented being treated on a level of parity with the rebels, thus setting the scene for anti-French demonstrations in Abidjan.[67] France, which has maintained a permanent military base in Côte d'Ivoire since the country's independence in 1960 as part of its neocolonial strategy in the region, deployed about 4,600 Licorne troops to monitor the ceasefire. By early 2003, the ECOWAS Mission in Côte d'Ivoire (ECOMICI) had deployed 1,288 largely francophone troops from Senegal, Niger, Togo, Benin, and Ghana, in what represented the fourth ECOWAS military mission to a West African country in thirteen years. Nigeria, which had provided the backbone for the ECOWAS missions in Liberia and Sierra Leone, would contribute just five troops to the UN mission in Côte d'Ivoire, underlining its historical rivalry for leadership of West Africa with both Paris and Abidjan.[68]

The ECOWAS mission in Côte d'Ivoire was largely financed and equipped by France, with other logistical and financial assistance provided by Belgium, Britain, the Netherlands, and the United States. ECOWAS promised to increase the number of its peacekeepers to 3,209 if funds could be secured. On a visit to New York in April 2003, its Ghanaian executive secretary, Mohammed Chambas, asked the Security Council to provide these funds.[69] Meanwhile, France also sought—like Britain in Sierra Leone—to use its permanent seat on the Security Council to secure a substantial UN peacekeeping force in Côte d'Ivoire.[70] Tensions over the US-British occupation of Iraq in March 2003 at first contributed to Washington's reluctance to sanction a large UN force in Côte d'Ivoire. After France overcame US opposition, the Council authorized a political assistance mission in Côte d'Ivoire (MINUCI),[71] which was then transformed in February 2004 into the $400 million a year, 6,240-strong UN Operation in Côte d'Ivoire (UNOCI).[72] The mission was mandated to work alongside the 4,600 French troops to maintain a "zone of confidence" between government and rebel troops and to implement the Marcoussis peace accord. UNOCI was also tasked to oversee the disarmament of twenty-six thousand Forces Nouvelles troops and four thousand government soldiers. The peacekeepers further provided security to opposition politicians in Abidjan. Senegalese general Abdoulaye Fall was named force commander of UNOCI, which also had a seven hundred–strong contingent from Morocco, one of France's most reliable African allies. By November 2004, the UN force, under Togolese special representative Albert Tévoédjré, had 5,995 peacekeepers. The small ECOWAS force was "rehatted" under this new UN mission, as had occurred in Sierra Leone and Liberia.

UNOCI was rocked in November 2004 when government soldiers attacked Forces Nouvelles positions and killed nine French soldiers in the northern city of Bouaké. French troops destroyed the entire Ivorian air force of nine planes, resulting in violent demonstrations against French interests and a mass evacuation of about ten thousand foreign (mostly French) citizens from Côte d'Ivoire. Jittery French troops killed at least fifty government-backed Young Patriot demonstrators outside Abidjan's Hotel Ivoire where many foreigners had taken shelter. These violent demonstrations by government-backed and other militias continued throughout the conflict, sometimes resulting in murders of innocent civilians. The distrust between the former colonial power and many Ivorians, fanned by a government that feared that Paris was bent on its removal, reached new heights. Gbagbo's supporters accused France of trying to "recolonize" the country by using "agents" like Burkina Faso.[73] The Forces Nouvelles rebels accused Guinea of backing the government militarily. While Gbagbo talked of leaving the French-dominated Communauté Financière Africaine (CFA) franc currency zone, his hard-line speaker of parliament, Mamadou Coulibaly, called for a complete break with the former colonial power. Gbagbo was further angered when France pushed the UN Security Council to impose an arms embargo and legal sanctions supported by largely francophone countries and Nigeria.[74] There were also splits between the Forces Nouvelles rebels which sometimes resulted in deadly military clashes. Both the UN and French Licorne troops came under attack and frequently had their freedom of movement restricted by the warring factions.

In July 2004, the Ivorian factions met with thirteen African heads of state. Ghana's president, John Kufuor, and UN Secretary-General Kofi Annan chaired the meeting. The Accra III accord that emerged set a new timetable for implementing the Marcoussis accord: amend discriminatory nationality and electoral laws by September 2004 and begin the disarmament process by October 2004. Both deadlines were missed.

Part of the complication of the Ivorian case lay in the proliferation of external mediators, which raised obvious questions about too many cooks spoiling the broth. Presidents John Kufuor of Ghana, Nigeria's Olusegun Obasanjo, Gabon's Omar Bongo, Sierra Leone's Ahmed Kabbah, Togo's Gnassingbé Eyadéma, and Niger's Mamadou Tandja were all involved in peacemaking efforts. South Africa, ECOWAS, the AU, the UN, and the Francophonie all nominated their own special envoys to Côte d'Ivoire. As AU Chairman, Obasanjo appointed South Africa's Thabo Mbeki as the organization's mediator to Côte d'Ivoire in November 2004, bringing some focus to the peacemaking process. After his appointment, Mbeki visited Abidjan and called the parties to Tshwane (Pretoria) to discuss their differences. With continuing delays in the implementation of these accords, the UN Security Council imposed an arms embargo on all the factions in November 2004[75] (followed a year later by an embargo on the trade of diamonds[76]) and unveiled the threat of travel sanctions and a freezing of the financial assets of individuals obstructing the peace process. Within the Council, France pushed strongly for individual sanctions, while Russia, China, and Algeria were opposed to these measures as well as to further actions to tighten the arms embargo.[77] Mbeki also successfully urged the Council to hold off individual sanctions to give his mediation efforts time to bear fruit. A tripartite monitoring group of ECOWAS, the AU, and the UN started submitting fortnightly monitoring reports. A major problem was that Gbagbo refused to empower his prime minister, Seydou Diarra, with decisionmaking powers and dragged his feet on amending laws that would have allowed his rival, Alassane Ouattara, to participate in national elections. Rebel leader Guillaume Soro, backed by the Coalition des Marcoussistes opposition parties, refused to disarm until the laws had been passed. Along with other opposition politicians, Soro frequently walked out of his post as communications minister in Abidjan to protest what they perceived to be Gbagbo's recalcitrance in implementing peace accords.

By 2005, the epicenter of conflict in West Africa appeared to have shifted from Liberia to Côte d'Ivoire. The country remained divided from 2002 between North and South, separated by UN and French forces. Côte d'Ivoire's volatile western region saw ethnic and community-based militias continue to clash violently, while the "zone of confidence" continued to be violated, mainly by the rebel Forces Nouvelles. In August 2005, the government-backed Young Patriots militia attacked the vehicle of the Swedish UN special representative Pierre Schori, who had replaced Tévoédjré in January 2005. The Togolese diplomat was no longer welcomed in West African capitals and was effectively seen as compromised by his proximity to the French government,[78] which continued to manipulate the UN presence in Côte d'Ivoire for its own parochial interests. UNOCI also reported an eight-fold increase in the limiting of its peacekeepers' freedom of movement between June and July 2005, and a Moroccan UN peacekeeper was murdered in the northern town of Bouaké a month later. The government of Laurent Gbagbo, Konan Bédié's Democratic Party of Côte d'Ivoire (PDCI), Alassane Ouattara's Rally of Republicans (RPR), and Guillaume Soro's Forces Nouvelles continued to squabble over implementation of the Pretoria Agreement of June 2005 that had been negotiated by Thabo Mbeki, setting timetables for implementing Marcoussis and Accra III. This resulted in the failure to achieve disarmament targets in August 2005 and the postponement by a year of elections that had originally been scheduled for October 2005.

Consistent with the Pretoria accord, Mbeki had urged Gbagbo to use his exceptional powers to amend discriminatory laws (on nationality, identification, the Human Rights Commission, and the print media) in July 2005 when it became clear that the Ivorian parliament would not amend them. After Gbagbo adopted these laws by decree, Soro and the Group of Seven opposition parties challenged these measures, as did Ouattara and Bédié. These politicians argued that certain groups in Côte d'Ivoire were still deprived of their rights under the nationality law and that the country's Independent Electoral Commission (IEC) needed to have clear primacy over the National Institute of Statistics in organizing elections. Gbagbo further amended the laws on the IEC, the nationality code, and the naturalization law—again by decree—in August 2005, but this still did not completely break the deadlock.

Aside from recalcitrant politicians and warlords, friction between some of the key mediators further complicated the resolution of the Ivorian crisis. French sensitivities at South Africa's lead role in the traditional Gallic *chasse gardée* (private hunting ground) erupted into the open when President Jacques Chirac, during a visit to Senegal in February 2005, complained that the peace process was too slow because the South Africans did not understand "the soul and psychology of West Africans." Regional actors, not least Mbeki, were taken aback by the cultural arrogance and political insensitivity of this statement, which underlined the continuing paternalism with which many Gaullistes still regarded their former colonies. Some in France also called for French troops to be withdrawn from Côte d'Ivoire, even as the South Africans quipped that they had achieved more in three months than Paris had done in two years.

After a South African statement blaming Soro for blocking the peace process, the Forces Nouvelles withdrew support from Mbeki's mediation efforts, accusing him of bias toward Gbagbo. The rebel group then urged the AU Chairman, Olusegun Obasanjo, to find an alternative way of resolving the impasse. These events coincided with tensions between South Africa and Nigeria over regional diplomatic issues and the acrimonious battle for an African seat on a reformed UN Security Council. At a meeting of the AU's fifteen-member Peace and Security Council on the margins of the UN General Assembly in September 2005, ECOWAS was tasked with overcoming this impasse: a clear attempt to shift the locus of peacemaking from South Africa to Nigeria.[79] Mbeki and Obasanjo jointly visited Côte d'Ivoire in November and December 2005 to meet with all the parties and were eventually able to convince them to agree on a new prime minister, technocrat Charles Konan Banny, to replace Diarra.

However, the stalemate over implementing disarmament and the amended laws continued, and elections continued to be delayed. The distrust between the Ivorian parties remained strong, and divisions between the regional mediators did not help. Kofi Annan had asked the Security Council to deploy an additional 1,226 peacekeepers in December 2005. The Council approved only 850 troops who arrived by January 2006. Annan, pushed by France, asked for a further 3,400 peacekeepers to maintain security in the volatile country. Washington agreed to consider an increase of 1,500 to 2,000 troops but resisted the increase that Paris was strongly pushing for. With other African members of the Council (Tanzania, Ghana, and Congo-Brazzaville), the United States insisted that the UN mission in Liberia should not be weakened by redeploying UNMIL troops to Côte d'Ivoire—as France had suggested—to bolster UNOCI.[80]

After UN and AU representatives called for the Ivorian parliament (whose term had expired) to be dissolved, violent demonstrations by the Young Patriots in Abidjan and the West of the country targeted UN and

French interests in January 2006. South Africa, which had earlier backed this position, reversed itself to support a parliamentary extension, raising questions again among rebel and opposition groups about Mbeki's bias toward Gbagbo.[81] In February 2006, a Security Council committee slapped targeted sanctions (a travel ban and a freeze on foreign assets) on two leaders of the Young Patriots, Charles Blé Goudé and Eugene Djué, as well as a Forces Nouvelles commander, Fofié Kouakou.[82] It seemed that the Council would have to continue these and other sanctions against spoilers, and a strengthened UN mission also appeared to be critical to achieving UNOCI's goals in Côte d'Ivoire. Prime Minister Banny was forced to dissolve his cabinet in September 2006 following riots after the dumping of toxic waste in Abidjan killed and hospitalized dozens of Ivorians. With both Obasanjo (privately) and Senegal's Abdoulaye Wade (publicly) increasingly critical of Mbeki's mediation, the South African president stepped down from the role at an AU meeting in October 2006 before he was pushed. UNOCI now had 8,045 peacekeepers in the country, though durable peace in Côte d'Ivoire remained elusive.

The situation in Côte d'Ivoire remained volatile in 2006 and 2007, and there were killings and the flight of civilians in the Western part of the UN- and French-monitored zone of confidence. The freedom of movement of the peacekeepers of the $491.8 million a year UN mission (whose main contingents came from Bangladesh, Pakistan, Jordan, Morocco, and Ghana by 2009), including a twelve hundred–strong civilian police unit, was also impeded by government and rebel-linked militias. At the UN Security Council in New York, France's permanent representative to the UN, Jean-Marc de La Sablière, used his country's permanent membership and close ties with Kofi Annan to push for continued support of the UN peacekeeping mission. The US permanent representative on the Council, John Bolton, felt that Paris was "micromanaging" the UN peacekeeping mission in Côte d'Ivoire, describing how the French were manipulating and dominating discussions on the Ivorian issue within the Council. He bluntly noted from his observations of Council discussions that "France did not like incumbent president Laurent Gbagbo."[83] Elections scheduled for October 2006 were again postponed. A potential breakthrough, however, appeared to have been brokered in Ouagadougou, Burkina Faso, in March 2007, when rebel leader Guillaume Soro was named prime minister by President Laurent Gbagbo. The Ouagadougou agreement called for removing the zone of confidence, reestablishing state administration throughout the country, dismantling militias and disarming combatants, merging the Forces Nouvelles and national defense and security forces, and organizing democratic elections. This period also saw the Ivorians seeking to take ownership of the peace process, privileging national institutions and reducing UNOCI's role: assisting vulnerable populations, protecting human rights, and promoting a stable political environment and economic recovery. The UN was also tasked to assist Bukinabè leader, Blaise Compaoré, the facilitator of the Ivorian peace process, to support the electoral commission, and to facilitate the DDR process and the dismantling of Ivorian militias.[84]

But key aspects of the ambitious Ouagadougou accord relating to disarmament and electoral issues were not implemented,[85] as the government continued to push for early disarmament while the rebels continued to insist on electoral reform. Meanwhile, South Korea's permanent representative at the UN and former UN Assistant Secretary-General for Peacekeeping, Young Jin Choi, replaced Pierre Schori as UN special representative in October 2007, working closely with regional mediators. Blaise Compaoré energetically hosted several meetings of the evaluation and monitoring committee of the Ivorian peace process with the key Ivorian political actors, once again postponing elections scheduled for November 2008. He also established an office in Abidjan under a special representative, Boureima Badini, funded through the UN Peacebuilding fund. At another meeting, in August 2009, Compaoré outlined the agreed priorities: providing security for elections, harmonizing the integration of the five thousand Forces Nouvelles troops into the national army, deploying the eight thousand–strong Integrated Command Center of mixed government and rebel brigades, and effectively centralizing the national treasury.[86] Elections scheduled for November 2009 were, however, postponed once again, even as crime and youth militia attacks continued to create instability.

The zone of confidence was dismantled in July 2008, restoring freedom of movement through Côte d'Ivoire in theory. However, in practice, the North still remained in the hands of the Forces Nouvelles with its own administration, judiciary, and currency. Frequent demonstrations took place in both government and rebel areas in 2008, with fighters demanding that allowances be paid. Funding remained a major problem for important projects: the national program for reinsertion and community rehabilitation received only $10 million out of $32.5 million sought in 2008, and no donors directly contributed to the fund.[87] Furthermore, armed militias and youth groups still operated in Abidjan, Yamoussoukro, and San Pedro.

Amid the continuing political impasse and military stalemate, the UN Security Council decided to reduce the peacekeeping mission's authorized strength from 8,115 to 7,450 in 2009. Two additional battalions were deployed to Abidjan and Yamoussoukro just before elections in October 2010. A French engineering company was replaced by an Egyptian one, while the French Licorne troops were halved from 1,800 to nine hundred. UNOCI continued to conduct joint patrols with the UN mission in Liberia to ensure security of the common border, and the force commanders of both missions continued to hold regular meetings.

As preparations for elections that had been postponed six times continued, President Laurent Gbagbo (without a legitimate mandate since 2005) accused the electoral commission of fraud in the registration of voters and replaced the body with a new one in February 2010. He also continued to warn ominously of non-Ivorians trying to smuggle themselves onto the electoral list. The same month also saw political violence in Abidjan, Gagnoa, Daloa, and Bouaké, which resulted in several fatalities. Elections scheduled for March 2010 were once again postponed for another seven months. Only in September 2010 did all parties agree to the issuance of national voter cards for the 5.7 million Ivorians found eligible to take part in the polls. After countless postponements, presidential elections eventually took place in October 2010, with 83.7 percent of the electorate voting. President Gbagbo won 38 percent of the vote, Alassane Ouattara 32 percent, and Henri Konan Bédié 25 percent.

With no candidate winning an outright majority, a second round was needed a month later. In an ironic twist, Bédié, who had vociferously promoted the toxic policy of Ivoirité to exclude Ouattara from the political process in 1995, asked his Baoulé supporters to back his former nemesis in the second round of voting. The electoral commission announced Ouattara as the winner with 54 percent of the vote to Gbagbo's 46 percent. As agreed beforehand, the UN special representative certified the election results based on government tallies and reports from UN peacekeepers deployed around the country to monitor the security situation. ECOWAS, AU, and EU electoral observers also declared Ouattara the winner. However, in a crude and dangerous act of political cynicism, the country's pro-Gbagbo Constitutional Council threw out votes from Ouattara's northern supporters and declared the incumbent the winner with 51 percent of the vote.[88] Both Gbagbo and Ouattara then declared themselves president and started to form separate administrations in Abidjan, with Soro appointed as Ouattara's "prime minister." The army pledged its support to Gbagbo, while the Forces Nouvelles threatened to remove him by force. The stalemate was complete: Gbagbo now had power without legitimacy, while Ouattara had legitimacy without power.

ECOWAS and the AU demanded that Gbagbo step down and that Ouattara be allowed to assume office. Both suspended Côte d'Ivoire from their institutions. ECOWAS, led by Nigeria, pushed for a more forceful military response to restore Ouattara's mandate, which Ghana and Gambia opposed.[89] At the UN Security Council, the United States and France called for Gbagbo to step down, while Russia (with economic interests in Abidjan), quietly backed by China, blocked a statement drafted by France calling for the announcement of the winner of the poll.[90] The election fueled ethnically motivated attacks and xenophobic text messages, effectively becoming a vehicle to wage war by other means. It left Côte d'Ivoire, with two declared presidents, more divided than ever.

The Forces Nouvelles rebaptized themselves the Republican Forces and pledged their loyalty to Alassane Ouattara.[91] In March and April 2011, they marched largely unimpeded from their northern stronghold to arrive at the seat of political power in Abidjan to oust the recalcitrant losing president, Laurent Gbagbo. The final battle proved to be a bloody but brief last stand, as the former history professor, Gbagbo, ironically failed to heed the lessons of the past: in 1990, Liberia's autocrat, Samuel Doe, had been captured by rebels in his capital of Monrovia and was tortured to death; a year later Somali strongman, Siad Barre, fled into exile as a rebellion approached the capital of Mogadishu; Zaire's despot, Mobutu Sese Seko, also fled his capital of Kinshasa in 1997 as rebels approached.

In a final storming of the presidential palace in April 2011, the Republican Forces (with help from French and UN forces) captured Gbagbo, whose troops were forced to surrender or flee. The fact that former rebels had restored Ouattara's democratic mandate stood in stark contrast to stolen elections in other African countries such as Kenya (2007) and Zimbabwe (2008). The elections in Kenya and Zimbabwe had resulted in messy "shot-gun weddings," in which cheating incumbents—Mwai Kibaki and Robert Mugabe—remained in power. Gbagbo was prevented from repeating this trend. The success of the Republican Forces in using force to realize Ouattara's democratic mandate could have profound and ambiguous implications for future electoral processes in Africa. It was clear that Ouattara would need to act as a gracious statesman in healing national divisions by bringing in some of Gbagbo's supporters and Southern politicians into a future government and building a genuinely integrated national army, with UN support.[92]

The UN's peacekeepers were rightly criticized for not doing more to protect civilians during the postelection violence in Côte d'Ivoire. By February 2011, three infantry divisions and two military helicopters had been transferred from the UN mission in Liberia to Côte d'Ivoire,[93] but they did not seem effective in protecting civilians. Governments contributing peacekeeping troops to Côte d'Ivoire as seen in other UN missions were reluctant to put their soldiers in harm's way. But with a peace-enforcement mandate reinforced by the UN Security Council (with France and Nigeria as co-drafters) in March 2011,[94] the world body was called to act decisively to protect civilians and halt human rights abuses, which had resulted in at least 1,500 deaths and an estimated one million internally displaced Ivorians. Both sides in the conflict were accused of atrocities. In March 2011, the Security Council imposed financial and travel sanctions on Gbagbo, his Lady Macbethian wife, Simone, and other associates. In the midst of the endgame in Abidjan, French troops increased their presence to about 1,200, taking over the airport in Abidjan and playing a major role in military and political developments in the country. Genuine suspicions persisted about the stance of pro-Ouattara France, whose previous self-interested interventions in Africa and continuing support for local autocrats cast the Gallic power in the role of a fox guarding a henhouse.

Regional actors also had an important part to play in stabilizing Côte d'Ivoire. With reports of over 100,000 Ivorian refuges spilling into Liberia, Mali, and Ghana, it was important to avoid the negative effects of earlier civil wars in Liberia and Sierra Leone. Nigeria, South Africa, and Angola often acted at cross purposes in Côte d'Ivoire. During the postelection crisis, Nigeria adopted a belligerent anti-Gbagbo posture that could have endangered the lives of thousands of its nationals in the country.[95] Angola reportedly provided funds and 300 soldiers to Gbagbo.[96] The Angolan tail was apparently wagging the South African dog, until Tshwane (pushed by Paris) belatedly rediscovered its moral compass and recognized Ouattara's electoral victory. Only through domestic reconciliation, regional consensus, and external diplomatic and military support will stability return to Côte d'Ivoire.

The Role, Impact, and Perceptions
of the UN in West Africa

I now return to the first three questions posed at the beginning of this chapter on the role, impact, and perceptions of the UN Security Council in Liberia, Sierra Leone, and Côte d'Ivoire, much of which has been covered in the three case studies. It is important to note at the outset that it was ECOWAS (and later the United States and Britain) and not the UN that drove the peace processes in Liberia and Sierra Leone for most of the duration of these conflicts. This was less the case in Côte d'Ivoire where France played a significant role from the beginning of the conflict, deploying troops, financing an ECOWAS force, hosting peace talks, and manipulating the UN presence for its own parochial interests. The Council's involvement in Liberia was slow and tentative: only thirteen months after the start of the conflict did the Council rouse itself to pass a resolution recognizing ECOMOG's efforts. It took the Council three years to impose an arms embargo on Liberia's recalcitrant warlords, and it took nearly four years from the start of the conflict to deploy UN military observers. In the second peacekeeping deployment to Liberia between 2003 and 2006, the Council, pushed by the United States, was involved in conflict management efforts from the start and thus played a more effective role. The second deployment stemmed a certain bloodbath in Monrovia and was more decisive than the lackadaisical and reluctant 1993 deployment during which the UN clearly played second fiddle role to ECOMOG.

In Sierra Leone, the UN Security Council adopted a policy of "malign neglect" to the conflict between 1991 and 1999, leaving ECOMOG again to improvise another effort at "peacekeeping on a shoestring" with predictable results. The British military and political role proved decisive in convincing the Council to replace the ECOMOG force with a UN mission. The Security Council thus helped to end the conflict in 2002, improvising a rare UN peacekeeping success in Africa. Finally, in the third case of Côte d'Ivoire, the French pushed the Security Council to transform a weak ECOWAS force into a UN force after a year by 2004. While the conflicts in Liberia and Sierra Leone had temporarily ended through the leadership of ECOWAS and the support of the UN by 2006, the crisis in Côte d'Ivoire continued until April 2011, when a rebel invasion, with help from France and the UN, installed Alassane Ouattara in power. The country's stability, however, remained fragile. All three Western Security Council members pushed for UN involvement in these three countries due to their historical relations, in the case of Britain and the United States, and strategic interests in the case of France.

Turning to the issue of the reaction of regional actors to the UN, in Liberia and Sierra Leone, some of the warlords often called for an increased role for the world body in order to counter the dominance of a Nigerian-led ECOMOG. However, some of the parties in Côte d'Ivoire—particularly the government of Laurent Gbagbo—viewed the UN with suspicion due to French influence within the Council. They thus sought to balance the French role by calling for a stronger AU and ECOWAS role. Significantly, no peace conference was held in France after 2003, and the center of peacemaking moved from Paris to Pretoria as Thabo Mbeki took up the reins of AU mediator. ECOMOG maintained a somewhat ambiguous attitude toward the Security Council in both Liberia and Sierra Leone. On the one hand, many of its leaders wanted a larger UN role to make up for its financial and logistical deficiencies; on the other hand, West African leaders were reluctant to hand over the credit for any peacekeeping success to the world body after nearly a decade of often thankless and frustrating peacekeeping in both countries.

Some ECOWAS countries such as Côte d'Ivoire and Burkina Faso opposed the Nigerian-led ECOMOG, backed rebels in Liberia and Sierra Leone, and contributed little to subregional peacekeeping efforts in both cases. Both therefore seemed to prefer a UN force and a stronger Security Council role. Similar splits were evident in Côte d'Ivoire, with Nigeria—France's traditional rival in West Africa—seeking to wield its influence through peacemaking within the AU (which it chaired in 2004 and 2005) and ECOWAS frameworks. Francophone countries such as Senegal, Niger, Togo, and Benin, which had deployed troops under a French-financed ECOWAS that was later subsumed under a UN mission, also felt that they had a stake in supporting the UN Security Council as well as French diplomatic and military efforts in Côte d'Ivoire.

Concluding Reflections

In discussing the lessons of UN/ECOWAS cooperation in Liberia, Sierra Leone, and Côte d'Ivoire, the three ECOWAS interventions underlined the importance of an active UN Security Council role in subregional peace-keeping efforts. In Liberia, the world body played a limited but useful monitoring role to ECOMOG and oversaw the country's 1997 election. The UN also deployed a peacekeeping mission to Liberia between 2003 and 2006. In Sierra Leone, the UN played a similar military monitoring role, as it did during the first intervention in Liberia until it took over peacekeeping efforts from ECOMOG in 1999. In Côte d'Ivoire, the world body took over ECOWAS's peacekeeping responsibilities after a year in 2004.

The creation of UN peacebuilding offices in Liberia and Sierra Leone represents a potentially significant innovation in the organization's conflict management strategy. However, these offices will in future have to be substantially bolstered with stronger mandates and greater staff and resources. Their cooperation with ECOWAS and civil society groups will also have to be strengthened and more clearly defined. The peacebuilding office in Liberia, established in 1997, was the first-ever such office established by the UN. However, as an internal UN report of July 2001 admitted, the peacebuilding office in Liberia was poorly resourced, and its mandate was weak and not politically intrusive due to the initial reluctance of the Security Council to establish the office.[97] The Liberian government had accepted the office as the lesser evil to a continued ECOMOG presence in the full knowledge that the UN would not interfere with its running of the country. The world body also established a peacebuilding office in Sierra Leone in January 2006.[98] These offices have been mandated to perform such tasks as providing electoral assistance; promoting human rights and the rule of law by working through both government and civil society actors; mobilizing donor support for disarmament, demobilization, and the reintegration of excombatants into local communities; supporting the rebuilding of administrative capacity; and rehabilitating local infrastructure.

Many of these goals have, however, often not been met in fragile situations in which donors have repeatedly failed to deliver on their pledges. The UN office in Liberia, under Gambian technocrat Felix Downes-Thomas, was regarded as too close to Charles Taylor's government. It narrowly interpreted its mandate as that of mobilizing donor support for peacebuilding and declined to work closely with civil society groups and to report on human rights abuses. It is vital that the UN collaborate with ECOWAS in its future peacebuilding tasks, particularly with the establishment of a thirty-one-member UN Peacebuilding Commission in December 2005 to mobilize resources for postconflict reconstruction, along with the African Development Bank, the World Bank, and the International Monetary Fund.

One approach that must be unequivocally rejected is the profoundly offensive idea of establishing a "trusteeship" in Africa's "failed states." British analyst Stephen Ellis has propounded this pseudoscientific cure in a crude treatise on "how to rebuild Africa." Ellis suggested ditching what he regarded as conventional methods by suspending the sovereignty of African states like Liberia and having external actors seize control of managing government revenues, with the whole project legitimized by the UN.[99] Needless to say, these Afro-pessimistic musings are based on the arrogant and patronizing assumptions of often deeply prejudiced analysts calling on the West to "craft strategies" for Africans who seemingly are unable to stand on their own feet in the difficult conditions of Western "civilization." It is a source of deep concern that jaundiced views like these actually receive a serious hearing in influential policy circles.

Following the recommendations of the UN's Inter-Agency Task Force on West Africa of May 2001, the decisions by the Security Council to establish a UN office in West Africa and to appoint a special representative of the UN Secretary-General, Mauritanian diplomat Ahmedou Ould-Abdallah, to head this office, both represented positive steps for UN/ECOWAS cooperation.[100] Algerian diplomat Said Djinnit was appointed as head of this office in February 2008. The Council mandated the office to help strengthen ECOWAS's peacekeeping and electoral capacities and to work with civil society groups in West Africa. The UN office was also tasked with performing the following specific tasks: assisting the UN and its subregional offices to coordinate strategies in West Africa; monitoring and reporting on political, humanitarian, and human rights developments; harmonizing UN activities with those of ECOWAS; monitoring ECOWAS's decisions and activities; and supporting national and subregional peacebuilding efforts.[101]

While these are all noble objectives, the curious decision not to locate this office in Abuja, site of the ECOWAS Secretariat, has reduced its effectiveness in fulfilling its mandate, particularly in light of the complications of communication and travel within West Africa. The one success of the office (with less than five professional staff in 2006 and about thirteen full-time posts in 2011) has been the organization of regular meetings between the political and military heads of UN missions in Liberia, Sierra Leone, Côte d'Ivoire, and Guinea-Bissau to discuss cross-border issues and to share comparative experiences as part of a regional approach to managing West Africa's conflicts. The UN office has also conducted research on youth unemployment in West Africa and has been engaged in private sector roundtables to attract investment to the subregion. UNOWA was further involved in the seventh EU/ECOWAS ministerial troika in Luxembourg in May 2005, where a Trilateral Framework of Action for Peace and Security was agreed to provide support for ECOWAS in the areas of security sector reform; electoral missions; mediation; peace support operations; and disarmament, demobilization, and reintegration.[102] By 2011, UNOWA was focusing on cross-border challenges, security sector reform, drug trafficking, organized crime, and human rights.

In concluding this chapter, it is important to note that a potentially useful mechanism that was employed in West Africa was the visits to the subregion by UN Security Council members. Five missions of UN Security Council permanent representatives visited Sierra Leone in October 2000; several West African countries in July 2003 and June 2004; Côte d'Ivoire in June 2007; and Liberia in May 2009. The Council also visited Liberia in May 2009. The main purpose of these visits was for Council members to gain a better understanding of the situation on the ground in this volatile subregion. These delegations thus met with regional heads of state, diplomats, rebels, and civil society actors. The missions urged more effective UN action in deploying peacekeepers and civilian staff, called for greater support for ECOWAS's peacemaking and peacekeeping efforts, saw the need for greater coordination of the UN's efforts in various subregional peacekeeping missions (the genesis of the world body's regional approach), advocated greater support for civil society actors, championed support of electoral and postconflict peacebuilding efforts, and called for an end to a "culture of impunity" by subregional warlords through targeted sanctions.[103]

These trips allowed the Security Council's ambassadors to gain first-hand experience of the situation on the ground and to assess for themselves the views and personalities of the key actors in West Africa's three destructive wars. These missions also provided Council members with insights that were useful in making decisions in New York. Such high-level field missions can bring home to parties in dispute the Council's serious intent to understand and address their conflicts. They can also bring hope to the populations of conflict-ridden regions like West Africa that they have not been abandoned by the international community.

Notes

This chapter builds on Adekeye Adebajo, "The Security Council and Three Wars in West Africa," in Vaughan Lowe, Adam Roberts, Jennifer Welsh, and Dominik Zaum, eds., *The United Nations Security Council and War: The Evolution of Thought and Practice Since 1945* (Oxford: Oxford University Press, 2008), pp. 466–493. The author would like to thank Ngozi Amu, James Jonah, Lansana Kouyaté, Musifiky Mwanasali, and Dominik Zaum for invaluable comments on an earlier version of the chapter.

1. James Jonah, "The United Nations," in Adekeye Adebajo and Ismail Rashid, eds., *West Africa's Security Challenges: Building Peace in a Troubled Region* (Boulder: Lynne Rienner, 2004), p. 331.

2. See Adebajo and Rashid, *West Africa's Security Challenges.*

3. See ECOWAS, *Protocol Relating to the Mechanism for Conflict Prevention, Management, Resolution, Peacekeeping and Security,* signed in Lomé, Togo, 10 December 1999.

4. For background to the Sierra Leone conflict, see Ibrahim Abdullah and Patrick Muana, "The Revolutionary United Front of Sierra Leone: A Revolt of the Lumpenproletariat," in Christopher Clapham, ed., *African Guerrillas* (Bloomington: Indiana University Press, 1998), pp. 172–193; Adekeye Adebajo, *Building Peace in West Africa: Liberia, Sierra Leone and Guinea-Bissau* (Boulder: Lynne Rienner, 2002); *African Development* 22, nos. 2 and 3 (1997), special issue on "Youth Culture and Political Violence: The Sierra Leone Civil War"; Kabral Blay-Amihere, *Between the Lion and the Elephant: Memoirs of an African Diplomat* (Tema, Ghana: Digibooks Ghana, 2010), pp. 89–158; John Hirsch, *Sierra Leone: Diamonds and the Struggle for*

Democracy (Boulder: Lynne Rienner, 2001); David Keen, *Conflict and Collusion in Sierra Leone* (New York: Palgrave, 2005); Mark Malan, Phenyo Rakate, and Angela McIntyre, *Peacekeeping in Sierra Leone: UNAMSIL Hits the Home Straight* (Tshwane: Institute for Security Studies, 2002); Adekeye Adebajo and David Keen, "Sierra Leone," in Mats Berdal and Spyros Economides, eds., *United Nations Interventionism, 1991–2004* (Cambridge: Cambridge University Press, 2007), pp. 246–273.

5. See, for example, Musifiky Mwanasali, "Africa's Responsibility to Protect," in Adekeye Adebajo and Helen Scanlon, eds., *A Dialogue of the Deaf: Essays on Africa and the United Nations* (Johannesburg: Jacana, 2006), pp. 89–110.

6. See, for example, Clement Adibe, "The Liberian Conflict and the ECOWAS-UN Partnership," *Third World Quarterly* 18, no. 3 (1997): 471–488; Norrie MacQueen, *United Nations Peacekeeping in Africa Since 1960* (London: Pearson Education, 2002); Binaifir Nowrojee, "Joining Forces: UN and Regional Peacekeeping, Lessons from Liberia," *Harvard Human Rights Journal* 18 (Spring 1995): 129–152; 'Funmi Olonisakin, "UN Co-operation with Regional Organizations in Peacekeeping: The Experience of ECOMOG and UNOMIL in Liberia," *International Peacekeeping* 3, no. 3 (Autumn 1996): 33–51; United Nations, *The United Nations and the Situation in Liberia,* revision one (New York: Department of Public Information, February 1997).

7. Though 712 ECOWAS troops from Benin, Gambia, Niger, and Togo intervened unsuccessfully in Guinea-Bissau in February 1999 before being withdrawn following fighting four months later, the UN did not deploy any military personnel into Guinea-Bissau, and the country did not experience the same level and duration of protracted fighting as the other three cases. I have therefore decided not to focus attention on Guinea-Bissau despite the UN's involvement in the country's postconflict peacebuilding efforts.

8. For accounts of the Liberian civil war, see Adekeye Adebajo, *Liberia's Civil War: Nigeria, ECOMOG and Regional Security in West Africa* (Boulder: Lynne Rienner, 2002); Abiodun Alao, John Mackinlay, and 'Funmi Olonisakin, *Peacekeepers, Politicians, and Warlords: The Liberian Peace Process* (New York: UN University Press, 1999); Alhaji M. S. Bah and Festus Aboagye, eds., *A Tortuous Road to Peace: The Dynamics of Regional, UN and International Humanitarian Interventions in Liberia* (Tshwane: Institute for Security Studies, 2005); Stephen Ellis, *The Mask of Anarchy: The Destruction of Liberia and the Religious Dimensions of an African Civil War* (London: Hurst, 1999); Karl Magyar and Earl Conteh-Morgan, eds., *Peacekeeping in Africa: ECOMOG in Liberia* (London: Macmillan, 1998).

9. This term also refers to soldiers who pretend to be rebels in order to loot and ambush.

10. For further details on ECOMOG's military shortcomings, see Herbert Howe, "Lessons of Liberia: ECOMOG and Regional Peacekeeping," *International Security* 21, no. 3 (Winter 1996/1997): 145–176; Cyril Iweze, "Nigeria in Liberia: The Military Operations of ECOMOG," in M. A. Vogt and A. E. Ekoko, eds., *Nigeria in International Peacekeeping 1960–1992* (Marina, Lagos: Malthouse, 1993); Robert Mortimer, "From ECOMOG to ECOMOG II: Intervention in Sierra Leone," in John W. Harbeson and Donald Rothchild, eds., *Africa in World Politics: The African State System in Flux,* 3rd ed. (Boulder: Westview, 2000), pp. 188–207.

11. Security Council (SC) Res. 1270, 20 October 1999, established UNAMSIL in Sierra Leone. SC Res. 1509, 19 September 2003, established UNMIL in Liberia.

12. See S/2001/434, 2 May 2001.

13. See Femi Aribisala, "The Political Economy of Structural Adjustment in Côte d'Ivoire," in Adebayo Olukoshi, Omotayo Olaniyan, and Femi Aribisala, eds., *Structural Adjustment in West Africa* (Lagos: Nigerian Institute of International Affairs, 1994); Yves A. Fauré, "Côte d'Ivoire: Analysing the Crisis," in Donal

Cruise O'Brien et al., eds., *Contemporary West African States* (Cambridge: Cambridge University Press, 1989), pp. 59–73.

14. For background to the current crisis, see Abdoulaye Bathily, "La Crise Ivoirienne: Elements pour Situer ses Origines et ses Dimensions Sous-regionales," *Democracy and Development* 3, no. 2 (2003): 93–99; Blay-Amihere, *Between the Lion and the Elephant,* pp. 180–234; Abdul Rahman Lamin, "The Conflict in Côte d'Ivoire: South Africa's Diplomacy, and Prospects for Peace," Occasional Paper no. 49, Institute for Global Dialogue, Johannesburg, South Africa, August 2005; Kaye Whiteman, "Côte d'Ivoire: The Three Deaths of Houphouet-Boigny," in *African Conflict, Peace and Governance Monitor* (Ibadan, Nigeria: Dokun Publishing House, 2005), pp. 43–59.

15. For an overview, see Shepard Forman and Andrew Greene, "Collaborating with Regional Organizations," in David Malone, ed., *The UN Security Council: From the Cold War to the 21st Century* (Boulder: Lynne Rienner, 2004), pp. 295–309.

16. James Jonah, "The United Nations," in Adebajo and Rashid, *West Africa's Security Challenges,* p. 325.

17. S/22133, 22 January 1991.

18. Jonah, "The United Nations," pp. 323–326.

19. SC Res. 788, 19 November 1992.

20. See Boutros Boutros-Ghali, *An Agenda for Peace,* 2nd ed. (New York: UN Department of Public Information, 1995).

21. SC Res. 866, 22 September 1993.

22. See "Report of the UN Secretary-General on Liberia," S/1994/1167, 14 October 1994.

23. See "First Progress Report of the Secretary-General on the UN Mission in Liberia," S/2003/1175, 15 December 2003.

24. Personal interview with Trevor Gordon-Somers, New York, May 1997.

25. Ibid.

26. "Report of the UN Secretary-General on Liberia," S/1995/158, 24 February 1995, p. 12.

27. "Report of the UN Secretary-General on Liberia," S/1995/781, 13 September 1995, p. 2.

28. "Final Report of the Secretary-General on the UN Observer Mission in Liberia," S/1997/712, 12 September 1997, p. 4.

29. The presence of ECOWAS and US troops was authorized by SC Res. 1497, 1 August 2003. UNMIL was established by SC Res. 1509, 19 September 2003.

30. SC Res. 1509, 19 September 2003.

31. "Third Progress Report of the Secretary-General on the UN Mission in Liberia," S/2004/430, 26 May 2004, p. 2.

32. See Ellen Johnson Sirleaf, *This Child Will Be Great: Memoir of a Remarkable Life by Africa's First Woman President* (New York: Harper, 2009).

33. This information has drawn upon "Ninth Progress Report of the Secretary-General on the UN Mission in Liberia," S/2005/764, 7 December 2005.

34. "Tenth Progress Report of the Secretary-General on the UN Mission in Liberia," S/2006/159, 14 March 2006, p. 7.

35. "Twentieth Report of the Secretary-General on the United Nations Mission in Liberia," S/2010/88, 17 February 2010, p. 15.

36. "Twenty-First Progress Report of the Secretary-General on the United Nations Mission in Liberia," S/2010/429, 11 August 2010, p. 3.

37. Ibid., p. 5.

38. "Twentieth Report of the Secretary-General on the United Nations Mission in Liberia," S/2010/88, 17 February 2010, p. 12.

39. "Nineteenth Report of the Secretary-General on the United Nations Mission in Liberia," S/2009/411, 10 August 2009; "Eighteenth Report of the Secretary-General on the United Nations Mission in Liberia," S/2009/86, 10 February 2009.

40. "Twenty-First Progress Report of the Secretary-General on the United Nations Mission in Liberia," S/2010/429, 11 August 2010, p. 13.

41. "Twenty-Second Progress Report of the Secretary-General on the United Nations Mission in Liberia," S/2011/72, 14 February 2011 (reissued 28 March 2011 for technical reasons).

42. Jonah, "The United Nations," p. 333.

43. SC Res. 1132, 8 October 1997.

44. SC Res. 1181, 13 July 1998.

45. Personal interview with an ECOMOG officer, Freetown, July 1999.

46. Jonah, "The United Nations," p. 331.

47. "Seventh Report of the Secretary-General on the UN Observer Mission in Sierra Leone," S/1999/836, 30 July 1999, p. 2.

48. See John Iliffe, *Obasanjo, Nigeria and the World* (Suffolk: James Currey, 2011).

49. "Eighth Report of the Secretary-General on the UN Observer Mission in Sierra Leone," S/1999/1003, 23 September 1999, p. 6.

50. SC Res. 1270, 22 October 1999. For a detailed history of UNAMSIL, see 'Funmi Olonisakin, *Peacekeeping in Sierra Leone: The Story of UNAMSIL* (Boulder: Lynne Rienner, 2008).

51. Jonah, "The United Nations," p. 330.

52. Ibid.

53. 'Funmi Olonisakin and Comfort Ero, "Africa and the Regionalization of Peace Operations," in Michael Pugh and Waheguru Pal Singh Sidhu, eds., *The United Nations and Regional Security: Europe and Beyond* (Boulder: Lynne Rienner, 2003), p. 246.

54. Jonah, "The United Nations," p. 331.

55. SC Res. 1289, 7 February 2000.

56. Jonah, "The United Nations," p. 330.

57. "Third Report of the UN Mission in Sierra Leone," S/2000/186, 7 March 2000, pp. 3–4; S/2000/751, 31 July 2000, p. 4.

58. "Fifth Report of the UN Mission in Sierra Leone," S/2000/751, 31 July 2000, p. 9.

59. See Lansana Fofana, "A Nation Self-destructs," *NewsAfrica* 1, no. 5 (31 July 2000): 25; Chris McGreal, "UN to Sack Its General in Sierra Leone," *Guardian Weekly,* 29 June–5 July 2000, p. 2.

60. John Hirsch, "Sierra Leone," in Malone, *The UN Security Council,* p. 528.

61. SC Res. 1306, 5 July 2000.

62. SC Res. 1343, 7 March 2001.

63. "Twenty-Fourth Report of the Secretary-General on the UN Mission in Sierra Leone," S/2004/965, 10 December 2004.

64. Personal discussions with senior UN officials, New York, February 2006.

65. "Twenty-Sixth Report of the Secretary-General on the UN Mission in Sierra Leone," S/2005/596, 20 September 2005.

66. "First Report of the Secretary-General on the UN Integrated Office in Sierra Leone," S/2006/269, 28 April 2006, pp. 2–3

67. Whiteman, "Côte d'Ivoire," p. 53.

68. See, for example, Adekeye Adebajo, "Nigeria: Africa's New Gendarme?" *Security Dialogue* 31, no. 2 (June 2000): 185–199; Adebayo Adedeji, "ECOWAS: A

Retrospective Journey," in Adebajo and Rashid, *West Africa's Security Challenges,* pp. 21–49; John Chipman, *French Power in Africa* (Oxford: Basil Blackwell, 1989).

69. See Mohammed Chambas, "The Security Council and ECOWAS: Facing the Challenges of Peace and Security," New York, 11 April 2003, Annex II of the New York–based International Peace Academy seminar report, "Operationalizing the ECOWAS Mechanism for Conflict Prevention, Management, Resolution, Peacekeeping and Security," based on a meeting in Dakar, Senegal, 12–13 August 2002, www.ipacademy.org.

70. See "Report of the UN Secretary-General on Côte d'Ivoire," S/2003/374, 26 March 2003.

71. SC Res. 1479, 13 May 2003.

72. SC Res. 1528, 27 February 2004.

73. Lamin, "The Conflict in Côte d'Ivoire," p. 27.

74. Whiteman, "Côte d'Ivoire," p. 57.

75. SC Res. 1572, 15 November 2004.

76. SC Res. 1643, 15 December 2005.

77. *Security Council Report,* "Monthly Forecast January 2006," 22 December 2005, p. 14; "Monthly Forecast April 2006," 30 March 2006, p. 8, www.security-councilreport.org.

78. Comfort Ero, "UN Peacekeeping in West Africa: Liberia, Sierra Leone and Côte d'Ivoire," in Adebajo, *From Global Apartheid to Global Village,* p. 299.

79. This information on Côte d'Ivoire has drawn upon "First Progress Report of the Secretary-General on the UN Operation in Côte d'Ivoire," S/2005/398, 17 June 2005, and "Sixth Report of the Secretary-General on the UN Operation in Côte d'Ivoire," S/2005/604, 26 September 2005.

80. *Security Council Report,* "Monthly Forecast May 2006," 27 April 2006, p. 9, and "Monthly Forecast March 2006," 24 February 2006, p. 12.

81. Francis Ikome, "Côte d'Ivoire Follow-up Dialogue," unpublished report of the Institute for Global Dialogue, South Africa, a seminar held 21 June 2006, p. 4.

82. "Eighth Report of the Secretary-General on the UN Operation in Côte d'Ivoire," S/2006/222, 11 April 2006, p. 5.

83. John Bolton, *Surrender Is Not an Option: Defending America at the United Nations and Abroad* (New York: Threshold, 2007), p. 361.

84. "Twenty-Fourth Report of the Secretary-General on the UN Operation in Côte d'Ivoire," S/2010/245, 20 May 2010, p. 12.

85. See "Thirteenth Progress Report of the Secretary-General on the UN Operation in Côte d'Ivoire," S/2007/275, 14 May 2007.

86. "Twenty-Second Progress Report of the Secretary-General on the UN Operation in Côte d'Ivoire," S/2009/495, 29 September 2009, p. 2.

87. "Nineteenth Report of the Secretary-General on the UN Operation in Côte d'Ivoire," S/2009/21, 8 January 2009, p. 3.

88. For a detailed analysis of these events, see " Twenty-Seventh Report of the Secretary-General on the UN Operation in Côte d'Ivoire," S/2011/211, 30 March 2011.

89. *The Economist,* "Coming to the Crunch," 31 March 2011, www.economist.com.

90. Louis Charbonneau, "UN Chief and Russia Bicker over Ivorian Poll Winner," *The Sunday Independent* (South Africa), 5 December 2010, p. 9.

91. This last section is based largely on Adekeye Adebajo, "After Gbagbo, What Next for Ivory Coast?" *The Guardian* (London), 6 April 2011, p. 32.

92. See David Smith, "Ivory Coast Settles into Tentative Peace Following Arrest of Laurent Gbagbo," *The Guardian* (London), 13 April 2011, www.guardian.co.uk; Mark John and David Smith, "Ivory Coast: Final Assault to Unseat Gbagbo Amid

Humanitarian Crisis," *The Guardian* (London), 5 April 2011, www.guardian.co.uk; "Basement Blues," *The Economist,* 9 April 2011, vol. 399, no. 8728, pp. 41–42.

93. "Twenty-Second Progress Report of the Secretary-General on the United Nations Mission in Liberia," S/2011/72, 14 February 2011, p. 13.

94. UN Security Council Resolution 1975, S/RES/1975, 30 March 2011.

95. See the article by Nigeria's foreign minister, Odein Ajumogobia, "Towards An Enduring Peace in Côte d'Ivoire," *This Day* (Nigeria), 24 January 2011, www.thisdayonline.com.

96. "Will the Bad Loser Be Squeezed Out?" *The Economist,* 12 March 2011, vol. 398, no. 8724, pp. 43–44.

97. See "Report of the Joint Review Mission on the United Nations Post-Conflict Peacebuilding Offices," Department of Political Affairs/United Nations Development Programme, 20 July 2001, p. 12.

98. SC Res. 1620, 31 August 2005.

99. Stephen Ellis, "How to Rebuild Africa," *Foreign Affairs* 84, no. 5 (September/October 2005): 135–148.

100. UN Security Council, "Report of the Inter-Agency Mission to West Africa," S/2001/434, 2 May 2001.

101. "ECOWAS-EU-UNOWA Framework of Action for Peace and Security," draft (no date).

102. Ibid.

103. See "Report of the Security Council Mission to Sierra Leone, 7–14 October 2000," S/2000/992, 16 October 2000; "Report of the Security Council Mission to West Africa, 26 June 2003," S/2003/688, 7 July 2003; "Report of the Security Council Mission to West Africa, 20–29 June 2004," S/2004/525, 2 July 2004; "Report of the Security Council Mission to the African Union, Rwanda, the Democratic Republic of the Congo and Liberia," S/2009/303, 11 June 2009.

6

The Conflicts of Identity:
The UN in the Horn of Africa

> Conflict of identities occurs when groups, or more accurately their
> elites, rebel against what they see as intolerable oppression by the
> dominant group, often expressed in denial of recognition, exclusion
> from the mainstream, marginalization, and perhaps the threat
> of cultural annihilation or even physical elimination.
> —*Francis Deng, Sudanese scholar-diplomat*[1]

In this chapter I assess four United Nations peacekeeping missions in the Horn of Africa: Somalia, Ethiopia-Eritrea, Sudan's Darfur region, and South Sudan. Since the UN's peacekeeping successes and failures are often contingent on the domestic, regional, and external dynamics of conflict situations, I examine these factors in detail in each case. I conclude by drawing broader lessons from the four cases for UN peacekeeping missions in Africa.

All four missions in the Horn of Africa were launched after the end of the Cold War, when the region had lost much of its strategic value to the great powers. The Somalia mission was launched under Chapter VII of the UN Charter as a peace-enforcement, large-scale mission in an anarchic civil conflict with uncertain consent from the warring parties and had nearly forty thousand soldiers at the height of the intervention. The two Sudan missions—at twenty-six thousand (Darfur) and ten thousand peacekeepers (South Sudan)—were launched to try to stabilize volatile regions in Africa's largest country at the time (just over a quarter of the size of the United States), as well as to allow the population of South Sudan to hold a self-determination referendum on secession from Khartoum by January 2011. The four thousand–strong Ethiopia-Eritrea UN mission was a classical peacekeeping mission, launched under Chapter VI of the UN Charter, to separate belligerents who had agreed to end an interstate conflict.

All four missions reveal the importance of the willingness of the parties to make peace to the success of UN peacekeeping missions. In Somalia between 1992 and 1995, the most powerful warlord, Mohammed Farah Aideed, was unwilling to share power and saw the presence of peacekeepers as obstructing his political ambitions. He thus attacked the peacekeepers as a strategy to force their withdrawal. In Ethiopia-Eritrea, the deployment of peacekeepers in 2000 after two years of bloody conflict was possible mainly because of the disastrous change in Eritrea's military fortunes and Ethiopia's willingness to accept a ceasefire. Continued problems in implementing the decision of an international boundary commission in April 2001 to demarcate the common border between both countries underlined the importance of the consent of warring parties to implementing peace agreements. In Sudan, the prospect of an oil-rich independent state and regional pressure on Khartoum led to a peace accord in 2005, though the situation remained fragile with rival groups in South Sudan also fighting for a share of the spoils. In Darfur, the splintering of rebel groups complicated peace efforts, while Khartoum often negotiated in bad faith, continuing to back antirebel militias who terrorized local populations.

The role of regional actors can be important to peace processes, as these four cases show. Ethiopia played an important, but not decisive, role in peacemaking efforts in Somalia in 1993, though regional actors, including Ethiopia itself, have subsequently played a more divisive role in backing rival Somali warlords, thus making peace more difficult to achieve. In Ethiopia-Eritrea, the Organization of African Unity—now the African Union—played a critical role under its chairman, Algerian leader Abdelaziz Bouteflika, in negotiating a peace accord in 2000 that led to the deployment of UN peacekeepers. In Sudan, regional leaders from the Intergovernmental Authority on Development (IGAD) contributed to peacemaking efforts through several conferences. Regional tensions between the leaders of Sudan and Chad, however, complicated these efforts, with Khartoum backing Chadian rebels and N'Djamena backing Darfuri rebels.

The role of external actors was also important in all four cases. The two most powerful members of the UN Security Council—the United States and the Soviet Union—fought over Somalia and Ethiopia during the Cold War era, and both countries served as clients of the two superpowers during different periods. Washington's decision to lead an intervention into Somalia in 1992 brought hope to the country and, for a while, stabilized parts of it, while its decision to withdraw its troops from Somalia after the killing of eighteen American soldiers in October 1993 effectively crippled the mission and left the country without peace for nearly two decades. In Ethiopia-Eritrea, the decision of the UN Security Council to send peacekeepers to implement the OAU's Algiers accord was crucial in freezing the conflict between both countries and providing space for working out the demarcation of the common border between the two neighbors. Washington—concerned about Khartoum supporting Islamic radicalism and with the Christian right in the United States advocating the rights of southern coreligionists—played an important role in the Comprehensive Peace Agreement (CPA) for South Sudan in 2005. France, another permanent member of the Security Council, supported its client, Idriss Déby, and manipulated the European Union and the UN to deploy peacekeepers to stabilize the Chad/Sudan border between 2008 and 2010. China—another of the five veto-wielding permanent members of the Security Council, whose third-largest trading partner in Africa is Sudan—played an instrumental role in convincing Khartoum to accept an AU/UN Hybrid Operation in Darfur (UNAMID) in 2007.

Finally, the role of the UN special representatives in Somalia and Ethiopia-Eritrea was important. In Somalia, US admiral Jonathan Howe was a military man with little diplomatic background and no prior experience with UN peacekeeping or understanding of Somali politics and culture. In contrast, Legwaila Joseph Legwaila, the UN special representative in Ethiopia-Eritrea, who had been deputy special representative on the UN mission in Namibia (UNTAG) and Botswana's long-serving permanent representative to the UN, enjoyed wide respect among the diplomatic community within and outside Africa. Former foreign minister of Congo-Brazzaville Rodolphe Adada was widely seen as ineffectual in the admittedly difficult environment of Darfur, while the dynamic Dutchman, Jan Pronk, fell foul of Khartoum and was expelled as head of the UN mission in Sudan.

Somalia

Background to Intervention

Somalia was an orphan of the Cold War in the era of intervention by external powers in Africa. Siad Barre, the country's autocratic leader since 1969, switched effortlessly from being a Soviet to a US client in 1978 until 1988.[2] Somalia's civil war erupted in full force in January 1991 after Barre fled Mogadishu. The central government collapsed, and Somalia joined the growing ranks of Cold War orphans. Two powerful warlords, Mohamed Farah Aideed and Ali Mahdi Mohamed, both members of the opposition United Somali Congress (USC), battled for control of the capital. In Kismayo, two rival warlords, General Siad "Morgan" and Colonel Omar Jess, fought for control, while northwestern Somaliland eventually declared itself an independent republic, which no state formally recognized.

With growing starvation in Somalia, the UN Security Council established the UN Operation in Somalia (UNOSOM I), deploying five hundred peacekeepers to protect food convoys. Egyptian UN Secretary-General Boutros Boutros-Ghali sent experienced Algerian diplomat Mohamed

Sahnoun to Somalia as his special representative in April 1992. Sahnoun sought to rebuild Somalia through a strategy of encouraging a legitimate political process based around Somalia's warlords, intellectuals, and elders. He eventually resigned in October 1992 following disagreements with Boutros-Ghali over UN tactics in Somalia.[3] As Somalia's warlords continued to blockade food convoys and with UNOSOM I's unarmed military observers unable to stop them, three hundred thousand deaths resulted, and one million refugees spilled into neighboring Kenya and Ethiopia.

Amid a worsening security situation, 38,301 peacekeepers, led by 25,426 Americans, entered Somalia in December 1992 as part of the Unified Task Force (UNITAF). Operation Restore Hope was mandated to facilitate the delivery of humanitarian goods to Somalia. The mission started well enough with the presence of the peacekeepers ensuring the delivery of food, reducing looting and banditry, rebuilding roads and bridges, and facilitating the repatriation of Somali refugees from neighboring countries. Between December 1992 and October 1993, a staggering $2 billion was spent on the international effort.

But Washington had quixotically assumed that it could deploy its troops and feed Somalis while avoiding any confrontation with the country's warlords. It refused Boutros-Ghali's frequent requests to disarm Somalia's factions. However, Aideed, who had been consolidating his military position before the UN's arrival, felt that the entry of the peacekeepers would deprive him of the presidency. He also feared that the intervention might seek to endorse his rival Ali Mahdi's questionable election as president of Somalia at a conference in Djibouti in 1991.[4] The mere presence of the UN force changed the military balance on the ground. While Aideed reluctantly accepted the peacekeepers, his less powerful rival Ali Mahdi enthusiastically supported their presence.[5] Further complicating the UN's tasks, Aideed distrusted Boutros-Ghali, whom he had considered pro-Barre since the latter's tenure as deputy foreign minister of Egypt. Aideed's suspicion of the UN was further heightened when a Russian plane with UN markings delivered military equipment to Ali Mahdi in northern Mogadishu.[6]

From "Operation Restore Hope"
to "Operation Return Home"
In May 1993, UNITAF was transformed into UNOSOM II, which still had four thousand US troops. The new UN "nationbuilding" mandate was ambitious in calling for the revival of national and regional institutions and the establishment of civil administration throughout Somalia.[7] Growing human rights abuses by UN peacekeepers, involving the killing of Somali civilians, soon resulted in the civilian population turning against the UN. After the killing of twenty-four Pakistani UN peacekeepers by Aideed's fighters in June 1993, Washington successfully championed a UN Security Council

resolution calling for the warlord's capture and trial. It was within this context that Admiral Howe virtually declared war on Aideed, sending US helicopters to kill or capture his supporters, including respected elders, in Mogadishu. Somalis were describing the UN at this stage as a warring faction, a militia of the Gal clan: rich and powerful, but dumb.

UNITAF's American special envoy Robert Oakley's discreet style, based on prior knowledge of Somalia, contrasted sharply with Howe's aggressive and confrontational tactics. Howe adopted "Wild West" tactics of placing a $25,000 bounty on Aideed's head. Sent out to carry out the sheriff's orders was a posse of US Army Rangers. The mission went disastrously wrong when the rangers became caught in a firefight with Aideed's men, resulting in the death of eighteen US soldiers and about one thousand Somalis, mostly civilians. In order to deflect the strong domestic backlash at the sight of a dead American soldier being dragged through the streets of Mogadishu by enraged Somalis, Bill Clinton's administration and much of the US media inaccurately blamed the botched mission—planned entirely under American command—on the UN. In early 1995, the UN withdrew all its peacekeepers from Somalia, leaving the country as anarchic as it had found it. Operation Restore Hope had become Operation Return Home. In the twilight of his career, Aideed died as he had lived: gunned down in a battle with a rival faction on the dusty streets of Mogadishu in 1996. The civil war continued a decade and a half after the end of the UN mission, and Somalia remained an acephalous state without a central government that controlled its entire territory, despite the energetic peacemaking efforts by IGAD and others.

Following the Somalia debacle, the administration of US president Bill Clinton placed severe restrictions on the approval of future UN missions through the heavy-handed Presidential Decision Directive (PDD) 25. Boutros-Ghali's requests for new UN peacekeeping missions in Burundi and Liberia met with an eloquent silence, even as the West continued to employ the UN for "rich men's wars"[8] in places that it considered to be of more strategic value to it such as Bosnia and Haiti. Undoubtedly the most tragic consequence of Somalia, however, occurred six months after the killing of the eighteen American soldiers. Washington led the opposition to a UN response to the genocide in Rwanda in which an estimated eight hundred thousand people were massacred in three months in a situation that was tragically and erroneously viewed through a tainted Somali prism (see Chapter 3).

Ethiopian troops invaded Somalia in December 2006, joined by a one thousand–strong Ugandan contingent under an African Union flag in 2007, to prop up a weak Transitional Federal Government (TFG). To many in Africa, this action represented a misguided mission that was utterly unable to stem the reckless bloodbath in Mogadishu and was more of an auxiliary of Pax Americana's erratic "war on terrorism" (with 1,700 US soldiers deployed in Djibouti) than a mission to promote sustainable peace. In what appeared to be a carefully coordinated military operation, a US gunship bombed a Somali village, and its special forces were reported to be operating on the ground in Somalia. Ethiopia, which had launched several incursions into Somalia since 1992, deployed troops to the country, seeking to protect its southern flank and to prevent a hostile government in Mogadishu from forging an alliance with Eritrea.[9] Ethiopia, however, failed to stem instability in Somalia and suffered hundreds of fatalities before withdrawing its troops from the country by December 2008.[10] The AU mission in Somalia (AMISOM), consisting largely of Ugandan and Burundian troops, struggled to keep peace in Mogadishu. The Nairobi-based United Nations Political Office for Somalia, under respected Tanzanian former permanent representative to the UN, Augustine Mahiga, supported the AU's peacemaking efforts in Somalia. The Department of Political Affairs in New York also provided assistance through the UN Support Office to AMISOM, while the Departments of Peacekeeping Operations and Field Support provided logistical support to the struggling AU mission in Somalia.

Ethiopia-Eritrea

The Roots of a Border Conflict

To many distant observers, the bloody brothers' war that was waged in the Horn of Africa by Ethiopia and Eritrea between 1998 and 2000 over barren, disputed border territories was akin to two bald men fighting over a comb.[11] Members of a UN Security Council mission who visited the region in May 2000 described the conflict as a "senseless war."[12] The territory being fought over had neither rich resources nor was it of vital strategic value to either side. Many Ethiopians and Eritreans share a common language, culture, religion, and history and have coexisted largely peacefully for centuries. The leaders of both countries, under the Eritrean People's Liberation Front (EPLF) and the Tigray People's Liberation Front (TPLF), had waged a successful thirty-year war against the dictatorship of the Soviet-backed Mengistu Haile Mariam, and Ethiopia's leader had strongly supported Eritrea's independence in 1993. So, what went wrong?

The border between the ancient empire of Ethiopia and the new nation-state of Eritrea became a metaphor for other divisions: personal divisions between former warlords in a friendship forged in the crucible of a long guerrilla struggle, monetary and trade divisions between two former allies, and political divisions between Tigrinya-speaking kinsmen in Ethiopia and Eritrea. After Italy's occupation of Eritrea by 1890, Ethiopia and Italy largely demarcated the border between the two territories. Benito Mussolini invaded Ethiopia in 1935 and ruled over both territories until Italy's defeat in World War II in 1941. Ethiopia regained its independence, and Eritrea came under British rule. After a decision by the UN, Eritrea was granted autonomous status under a federation with Ethiopia in 1952. Emperor Haile Selassie unilaterally incorporated the region into Ethiopia in 1962.[13]

Despite their military and ideological differences, the TPLF's Meles Zenawi kept his promise to EPLF leader Isaias Afwerki to support Eritrea's right to self-determination. Following a referendum in 1993, Eritrea became Africa's first territory to secede from a postcolonial state. This was seen at the time as a "velvet divorce." But Meles—himself a Tigrinya-speaker like Afwerki—was widely regarded by Ethiopians as being too close to Eritrea. He was often accused of being subservient to his former brother in arms. In the early years of Eritrea's independence, Addis Ababa and Asmara continued their war-time alliance. Rendered landlocked as a result of Eritrea's independence, Ethiopia was granted access to the key Eritrean ports of Assab and Massawa. Both countries were also united in opposing Sudan's Islamist government, and both were staunch US allies.

But relations started to sour from early 1997, when Ethiopia and Eritrea accused each other of blocking the free flow of trade and investment. The development needs of Meles's home province of Tigray had been neglected by past regimes in Addis Ababa. A major goal of the TPLF struggle was to redress this situation. Tigray's development, however, was felt to require the curtailing of Eritrean exports to Ethiopia, since Eritrean textiles, beverages, and finished products could also be produced locally in Tigray. Tensions came to a head after Eritrea, which had been using the Ethiopian *birr* as its national currency, introduced the *nakfa* in November 1997. Addis Ababa introduced new currency notes and insisted that bilateral trade be conducted in hard currency. The nakfa fell sharply against the birr, with a devastating impact on Eritrea's economy. Eritrea retaliated by increasing duties on goods destined for Ethiopia through Assab.[14] Though there were other sources of division, Ethiopia's refusal to guarantee the nakfa's value provided one of the principal casus belli for the border war that erupted shortly after this currency dispute.[15]

A Bloody War in the Horn of Africa, May 1998–December 2000

Before full-scale war erupted between Ethiopia and Eritrea, both countries had experienced border clashes that were regarded at the time as insignificant local disputes. On 6 May 1998, Eritrean troops attacked and took over Ethiopian-administered Badme. After overwhelming Ethiopian forces, Eritrean troops launched attacks on several fronts to retake what Asmara described as its territories that were under Ethiopian control. Ethiopia mobilized 450,000 soldiers to fight a 350,000-strong Eritrean army. About 350,000 Ethiopians were expelled from Eritrea, while 250,000 Eritreans were expelled from Ethiopia. Addis Ababa and Asmara launched a poisonous propaganda war against each other and supported rebels from each other's country. Regional alliances were hastily reshuffled, as Djibouti and Sudan moved closer to Addis Ababa, while Asmara scrambled to avoid diplomatic isolation by settling a border dispute with Yemen and supporting warlords in Somalia. (Ethiopia also backed rival Somali factions.[16])

Military and diplomatic stalemate ensued after Meles refused to negotiate until Eritrea had withdrawn its troops, and Afwerki refused to withdraw his troops until Ethiopia had negotiated over disputed territories. Both sides used different legal arguments to buttress their claims. Eritrea based its claims on the three treaties signed between colonial Rome and imperial Addis Ababa between 1900 and 1908 and called for the territory to be demarcated based on these maps. Ethiopia, on the other hand, argued for the principle of *uti possedetis* or effective occupation, noting that the disputed areas were under its peaceful occupation before May 1998.

In a fit of *folie de grandeur,* Afwerki had become convinced of his military invincibility, having battled a Soviet-backed Ethiopian army during the EPLF's liberation struggle. Eritrea's early foreign policy was aggressive, and there was a sense that, having built up a strong army, it could settle disputes through the use of force. Before its border war with Ethiopia, Eritrea had clashed militarily with Djibouti and Yemen. With the forcible annexation of Badme, Lilliputian Eritrea, with a population of about four million, was challenging the regional Gulliver with a population fifteen times larger. Afwerki's action, probably designed to force international arbitration, turned out to be a disastrous error of judgment. He had concluded that, having demobilized five hundred thousand soldiers inherited from the Mengistu regime, Ethiopia would be too weak to fight back. Meles, who had often been depicted by non-Tigrayan Ethiopians as an Eritrean stooge and harshly criticized for backing Eritrean independence, was provided with an opportunity to ride on a backlash of Ethiopian nationalism against Eritrea. Ethiopia's premier felt personally betrayed by Afwerki, having supported Eritrean independence at great political cost to himself at home.

Susan Rice, the US assistant secretary of state for African affairs, launched a peace initiative in May 1998, as part of a US-Rwanda mediation effort. She offered a plan that called for the settlement of the dispute through border demarcation based on colonial treaties and international law; the withdrawal of Eritrean troops from Badme, followed by the deployment of a small observer force, and resumption of Ethiopian administration; and the demilitarization of the common border. While Meles accepted the plan, Afwerki rejected it, criticizing the US team for exceeding its mandate of facilitation of contacts to engage in actual mediation and for trying to pressure Eritrea to make concessions based on Meles's apparently weak political position at home. The OAU thereafter took over leadership of international mediation efforts.

After maintaining a low profile in the conflict, the UN Security Council roused from its deep slumber to pass several resolutions supporting the OAU's mediation efforts from June 1998. With the UN involved in other areas like the Balkans and East Timor, which were considered to be of more strategic value to the Western powers, the Council was content to leave peacemaking largely to the Africans. The Security Council, however, endorsed Ghanaian UN Secretary-General Kofi Annan's decision to send Mohammed Sahnoun, a veteran Algerian troubleshooter who had served as the UN's special representative in Somalia, to the region in 1999. Sahnoun expressed his frustration at the low priority accorded to this conflict by the Council: "the United Nations should be given more means to address such issues and . . . the international community should be more involved. It was not enough to pass a resolution and forget about the issue."[17]

Following the lethargy of the UN and the failure of the US initiative to end the conflict, the OAU sent a high-level delegation to Addis Ababa and Asmara in June 1998. The delegation met again with Meles and Afwerki in Burkina Faso in November 1998 and devised a peace plan that came to be known as the Framework Agreement. The accord called for the withdrawal of Eritrean troops from Badme; the deployment of military observers by the OAU, with the support of the UN; the redeployment of Ethiopian and Eritrean troops from all contested areas; the delimitation and demarcation of the border with UN assistance; and the establishment of an OAU follow-up committee, with UN assistance, to implement the peace plan, which would be guaranteed by both organizations. The fact that the plan kept invoking UN assistance was a clear recognition that this was an *international* and not just an *African* problem but also reflected the OAU's financial and logistical constraints in implementing the accord.

In the largest military engagement in Africa since World War II ended in 1945, Ethiopia broke through Eritrean defenses at Badme in February 1999, forcing a hasty Eritrean retreat. Afwerki immediately accepted the OAU peace plan he had spent the last year deriding as biased. But Eritrea rejected Ethiopia's demands to withdraw from other disputed areas like Zalambessa and Alitena. Fighting continued in March and April 1999, before resuming in June 1999. The military balance shifted in Ethiopia's favor, and Addis Ababa would eventually use its overwhelming manpower to remove Eritrean troops from most of the disputed territories. At the OAU summit in Algiers in July 1999, African leaders endorsed the Modalities for the Implementation of the OAU Framework Agreement calling for a cease-fire, the withdrawal of both sides from disputed territory, and the deployment of military observers to supervise the withdrawals.

After the Algiers summit, representatives from the OAU, the UN, Algeria, and the United States—led by Anthony Lake, former US national security adviser—met and hammered out the technical details for implementing an accord, which included the deployment of a UN peacekeeping force. A UN Security Council mission was visiting Africa's Great Lakes region in May 2000, led by US ambassador Richard Holbrooke. They shuttled unsuccessfully between Addis Ababa and Asmara in a bid to halt the fighting.[18] In the same month, acting under Chapter VII of the UN Charter, the Council imposed an arms embargo on both parties, which several countries, including a permanent member of the Security Council, China, violated.[19] During a trip to Africa two years earlier, US president Bill Clinton had brashly named Meles and Afwerki as belonging to a group of Africa's "new leaders." American frustration at its failure to restrain two of its key African allies was clearly evident in the fact that Washington sponsored the UN resolution calling for the arms embargo on both countries.

As fighting continued, Algerian leader and OAU chairman Abdelaziz Bouteflika sent his special envoy, Ahmed Ouyahia, on a diplomatic shuttle between Addis Ababa and Asmara. Proximity talks finally resumed in Algiers in May 2000, with Anthony Lake and, to a lesser extent, the EU special envoy Rino Serri actively involved in the negotiations. These talks culminated in the signing of the Algiers agreement in June 2000, under which both parties called on the UN to establish a peacekeeping force, in cooperation with the OAU, to implement the Framework Agreement. In July 2000, the UN Security Council authorized the deployment of the UN Mission to Ethiopia and Eritrea (UNMEE).[20] The signing of another agreement in December 2000 in Algiers committed both parties to implementing the OAU Framework Agreement; to release prisoners of war; to allow an independent investigation into the origins of the conflict; and, most significantly, to agree to a neutral boundary commission to demarcate the common border between both countries, as well as another commission to decide on claims for damages.

The UN force, established at an annual cost of about $200 million, was mandated to monitor and verify the withdrawal of troops from both sides to prewar positions, monitor a zone of separation known as the Temporary Security Zone (TSZ), and assist in clearing landmines. Created under a Chapter VI mandate, the peacekeepers were authorized to use force in self-defense and to protect international civilians. The agreement also called for the establishment of a UN-chaired Military Coordination Commission (MCC) to resolve problems in implementing the accord. The MCC was to be composed of the UN, the OAU, and representatives of both parties. Botswana's long-serving permanent representative to the UN in New York since 1980, Legwaila Joseph Legwaila, was appointed as special representative of the Secretary-General to lead the UN mission. He was assisted by two deputies in Addis Ababa and Asmara. Dutch general Patrick Cammaert was appointed as UNMEE's first force commander. The 4,200-strong UN peacekeeping force, including 220 military observers, was to be withdrawn after the demarcation of the border between both countries.

UNMEE's largest contingents were initially from the Netherlands, Jordan, Kenya, Canada, and Denmark. For the first time in its history, the UN's Standby High Readiness Brigade (SHIRBRIG) arrangement was used and contributed to a quicker deployment of UN peacekeepers to the field. Western countries that initially contributed the largest contingents as part of the SHIRBRIG arrangement gradually reduced their presence in UNMEE, leaving India, Jordan, and Kenya as the largest contingents. The OAU Liaison Mission in Ethiopia-Eritrea (OLMEE), with forty-three military and civilian officials from Algeria, Ghana, Kenya, Nigeria, Tunisia, and South Africa, deployed alongside UN peacekeepers by December 2000 to undertake monitoring tasks similar to those of UNMEE.[21] A war that had resulted in nearly 100,000 deaths, displaced more than 1.2 million people, and put 10 million people at risk of famine, finally seemed to be over.

The early invisibility of the UN and the credibility of the OAU were questioned in the course of this dispute. Eritrea had always had a strained relationship with the OAU, an organization that had treated secession as taboo throughout its history and strongly supported the inviolability of colonial borders for the first three decades of its existence. Afwerki had described the OAU in 1993 as "a complete failure for thirty years,"[22] and regarded the Addis Ababa–based organization as pro-Ethiopia. During peace talks in Algiers, Ethiopia had insisted on a central monitoring role for the OAU. After disagreements erupted on the implementation of the Algiers accord in December 2000, Meles appealed to the OAU, while Afwerki appealed to the UN. It was clear that the participation of both the UN and the OAU would be essential to implementing the Algiers accords.

Implementing the Algiers Accords, January 2001–March 2002

By April 2001, UNMEE had verified the redeployment of Ethiopian and Eritrean troops. The Temporary Security Zone was established by April 2001, and the UN presented the final map of the zone to both sides two months later. But though the military battle had ended, both sides refused formally to recognize the TSZ and created obstacles to the full implementation of the Algiers accords. Eritrea particularly restricted the freedom of movement of UN peacekeepers in the fifteen-kilometer areas adjacent to the TSZ. The parties denied the UN permission to establish a direct high-altitude flight route between Asmara and Addis Ababa. Both sides questioned the boundaries of the security zone. Eritrea failed to provide information on its militia and police presence in the zone and refused to sign a status-of-forces agreement with the UN.

The MCC tried to resolve differences on the ground between the parties, with decidedly mixed results. By February 2002, the commission had held eleven meetings in Nairobi, Djibouti, and the Mareb River Bridge, a frontier between Ethiopia and Eritrea. The meetings discussed issues like ensuring freedom of movement for UNMEE soldiers, monitoring militia and police in the TSZ, establishing joint investigation teams for military incidents, providing mine information to the UN, overseeing the return of internally displaced persons, and repatriating the remains of soldiers from both sides. Despite the obstacles created by the two sides to resolving these issues, the ceasefire largely held, and Ethiopia and Eritrea respected the TSZ in practice if not always in principle.

An important innovation in this mission, and a lesson learned from previous UN peacekeeping efforts, was the provision of $700,000 to undertake quick impact projects in the areas of health, water, sanitation, education, and training during the first year of UNMEE's presence. The idea was to "win hearts and minds" by giving local populations a stake in the peace process through providing tangible signs of socioeconomic progress as a result of the presence of UN peacebuilders. To support its work after the initial funds had been disbursed during the first year of the mission, the UN Security Council established a special Trust Fund to Support the Peace Process in Ethiopia and Eritrea in July 2001. But these initiatives could only represent small gestures in the context of the huge development needs of both countries.

The boundary commission called for as part of the peace process was established by March 2001. The commission heard arguments from both sides in December 2001. Its decision on the demarcation of the border, scheduled for February 2002, was however postponed for two months due to logistical difficulties. One of the important observations that a boundary commission reconnaissance team made was that, since many border areas between Ethiopia and Eritrea were heavily mined, the demarcation of the boundary would necessarily be a slow and laborious process. These dangers were clearly demonstrated with twenty civilians being killed and fifty-six being injured by mines and unexploded ordnance between December 2001 and February 2003.

The Boundary Commission Decision and Its Aftermath, April 2002–July 2008

The boundary commission issued its decision on the delimitation of the Ethiopia-Eritrea border on 13 April 2002.[23] Both parties immediately rhetorically accepted the "April decision," which they had agreed beforehand would be binding. But soon after, Ethiopia, in particular, obstructed the implementation of the peace plan. Between 26 April and 6 May, Addis Ababa refused to allow UNMEE and boundary commission staff to cross from Eritrea into Ethiopia. The Ethiopians also questioned the impartiality of the commission and refused to deal with UNMEE force commander General Cammaert, holding him personally responsible for authorizing a flight by two international journalists to Badme from Asmara. As a result, the MCC did not meet for seven months. The border that had been delimited could also not be demarcated. After completing his tour of duty, Cammaert was replaced by British general Robert Gordon in October 2002.

In March 2003, the UN reported that Meles had threatened to reject the decision of the boundary commission if Ethiopia's concerns were not properly addressed. In response to a commission request for technical comments on its map for demarcating the border, Ethiopia submitted a 141-page report outlining its views of the measures needed to be taken to complete the demarcation process. In unusually strong language, the commission described Ethiopia's comments as "an attempt to reopen the substance of the April Decision . . . and to undermine not only the April Decision but also the peace process as a whole."[24] The commission further noted that it did not have the power to vary the boundary in ways that would avoid dividing local communities and transferring populations, but that it would be prepared to consider such boundary variations at the request, and with the agreement, of both parties.

Ethiopia and Eritrea finally released their remaining prisoners of war and civilian detainees by November 2002. A glimmer of hope lay in the fact that both sides had stopped shooting at each other for three years and were now waging war through other means, as occurred in Western Sahara (see Chapter 2). But amid the difficulties of implementing the Algiers accords, the humanitarian situation in both Ethiopia and Eritrea remained dire. Drought and the failure of the rains had led to massive crop failure and the death of livestock in both countries. Cereal production was also decimated in regions that were previously self-sufficient. Even the vengeful rain gods seemed to be expressing their rage at the manmade disaster wrought by two strong-headed guerrilla leaders.

A final resolution of the Ethiopia-Eritrea conflict was further complicated by the domestic political challenges that both Meles and Afwerki faced. A split in the TPLF in 2001 culminated in the arrest of senior party cadres after they had openly challenged Meles's leadership. Ethiopian security forces killed several students in 2001 and other protesters in 2002. After flawed elections in Ethiopia in 2005, about two hundred people were killed and thousands imprisoned.[25] The town of Badme had, however, become a lightning rod for the Ethiopian public. Their opposition to the boundary commission's apparent decision to award Eritrea sovereignty over this area was one of raw, deep-felt anger, and much of this rage was directed at Meles. Having sacrificed so much in the conflict to recover a territory invaded by Eritrea, many Ethiopians questioned why they had mobilized to fight for territory that now had to be surrendered to the "aggressor." Meles was in danger of losing face among his own people in a struggle that was very much about his political survival. Following his decision to agree to an impartial arbitration panel, old accusations of being an Eritrean Trojan horse were resurrected in Addis Ababa.[26] In Eritrea, Afwerki clamped down harshly on dissent and muzzled the independent media. In 2001, politicians, party cadres, and journalists were jailed for criticizing government policies. National elections were indefinitely postponed in December 2001. The government also shut down several churches and banned some religious denominations.

Ethiopia hosted a meeting of exiled Eritrean groups in October 2002, and Meles met with the leaders of Sudan and Yemen during the same month in a bid to isolate Eritrea diplomatically. Eritrea subsequently dubbed the trio an "axis of belligerence." Ethiopia's embassy in Asmara was closed down in December 2002. Addis Ababa's rejection of Asmara's offer to open Assab and Massawa ports to food aid in November 2002 provided more proof of how profound the resentment and distrust had become between the two countries. With both regimes facing internal governance challenges, Addis Ababa and Asmara massed troops near their common border, with Eritrea demanding the return of Badme as decided by the international boundary commission in 2002.

UN special representative Joseph Legwaila sought to push the Security Council to act in October 2005 when he noted: "I just hope people wake up and realize it is important we should deal with the [border] stalemate decisively to make sure it ends."[27] However, despite a UN Security Council threat to impose further sanctions on both parties in November 2005, Eritrea expelled Western UN staff from its country a month later, leaving mostly Asian and African peacekeeping contingents. The UN reduced its mission in Ethiopia-Eritrea from 2,300 to 1,700 by April 2007, as the security situation became increasingly tense with Eritrea deploying two thousand troops, tanks, and weapons in the UN-monitored TSZ from October 2006. Ethiopia also deployed troops near the TSZ as both sides dangerously rattled their sabers. In the Security Council, the pugnacious US permanent representative to the UN, John Bolton, rallied support from France, Japan, and others to consider a complete withdrawal of the mission. British ambassador Emyr Jones-Parry and UN Secretary-General Kofi Annan led the opposition to withdrawal.[28] With Ethiopia and Eritrea remaining intransigent, however, UNMEE was eventually withdrawn in July 2008, even as tensions remained high between both governments.

The role of the United States, a traditional ally of both Ethiopia and Eritrea and permanent member of the UN Security Council, could be vital in achieving durable peace in this dispute. The US "war on terrorism" under the George W. Bush administration between 2001 and 2008 massively increased the strategic value of the Horn of Africa. The establishment of an American base in Djibouti with 1,700 soldiers to track suspected terrorists in Somalia and Yemen was followed by US negotiations for the establishment of a military base in Eritrea. Washington also maintained close ties with Ethiopia, the preeminent military power in the Horn, in order to benefit from Addis Ababa's experience and intelligence in fighting Islamist networks in the region. In March 2003, Ethiopia had granted the United States overflight and basing rights to assist its invasion of Iraq. Both countries were also among only a handful of African states that had supported the US invasion of Iraq in 2003. Ethiopian troops had invaded Somalia at the behest of their American patron in 2006 but had failed to stabilize the country.

Sudan

In this next section I assess the dynamics of the conflict in Sudan, Africa's geographically largest country in June 2011 with nine neighbors (Egypt, Libya, Ethiopia, Eritrea, Kenya, Uganda, the DRC, the Central African Republic, and Chad) and a nation the size of Western Europe. I examine the conflicts in South Sudan—which raged since independence in 1956 with an interlude between 1972 and 1983, until a peace accord in 2005—and also the conflict in the western Darfur province that erupted in 2003. I address four key questions: First, what were the main domestic, regional, and external factors that fueled the conflicts in South Sudan and Darfur? Second, what were the key domestic, regional, and external factors that enabled the UN to deploy peacekeepers to both conflicts? Third, what have been the main challenges of implementing the peace accords in both cases? Fourth, what factors are likely to determine success or failure in South Sudan and Darfur?

Sudanese scholar-diplomat Francis Deng described his country's crisis, in 1995, as a "conflict of identities" in which marginalized groups rebel against intolerable domination from a dominant elite in control of both state and society.[29] He noted the irony of Africa's geographically largest state, with nine neighbors and a microcosm of the continent's Afro-Arab and religious diversity, being embroiled in a seemingly endless series of civil conflicts. At the core of the conflict is a Northern Sudanese elite that sees itself as Arab and has, in recent times, adopted a *jihadist* ideology that has sought not only forcibly to Islamize and Arabize other populations—particularly through a *sharia* decree in 1983 and also after Brigadier Omar al-Bashir's 1989 coup—but to subjugate them politically, militarily, culturally, and economically.[30] It should be noted, however, that there are also differences within this Northern Sudanese elite, and some of its members have worked with Southern Sudanese political groups.

It is often said that behind every "plot" is a British hand, and colonial social engineering by "perfidious Albion" between 1899 and 1956 also helped sharpen divisions between the Northern two-thirds and Southern third of Sudan, leaving the latter as an underdeveloped backwater that lacked both infrastructure and access to education, health, and other social services. Khartoum's rulers effectively inherited the British colonial tools of "divide and rule" policies in Sudan's provinces. Divisions within the South, Darfur, and other areas hindered efforts to forge a common front to their common oppressors in the capital.

Roots of the Conflict

Since independence in January 1956, Sudanese leaders in Khartoum have ruthlessly suppressed the country's "peripheries" in the South, East, and West. In the case of the South, this was done through the ideology of forced Arabization. A sectarian Afro-Arab Northern elite claimed to be *awlad al-balad* (children of the land) and, from the seventh century, treated other areas as *dar fertit* (lands of enslavable communities).[31] Squabbling, unstable political coalitions in Khartoum often fell from power after 1956, largely as a result of an inability to resolve the war with the South. By the 1960s, most of Khartoum's major parties were advocating an Islamic state. The wily autocrat Colonel Ja'far al-Numeiri seized power in May 1969 and eventually negotiated an autonomy agreement with the South in 1972, which Khartoum unilaterally abrogated in 1983, having exploited Southern divisions. Numeiri then cynically imposed sharia Islamic laws on the whole country in 1983 in order to outflank his Islamist opponents, before being overthrown in April 1985. John Garang's Sudan People's Liberation Movement/Army (SPLM/A) led the Southern rebellion after 1983, winning major military victories in 1988 and 1989. Khartoum responded by arming ethnic militias and turning them on Dinka populations in Jonglei and Lake provinces. The humanitarian crisis would force the UN to launch Operation Lifeline Sudan (OLS) in April 1989 to assist two million people facing famine in the South.[32]

Just as the military was pushing Prime Minister Sadiq al-Mahdi to end the war in South Sudan, Brigadier (later, General) Omar al-Bashir, in concert with the radical Islamist Hassan al-Turabi's National Islamic Front, seized power in Khartoum through a military coup in June 1989. He introduced *sharia* laws even more virulently than his predecessors, extending them even to non-Muslims in South Sudan. The simultaneous Islamization and militarization of society reflected the military-religious alliance that had seized power. Even as the war in South Sudan continued, rebellions eventually erupted against these oppressive policies by groups in Southern Kordofan, Blue Nile, Eastern Sudan, and Darfur. By 1991, Bashir sought to exploit splits in the South by arming Nuer groups against the majority Dinka. Khartoum's atrocities against its own citizens across the country were many: a massacre in the Darfurian town of ed Da'ien in 1987; killings and deliberate starving of displaced populations in Bahr el Ghazal in 1989; a massacre in the Southern city of Juba in 1992; and forced relocation of populations in the Nuba Mountains in 1992–1993, in which the systematic, grisly use of rape was employed in an attempt to destroy groups and create new identities more favorable to Khartoum's diabolical political, economic, and cultural hegemony.[33] The militias often became Frankenstein-like monsters that broke free of their deranged puppeteer-political masters in Khartoum to spread death and destruction across the country. Bashir oversaw a jihad against the South in which over two million people have been killed since 1956. It should also be noted that military groups in South Sudan, including the SPLM, also committed human rights abuses, though not on the scale of Khartoum. Khartoum also forged close economic ties with China, which helped it to increase its oil production and cemented economic ties with the rapidly industrializing Asian giant and permanent member of the UN Security Council.[34]

Regional Rivalries

Regional rivalries have also played an important role in Sudan's complex civil wars, with Egypt, Libya, Chad, Ethiopia, Eritrea, Uganda, and Kenya all playing a role in this extensive security complex that spans the Horn of Africa, East Africa, Central Africa, North Africa, and the Middle East.

Uganda's Idi Amin and Ethiopia's emperor Haile Selassie supported the Southern rebellion in the early 1970s. Khartoum was allied at this time with governments in Libya and Egypt. After Mengistu Haile Mariam's regicide against Emperor Haile Selassie in 1974, Ethiopia became the strongest supporter of South Sudan's rebel groups, and especially of John Garang's SPLM/A after 1983. Addis Ababa accused Khartoum of backing Eritrean secessionists. After 1989, Bashir moved closer to Libya and away from Egypt. Following Mengistu's fall in 1991, the SPLM lost its main backer and moved closer to Uganda and Kenya, both of which worried about Khartoum's jihadist ideology. Uganda and Eritrea broke off diplomatic relations with Sudan by 1995 as a result of such concerns. Sudan's relations with Ethiopia and Egypt also suffered following an assassination attempt on former Egyptian leader Hosni Mubarak in Addis Ababa in 1995 that was linked to Sudanese militants. With Turabi increasingly spreading a gospel of radical Islam and backing terrorist groups as well as supporting Iraq's invasion of Kuwait in 1990, Algeria, Egypt, and Tunisia also started to distance themselves from Khartoum.[35]

Nigerian leader General Ibrahim Babangida hosted peace talks in Abuja between May 1992 and May 1993 with Bashir's encouragement. Khartoum perhaps calculated that the Nigerians, having been through a bloody civil war between 1967 and 1970 in a conflict triggered by events between a largely Muslim North and Christian East in which the unity of the country had been preserved, would be sympathetic to its antisecessionist position. The Nigerians tried to draw Uganda and Kenya into the mediation to put pressure on both parties. The issues discussed included national identity, citizenship, and fundamental rights; power and wealth-sharing; and interim arrangements to draft a permanent constitution. Khartoum, however, insisted on an Islamic state and refused to allow the South any chance to assert a right to self-determination.[36]

From 1993, IGAD—a subregional body initially set up in 1986 to tackle drought—took the lead in efforts to mediate an end to Sudan's conflict. IGAD's Standing Committee on Peace in Sudan consisted of Kenya, Uganda, Ethiopia, and Eritrea. Western donors through the IGAD Partners Forum also played an important political and economic role, funding peace efforts and shielding the process from being wrecked by Libyan and Egyptian rival initiatives.[37] It was Bashir that had invited IGAD to lead mediation efforts. He thought key regional states would support him and hoped to use the weaker regional body to prolong the process and exploit divisions between its members, as he would later do in insisting on a weaker AU force in Darfur in 2004 over a more effective UN force.

IGAD mediators prepared a Declaration of Principles (DOP) in May 1994, covering such issues as self-determination and unity, state and religion, democracy and human rights, and political decentralization. The key point, however, was that the principle of self-determination for South Sudan through a referendum had been put on the table. Khartoum predictably rejected a secular state and the South's right to self-determination, seeking to play to African fears of a "domino effect" resulting from a chaotic unraveling of the colonial boundaries. Uganda and Eritrea blamed Khartoum for the breakdown of talks in September 1994 and subsequently withdrew from the negotiation committee. Kenyan leader Daniel arap Moi pushed Bashir to accept the DOP as a basis of negotiations in 1997. Complicating these efforts was a new parallel Egyptian-Libyan initiative, as Cairo undertook a rapprochement with Khartoum based on its longstanding fears about instability in Sudan negatively affecting its lifeline: the waters of the Nile. Egypt at this stage, along with Libya, publicly and vocally opposed the secession of the South and expressed its determination to seek to prevent it.[38]

By May 1998, war and drought threatened 350,000 Southern Sudanese as further peace talks resumed in Nairobi, the opening of which Ghanaian UN Secretary-General Kofi Annan attended. Further peace talks in Addis Ababa in August 1998 were attended by the Tanzanian secretary-general of the OAU, Salim Ahmed Salim, who would later play a leading mediating role on Darfur. The treacherous, shifting alliances of the Horn of Africa saw a rapprochement between Khartoum and Addis Ababa and, to a lesser extent, Asmara by 1999. The IGAD Partners Forum pressured the body to establish a dedicated secretariat for peace talks and to appoint a special envoy: Kenya's Daniel Mboya. In March 2000, the SPLA suspended its participation in talks after Khartoum bombed Southern civilian areas. Talks also stalled as Kenya, Eritrea, and Egypt squabbled for leadership of peace efforts.

The dynamic General Lazaro Sumbeiywo was appointed IGAD's chief mediator in 2001. He rallied mediators from Eritrea, Ethiopia, and Uganda, assisted by the UN, along with observers from the United States, Britain, Norway, and Italy to renew talks in May 2002 based mainly on the DOP.[39] The Machakos Protocol of July 2002 that emerged from these talks set out the status of state and religion and agreed to the right of self-determination of South Sudan. *Sharia* laws would be applied in the North but not in the South. Both North and South political leaders agreed to address the root causes of the conflict and to share power and wealth. The unity of Sudan was to be made "attractive" by both sides, and a six-year interim period was agreed, after which Southerners would vote for unity or secession from the North. In 2003, conflict broke out in Darfur that distracted Khartoum during the peace negotiations. But between September 2003 and September 2004, direct talks in the Kenyan town of Naivasha led to agreement on various issues, including power- and wealth-sharing and security arrangements, without IGAD mediators. Further talks took place in Nairobi resulting in both sides signing the Comprehensive Peace Agreement in January 2005.

External Friends and Foes

Sudan was a pragmatic US ally during the Cold War and supported the Camp David process that led to a peace treaty between Egypt and Israel. After Marxist Mengistu Haile Mariam seized power in Ethiopia in 1974, Ja'far Numeiri's autocratic regime became the main US regional counterbalance to Addis Ababa, receiving much economic and military support, despite the human rights rhetoric of the Jimmy Carter administration between 1977 and 1980. Washington also backed regimes in Egypt and Somalia to counter Soviet support of Libya and Ethiopia.[40] The right-wing regime of the Cold War–mongering US president Ronald Reagan between 1981 and 1988 massively increased this support, with Sudan receiving $900 million worth of aid in 1988–1989 and Washington training the seventy thousand–strong Sudanese army.[41] After the end of the Cold War, it was Bashir who had encouraged the United States to become involved in peace-making in his country under its assistant secretary of state for African affairs Herman Cohen.

US oil giant Chevron had discovered Sudan's oil resources in 1978. Due to political pressure from Washington, however—which branded Khartoum, whose leaders had hosted Al-Qaida chieftain Osama bin Laden between 1991 and 1996, as a "sponsor of state terrorism" in 1993— Chevron sold its concessions in 1992. The Bill Clinton administration (1993–2000) sought to isolate the regime in Khartoum for its human rights abuses and for supporting international terrorism. The Bashir government was accused of complicity in the World Trade Center bombing in June 1993, and Washington also frowned on its close ties with Iran and Iraq. The Clinton administration thus banned all bilateral aid and foreign assistance to

Sudan, and the US-dominated International Monetary Fund suspended Sudan's membership in August 1993 for its failure to repay its loans on a $17 billion external debt.[42]

The chair of the US House Foreign Affairs Subcommittee on Africa, Harry Johnston, also played an important role in temporarily uniting squabbling SPLM factions in 1993. President Bill Clinton appointed Melissa Wells as his special envoy to the IGAD peace talks in June 1994. To put pressure on Khartoum to negotiate an end to the conflict and to desist from supporting international terrorism, Clinton launched the frontline strategy in 1995 providing economic and military backing to Eritrea, Ethiopia, and Uganda with $20 million a year in "defensive weapons." In 1996, Washington withdrew its embassy staff from Khartoum and pushed the UN Security Council to impose sanctions limiting the travel of some Sudanese government officials as well as a ban on holding international conferences in Khartoum. Squeezing the noose tighter, Washington froze Sudanese assets in the United States and banned financial transactions with the country in November 1997. In response to the bombing of two US embassies in Nairobi and Dar-es-Salaam in August 1998, which resulted in scores of mostly African fatalities, the Clinton administration launched a cruise missile attack on Sudan's Al-Shifa pharmaceutical plant, which it erroneously described as a chemical weapons manufacturing site. Clinton appointed US congressman Harry Johnston as his special envoy to Sudan in May 1999. The legislator-turned-diplomat sought to unite Sudan's fractious opposition, to bring Egypt into the peace process as an observer, and to marginalize Libya.[43] But the Clinton strategy did not really achieve many results, devoting neither enough attention nor resources to this case.

George W. Bush took over the US presidency in January 2001. The terrorist attacks on New York and Washington, DC, nine months into his tenure, would radically alter Clinton's former approach of sticks-without-carrots, as Washington sought Khartoum's help in its "war on terror." After the 11 September 2001 terror attacks, Sudan also distanced itself from its former terrorist networks in a bid to end its international isolation and avoid incurring the wrath of the United States. SPLM leader John Garang skillfully exploited the sympathies of the "religious right" in the United States—a key constituency of the Bush Republican administration—portraying the South Sudanese conflict as oppression by a Northern Muslim oligarchy of a Southern Christian minority. Senator John Danforth had been appointed US special envoy for Sudan a week before the September 11 attacks. He at first pushed for an end to aerial bombing of civilians in South Sudan, a ceasefire to allow delivery of humanitarian assistance in the Nuba mountains, and an end to slave raiding. The US envoy was able to bring together government and SPLA delegations in the Swiss town of Buergenstock in January 2002 to agree to a ceasefire in the Nuba Mountains, which provided momentum to the IGAD talks.

Reflecting this new-found focus, the US Congress passed the Sudan Peace Act in October 2002, which required that the American president submit a six-monthly report to Congress on progress in the peace talks. Washington also used its presidency of the UN Security Council in November 2004 to convene a special session to push the Sudanese parties to reach agreement by the end of the year. But the US policy was somewhat schizophrenic: even as Washington accused Khartoum of committing "genocide" in Darfur, it continued to support the negotiation of the CPA with the regime and to cooperate closely with Sudan's security services to fight international terrorism.

The other key external actor in Sudan was China, another veto-wielding permanent member of the UN Security Council. One significant issue that has often been overlooked in the relationship between China and Sudan is that Khartoum actually appears to have initiated this courtship of the Asian dragon. Following its military coup in June 1989, the Bashir regime found itself financially bankrupt and diplomatically isolated. Within fifteen months of taking office, Sudan's leader visited Beijing. A $300 million arms deal with China emerged the following year, and Beijing would become in the next decade and a half the largest importer of, and investor in, Sudanese oil.[44] The malevolent guile and far-sightedness of Khartoum's diplomacy is one of the reasons why Bashir and his regime have been able to survive economically better than others, such as Zimbabwe's Robert Mugabe.

Having provided a background of the domestic, regional, and external dynamics of Sudan's conflict, the next focus will be on the role of two UN peacekeeping missions, assessing their performance. I begin with South Sudan before turning to Darfur.

South Sudan

The Peace Process

A power-sharing agreement was reached between Khartoum and the SPLM in Naivasha, Kenya, in May 2004, with US pressure and regional diplomacy by IGAD playing important roles. A Comprehensive Peace Agreement was subsequently signed in January 2005 with a three-headed presidency under the leadership of Omar al-Bashir. SPLM/A leader John Garang and Bashir's vice president, Ali Osman Taha, were the two principal negotiators who completed this triumvirate. The accord sought to end a conflict in which over two million people had been killed, four million internally displaced, and six hundred thousand rendered refugees in neighboring countries.[45]

The CPA consisted of four protocols, two framework agreements, and two annexes on implementation modalities. The parties agreed to redeploy their armed forces and establish a 39,000-strong joint integrated unit of soldiers from both sides; they agreed to disarmament, demobilization, and reintegration programs; an Agreement on Wealth Sharing dealt with the creation of wealth-sharing mechanisms for Sudan's provinces, while the Protocol on Power Sharing agreed to create a Government of National Unity and to devolve power to provinces and the government of South Sudan. Specific protocols were also agreed to for Southern Kordofan and Blue Nile provinces on administration and popular consultation. Another protocol was agreed to on the Abyei area on administration and a referendum in January 2011 as to whether or not the inhabitants of the territory would join an independent South (following a referendum) or remain in the North. An assessment and evaluation commission was to be established to monitor implementation of the CPA and to help support the idea of "making unity attractive." The commission was chaired until December 2007 by the seasoned Norwegian diplomat-politician and the UN Secretary-General's special envoy for humanitarian affairs for Sudan between 1998 and 2004, Tom Vraalsen. British diplomat Derek Plumbly replaced Vraalsen as chair in February 2008. Under the CPA, the international donor community agreed to finance postconflict reconstruction tasks and to act as guarantors against unilateral abrogation of the accord.

UN Secretary-General Kofi Annan appointed the dynamic Dutch former minister for development cooperation, Jan Pronk, as his special representative to Sudan, and Pronk assumed his duties in August 2004. The Dutch politician had been involved in the IGAD Group of Friends and known Bashir and several of his senior officials since the 1990s, having been closely involved in supporting the UN's Operation Lifeline Sudan.[46] The UN had sent a team to attend the final stages of the peace talks in Naivasha to ensure that implementation of peacekeeping was not delinked from peacemaking as had occurred, for example, with the Arusha accord in Rwanda in 1993 (see Chapter 3). Before accepting his appointment, Pronk had made two requests of Annan: to give him overall head of both the peacekeeping and development aspects of the UN mission in terms of management, policy guidance, and coordination and to be able to promote peace efforts in Darfur, which he rightly regarded as inseparable from peace in the South.[47] Both requests were granted, and Pronk sought to lead the UN's fractious fiefdoms to coordinate political and humanitarian efforts as well as to collaborate with Nigerian diplomat Baba Gana Kingibe, the AU special representative in Darfur, who was said not to have spent sufficient time with his troops in Darfur, preferring instead the comforts of Khartoum.[48]

The $1 billion a year United Nations mission in Sudan (UNMIS) was established as a multidimensional peace support operation. Headed by a special representative and two deputies, the mission was headquartered in Khartoum with offices in Southern Sudan, Darfur in the West, and Kassala in the East. Its main contingents were initially from Bangladesh, India, Nepal and Pakistan, and by 2010 regional states like Egypt, Zambia, and

Kenya had also contributed significant troops, as had China. Indian general Jasbir Singh Lidder (the former military chief of staff of the UN mission in Mozambique and the deputy special representative of UNMIS since January 2010) was appointed force commander to head the military mission, a position he held for two years. The UN peacekeepers were mandated to deploy a force with a maximum mandated strength of 10, 130 to the six areas of Equatoria, Bahr el Ghazal, Upper Nile, Nuba Mountains, Southern Blue Nile, and Abyei.

UNMIS was tasked to perform the following responsibilities: support implementation of the CPA by assisting both parties politically as well as helping to manage local disputes; support the assessment and evaluation commission in its mandate; cooperate with the AU in implementing the Abuja peace process on Darfur; monitor the ceasefire; protect civilians within the capability of the UN peacekeeping mission; assist the government of South Sudan in its development and governance tasks; help Sudan to reform its police service as well as implement disarmament, demobilization, and rehabilitation programs; assist in the conduct of elections in Sudan and referenda in the South and Abyei; establish a strong human rights presence in Darfur and monitor human rights throughout the country; assist humanitarian efforts as well as the return of refugees; and help mobilize international resources for Sudan's socioeconomic development. The UN was also mandated to participate in the ceasefire political commission, a ceasefire joint military committee, and area joint military committees.[49]

In May 2005, Kofi Annan visited the Horn of Africa. In Addis Ababa, he cochaired a meeting with Malian AU Commission head Alpha Oumar Konaré, where both called on the international donor community to support the expansion of the AU mission in Darfur. The UN Secretary-General then went on to Sudan where he urged both sides to ensure an inclusive approach to the CPA that involved parties that were not signatories of the accord.[50]

The urbane, but sometimes ruthless, SPLM leader, John Garang, had consistently been the most articulate proponent of the vision of a "New Sudan": mobilizing the country's "peripheries" to challenge Khartoum in creating a multiparty state in which the political, cultural, and socioeconomic rights of all citizens would be respected. Garang's death in a helicopter crash in July 2005 threatened to lead to further instability as violence erupted in Khartoum, Juba, and Malakal. But the situation was eventually calmed, and the vice president of South Sudan, Salva Kiir, took Garang's place in the interim government. By September 2005, the government of national unity was established. All the key political and military commissions of the CPA—such as the ceasefire political commission and the assessment and evaluation commission—also started functioning, while reconstruction efforts were initiated in the South under its own autonomous government. These efforts, however, remained daunting and clearly required enormous resources and capacity building to develop skilled personnel in South Sudan, which, though oil-rich, had very little infrastructure. The area had only sixty kilometers of asphalt roads in 2010.[51] International attention and resources were unfortunately diverted to Darfur, rendering much of the commissions and institutions of the CPA underresourced in a country in which 75 percent of females (90 percent in South Sudan) are illiterate.[52]

Challenges in the Implementation of the CPA

Despite its mandate's having been agreed to in January 2005, UNMIS started deploying only three months later. By December 2005, only 40 percent of UN peacekeepers had been deployed. Only in September 2006—twenty-one months after the UNMIS mandate had been approved—the mission reached its full strength. UNMIS tried, within its limited capacity, to defuse conflict situations and continued to conduct patrols. One positive development was, however, that the mission sought to coordinate its efforts with other UN missions and offices in the DRC, Kenya, Ethiopia-Eritrea, and CAR-Chad, trying to adopt the essential regional approach that the UN was pursuing in West Africa (see Chapter 5) and the Great Lakes region (see Chapter 3). This coordination, however, did not translate into a genuine regional strategy despite more frequent meetings. An internal UN review of UNMIS's mandate in February 2008 revealed that its greatest impact had been in areas where both sides had sought its assistance, but the document acknowledged that the peacekeepers were less effective when one side was unwilling to have the UN participate in local peace efforts. The review concluded that it was political will by both parties rather than any limitations in UNMIS's mandate that remained the major challenge to the mission's success.[53]

Though UNMIS met regularly with both parties and sought to bring political actors together across the country to resolve local issues, many problems hampered the implementation of the CPA. The SPLM sometimes looked to the region and external actors for support against Khartoum. In January 2007, Salva Kiir appealed to IGAD and its Partners Forum to implement the Protocol on the Resolution of the Conflict in the Abyei Area.[54] The SPLM suspended its participation from the government for two months in October 2007 over issues concerning the failure of the ruling National Congress Party (NCP) to consult the SPLM on key decisions, the disputed region of Abyei, the North-South border, sharing of oil revenues, and organizing a national census and elections. Bashir's NCP also accused the SPLM of siding with the Northern opposition to the government of national unity, of exceeding its powers in the government of South Sudan, and of delaying the redeployment of its forces from the southern Blue Nile and Southern Kordofan.[55]

The ceasefire joint military commission is one of the few bodies of the CPA that has had an impact on the peace process, having met one hundred times by October 2009. The important assessment and evaluation commission had held its fourth meeting by February 2006, and UNMIS joined as an exofficio member six months later. The ceasefire political commission started meeting in February 2006. The fiscal and financial allocation and monitoring commission and the national petroleum commission were also established by March 2006. Many of the bodies called for under the accord were established late and have not always met regularly or functioned effectively.

Local disputes in Sudan, fueled by the proliferation of small arms, led to thousands of fatalities in disputes over power struggles, forced disarmament, nonpayment of salaries, ill-disciplined soldiers, banditry, looting of food trucks, natural resources, land, water, and grazing rights in Western and Eastern Equatoria, Upper Nile, Jonglei, Warrab, Lakes, Unity, Bahr Al Ghazal, and Southern Kordofan. In a particularly egregious incident, over 450 civilians were killed in interethnic feuds in the Jonglei state in March 2009.[56] Between July and October 2009, at least 316 people lost their lives in fifty-four clashes in Jonglei, Upper Nile, and Lakes states.[57] Between January and July 2010, over seven hundred people were killed and more than 150,000 displaced in South Sudan.[58] UN peacekeepers were often powerless to stop most of these atrocities, even though they sometimes played a role in helping to stabilize volatile situations. In a clear sign of the dissipation of the "spirit of Naivasha," one of the most serious breaches of the ceasefire occurred in November 2006 when at least 150 people, including civilians, were killed following fighting in Malakal, Upper Nile, between the Sudan Armed Forces (SAF) and the SPLA.[59] The UNMIS-chaired joint military committee eventually helped end the fighting. The July 2007 deadline for the redeployment of the SAF north of the 1956 boundary was, however, also missed.

The SPLA disarmament programs in Upper Nile, which the UN supported, experienced many difficulties. In January 2006, a heavy-handed SPLA disarmament program in Jonglei led to clashes between its largely Dinka forces and local Nuer and Murle groups.[60] Similar exercises of civilian disarmament led to violence in Jonglei in May 2008. In April 2009, there was further heavy fighting between the Dinka and Nuer in Jonglei in which 195 civilians were killed. Two months later in the same province, thirty civilians and eighty-nine SPLA troops were killed when a food convoy was attacked.[61] By 2008, local communities in Eastern Equatoria refused to disarm due to the threat of attacks from Uganda's rebel Lord's Resistance Army (LRA) while continued violence in Jonglei and Lakes states ended comprehensive disarmament. Though protocols for Southern Kordofan and Blue Nile were implemented, the one on the disputed territory of Abyei continued to be obstructed.[62]

By March 2006, anti-UN campaigns were launched in Khartoum and other cities, which included vitriolic personal attacks on Jan Pronk.[63] Seven months later, Pronk met with rebel commanders in Darfur to urge them not to attack government positions. Before he could communicate his discussions to Khartoum, government troops had bombed the areas where he had met with the rebels. An enraged Pronk described this as a betrayal and indifference to the peace process on the part of Khartoum. The Dutch diplomat also unwisely kept a blog that highlighted some of the military weaknesses of the Sudan Armed Forces.[64] In the same month as this incident, Khartoum informed Kofi Annan that it had "terminated" Jan Pronk's mandate, declared him persona non grata, and given him seventy-two hours to leave the country. Despite the UN's protests, the Dutch politician was forced to leave, coming back for a brief farewell tour before his contract expired in December 2006. Pronk's Ethiopian deputy, Tayé-Brook Zerihoun, took over as acting special representative, until the Pakistani diplomat Ashraf Jehangir Oazi was appointed the substantive special representative in September 2007. After Pronk left, there was a lack of dynamism in the mission until February 2010, when Eritrean diplomat and former deputy UN special representative to the DRC Haile Menkerios replaced Oazi.[65]

On his visit to Sudan in September 2007, South Korean UN Secretary-General Ban Ki-moon appealed to both sides to resolve their differences peacefully and noted the UN's readiness to assist them in doing so. Government officials complained to Ban about the failure of donors to fulfill their pledges and called for the SPLM to play a fuller part in implementing the CPA. The SPLM, for its part, expressed frustration about the government's delay in redeploying its forces, in resolving the Abyei issue, in demarcating the border, and in sharing oil revenues in a transparent manner.[66] As the UN itself frankly admitted, the ceasefire political commission—which has met infrequently—failed to become a genuine decision-making body able to resolve issues referred to it by the ceasefire joint military committee.[67]

Despite the establishment of the government of Southern Sudan in October 2005, there were continued capacity constraints (lack of skilled personnel and physical infrastructure) as well as concerns about widespread government corruption. For example, between January and August 2007, the government of South Sudan received $778 million in oil revenues,[68] though it had limited administrative absorptive capacity and lacked well-established accountability systems. The overrepresentation of Dinkas in the government also created tensions with other ethnic groups and led to some of the divisions that Khartoum had been able to exploit within the autonomous Southern government between 1972 and 1983, when Equatorians had complained of the domination of the Dinka.[69] Nuer groups had also expressed similar sentiments.[70]

There were also tensions between Khartoum and Juba on the issue of wealth sharing, with regular complaints of delays in Khartoum transferring oil revenues to the government of Southern Sudan. By February 2009, oil arrears to the government in Juba had reached $210.65 million.[71] Instability was also often reported in oil-producing and exploration areas such as Upper Nile, with the SPLA accusing the Sudan Armed Forces of continuing to deploy in oilfields. (By the SAF's admission, 3,600 troops remained in South Sudan in August 2007, apparently to protect oil fields.[72])

Under the CPA, Abyei was to have been a bridge between North and South Sudan, but the area turned out to be very different in efforts to implement the accord, with UN peacekeepers' freedom of movement hampered from 2006. Tensions continued between Dinka Ngok and Massiriya groups in Abyei over cattle migration of these groups as well as land ownership disputes. Both Khartoum and Juba also squabbled over the report of the Abyei boundaries commission in July 2005 about the demarcation of the country's borders, which Khartoum rejected in March 2006. The case eventually ended up in the Hague-based Permanent Court of Arbitration by March 2009. The Court's ruling four months later led to further controversy by placing Higlig oilfields in the North outside the Abyei area, a decision the SPLM in turn challenged.[73] Khartoum's failure to appoint a local Executive Council in Abyei also delayed the delivery of social services to the people of this area.[74]

One of the most serious breaches of the ceasefire occurred in Abyei in May 2008 when a week of fighting between the SAF and SPLM effectively destroyed most of Abyei town, resulting in eighty-nine deaths and the displacement of over fifty thousand inhabitants. UNMIS was widely criticized for withdrawing its peacekeepers and not doing more to protect the town and its inhabitants. The UN noted that the mission had sheltered and escorted more than one hundred civilians in its compound to safety.[75] But many saw this as too little, too late. A UN Security Council delegation visited Khartoum and Juba in June 2008, with both parties agreeing to the deployment of new Joint Integrated Units and police as well as the redeployment of the SAF and SPLM from the area and free movement for UNMIS peacekeepers.

An Abyei Joint Integrated Unit became operational in August 2008, and SAF and SPLM troops started leaving the area. A UN Department of Peacekeeping Operations fact-finding team led by Dutch general Patrick Cammaert, former UN force commander to Ethiopia-Eritrea and UN force commander to the Eastern DRC, visited Sudan in August 2008 following criticisms of the peacekeepers in Abyei. The team noted that while most of Abyei's population had left the town before the fighting peaked, UNMIS had been able to protect some civilians in its compound. It also recommended a reinforcement of the UN mission in this area.[76] But more independent observers remained unconvinced about UNMIS's performance in Abyei.

The fragility of this area was again demonstrated in December 2008 when fighting erupted between members of the misnamed Joint Integrated Unit and Joint Integrated Police Unit, killing one person and injuring nine. UNMIS reacted more quickly this time, deploying armored personnel carriers. One positive development from these events was the establishment of the Abyei Area Administration in November 2008, which received some capacity-building support from UNMIS and UN development agencies.

Some progress was also reported in the implementation of the CPA. The SPLA had withdrawn from eastern Sudan by September 2006. Eighty percent of SAF troops had been redeployed by October 2007; and 81 percent of the Joint Military Teams had been established, though without the requisite trust and cohesion. Power had been peacefully transferred from the NCP to the SPLM in Blue Nile, and from the SPLM to the NCP in Southern Kordofan by 2007. All 46,403 SAF troops had been redeployed south of the border line by November 2009, and SPLA troops redeployed from Blue Nile and Southern Kordofan, though only 33.7 percent of their 59,168 troops had been redeployed by the same date.[77] The Joint Integrated Unit had also reached 84.7 percent of its authorized strength of 39,639 by October 2008,[78] though these units lacked proper communication, transport, weapons, and accommodation. UNMIS civilian police had also trained about eight thousand Southern Sudanese and Sudanese police officers in election security by January 2010.[79]

In July 2008, the Argentinian prosecutor of the Hague-based International Criminal Court, Luis Moreno-Ocampo, recommended that the Court issue an arrest warrant for Bashir for genocide, crimes against humanity, and war crimes in Darfur. Senior Sudanese government officials warned of dire consequences for UNMIS if their leader were indicted. In his report to the UN Security Council in January 2009, Ban Ki-moon sounded irritated with the ICC, noting that its "actions have a major impact on Sudanese political dynamics and have diverted much attention at a time when outstanding issues related to the Comprehensive Peace Agreement require the parties' cooperation and renewed commitment."[80] As expected, the arrest warrant was issued by the ICC in March 2009 on two counts of war crimes and five counts of crimes against humanity against the Fur, Masalit, and Zaghawa ethnic groups (and a second arrest warrant was issued in July 2009). In retaliation, Bashir expelled thirteen international NGOs, and demonstrations were held outside UN offices in Khartoum. The Barack Obama administration in the United States (though itself, like Sudan, not a member of the ICC) led opposition within the UN Security Council to a twelve-month suspension of the warrant as demanded by the AU.

Exposing again the huge mistrust between the parties and the continuing fragility of the CPA, fighting erupted again between SAF and SPLA elements of the misnamed Joint Integrated Unit in Malakal in Upper Nile State in 2009. At least sixty-two people were killed, about half of them civilians.[81] Even Ban Ki-moon admitted in a report to the UN Security Council in January 2010—a year before scheduled referenda in South Sudan and Abyei—that "a return to conflict remains a very real possibility" due to what he described as "the current atmosphere of pervasive mistrust."[82] In October 2009, the SPLM withdrew its parliamentarians from the National Assembly until outstanding issues relating to the referendum, Abyei, national security, and popular consultations had been settled. The national security and referendum bills were subsequently passed in December 2009. Juba also dropped its objections to the 2008 census results in exchange for forty additional Southern seats in the National Assembly, which effectively gave it a veto over legislation that it found unpalatable,[83] though these additional seats were not provided. The UN received reports of human rights abuses by security services in both North and Southern Sudan.[84]

The national elections commission—to which UNMIS provided technical support—had registered 16.5 million voters by December 2009. Thrice postponed national elections (originally scheduled for 2008) were eventually held in April 2010. Bashir won the presidential election with 68 percent of the vote. Despite SPLM presidential candidate Yassir Arman's late withdrawal from the poll, he still won 21.6 percent of the vote. In the Southern Sudan vote, Salva Kiir won the presidential election with 92.99 percent of the vote. Bashir's NCP won 72 percent of seats in the National Assembly to the SPLM's 22 percent. In the Southern legislature, the SPLM secured a 93.52 percent majority. After losing the poll, Jonglei gubernatorial candidate General George Athor began an armed rebellion, another sign of possible dangers to come in the fractious South.

In May 2010, a high-level strategic meeting between the AU and the UN (also involving IGAD, the League of Arab States, the Organisation of the Islamic Conference, the European Union, the five permanent members [P-5] of the Security Council, the assessment and evaluation commission, Finland, Italy, Japan, Norway, Qatar, and Sweden) in Addis Ababa agreed to establish a consultative forum to harmonize international efforts to implement the CPA, to shape postreferendum efforts, and to assist peace efforts in Darfur. The AU and the UN would chair the forum, which would meet every two months. In a sign of further progress, a referendum commission was appointed in June 2010. The parties could not agree on the referendum in Abyei and progress on the popular consultations in Southern Kordofan remained slow, due largely to the delayed census and elections in the state. The SAF and SPLA fired on each other across the border of Upper Nile and Sennar states in October 2010. Two months before the South Sudan referendum, Khartoum bombed the Southern Darfur/Northern Bahr El Ghazal border in November 2010 (claiming to be targeting Justice and Equality Movement [JEM] fighters), wounding four SPLM soldiers. The Bashir government subsequently accused the SPLM in the same month of harboring Darfur rebel groups (Juba retorted that it had merely treated wounded JEM soldiers).[85] All of these incidents suggested continuing profound mistrust between the two sides.

Regional Difficulties

There have also been regional issues that have complicated the UN's peace-keeping efforts in South Sudan. Having been pushed out of northern Uganda in a protracted two-decade conflict, the country's rebel Lord's Resistance Army and its splinter groups continued to employ its brutal tactics against civilians in South Sudan's Western Equatoria state, pillaging and killing innocent civilians, as well as abducting women and children along Sudan's borders with Uganda and the DRC. By 2010, over two thousand civilians had been killed, 2,600 abducted, and 440,000 displaced by the actions of the LRA.[86]

The Juba peace process was launched in 2006, but by 2007, LRA elements were operating in the DRC's Garamba Park. Peace talks continued periodically between the LRA and Kampala, though the rebel movement sometimes opposed South Sudan's government as an impartial mediator. Former Mozambican president, Joaquim Chissano, acted as the UN's special envoy for the LRA-affected areas. Six key protocols of a peace deal were signed by the LRA and Kampala in March 2008 but not the final accord. LRA leader Joseph Kony maintained sporadic contact with Chissano and the SPLM. The Ugandan warlord refused to sign the Juba Final Peace Agreement in November 2008, resulting in Ugandan, Congolese, and Southern Sudanese forces launching a joint military operation against the LRA in northern DRC. The resulting destruction of some LRA bases in the Congo forced the rebels to operate mainly in Western Equatoria, though the rebel movement still launched attacks from both the DRC and the CAR (see Chapter 3).

Ethiopia and Eritrea, having fought a devastating war between 1998 and 2000, continued to experience sporadic tensions. Sudan and Ethiopia, however, sought to improve ties by agreeing to closer cooperation in the areas of security, trade, agriculture, and health in March 2009. Egypt—which remained opposed to South Sudanese independence due to its fears of the diversion of the Nile waters—hosted meetings between both parties and pragmatically established an office in Juba. The fall of the regime of Hosni Mubarak following street protests in February 2011 meant that Cairo would for a while be faced with its own domestic political issues. Following an improvement in previously strained diplomatic relations between Khartoum and Asmara (full diplomatic relations were restored by June 2006), Eritrea also eventually played an active role in seeking to curb the violence in eastern Sudan, bringing the Eastern Front leadership to the negotiating table with Khartoum in June 2006, resulting in the signing of the Eastern Sudan Peace Agreement four months later. Through this deal, the Eastern Front gained posts in the Government of National Unity, and the state of emergency over Kassala and Red Sea provinces was lifted. A five-year $600 million Eastern Sudan reconstruction and development fund was established by April 2008. IGAD also continued to pursue an active role through its Ethiopian special envoy in Khartoum, Lissane Yohannes, continuing to warn both sides not to use border demarcation as an excuse to postpone the January 2011 referenda in South Sudan and Abyei.[87] But the subregional body's political divisions on Sudan among its members limited its influence on both parties.

External Actors

Despite a donor conference for Sudan held in the Norwegian capital of Oslo in April 2005, which pledged $4.5 billion, international funding of the CPA has been erratic. By December 2005, only 52.5 percent of funding needs for Sudan had been met.[88] The four largest funders were the United States, Britain, the European Union, and the Netherlands. The gap between pledges and delivery continued to be large, and by August 2008 only $1.24 out of $2.37 billion pledged for humanitarian programs in Sudan in 2008 had been delivered.[89]

Two external actors have played an important role in Sudan and the Greater Horn region: the United States and China. In December 2008, three weeks before the end of the George W. Bush administration, Washington had provided intelligence and logistical support and advisers for the Ugandan army to crush the LRA rebellion in the DRC, but the intervention failed to destroy the rebel group.[90] In May 2010, President Barack Obama signed into law the Lord's Resistance Army Disarmament and Northern Uganda Recovery Act, making it US policy to kill or capture LRA warlord Joseph Kony and to defeat his rebellion.[91]

In the area of peacemaking, by 2009 the US special envoy to Sudan, General Scott Gration, was using the tripartite mechanism to meet in Khartoum and Juba with the NCP and the SPLM, seeking to focus on the implementation of deadlines for elections, referenda, popular consultations, and border demarcation. In 2010, the number of American officials in Juba was tripled, and US secretary of state Hillary Clinton was talking of the "inevitable" secession of South Sudan by September 2010. During the UN General Assembly in New York in the same month, President Barack Obama met with Sudanese vice president Ali Osman Taha and president of Southern Sudan, Salva Kiir, with the US president insisting that the CPA be fully implemented in a timely fashion.[92] In November 2010, John Kerry, the chair of the US Senate foreign affairs committee, went to Khartoum and informed Bashir—on behalf of Barack Obama—that Washington would remove Sudan from its list of state sponsors of terrorism if he allowed a referendum to take place in the South in January 2011.[93] Washington later also promised restoration of diplomatic relations and an annulment of part of Sudan's $40 billion external debt.[94]

The dangers of China's high-profile role in Sudan were exposed when nine of its oil workers were kidnapped in Southern Kordofan in October 2008, and four of them subsequently killed after a botched rescue attempt.[95] Beijing had, by 2010, reduced its dependence on Sudanese oil, accounting for only 6 percent of its oil imports,[96] though China remained among the largest importers of Sudanese oil. Beijing did, however, establish a diplomatic presence in Juba in a bid to ensure a balanced relationship in the event of the emergence of an independent South.

A UN Security Council delegation visited Sudan in October 2010, stressing that the two referenda be held as scheduled in January 2011. The referendum in South Sudan was held on schedule and resulted in over 95 percent of voters choosing to secede in a serious indictment of Khartoum's fifty-year misrule. The AU and the UN urged a speedy demarcation of the border and the creation of a "soft border" regime that would foster continued trade and cooperation between North and South. But instability continued in the volatile Abyei area in June 2011, and the UN Security Council requested that Khartoum withdraw its troops from the area and an Ethiopian peacekeeping force be deployed amid reports of deaths and widespread displacement.

Darfur

Background to Conflict

Turning from the South to the West, Sudan's volatile, landlocked Darfur region (consisting of the three states of West, South, and North Darfur) has seen one of the worst humanitarian tragedies in the world. This represented the biggest test case for the African Union's new peacekeeping ambitions, and the organization did not emerge from this situation with flying colors. AU Commission chair Alpha Konaré and his commissioner for peace and security, Algeria's Said Djinnit, overestimated their organization's peacekeeping capabilities and clearly failed to learn lessons from previous difficult regional initiatives in places like Liberia, Sierra Leone, and Burundi, which the UN took over (see Chapters 3 and 5). An estimated three million people were internally displaced in Darfur, while over two hundred thousand sought refuge across the border in Chad. An estimated three hundred thousand people have also reportedly died as a result of conflict-related violence since 2003. Though an earlier SPLA-led rebellion in Darfur had been ruthlessly crushed by Khartoum in 1991, the fuse of the current crisis was lit in February 2003 when two mainly "non-Arab" rebel groups—the Justice and Equality Movement and the Sudan Liberation Movement/Army (SLM/A)—attacked government installations in Darfur. The rebels received support from Chad, Libya, Eritrea, and the SPLA. Khartoum was itself implicated in backing militias in Chad, the CAR, Uganda, Ethiopia, and Eritrea.[97]

Khartoum's Popular Defense Force (PDF) in Darfur was bolstered with "Arab" militias in the area who came to be known as Janjaweed: armed devils on horseback. These militias were provided with training, arms, and air cover by the government. They committed massive human rights abuses, burning "African" villages, raping women, and pillaging. The difficulty in calls for Khartoum to disarm the Janjaweed lay in the fact that the government had relied heavily on the militia in the early days of the conflict and only had tenuous control over many of its members. Bashir was also concerned that a weakening of his allies would strengthen the two rebel groups in Darfur.[98]

International attention on the Darfur crisis increased significantly in 2004. A ceasefire was negotiated in N'Djamena between all sides in April 2004 by host Chadian leader Idriss Déby, and the AU sent sixty military observers and a three hundred–strong protection force to observe it. The troops started arriving in June 2004 and were known as the African Union Mission in Sudan (AMIS I). AU commission chair between 2003 and 2008, Alpha Konaré, blazed the diplomatic trail to Darfur, closely followed by then UN Secretary-General Kofi Annan and the African American US secretary of state at the time, Colin Powell, in June 2004. The US House of Representatives voted unanimously to describe the situation in Darfur as "genocide" in July 2004, deeply conscious of the shame of the Bill Clinton administration in having instructed its officials not to describe the massacres in Rwanda as "genocide" in 1994 (see Chapter 3). The resolution called for action to stop the massacres, but Washington did not take any military action to enforce it. In the same month, the UN Security Council, having cynically ignored the crisis in Darfur for a year during the worst killings so as not to jeopardize the Naivasha peace process for South Sudan, finally roused itself to pass a resolution calling for the Janjaweed to be disarmed by August 2004. The AU and the UN both recognized that war crimes had taken place but stopped short of describing the situation in genocidal terms.[99]

An expanded AU mission in Darfur (AMIS II), composed mainly of soldiers from Nigeria and Rwanda, was authorized by the fifteen-member AU Peace and Security Council (PSC) in October 2004. The AU force included civilian police units to protect refugee camps, with the UN dispatching a handful of human rights monitors. The mission's mandate was to monitor and observe compliance with the ceasefire, build confidence among the parties, help establish a secure environment to deliver humanitarian relief and facilitate the return of internally displaced persons (IDPs) to their homes, and contribute to improving security in Darfur. AMIS II took over six months to deploy and was hampered by a failure to devise a sound logistics plan; weak capacity for financial management; lack of vehicles, furniture, oil, stationery, and communication equipment; bureaucratic red tape; lack of strategic intelligence and a clear mandate to use force; lack of linguistic and driving skills; and difficulties with securing accommodation. The US firm Pacific Architects and Engineers (PAE) was belatedly called in to provide logistical support, and by April 2005 the mission—under Nigerian force commander General Festus Okonkwo—had 328 vehicles. AMIS II had been authorized to deploy 2,341 military personnel, 450 military observers, 815 civilian police, and 26 civilian staff. Based largely on the recommendations of an AU-led assessment mission to Darfur, this number was increased to 6,170 military personnel and 1,560 civilian police.[100] Senior AU officials, however, rarely visited Darfur, a lack of visibility that may have demoralized their troops.[101]

The UN Security Council passed a resolution in July 2004 calling on Khartoum to disarm the Janjaweed and to arrest their leaders for human rights abuses. A joint implementation mechanism was also established to monitor progress, cochaired by Sudan's foreign minister at the time, Mustafa Osman Ismail, and then Dutch UN special representative to Sudan Jan Pronk. The mechanism involved the AU and the League of Arab States. By October 2004, all sides in Darfur were still dragging their feet in providing information on their fighters to the joint implementation mechanism. The security situation also deteriorated, with attacks and killings of civilians and policemen by government-backed and rebel fighters, as well as incidences of highway robbery and banditry. Pronk noted that Khartoum did not really take the UN Security Council very seriously, often dismissing it as an anachronistic body that frequently picked on Arab countries and selectively implemented its resolutions on Palestine, Lebanon, and Iraq.[102] Having uniquely deployed two peacekeeping missions in one country, the UN was also not used to dealing with a government as strong and wily as Khartoum.[103]

Between June 2004 and April 2005, over 179 ceasefire violations had been reported, and more than seven hundred more people killed in Darfur.[104] Most violations at this stage were attributed to the SLM/A.[105] Government forces fought the SLM/A in North and South Sudan, while rebel attacks were launched in eastern Darfur and in the area of oil facilities in west Kordofan. The Sudan Armed Forces used often indiscriminate air bombardment and helicopter gunships in pursuing the rebels, leading to countless civilian deaths. It often worked with the brutal Janjaweed militia to burn and terrorize villages.[106] Attacks on camps of internally displaced persons (from which rebel groups sometimes recruited) also resulted in countless deaths of innocent civilians. The rebels kidnapped and killed humanitarian workers and seized their vehicles, shot at their helicopters, as well as attacked humanitarian relief trucks. Adding to this anarchic situation, clan-based militias also staged armed attacks against each other, with civilians often caught in the crossfire. AU peacekeepers were also killed: five lost their lives in October 2005 after a suspected attack by SLM/A militia. As in South Sudan, cattle rustling was also a major casus belli between local groups.

By 2005, 2.5 million people in Darfur needed humanitarian assistance, and 1.6 million had been internally displaced.[107] The agreement that Khartoum had reached with UN Secretary-General Kofi Annan during his visit to Sudan in July 2004 was being continually violated: the Janjaweed were not disarmed but integrated into Khartoum's army and police,[108] and they continued to attack civilians, while Khartoum did not deploy a strong and credible police force nor keep militias out of the vicinity of camps for internally displaced persons. The UN Security Council continued to pontificate from New York in declaring the conflict a "threat to international peace and security" and demanding that Khartoum fulfill its commitments. But such paper resolutions were meaningless to changing the volatile situation on the ground. More positively, permanent Security Council members the United States and Britain (along with the Netherlands and Canada) assisted AMIS with meals, accommodation, vehicles, and helicopters, though not to the required needs. A joint commission involving the Sudanese parties, the AU, the UN, and regional governments such as Chad, Gabon, Congo-Brazzaville, Libya, Nigeria, and Egypt continued to meet regularly to seek implementation of peace accords, but agreements were often violated even before the ink had dried on them.

The SLA/JEM and some civilians called for the UN to take over the AU's peacekeeping tasks. Seven rounds of inter-Sudanese peace talks were held in Addis Ababa and then mostly in the Nigerian capital of Abuja between 2004 and 2006, many of them while Nigerian president Olusegun Obasanjo chaired the AU.[109] These talks were eventually held under AU chief mediator and former OAU secretary-general Salim Ahmed Salim from June 2005. A declaration of principles was eventually devised that built on the N'Djamena ceasefire agreement of March 2004, which had established an AU-chaired ceasefire commission. The talks, as in South Sudan, focused on security, wealth sharing, power sharing, and the reconstruction of Darfur. But unlike in the South, there was no opportunity for self-determination for the rebel groups.

The Abuja talks led to the crafting of the Darfur Peace Agreement (DPA) in May 2006, which only the government in Khartoum and one of the SLM factions—headed by Minni Minnawi—signed, but not the France-based Abdul Wahid Al-Nur's SLM faction nor the JEM of Khalil Ibrahim.[110] Both warlords refused to sign, partly because the text did not envisage an autonomous Darfur region.[111] Fighting also continued during most of the negotiations, while the SLM split further complicated issues. Senior representatives from the United States, Britain, Canada, and the EU parachuted into Abuja for the final stages of the talks in a vainglorious bid to knock heads together to reach a deal. Rather than working with the AU team, they effectively took over the negotiation. Nigerian president Olusegun Obasanjo, famously lacking diplomatic finesse, scolded recalcitrant warlords like a hectoring schoolmaster. Deputy US secretary of state Robert Zoellick threatened nonsignatories whom he referred to as "outlaws" and arrogantly read letters from President George W. Bush to them while ignoring their genuine grievances.[112] The accord was unsurprisingly soon rendered a dead letter.

The proliferation of mediators in Sudan has also often encouraged rebel factions to engage in "forum shopping." UN special representative Jan Pronk tried to bring some coordination to these efforts by convening a meeting of special envoys on Darfur in Khartoum in November 2005 with troubleshooters from the AU, the EU, the League of Arab States, the United States, Britain, France, Germany, Norway, Canada, and the Netherlands. UNMIS also continued to provide AMIS with logistics, communications, transport, and assistance in public information and humanitarian issues. Pronk would, however, later note that there was not much enthusiasm for the Abuja accord within the UN Secretariat in New York.[113] Even after the talks in Abuja, Khartoum continued its heavy-handed response to protests, killing at least six internally displaced persons in the first six months of 2006 as demonstrations occurred in camps in Zalingei, Nyala, and El Fasher. Armed attacks also continued against villagers and other unarmed Darfuris.[114]

The situation in Darfur has also been complicated by regional rivalries. The SPLA and Eritrea were early suppliers of arms to the SLA, and the Chadian military has armed JEM.[115] By November 2005, there were reports of defections from the Chadian army to join rebellions of their ethnic kinsmen based in Darfur.[116] Difficult relations between Sudan and Chad were further strained by reports of an attack by Chadian opposition groups on the country's border town of Adre in December 2005, leading to both countries mobilizing their troops along their common border.[117] While Sudan hoped to use Chadian rebels to curb the rebellion in Darfur, Chad sought to use Sudanese rebels to secure its border. Libya had long played a historical role in Chad: Muammar Qaddafi had regularly sent troops and backed assorted warlords in the country from the 1970s. Libya even occupied Chad's Aouzou strip between 1973 and 1994, claiming it as part of its country until the issue was settled through international arbitration in favor of Chad. More recently, Qaddafi hoped to use a mediating role to raise his profile following years of Western-led diplomatic isolation.[118] France—a permanent

UN Security Council member—had also traditionally played a role in this region, supporting the autocratic regime of Idriss Déby (providing him with logistics and intelligence after a rebel attack in December 2005[119]) and helping, with Chadian rebels, to install General François Bozizé in neighboring CAR in March 2003.[120] France had kept troops in Chad and intervened there since the 1960s.

The Evolution of an AU/UN Hybrid Force

The UN sent an assistance cell to Addis Ababa under General Henry Anyidoho, the Ghanaian former deputy UN force commander in Rwanda during the 1994 genocide, to work with the AU in planning the military mission to Darfur. Only one full-time professional staff was dedicated to Darfur in the AU commission in Addis Ababa. Anyidoho started work in January 2005 and quickly won the trust and confidence of AU officials in Addis Ababa.[121] Following a meeting in New York between Kofi Annan and the chair of the AU commission, Alpha Konaré, in February 2005, the AU led an assessment mission to Sudan also involving the UN, the EU, and the United States. The mission suggested a three-phase support of AMIS: first, AMIS should reach operational effectiveness by the end of May 2005; second, the force would be expanded to 5,887 soldiers and 1,560 police between June and August 2005; and third, a multidimensional mission of twelve thousand peacekeepers (military and police) would be established to stabilize Darfur.[122]

In late 2005, the EU announced that it would no longer fund AMIS, and Brussels, along with Kofi Annan (and the UN Department of Peacekeeping Operations), pushed for a UN force to replace the AU mission.[123] John Bolton, the US permanent representative to the UN at the time, noted that France was skeptical of a purely UN mission in Darfur as it feared that such a force would drain resources from more strategic missions for Paris, such as the one in Côte d'Ivoire. Bolton further noted that French ambassador Jean-Marc de La Sablière only fully supported the role of the world body in Darfur when the French-backed regime of Idriss Déby was in danger of being toppled by the instability between Sudan and Chad.[124] Both China and Russia, having earlier opposed a UN force in Darfur (partly out of fear that it would have Chapter VII peace-enforcement powers[125]), eventually supported the hybrid force with an "African character" that emerged as the compromise solution. Two African permanent representatives—Ghana's Nana Effah-Apenteng and Tanzania's Augustine Mahiga—also pushed strongly for the hybrid force.

The world was finally waking up to the tragedy in Darfur. AMIS's troop strength had reached 6,706 by October 2005. The clashes between government forces and their allied militias and rebels, however, continued throughout 2006, again resulting in hundreds of civilian casualties and the burning and pillaging of villages. The Sudan Armed Forces, SLM-Abdul Shafi, the SLM-Minnawi, and JEM were often the most prominent groups in these attacks. Eleven AMIS peacekeepers were killed in armed attacks between February and July 2007, as well as a UN peacekeeper from the advanced team for the light support package for AMIS.[126] A tripartite committee consisting of Sudanese government officials, the UN, and the AU also started to meet in December 2006 and was helpful in resolving some of the deadlocks involving harassment of UN staff and delays in releasing UN equipment in ports but not in addressing the fundamental conflict in Darfur.

The cross-border situation between Sudan and Chad also worsened the security situation in Western Darfur, as each side continued to support each other's rebels who were based on its territory. Following a rebel attack on the Chadian capital of N'Djamena that nearly led to the ouster of Idriss Déby in April 2006, Chad severed diplomatic relations with Khartoum and subsequently declared itself to be in a "state of war" with Sudan. JEM fought alongside its fellow ethnic Zaghawa clansmen to protect the Chadian government. France again provided military support to prop up Déby's autocratic regime.[127] Chadian armed rebels continued to launch attacks into the country from Darfur, which were repelled, with the Chadian army then launching attacks into Sudanese territory in pursuit of the rebels. Tripoli often sought to mediate between Khartoum and N'Djamena. A particularly horrific attack by Arab militia from Chad on two Sudanese villages in Western Darfur resulted in about three hundred deaths in March 2007.[128] Armies from both sides clashed directly on Sudanese territory a month later, raising the specter of full-scale war between the two countries. An accord brokered by Saudi Arabia in Riyadh in May 2007 saw Déby demanding that Sudanese troops withdraw from Chadian territory. Only in November 2008 did Khartoum and N'Djamena restore diplomatic relations, but within two months tensions were again reported after the unification of several Chadian armed groups in Sudan and provocative statements by Déby during a visit to the border area.[129]

In order to maintain stability in Chad, France manipulated the deployment first of an EU bridging force (EUFOR) in the border area of Chad and the CAR between 2008 and 2009, before using its permanent seat on the UN Security Council to ensure the deployment of a self-interested UN force between 2009 and 2010. In both cases, Paris was effectively multilateralizing its previous unilateral interventions in Africa, which had become widely discredited after the Rwandan genocide of 1994 (see Chapter 3). France was effectively getting its European partners and the broader international community to pay for its policies of keeping the autocratic but shaky regime of Déby in power. Historically, France had pushed the UN Security Council to approve a 1,350-strong UN Mission in the Central African Republic (MIN-

URCA)—consisting largely of francophone troops from Gabon, Burkina Faso, Chad, Mali, Togo, and Senegal, who had been part of a French-funded eight hundred–strong force deployed in 1997—which sought to provide stability to an important French neocolony between April 1998 and February 2000. Meanwhile, 1,400 French troops based in the CAR departed a country in which Paris had maintained a military base until 1998.[130] The more recent 2,159-strong UN Mission in the Central African Republic and Chad (MINURCAT)—consisting largely of troops from Nepal, Ghana, Togo, and Mongolia—replaced the EU force and was deployed between July 2009 and December 2010. The UN mission trained Déby's security forces, patrolled refugee camps and IDP sites, and protected UN humanitarian convoys seeking to assist 255,000 refugees and 137,500 IDPs in eastern Chad.[131]

Returning to Darfur, working with the AU/UN Joint Mediation Support Team (JMST), Salim Salim and Jan Eliasson, the AU and UN special envoys, embarked on continuous mediation efforts in a bid to make the Darfur process more inclusive of other warring groups, civil society, and traditional leadership. They traveled to Sudan frequently and held meetings with key regional and external actors in Geneva, which the permanent members of the Security Council also attended. Both envoys attended meetings with regional players (Sudan, Chad, Egypt, and Eritrea) often hosted by Libya.

On assuming office as UN Secretary-General in January 2007, one of Ban Ki-moon's first meetings was with Salim and Eliasson in New York that month to discuss Darfur, which he identified early in his tenure as a key priority. In the same month, Ban attended the AU summit in Addis Ababa where he met with key leaders, including Omar Bashir, to discuss the proposed AU/UN hybrid peacekeeping force to be deployed in Sudan's volatile province. The Secretary-General sought to confirm Khartoum's acceptance of the three-phase UN support of AMIS: first, providing a small number of advisers; second, delivering a "heavy" package of support to AMIS involving 2,250 military personnel, three police units, as well as transport and engineering units, aircraft and helicopters; and, third, the deployment of a full hybrid force. He also reiterated Kofi Annan's agreement to retain the "African character" of the hybrid force, with the core remaining troops coming from the continent.

The Bashir government in Khartoum had long resisted a strong UN presence in Darfur (despite the existence of a ten thousand–strong UNMIS force largely in South Sudan to oversee the implementation of the CPA), branding it an effort by the West to extend its "neocolonial" influence to the area. Instead, Bashir insisted on the continued presence of an ineffectual AU force that was clearly unable to keep the peace. Diplomatic pressure exerted by China—one of five veto-wielding permanent members of the UN

Security Council—appears to have been instrumental in twisting Bashir's arm by June 2007. Beijing reversed its traditional, largely rhetorical policy of "nonintervention" in internal African affairs to convince Khartoum—from which China buys much of its oil in Africa—to accept a UN force, apparently under Western threats of a boycott of China's showpiece Olympics in 2008.[132] The AU was also critical to convincing Bashir to accept the force, with its commission chair, Alpha Konaré, supporting Khartoum's insistence on retaining the "African character" of the mission.[133]

Critics like Ugandan scholar Mahmood Mamdani employed the same argument as Bashir in depicting a UN intervention as a "civilizing mission" that would be "imperial."[134] This argument showed a startling lack of basic understanding of international peacekeeping. It was also a bizarre depiction for a force that was led by the UN—the most legitimate global intervener with six other missions in Africa in 2007 and over 70 percent of its peacekeepers having been deployed on the continent—and consisted mostly of African troops. Mamdani aimed much of his vitriol at the American strawmen of the Save Darfur advocacy movement, crudely and insultingly describing the movement as "the humanitarian face of [George W. Bush's] . . . War on Terror."[135] The Ugandan scholar's dismissal of this movement seemed about as intelligent as dismissing the antiapartheid movement on US college campuses in the 1980s as Cold Warrior allies of the conservative President Ronald Reagan. There were, of course, many naive individuals in both groups who did not properly understand the dynamics of the conflicts in Darfur and South Africa, but was this really a reason to denigrate well-meaning individuals wanting to help their fellow human beings?

Mamdani also rather insensitively noted that there were more deaths from the US-led occupation of Iraq than in Darfur, as if this somehow wiped away the millions of displaced and dead in Darfur. The Ugandan scholar's counterproductive approach is, of course, unlikely to build necessary support for genuine suffering in African conflict situations from Western governments and populations. It also ignored the lack of financial and logistical capacity of African peacekeepers that led the UN to take over regional missions not only in Darfur but also in Burundi, Liberia, and Sierra Leone (see Chapters 3 and 5). Schizophrenic African scholars really must make up their minds about Western intervention: when the West did not intervene in Rwanda in 1994, they charge racism; when Western actors try to push for intervention in Darfur, they charge "imperialism." In both cases, there are millions of victims who suffer, even as scholars in ivory towers conduct esoteric academic debates totally divorced from the realities of widespread suffering on the ground. Nigerian Nobel literature laureate Wole Soyinka was much closer to the mark than Mamdani in describing Darfur as "the greatest crime against humanity on the African continent since the killing spree of Rwanda."[136]

Returning to the Darfur peace process, in July 2007, the UN Security Council approved the deployment of twenty-six thousand peacekeepers to the province to take over AMIS's mission by December 2007.[137] The former foreign minister of Congo-Brazzaville, Rodolphe Adada, was appointed joint special representative of the AU/UN Hybrid Operation in Darfur. Nigeria's respected former chief of defense staff and former deputy UN force commander in Sierra Leone, General Martin Luther Agwai, was appointed its force commander. Both arrived in the mission area in July 2007. General Henry Anyidoho, who had been heading the UN's assistance cell to AMIS since 2005, was appointed as Adada's deputy.

UNAMID's Baptism of Fire

The $1.8 billion-a-year AU/UN Hybrid Operation in Darfur's main mandate was to oversee the implementation of the Darfur Peace Agreement of May 2006 and to protect civilians.[138] Though there was agreement that the force should have a "predominantly African character," there were serious doubts whether Africa's overstretched armies had sufficient military capacity to undertake such a mission successfully. The main contingents would be formed from AMIS's backbone: four battalions each from Nigeria and Rwanda; one each from South Africa and Senegal; and additional troops came from Ethiopia, Egypt, Burkina Faso, Gambia, Tanzania, Sierra Leone, as well as Bangladesh, Nepal, China, and Thailand. Khartoum refused to allow the deployment of a Nordic contingent, again highlighting its desire to have a logistically weak force. UNMIS provided some financial and logistical support to UNAMID's initial efforts due to the delay in approving the mission's budget. The force, though, struggled with poor military equipment, with donors having to support several contingents. The peacekeepers also struggled with a lack of helicopters and poor transport.[139] Much of the initial period of the mission was spent equipping and training rehatted AU contingents. Accommodation was scarce and tents had to be set up for the peacekeepers across Darfur.

A month after the mandating of UNAMID, twelve AMIS peacekeepers were brutally murdered at their group site in Southern Darfur in September 2007, underlining the dangerous environment in which peacekeepers were being deployed in which there was no peace to keep. The ceasefire commission continued to meet, but the warring parties continued to talk peace while waging war. Fighting continued and even spread to the oil field of Abyei by December 2007. JEM and regular Chadian soldiers launched joint attacks into Western Darfur in the same month.[140] A week after the transfer of authority from AMIS to UNAMID, the peacekeepers faced a baptism of fire as the warring factions sought to test their mettle. The lack of helicopters and logistical equipment would also prove particularly problematic for UNAMID, limiting its ability to conduct effective military patrols and evacuate wounded staff and civilians. To compound the problem, Darfur also had notoriously bad roads with 1,400 miles separating the UN supply line between Port Sudan and Darfur.

Continuing the proliferation of peacemaking initiatives that sometimes made the Sudan case resemble a moving diplomatic circus, France had convened a meeting of the enlarged contact group for Darfur in June 2007. A Dakar contact group, the League of Arab States, and the governments of the Netherlands, Qatar, and Russia were also involved in mediation efforts. Further peace talks were held in Arusha, Tanzania, in August 2007, led by Salim Salim and Jan Eliasson, with Darfuri rebel groups that had not signed the DPA. In attendance were JEM, the Sudan Federal Democratic Alliance, the National Movement for Reformation and Development, SLM-Unity, SLM-Abdul Shafi, and SLM-Khamis. Abdul Wahid, leader of another SLM faction, was absent from the discussions. Representatives of Chad, Egypt, Eritrea, and Libya were also present. Issues of wealth sharing, power sharing, land, security, and humanitarian assistance were discussed.

But despite these efforts, the security situation deteriorated while UNAMID's freedom of movement and ability to monitor or prevent the violence continued to be hampered by both the government and rebels. Peace talks were held in the Libyan town of Sirte in October 2007 in efforts to unify some of the rebel movements to be able to assist facilitation efforts.

The security situation in Western Darfur continued to worsen, and tensions between Chad and Sudan were also heightened even as the SAF continued to fight JEM and SLM/A-Abdul Wahid rebels. Men on horses and camels also attacked villages in interclan fights in Southern Darfur. Cattle continued to be rustled, fueling further communal conflicts. In January 2008, Chadian armed groups attacked N'Djamena in a bid to topple Déby before the rebels retreated into Western Darfur. In an attack of stunning audaciousness in retaliation, Darfur's JEM rebel group attacked Khartoum's twin city of Omdurman with about one thousand fighters in May 2008, an attack eventually repulsed by government troops. A reported fifty-seven civilians, seventy-nine government soldiers, and 329 JEM rebels died in this attack.[141] Sudan accused Chad of supporting JEM rebels and cut off diplomatic relations with N'Djamena. Chad retaliated by closing its border with Sudan. Khartoum and N'Djamena were still unleashing their "dogs of war"—proxy rebels—against each other from their territory in a macabre game of tit for tat. UN Security Council permanent member France again intervened to save the Déby regime from falling in 2008. Many questioned whether the French-led EUFOR in Chad/CAR was not an attempt to multilateralize Paris's historical support for African autocrats. Diplomatic relations were fully restored between Sudan and Chad in November 2008, and both countries started joint patrols of their common border. By July 2009, however, Chadian government forces were reported to have attacked Sudanese border villages, with soldiers from both countries exchanging fire,[142] and cross-border incursions by both sides were still being reported in November 2009.[143]

In April 2008, the clashing egos of competing warlords continued to stall progress in peacemaking: SLM/A's Abdul Wahid insisted that he would only negotiate if the security situation improved; JEM's Khalil Ibrahim argued that only his group and the SLM/A be represented at peace talks; while SLM/A's Abdul Shafie complained about the format, location, and timing of talks.[144] Former Burkinabè foreign minister Djibrill Yipène Bassolé started work as the new AU/UN chief mediator for Darfur in August 2008, ending the previous two-headed mediation team of Salim and Eliasson. While Bassolé shuttled between capitals and factions, instability continued in this volatile region in the second half of 2008. Bassolé convened two meetings in the Qatari capital of Doha between Khartoum and JEM between February and June 2009. The talks were deadlocked as JEM insisted that the government release its prisoners before peace talks, while the government insisted on a ceasefire before releasing JEM prisoners. Bassolé also met with the Tripoli Group (five Darfuri rebel movements) in Sirte in June 2009 and sought to consult Darfuri civil society and traditional leadership. The Burkinabè diplomat appeared to be far more active than Adada, the Congolese UN special representative. The United States also sought to unite various SLA factions in Addis Ababa,[145] as the splintering of unstable factions continued to complicate peacemaking efforts, while the EU's conflict management efforts were led by seasoned Danish diplomat Torben Brylle.

UNAMID's civilian staff was harassed by Sudanese security officials and its peacekeepers also started to be murdered: in a ghastly attack in July 2008, seven peacekeepers on a patrol were killed and twenty-two wounded. In a particularly horrific incident in Kalma camp in August 2008, Sudanese government troops killed thirty-two IDPs and wounded at least eighty-five more in an apparent search for arms.[146] UNAMID only had 12,541 peacekeepers deployed (64 percent of its authorized strength of 19,555) by January 2009, a year after it had taken over peacekeeping responsibilities from AMIS. The United States helped airlift some of the troops without charging the UN. Between July and November 2009, UNAMID peacekeepers were attacked in four separate actions, leading to one death and two serious injuries.[147]

The AU High-level Panel on Darfur, led by former South African president Thabo Mbeki, was inaugurated in March 2009 and issued its report in October 2009. The panel did not pull its punches on what it described as the "extreme violence and gross human rights abuses" that have taken place in Sudan. The AU heads of state, though not the UN Security Council, endorsed Mbeki's report. The role of this panel was then extended to one of attempting to coordinate international diplomatic efforts on Sudan alongside the UN. This development understandably created tensions, and some saw as a "power grab" the fact that a high-level blue-ribbon panel could transform itself into an implementing one. Though Mbeki enjoyed the confidence of Khartoum, some in Juba were wary of his perceived closeness to Bashir.[148] There was also some history that threatened to complicate diplomatic efforts: as South African president, Mbeki had unceremoniously stepped down as the chief mediator in Côte d'Ivoire in October 2006 after prodding by ECOWAS (see Chapter 5). He had been replaced by Burkina Faso with its foreign minister, Djibrill Bassolé, who was now working as the UN/AU chief mediator for Darfur, playing a lead role. Concerns were therefore raised that the famously politically ruthless Mbeki might use his position as a chance for diplomatic one-upmanship over Bassolé.[149]

Both UN special representative Rodolphe Adada and force commander General Martin Agwai completed their tours of duty in August 2009. Adada proved to be somewhat ineffectual in his role and did not enjoy much visibility or spend that much time with his troops or visiting camps for the internally displaced.[150] There were also reports of tensions between the Congolese diplomat and his Ghanaian deputy, General Henry Anyidoho, who was apparently often not kept in the loop.[151] Agwai—who was criticized for frequent travel abroad to attend seminars—raised eyebrows on the eve of his departure when he publicly noted that the conflict in Darfur was over, arguing that: "Banditry, localized issues, people trying to resolve issues over water and land at a local level. But real war as such, I think we are over that." The Nigerian general further opined that only JEM posed a real threat as a rebel group, but that even it could no longer hold and conquer territory.[152] Continuing fighting between the government and rebels in Northern and Western Darfur resulting in dozens of deaths of soldiers and civilians, border incursions by Sudanese and Chadian government soldiers, and the killing of five UNAMID peacekeepers between November 2009 and January 2010 all appeared to contradict Agwai's curious claim.

General Henry Anyidoho, Adada's deputy who had lived in Darfur since October 2006, acted as the UN special representative until the arrival of veteran Nigerian diplomat and former UN special representative to Angola, Ibrahim Gambari, in January 2010. Abuja was rewarded for the loss of the force commander position. In September 2009, Somali diplomat Mohamed Yonis was appointed deputy special representative, while Rwandan general Patrick Nyamvuba was made force commander. Within a week of arriving in Sudan, Gambari met Bashir and assured him that he would sometimes need to speak bluntly to maintain the credibility of his mission.[153]

By January 2010, UNAMID continued to conduct patrols in the territory. But as in South Sudan, the lethargic pace of UN deployment in a territory the size of France appeared to suggest a lack of urgency on the part of the UN Security Council in resolving this complicated case. In February 2010, yet another accord was signed by Khartoum and JEM in Doha. The agreement had incredibly been negotiated by Idriss Déby, himself effectively one of the warring factions and fuelers of the Darfur conflict. More positively,

Déby visited Khartoum in February and May 2010, and both countries agreed to deploy a joint three thousand–strong contingent to patrol their common border.

Khartoum and the JEM signed a framework agreement in February 2010, sponsored by Chad, but three months later the rebel movement had frozen its cooperation with the Doha peace process, insisting on the release of prisoners. JEM leader Khalil Ibrahim was detained at N'Djamena airport in May 2010, forcing him to relocate to Tripoli as the shifting regional diplomatic dynamics continued further to complicate the factionalism of the rebel movements. Bassolé was reduced to negotiating between Khartoum and the Liberation and Justice Movement (LJM) by June 2010 as most of the other warlords deserted the negotiation table. The Burkinabè diplomat visited Darfur and Chad in November and December 2010, while Ibrahim Gambari and Thabo Mbeki sought to steer Khartoum to engage in a more fruitful political process with Darfuri groups.[154] But military events on the ground failed to conform with these diplomatic efforts. The Sudan Armed Forces launched airstrikes against JEM positions in October and November 2010, while JEM retaliated by killing 40 police personnel. Fighting also occurred between the Sudan Armed Forces and the SLA-MM in December 2010, which continued throughout January and February 2011.[155] UNAMID tried to continue its long-range patrols, but its freedom of movement was restricted 123 times in 2010, and its peacekeepers continued to be shot at and kidnapped in several incidents in October 2010. Deficiencies were also identified in the 17,912-strong UN peacekeeping force's contingency-owned equipment.[156] Bassolé resigned as the AU/UN joint chief mediator in Darfur in April 2011.

As in South Sudan, Washington's conflicting role also complicated this case. As earlier noted, the terrorist attack on the United States on 11 September 2001 had made Washington adopt a pragmatic approach toward Khartoum. Under the George W. Bush administration, the Department of State, the Central Intelligence Agency, and the Defense Intelligence Agency (DIA) were working closely with Sudan's national intelligence and security agencies to garner information on global terrorist networks. The US Congress and the US Agency for International Development (USAID)—though part of the Department of State—however, pushed for pressure to be maintained on Khartoum to fulfill commitments on peace accords, human rights, and humanitarian assistance.[157] As in South Sudan, Bush also faced domestic civil society groups demanding action on Darfur during a bid for reelection in 2004. There was a recognition within the US administration that Khartoum was concerned that Washington could adopt a policy of "regime change" in Sudan if it continued to back international terrorism.[158] Richard Williamson, Bush's special envoy for Sudan between January 2008 and January 2009, successfully pushed strongly against deferring the ICC indictment of Bashir in the UN Security Council.

Barack Obama appointed General Scott Gration as his special envoy to Sudan in March 2009. Though Obama and many of his officials vowed to be tough on Khartoum while in office, discordant voices were visible. Secretary of State Hillary Clinton and Gration seemed to favor accommodation with Khartoum, while Susan Rice, the US permanent representative at the UN—who had reportedly opposed action against *génocidaires* during the Rwandan genocide in 1994 while serving on Bill Clinton's National Security Council (see Chapter 3)—called for stronger action. Gration was widely seen to be out of his depth and not conversant with the intricacies of the treacherous Sudanese landscape. In June 2009, Senator Russ Feingold, chair of the US Senate Subcommittee on African Affairs, along with six senators, wrote to Obama warning him that Khartoum had been an untrustworthy ally in the past and that pressure and a willingness to impose sanctions were also needed in dealing with the regime.[159] They urged that diplomatic sticks be employed and not just carrots. Princeton Lyman, a former US ambassador to South Africa and Nigeria, was dispatched to Sudan in 2010, an act that was seen by some as a loss of confidence in Gration's approach. The United States chaired talks on Abyei in Addis Ababa in October 2010, remaining involved in the peace process.

UN special representative Ibrahim Gambari sought to involve the UN Security Council's five permanent members and key donors in the Darfur process, inviting them to a retreat in Kigali in February 2010. But events on the ground still refused to match the lofty efforts of the peacemakers in Sudan. During national elections in April 2010, less than half of registered Darfuris voted,[160] and several Darfuri rebel groups threatened to disrupt the polling. In March 2010, clashes in Western and Southern Darfur had led to 182 deaths;[161] two months later, over four hundred conflict-related fatalities were recorded (compared to 295 conflict-related deaths, excluding 134 intra-clan clashes, recorded by UNAMID for all of 2009[162]): the largest number in a month since UNAMID deployed two and a half years earlier.[163] UN peacekeepers, 88 percent (17,308) of whom had been deployed by July 2010, were observing rather than preventing killings, barely being able to protect themselves let alone Darfuris. Between July 2009 and July 2010, UNAMID peacekeepers were attacked twenty-eight times, resulting in ten dead and twenty-six injured,[164] while Khartoum still placed restrictions on UN helicopter flights. An incredible 25 percent of Darfur's population—2 million—were still displaced and needing international assistance to survive by July 2010.[165]

Concluding Reflections

For many observers, the UN Security Council's abandonment of Somalia to its fate in 1995 and its lethargic response to the Ethiopia-Eritrea conflict in 1998 were yet additional examples of the neglect of African conflicts by the Council. Similar accusations were made against the UN in South Sudan and

Darfur. Despite these disappointments, the dispatch of peacekeepers to Ethiopia and Eritrea, however, provided an opportunity for the UN to reengage with Africa. This was a classical peacekeeping mission in which both sides had agreed to stop fighting and to work with an interpositional force. Western armies that had abandoned Africa during its greatest hour of need after the Somali debacle in 1993 and the Rwandan genocide of 1994 now took their first tentative steps back into the continent.

But while Somalia represented the cynical abandonment of peacekeeping in Africa and the UN's retreat from Ethiopia-Eritrea may signify further neglect of the continent, the UN deployed nearly forty thousand peacekeepers to two missions in Sudan between 2005 and 2011. The world body's peacekeeping efforts in Ethiopia-Eritrea and Sudan and the crucial support of the United States and the EU for peace efforts demonstrate the importance of external actors to peace processes in Africa. Regional actors still lack the financial, diplomatic, and logistical muscle of outsiders as the Somalia, Ethiopia-Eritrea, South Sudan, and Darfur cases demonstrated. The international community—symbolized most powerfully by the UN— must continue to support the efforts of African actors to maintain peace on their own continent.

The conflicting role of domestic, regional, and external actors was again critical to the outcomes of the cases of South Sudan and Darfur. At the domestic level, the government of Khartoum's historical brutal repression against different groups across this vast country resulted in rebellions in the South and Darfur. The splintering of armed factions in Darfur also complicated peacemaking and peacekeeping efforts. Regional and external actors effectively imposed a peace deal in the South that forced Khartoum to accept the region's right to secede. These actors were less effective at forcing Bashir's hand in Darfur, where repression and rebel attacks continued.

At the regional level, Kenya and other IGAD states played an important mediating role in South Sudan. Eritrea also led mediation efforts in eastern Sudan. But these actors had also played more negative conflict-fueling roles in the past, with Ethiopia, Uganda, and Kenya having backed the SPLA, and Khartoum being backed by Libya and Egypt.

At the external level, several veto-wielding permanent members of the UN Security Council played critical roles in the two Sudanese conflicts. The United States had supported Sudan during the Cold War, before branding it a sponsor of terrorism after the end of the Cold War. Washington played an important role in pressuring Khartoum to accept the CPA in 2005, and the conflict became "ripe for resolution" after US pressure on Sudan started to pay off in the wake of the 11 September 2001 terrorist attacks on the United States and Khartoum's own desire to cooperate with Washington. China, the largest investor in, and importer of, Sudanese oil, also played an important role in pressuring Khartoum to accept a UN mission in Darfur in 2007. Beijing further deployed troops to the UN missions in south Sudan and Darfur. Britain played an important role, along with the United States and Norway, in the IGAD Partner's Forum, which supported peacemaking efforts in South Sudan. More negatively, France, another permanent member of the Security Council, provided support to the autocratic regime of Idriss Déby in Chad, helping him to stay in power through military and intelligence support.

The UN deployed peacekeepers to both South Sudan and Darfur. Since the AU was deployed first in Darfur due to the reluctance of Bashir to accept UN peacekeepers, and since South Sudan voted overwhelmingly to become an independent country in January 2011, the unusual phenomenon of the UN operating two independent missions in one country may have been an accident of history that may never be repeated. It is important to stress the indivisible link between peace in South Sudan and Darfur. (Southern Kordofan and Abyei, after all, border Southern Darfur.) The UN Security Council largely ignored Darfur during the worst human rights abuses between 2003 and 2005 for fear of destabilizing the CPA process and then focused attention on Darfur to the detriment of the South after 2007.[166] The historical roots of Sudan's problems have involved disputes between an often domineeringly brutal center in Khartoum and its subordinate peripheral regions. The independence of the South will not dissipate these problems and may in fact harden Khartoum's resolve to keep other provinces from seceding in future. The deployment of the Sudanese army into oil-rich Abyei by May 2011 provided some evidence of this approach.

With about ten thousand troops in a large area, it was clear that UNMIS would struggle with South Sudan's poor communications, impassable roads (particularly during the eight-month rainy season), and inoperable railway system. This case resembled the UN's peacekeeping travails in Africa's third largest country—the DRC—with equally dilapidated transport and communications infrastructure (see Chapter 3). The 26,000 UN peacekeepers in Darfur faced similar difficulties, as well as continued fighting among the warring parties and regional destabilization.

But even after the successful conduct of the self-determination referendum in South Sudan in January 2011, much uncertainty remains over the independence of the South. With leaders in Khartoum having unilaterally abrogated the 1972 Addis Ababa accord with the South, it is unclear whether Bashir and his allies will allow the oil-rich South to thrive as an independent state. Khartoum could well attempt to play a similar obstructionist role to the one that Morocco has played in frustrating self-determination aspirations in Western Sahara (see Chapter 2). Before the declaration of Southern independence in July 2011, tough negotiations occurred on sharing oil revenues, the management of assets and debt, citizenship issues, border security, and joint control of disputed areas.[167] Abyei still remains a potential tinderbox. This is the history that has left Sudan in a precarious state, with the South grabbing the chance for a bitter divorce in anticipation that a vengeful northern spouse could still in the future seek to resort to domestic violence to prevent the other partner from completely walking out of an unhappy marriage. Non-Arab areas in southern Kodorfan, southern Blue Nile, and Darfur have also borne the brunt of Northern attempts at forcible cultural and religious assimilation.

But while Somalia represented the cynical abandonment of peacekeeping in Africa and the UN's retreat from Ethiopia-Eritrea may signify further neglect of the continent, the UN deployed nearly forty thousand peacekeepers to two missions in Sudan. The world body's peacekeeping efforts in Ethiopia-Eritrea and Sudan and the crucial support of the United States and the EU for peace efforts demonstrate the importance of external actors to implementing peace agreements in Africa. Regional actors still lack the financial, diplomatic, and logistical muscle of outsiders, as these cases clearly demonstrate. These external actors also often have contradictory agendas that have frequently exacerbated conflicts, even as some states have played constructive roles.[168]

Finally, a potentially useful mechanism that was employed in these cases was the two visits to the Horn of Africa by UN Security Council members in May 2000 and February 2002. The Security Council also visited Sudan in June 2006, June 2007, June 2008, and October 2010. These six trips allowed the Council's ambassadors to gain firsthand experience of the situation on the ground and to assess the views and personalities, particularly of regional leaders. These missions provided Council members insights that were useful for making decisions in New York. The six visits to the Horn of Africa and others to the Great Lakes region, West Africa, and Western Sahara, are an important diplomatic tool in the Council's conflict management armory. Such high-level field missions can bring home to parties in dispute the Council's seriousness about understanding and addressing regional conflicts of identity.

Notes

The title of this chapter is borrowed from Francis Deng, *War of Visions: Conflict of Identities in the Sudan* (Washington, DC: Brookings Institution, 1995). The author would like to thank Francis Deng, Daniel Large, Musifiky Mwanasali, Sharath Srinivasan, Solomon Gomes, Alem Habtu, Ruth Iyob, the late Dominique Jacquin-Berdal, Ian Martin, and Aida Mengistu for extremely useful comments on an earlier version of sections of this chapter.

1. Francis Deng, *War of Visions: Conflict of Identities in the Sudan* (Washington, DC: Brookings Institution, 1995), p. 1.

2. See Hussein Adam, "Somalia: A Terrible Beauty Being Born?" in I. William Zartman, ed., *Collapsed States: The Disintegration and Restoration of Legitimate Authority* (Boulder: Lynne Rienner, 1995), pp. 69–78. See also Ioan Lewis and James Mayall, "Somalia," in Mats Berdal and Spyros Economides, eds., *United*

Nations Interventionism, 1991–2004 (Cambridge: Cambridge University Press, 2007), pp. 108–138.

3. See Mohamed Sahnoun, *Somalia: The Missed Opportunities* (Washington, DC: US Institute of Peace, 1994), pp. 25–41.

4. Walter Clarke, "Failed Visions and Uncertain Mandates in Somalia," in Walter Clarke and Jeffrey Herbst, eds., *Learning from Somalia: The Lessons of Armed Humanitarian Intervention* (Boulder: Westview, 1997), p. 5.

5. John L. Hirsch and Robert B. Oakley, *Somalia and Operation Restore Hope: Reflections on Peacemaking and Peacekeeping* (Washington, DC: US Institute of Peace Press, 1995), p. 54.

6. Sahnoun, *Somalia,* p. 39.

7. See Ameen Jan, "Peacebuilding in Somalia," IPA Policy Briefing Series, July 1996.

8. This expression was coined by Boutros Boutros-Ghali.

9. See Roland Marchal, "Horn of Africa: New War, Old Methods," *The Africa Report,* no. 8 (October–December 2007): 47–50.

10. See Paul D. Williams, "Into the Mogadishu Maelstrom: The African Union Mission in Somalia," *International Peacekeeping* 16, no. 4 (August 2009): 514–530.

11. This section is based on Adekeye Adebajo, "Ethiopia/Eritrea," in David M. Malone, ed., *The UN Security Council: From the Cold War to the 21st Century* (Boulder: Lynne Rienner, 2004), pp. 575–588.

12. UN Security Council special mission visit to Eritrea and Ethiopia, S/2000/413, 9 and 10 May 2000, p. 2.

13. See Dominique Jacquin-Berdal and Martin Plaut, eds., *Unfinished Business: Ethiopia and Eritrea at War* (Trenton: Red Sea, 2004); David Pool, "The Eritrean People's Liberation Front," in Christopher Clapham, *African Guerrillas* (Bloomington: Indiana University Press, 1998), pp. 19–35; Tekeste Negash and Kjetil Tronvoll, *Brothers at War: Making Sense of the Eritrean-Ethiopian War* (Oxford: James Currey, 2000), pp. 12–21; Peter Woodward, *The Horn of Africa: Politics and International Relations* (London: I. B. Tauris, 2003); John Young, "The Tigray People's Liberation Front," in Christopher Clapham, *African Guerrillas,* pp. 36–52.

14. Dominique Jacquin-Berdal and Aida Mengistu, "Nationalism and Identity in Ethiopia and Eritrea," in Dorina A. Bekoe, ed., *East Africa and the Horn: Confronting Challenges to Good Governance* (Boulder: Lynne Rienner, 2006), pp. 81–100.

15. See Christopher Clapham, "The Ethiopia-Eritrea Conflict," in *South African Yearbook of International Affairs 1999/2000* (Johannesburg: South African Institute of International Affairs, 1999), pp. 351–356; Aida Mengistu, "Uneasy Peace," *The World Today,* May 2001, pp. 9–10.

16. See Christopher Clapham, "The Ethiopia-Eritrea Conflict (Continued)," in *South African Yearbook of International Affairs 2000/2001* (Johannesburg: South African Institute of International Affairs, 2000), p. 298; Ruth Iyob, "The Foreign Policies of the Horn: The Clash Between the Old and the New," in Gilbert Khadiagala and Terrence Lyons, eds., *African Foreign Policies* (Boulder: Lynne Rienner, 2001), pp. 107–129; Terrence Lyons, "The International Context of Internal War: Ethiopia/Eritrea," in Edmond J. Keller and Donald Rothchild, eds., *Africa in the New International Order* (Boulder: Lynne Rienner, 1996), pp. 85–99.

17. Quoted in Negash and Tronvoll, *Brothers at War,* p. 82.

18. Jeremy Greenstock, "The Security Council in the Post–Cold War World," in Vaughan Lowe, Adam Roberts, Jennifer Welsh, and Dominik Zaum, eds., *The*

United Nations Security Council and War: The Evolution of Thought and Practice Since 1945 (Oxford: Oxford University Press, 2008), p. 256.

19. Ian Taylor, "The 'All Weather' Friend? Sino-African Interaction in the Twenty-First Century," in Ian Taylor and Paul Williams, eds., *Africa in International Politics: External Involvement on the Continent* (London: Routledge, 2004), pp. 83–101.

20. See UN Security Council Resolution 1312, S/RES/1312, 31 July 2000.

21. See Festus Aboagye, "Towards New Peacekeeping Partnerships in Africa? The OAU Liaison Mission in Ethiopia/Eritrea," in *African Security Review* 10, no. 2 (2001): 19–33.

22. Quoted in Clapham, "The Ethiopia-Eritrea Conflict," p. 354.

23. For details, see "Eritrea/Ethiopia Boundary Commission Decision Regarding Delimitation of the Border Between the State of Eritrea and the Federal Democratic Republic of Ethiopia" (The Hague: Eritrea/Ethiopia Boundary Commission, 13 April 2002).

24. "Eighth Report on the Work of the Eritrea/Ethiopia Boundary Commission," Annex I, "Report of the UN Secretary-General on Eritrea and Ethiopia," S/2003/257, 6 March 2003, pp. 10–11.

25. "Anxious Ethiopia: Jangling Nerves," *The Economist,* 23 January 2010, p. 37.

26. I am grateful to Professor Alem Habtu for raising these points during a lecture at Columbia University, New York, in April 2003.

27. Quoted in John Bolton, *Surrender Is Not an Option: Defending America at the United Nations and Abroad* (New York: Threshold, 2007), p. 345.

28. Bolton, *Surrender Is Not an Option,* pp. 146–148.

29. See Deng, *War of Visions.*

30. See, for example, ibid.; Francis Deng, *Sudan at the Brink: Self-Determination and National Unity* (New York: Fordham University Press, 2010); Dunstan M. Wai, *The African-Arab Conflict in the Sudan* (New York: Africana Publishing, 1981); Peter Woodward, *Sudan, 1898–1989: The Unstable State* (Boulder: Lynne Rienner, 1990).

31. Ruth Iyob and Gilbert M. Khadiagala, *Sudan: The Elusive Quest* (Boulder: Lynne Rienner, 2006), pp. 15–16.

32. See David Keen, *The Benefits of Famine: A Political Economy of Famine and Relief in Southwestern Sudan, 1983–1989* (Princeton, NJ: Princeton University Press, 1994).

33. See Alex de Waal, "Sudan: The Turbulent State," in Alex de Waal, ed., *War in Darfur and the Search for Peace* (London: Justice Africa, 2007), p. 6; Keen, *The Benefits of Famine.*

34. "Sudan's Coming Elections: How Did It Come to This?" *The Economist,* 16–22 January 2010, p. 37.

35. Iyob and Khadiagala, *Sudan,* p. 102.

36. I am grateful to Iyob and Khadiagala, *Sudan,* pp. 79–97, for the information used in the above two paragraphs.

37. Iyob and Khadiagala, *Sudan,* p. 101.

38. Ibid., p. 117.

39. See Waithaka Waihenya, *The Mediator: Gen. Lazaro Sumbeiywo and the Southern Sudan Peace Process* (Nairobi: Kenway, 2006).

40. See Woodward, *The Horn of Africa,* pp. 117–133.

41. De Waal, "Sudan," p. 17.

42. Iyob and Khadiagala, *Sudan,* p. 102.

43. Ibid., p. 115.

44. See Daniel Large, "China and the Contradictions of 'Non-Interference' in Sudan," *Review of African Political Economy* 35, no. 115 (March 2008): 93–106; Sharath Srinivasan, "A Marriage Less Convenient: China, Sudan, and Darfur," in Kweku Ampiah and Sanusha Naidu, eds., *Crouching Tiger, Hidden Dragon? Africa and China* (Scottsville, South Africa: University of KwaZulu-Natal Press, 2008), pp. 55–85.

45. "Report of the UN Secretary-General on Sudan to the Security Council," S/2005/57, 31 January 2005, p. 1.

46. Personal interview with Jan Pronk, special representative of the UN Secretary-General, 2004–2006, Cape Town, 26 August 2010.

47. Ibid.

48. Confidential interview.

49. "Report of the UN Secretary-General on Sudan to the Security Council," S/2005/57, 31 January 2005, pp. 8–9.

50. "Report of the UN Secretary-General on Sudan to the Security Council," S/2005/411, 23 June 2005, p. 4.

51. Jeremy Clarke, "Breaking Up but Stuck Together," *The Africa Report,* no. 26 (December 2010–January 2011): 50.

52. "Sudan's Coming Elections," *The Economist,* p. 37.

53. "Report of the UN Secretary-General on Sudan to the Security Council," S/2008/267, 22 April 2008, p. 6.

54. "Report of the UN Secretary-General on Sudan to the Security Council," S/2007/42, 25 January 2007, p. 4.

55. "Report of the UN Secretary-General on Sudan to the Security Council," S/2007/624, 23 October 2007, p. 4.

56. "Report of the UN Secretary-General on Sudan to the Security Council," S/2009/211, 17 April 2009, p. 2.

57. "Report of the UN Secretary-General on Sudan to the Security Council," S/2009/545, 21 October 2009, p. 1.

58. "Report of the UN Secretary-General on Sudan to the Security Council," S/2010/388, 19 July 2010, p. 12.

59. "Report of the UN Secretary-General on Sudan to the Security Council," S/2007/42, 25 January 2007, p. 1.

60. Medhane Tadesse, "UN Peacekeeping in the Horn of Africa: Somalia, Ethiopia/Eritrea and Sudan," in Adekeye Adebajo, ed., *From Global Apartheid to Global Village: Africa and the United Nations* (Scottsville, South Africa: University of KwaZulu-Natal Press, 2009), pp. 330–333.

61. "Report of the Secretary-General on the United Nations Mission in Sudan," S/2009/357, 14 July 2009, p. 1.

62. Musifiky Mwanasali, "Building Peace in Sudan: A Daunting Task," paper presented at a seminar on "Peacebuilding in Africa" held in Botswana on 25–28 August 2009, cohosted by the Centre for Conflict Resolution, Cape Town, University of Botswana, and University of Cambridge, England.

63. "Report of the UN Secretary-General on Sudan to the Security Council," S/2006/160, 14 March 2006, p. 17.

64. Personal interview with Jan Pronk, special representative of the UN Secretary-General, 2004–2006, Cape Town, 26 August 2010.

65. Confidential interview.

66. "Report of the UN Secretary-General on Sudan to the Security Council," S/2007/624, 23 October 2007, pp. 1 and 3.

67. "Report of the UN Secretary-General on Sudan to the Security Council," S/2007/42, 25 January 2007, p. 4.

68. "Report of the UN Secretary-General on Sudan to the Security Council," S/2007/624, 23 October 2007, p. 6.

69. Woodward, *The Horn of Africa*, p. 45.

70. Ibid., p. 51.

71. "Report of the UN Secretary-General on Sudan to the Security Council," S/2009/211, 17 April 2009, pp. 5–6.

72. "Report of the UN Secretary-General on Sudan to the Security Council," S/2007/500, 20 August 2007, p. 2.

73. "Report of the UN Secretary-General on Sudan to the Security Council," S/2009/545, 21 October 2009, pp. 3–4.

74. "Report of the UN Secretary-General on Sudan to the Security Council," S/2006/728, 12 September 2006, p. 3.

75. "Report of the UN Secretary-General on Sudan to the Security Council," S/2008/485, 23 July 2008, p. 6.

76. "Report of the UN Secretary-General on Sudan to the Security Council," S/2008/662, 20 October 2008, p. 7.

77. "Report of the UN Secretary-General on Sudan to the Security Council," S/2010/31, 19 January 2010, p. 5.

78. "Report of the UN Secretary-General on Sudan to the Security Council," S/2008/662, 20 October 2008, p. 4.

79. "Report of the UN Secretary-General on Sudan to the Security Council," S/2010/31, 19 January 2010, p. 9.

80. "Report of the UN Secretary-General on Sudan to the Security Council," S/2009/61, 30 January 2009, p. 17.

81. "Report of the UN Secretary-General on Sudan to the Security Council," S/2009/211, 17 April 2009, p. 1.

82. "Report of the UN Secretary-General on Sudan to the Security Council," S/2010/31, 19 January 2010, p. 17.

83. "Report of the UN Secretary-General on Sudan to the Security Council," S/2010/168, 5 April 2010, pp. 1–2.

84. Ibid., p. 2.

85. "Report of the UN Secretary-General on Sudan to the Security Council," S/2010/681, 31 December 2010, pp. 6–7.

86. "Lords of Woe," *The Economist,* 13 November 2010, p. 51.

87. Lissane Yohannes, "Regional Implications of the Referendum in South Sudan," presentation at the Centre for Conflict Resolution, Cape Town, policy advisory group seminar "Stabilizing Sudan: Domestic, Sub-regional, and Extra-regional Challenges," 23–24 August 2010, Western Cape, South Africa.

88. "Report of the UN Secretary-General on Sudan to the Security Council," S/2005/821, 21 December 2005, p. 15.

89. "Report of the UN Secretary-General on Sudan to the Security Council," S/2008/662, 20 October 2008, p. 9.

90. "Lords of Woe," *The Economist,* p. 52.

91. Ibid.

92. Cited in Centre for Conflict Resolution, "Stabilising Sudan: Domestic, Sub-regional, and Extra-regional Challenges," Policy Advisory Group Seminar Report, 23–24 August 2010, Cape Town, Western Cape, South Africa, www.ccr.org.za.

93. "Pressing the North to Let the South Go," *The Economist,* 13 November 2010, p. 52.

94. "Independence Beckons," *The Economist,* 8 January 2011, p. 33.

95. "Report of the UN Secretary-General on Sudan to the Security Council," S/2009/61, 30 January 2009, p. 2.

96. "Pressing the North to Let the South Go," *The Economist,* p. 52.

97. De Waal, "Sudan," pp. 23 and 28.

98. For this summary, I have relied on the excellent report by Francis Deng, "Specific Groups and Individuals: Mass Exoduses and Displaced Persons; Report of the Representative of the Secretary-General on Internally Displaced Persons; Mission to the Sudan: The Darfur Crisis; UN Economic and Social Council," E/CN.4/2005/8, 27 September 2004. See also Sharath Srinivasan, "Minority Rights, Early Warning and Conflict Prevention: Lessons from Darfur," Minority Rights Group International Report, September 2006; International Crisis Group, "Darfur: Revitalising the Peace Process," Africa Report, no. 125, 30 April 2007.

99. See, for example, Richard Cockett, *Sudan: Darfur and the Failure of an African State* (New Haven: Yale University Press, 2010).

100. I am indebted for much of this information to the excellent article by the head of the AU mission in Sudan, Cdr. Seth Appiah-Mensah, "AU's Critical Assignment in Darfur: Challenges and Constraints," in *African Security Review* 14, no. 2 (2005): 7–21.

101. Confidential interview.

102. Personal interview with Jan Pronk, special representative of the UN Secretary-General, 2004–2006, Cape Town, 26 August 2010.

103. Personal interview with General Henry Anyidoho, deputy special representative of the UN Secretary-General in Darfur, 2006–2010, Cape Town, 22 August 2010.

104. Appiah-Mensah, "AU's Critical Assignment in Darfur," p. 14. See also "Report of the Chairperson of the AU Commission on Conflict Situations in Africa," Executive Council, Seventh Ordinary Session, 28 June–2 July 2005; Sirte, Libya. EX.CL/191 (VII).

105. "Monthly Report of the UN Secretary-General on Darfur," S/2005/719, 16 November 2005, p. 1.

106. See, for example, "Report of the UN Secretary-General on Sudan to the Security Council," S/2005/68, 4 February 2005, p. 2; "Report of the UN Secretary-General on Sudan to the Security Council," S/2005/140, 4 March 2005, p. 3.

107. "Report of the UN Secretary-General on Sudan to the Security Council," S/2005/57, 31 January 2005, p. 7.

108. Gérard Prunier, *Darfur: A 21st Century Genocide* (Ithaca: Cornell University Press, 2008), p. 117.

109. See Dawit Toga, "The African Union Mediation and the Abuja Peace Talks," in de Waal, *War in Darfur and the Search for Peace,* pp. 214–244.

110. For an informative insider perspective of the peace talks, see Alex de Waal, "Darfur: The Inside Story," *NewAfrican,* no. 461 (April 2007): 28–33. See also, Gérard Prunier, "Buying Time in Darfur," *Mail and Guardian,* 22 August 2007, p. 18.

111. De Waal, "Sudan," p. 21.

112. See the entertaining insider account, Alex de Waal, "Darfur's Deadline: The Final Days of the Abuja Peace Process," in de Waal, *War in Darfur and the Search for Peace,* pp. 267–283.

113. Personal interview with Jan Pronk, special representative of the UN Secretary-General, 2004–2006, Cape Town, 26 August 2010.

114. "Report of the UN Secretary-General on Sudan to the Security Council," S/2006/426, 23 June 2006, pp. 3–4.

115. Roland Marchal, "The Unseen Regional Implications of the Crisis in Darfur," in de Waal, *War in Darfur and the Search for Peace,* p. 191.

116. "Monthly Report of the UN Secretary-General to the Security Council on Darfur," S/2005/719, 16 November 2005, p. 2.

117. "Report of the UN Secretary-General on Sudan to the Security Council," S/2006/160, 14 March 2006, p. 3.

118. Marchal, "The Unseen Regional Implications of the Crisis in Darfur," pp. 174–175.

119. Ibid., p. 194.

120. Ibid., p. 175.

121. See Henry Kwami Anyidoho, *My Journey . . . Every Step* (Accra: Sub-Saharan Publishers, 2010), pp. 330–346.

122. "Report of the UN Secretary-General to the Security Council on United Nations Assistance to the African Union Mission in Sudan," S/2005/285, 3 May 2005, p. 2.

123. Bolton, *Surrender Is Not an Option,* p. 350.

124. Ibid.

125. Ibid., p. 353.

126. "Report of the UN Secretary-General to the Security Council on Darfur," S/2007/462, 27 July 2007, p. 2.

127. "Central Africa: On the Brink," *Africa Confidential,* 12 January 2007, p. 6.

128. "Report of the UN Secretary-General to the Security Council on Darfur," S/2007/462, 27 July 2007, p. 4.

129. "Report of the UN Secretary-General on Sudan to the Security Council," S/2009/211, 17 April 2009, p. 3.

130. See Norrie MacQueen, *United Nations Peacekeeping in Africa Since 1960* (London: Pearson Education, 2002), pp. 96–104.

131. See "Report of the Secretary-General on the UN Mission in the Central African Republic and Chad," S/2010/611, 1 December 2010; "Report of the Secretary-General on the UN Mission in the Central African Republic and Chad," S/2010/529, 14 October 2010; Amnesty International, *Chad: "We Too Deserve Protection"* (London: Amnesty International, July 2010).

132. See, for example, Richard Dowden, "China's Healing Power," *Time* 170, no. 6 (13 August 2007): 13.

133. I thank a confidential source for these insightful observations.

134. Mahmood Mamdani, "Darfur: The Politics of Naming," *Mail and Guardian,* 16–22 March 2007, pp. 23 and 26.

135. Mahmood Mamdani, *Saviours and Survivors: Darfur, Politics, and the War on Terror* (Cape Town: Human Sciences Research Council, 2009), p. 6.

136. Wole Soyinka, "Darfur: Anything to Do with Slavery?" in Wole Soyinka, *Interventions,* Vol. 2 (Ibadan, Nigeria: Bookcraft, 2010), p. 65.

137. See Seth Appiah-Mensah, "The African Union Mission in Sudan: Darfur Dilemmas," *African Security Review* 15, no. 1 (2006): 2–19; Kristiana Powell, *The African Union's Emerging Peace and Security Regime: Opportunities and Challenges for Delivering on the Responsibility to Protect,* Institute for Security Studies (South Africa) Monograph Series no. 119, May 2005.

138. UN Security Council Resolution 1769, S/RES/1769, 31 July 2007.

139. "Report of the UN Secretary-General on Sudan to the Security Council on the Deployment of the AU/UN Hybrid Operation in Darfur," S/2008/249, 14 April 2008, p. 7.

140. "Report of the UN Secretary-General on Sudan to the Security Council on the Deployment of the AU/UN Hybrid Operation in Darfur," S/2008/98, 14 February 2008, p. 1.

141. "Report of the UN Secretary-General on Sudan to the Security Council," S/2008/485, 23 July 2008, p. 1.

142. "Report of the UN Secretary-General on the AU/UN Hybrid Operation in Darfur," S/2009/592, 16 November 2009, p. 3.

143. "Report of the UN Secretary-General on the AU/UN Hybrid Operation in Darfur," S/2010/50, 29 January 2010, p. 5.

144. "Report of the UN Secretary-General on Sudan to the Security Council on the Deployment of the AU/UN Hybrid Operation in Darfur," S/2008/249, 14 April 2008, p. 9.

145. "Report of the UN Secretary-General on Sudan to the Security Council," S/2009/545, 21 October 2009, p. 7.

146. "Report of the UN Secretary-General on Sudan to the Security Council on the Deployment of the AU/UN Hybrid Operation in Darfur," S/2008/781, 12 December 2008, p. 4.

147. "Report of the UN Secretary-General on the AU/UN Hybrid Operation in Darfur," S/2009/592, 16 November 2009, p. 2.

148. Confidential interview.

149. Confidential interviews.

150. Confidential interviews.

151. Confidential interviews.

152. Quoted in BBC News, "War in Sudan's Darfur 'Is Over,'" 27 August 2009, http://newsvote.bbc.co.uk (accessed 23 November 2010).

153. Personal interview with Ambassador Abiodun Bashua, director, Political Affairs Division, AU/UN Hybrid Operation in Darfur, Cape Town, 23 August 2010.

154. "Report of the UN Secretary-General on the Implementation of the Darfur Political Process," S/2011/252, 15 April 2011.

155. "Report of the UN Secretary-General on the AU/UN Hybrid Operation in Darfur," S/2011/244, 14 April 2011.

156. "Report of the UN Secretary-General on the AU/UN Hybrid Operation in Darfur," S/2011/22, 18 January 2011.

157. Prunier, *Darfur,* p. 139.

158. Personal interview with Richard W. Williamson, US special envoy to Sudan, January 2008–January 2009, Cape Town, 26 August 2010.

159. Quoted in Richard W. Williamson, "Sudan and the Implications for Responsibility to Protect," Stanley Foundation Policy Brief, October 2009, p. 5.

160. "Report of the UN Secretary-General on the AU/UN Hybrid Operation in Darfur," S/2010/382, 14 July 2010, p. 1.

161. "Report of the UN Secretary-General on the AU/UN Hybrid Operation in Darfur," S/2010/213, 28 April 2010, p. 6.

162. "Report of the UN Secretary-General on the AU/UN Hybrid Operation in Darfur," S/2010/382, 14 July 2010, p. 5.

163. Ibid., p. 5.

164. Ibid., p. 7.

165. Ibid., p. 8.

166. I thank Daniel Large for this important point.

167. "Special Report of the UN Secretary-General on the Sudan," S/2011/314, 17 May 2011.

168. I thank Musifiky Mwanasali for this important point.

7

Conclusion: From Burden Shedding to Burden Sharing

> Combining the principle of neighbourhood with the
> principle of distant impartiality . . . is critical because at times
> keeping neighbours out of each other's problems carries
> the risk of fomenting suspicion and resentment.
> —*Salim Ahmed Salim, OAU secretary-general, 1989–2001*[1]

In this book, I have systematically investigated fifteen cases of United Nations peacekeeping efforts in Africa over the last five and a half decades. I noted from the outset that three key factors have most often contributed to success in UN peacekeeping missions in Africa: (1) the interests of key permanent members of the UN Security Council needing to be aligned to efforts to resolve the conflict in question, and their willingness to mobilize diplomatic and financial support for peace processes; (2) the willingness of belligerent parties to cooperate with the UN to implement peace accords or, in cases where such cooperation is not forthcoming, the development of an effective strategy to deal with potential "spoilers" who are prepared to use violence to wreck peace processes; and (3) the cooperation of regional players in peace processes, as well as their provision of diplomatic and/or military support to UN peacekeeping efforts. It is the alignment of interests at these three interdependent levels—domestic, regional, and external—that has often shaped the course and outcome of the fifteen cases examined in this book. In addition, I have stressed the importance of unforeseen contingencies in determining peacekeeping outcomes. A brief summary of the domestic, regional, and external factors that obstructed or assisted UN peacekeeping efforts in the fifteen cases will highlight these points.

Starting in North Africa, the Suez crisis of 1956 demonstrated how four powerful veto-wielding members of the Security Council—the United States, the Soviet Union, Britain, and France—shaped the outcome of the first armed UN peacekeeping mission in the world and how divisions between these powers can actually sometimes help reach a solution to difficult issues. The peacekeeping mission represented a face-saving response to the invasion of Egypt by Britain, France, and Israel, with Washington and Moscow opposing the intervention for their own strategic interests. Reinforcing the point about contingencies, the roles of three personalities were also important in shaping this conflict: Egyptian leader Gamal Abdel Nasser, British prime minister Anthony Eden, and US secretary of state John Foster Dulles. The Western Sahara issue, despite being a classic case of self-determination, much like Namibia, saw French and American support of the occupying power—Morocco—frustrating the UN's efforts to organize a self-determination referendum since 1991. Rabat remained particularly intransigent while its regional rival, Algeria, continued to back POLISARIO Front liberation fighters.

Turning to Africa's Great Lakes region, the UN mission in the Congo in 1960–1964 succeeded in reuniting a fractious country despite regional divisions and external meddling. US client Mobutu Sese Seko won power in 1965, an outcome accepted by domestic parties and regional states. The UN mission in Burundi in 2004–2006 also succeeded in its peacekeeping tasks through determined regional mediation and an African Union–led peacekeeping force, which the UN took over by 2004. Domestic spoilers were eventually isolated through a government of national unity involving the main military factions. The UN mission in Rwanda was, from the start, based largely on ill-equipped armies from developing countries that lacked strong political and financial backing from the UN Security Council. This weakness encouraged the country's extremist factions to seek to force the withdrawal of the mission by killing its peacekeepers. France, which had trained and provided military support to the genocidal regime, was considered a partisan and compromised intervener. Regional actors were too weak to impose peace on the belligerents, and their roles were sometimes compromised by past and continuing support to individual factions. The UN mission in the DRC in 2000–2011 saw the Security Council failing to send insufficient peacekeepers (only about 20,000) to a territory the size of Western Europe. France played a positive role in leading European Union forces to help stabilize Bunia in 2003 and Kinshasa in 2006. During the conflict, however, the country's riches were exploited by the warring factions, as well as by Rwanda, Uganda, and Zimbabwe. Regional actors were also deeply divided, with Rwanda and Uganda sending troops to support a rebellion against the government in Kinshasa in 1998, which in turn was provided with military support by troops from Zimbabwe, Angola, and Namibia. Only when regional states cooperated against "negative forces" in the Congo by 2008 was a modicum of stability restored to most parts of the country, though the Kivu and Orientale provinces remained volatile.

The three Southern African cases, Namibia, Angola, and Mozambique ("orphans of the Cold War"), demonstrate again the importance of external actors in fueling conflicts and obstructing peaceful solutions to crises. These cases, however, also demonstrate the important role that powerful states can play in ensuring the success of UN peacekeeping missions. The United States delayed implementation of a peace plan for Namibia in favor of its Cold War focus on Cuban and Soviet expansionism. Only after US-Russian rapprochement, with the advent of the reformist administration of Mikhail Gorbachev in Moscow in 1985—another unforeseen contingency— did Washington pressure its South African client to withdraw from the territory and facilitate Namibia's independence by 1990. The improved post–Cold War environment made deployment of UN peacekeepers in Mozambique possible in 1992. Both Angola and Mozambique had spoiler warlords—Jonas Savimbi and Afonso Dhlakama, respectively—who seemed determined to wreck peace processes. However, the presence of economic resources in Angola and the greater cooperation of the warring parties in Mozambique were crucial in explaining the different outcomes in the two cases. The sustained interest and cooperation of the powerful members of the UN Security Council and their contribution of financial, diplomatic, and logistical support to the UN missions were important to success in Namibia and Mozambique and mostly lacking in the first peacekeeping mission in Angola. Even after the deployment of a stronger peacekeeping mission in Angola in 1995, the continued recalcitrance of Jonas Savimbi— another unforeseen contingency—continued to obstruct peace efforts until his assassination by Angolan government forces in 2002.

In West Africa, the three interventions in Liberia, Sierra Leone, and Côte d'Ivoire underlined the importance of an active UN Security Council role in subregional peacekeeping efforts. The United States, Britain, and France eventually pushed for interventions in former or current spheres of influence. In Liberia, the UN played a limited but useful monitoring role to the West African force, ECOMOG, and oversaw the country's 1997 election. The UN, pushed by Washington, also deployed a peacekeeping mission in Liberia in 2003, which has helped stabilize nearly two decades of civil conflicts. In Sierra Leone, the world body played a similar military monitoring role, as it had done during the first intervention in Liberia until it took over peacekeeping efforts from ECOMOG in 1999. British troops also helped stabilize a crumbling UN mission in 2000. In Côte d'Ivoire, the UN took over ECOWAS's peacekeeping responsibilities in 2004, while between 900 and 4,600 French troops worked alongside UN peacekeepers. West Africa's regional hegemon, Nigeria, closely supported by Ghana, played an important role in Liberia and Sierra Leone, providing the military backbone and financial support for both missions. However, some of Nigeria's neighbors accused it of pursuing a self-interested domineering agenda. Countries such as Burkina Faso, Côte d'Ivoire, Senegal, and Liberia sometimes obstructed peace efforts in both cases, forging alliances with domestic warlords—as did Nigeria—which prolonged the conflicts.

Finally, all four cases on the Horn of Africa—Somalia, Ethiopia-Eritrea, South Sudan, and Darfur—again revealed the importance of the role of powerful members of the UN Security Council in determining peacekeeping outcomes. The superpowers—the United States and the Soviet Union—had fought over both Somalia and Ethiopia during the Cold War. Washington's decision to lead a military intervention into Somalia in 1992 brought hope to the country and, for a while, stabilized parts of it until the United States withdrew from Somalia in 1993 after the killing of 18 of its soldiers, effectively crippling the mission by 1995. In Ethiopia-Eritrea, the Security Council's decision to send peacekeepers to the two countries in 2000, following regional and American intervention, was important in ending a bloody two-year conflict. In South Sudan, the United States was instrumental in pressuring Khartoum to sign a Comprehensive Peace Agreement in 2005, while China, with large economic interests in Sudan, also played a crucial role in convincing Khartoum to accept an AU/UN Hybrid Operation in Darfur in 2007. France played a more negative role by assisting the autocratic regime of Chad's Idriss Déby to remain in power and by manipulating the deployment of EU and UN peacekeeping missions in Chad–Central African Republic in 2008–2010 for self-interested reasons.

These four missions also revealed the importance of the willingness of the parties to make peace. In Somalia, the most powerful warlord, Mohammed Farah Aideed, was unwilling to share power and regarded the presence of peacekeepers as obstructing his political ambitions. He attacked UN troops in a bid to force their withdrawal. In Ethiopia-Eritrea, the refusal of both Addis Ababa and Asmara to implement an international boundary commission's 2002 decision to demarcate their common border eventually forced the Security Council to withdraw the UN mission in 2008. In South Sudan, rival groups fighting for a share of the spoils often made peacekeeping hazardous, though the prospect of an oil-rich independent state kept the process on track. In Darfur, the splintering of rebel groups complicated peace efforts, while Khartoum often negotiated in bad faith and continued to back antirebel militias who terrorized local populations. Ethiopia played an important, but not decisive, role in peacemaking efforts in Somalia in 1993, before subsequently backing rival Somali warlords and intervening militarily but ineffectually in the country in 2006, strongly supported by the United States. In Sudan, regional leaders from the Intergovernmental Authority on Development contributed to peacemaking efforts, though regional tensions between the leaders of Sudan and Chad often complicated these initiatives. Regional tensions also complicated the Ethiopia-Eritrea case as Asmara perceived the OAU to be biased toward Addis Ababa.

Based on these fifteen cases, I next offer five lessons for the UN's future efforts at managing conflicts in Africa and beyond. First, there is a need to encourage external actors—particularly the powerful members of the Security Council—to ensure an effective UN role in regional conflicts. Second, there must be an effective division of labor between the UN and African regional organizations such as the Economic Community of West African States, the Southern African Development Community, the Intergovernmental Authority on Development, and the African Union. Third, the UN should cooperate with local hegemons like Nigeria and South Africa, which possess relative political and military clout in their regions, in undertaking multilateral UN missions. Fourth, the UN should develop effective strategies to deal with domestic and regional "spoilers," who are determined to wreck peace processes.[2] Finally, able UN special representatives should be selected to head peacekeeping missions. These five lessons are elaborated below.

The Security Council's Great Powers

As emphasised throughout this study, the games that great powers (the five veto-wielding powers on the Security Council) play often determine the birth and fate of UN peacekeeping missions. As noted earlier, these fifteen cases have clearly demonstrated that the commitment of important members of the Council to UN peacekeeping in Africa and the politics surrounding their interactions within the Council are often vital to the outcome of these missions. The role of the United States and the Soviet Union was critical in forcing France and Britain to disgorge the Suez canal in 1956, after both European powers had invaded Egypt alongside Israel. This led to the birth of armed UN peacekeeping as a face-saving mechanism for the withdrawal of Anglo-French-Israeli troops and a way of keeping Egyptian and Israeli soldiers apart. In the case of the former Spanish colony of Western Sahara, the United States and France obstructed UN efforts to organize a self-determination referendum that they feared Morocco would lose. Washington and Paris appeared to be more concerned about the stability of their Moroccan ally than the rights of the people of Western Sahara.

The United States was able to delay the implementation of a peace plan for Namibia for twelve years, between 1978 and 1989, due to Cold War calculations of curbing Cuban and Soviet military support for the socialist regime in Angola. Washington played a critical role in obstructing UN action to stop the genocide in Rwanda in which about eight hundred thousand people were killed in 1994. The critical decision to send a UN peacekeeping force to Rwanda in 1993 was pushed strongly in the Security Council by France, which hoped to use the peacekeepers for its own parochial national interests in keeping Juvénal Habyarimana in power. France provided support to the autocratic regime of Idriss Déby in Chad, pushing the UN to deploy a peacekeeping force there from July 2009 to December 2010, having earlier manipulated the UN to dispatch troops to the Central African Republic between 1998 and 2000 in promotion of efforts to stabilize another traditional Gallic sphere of influence in Africa.

More positively, the sustained interest and cooperation of the powerful members of the UN Security Council and their contribution (particularly the United States and Russia) of financial, diplomatic, and logistical support to UN missions was important to success in Namibia (1989–1990) and Mozambique (1992–1994). The US role in Somalia in 1993 and Liberia in 2003; the British role in Sierra Leone in 1999; the French role in Côte d'Ivoire in 2004; and the Chinese role in Sudan's Darfur region in 2007 were all crucial to the establishment of UN missions in these countries. The American leadership of the UN mission in Somalia in 1992–1993, the more limited British intervention in Sierra Leone in 2000, and the French intervention in Côte d'Ivoire in 2002 also demonstrated that, even if only to provide military support to weak peacekeeping missions, the involvement of such armies is crucial in filling gaps created by the deficiencies of militaries from developing countries. It was, however, grossly irresponsible that Washington, London, and Paris—three permanent members of the Security Council—did not place their troops under UN command, choosing instead a desire to maintain their own independence of action over the need to strengthen global UN peacekeeping missions. Though these countries would argue about the weakness of UN command and control, their presence in the command structures of these missions could have done much to improve the effectiveness of the UN's peacekeeping efforts.[3] In the DRC, France played an important role in leading two European Union forces in 2003 and 2006 that helped to stabilize Bunia and Kinshasa respectively, while the United States played an important role in pressuring its Rwandese and Ugandan allies to withdraw their troops from the country in 2002. Despite the presumed domestic political risks of participating in such missions, it is important that a new "aristocracy of death" not be established where the lives of Western soldiers are worth more than those of non-Western peacekeepers and African civilians.

The two UN peacekeeping missions in Sudan also demonstrated the positive role that great powers can play in helping to support the world body's peacekeeping efforts. In South Sudan, the United States played an important role in pressuring Khartoum to accept the Comprehensive Peace Agreement in 2005. China—another veto-wielding permanent member of the Council and the largest investor in, and importer of, Sudanese oil—also played an important role in pushing Khartoum to accept a UN mission in Darfur in 2007. Beijing further deployed troops to the UN missions in South Sudan and Darfur. A third permanent member, Britain, also played an important role—along with the United States and Norway—in the Intergovernment Authority on Development Partner's Forum, which supported peacemaking efforts in South Sudan. The UN Security Council must also deploy peacekeepers and provide regional actors in Africa in a timely manner, with the logistical and financial resources that they need if such missions are to achieve their goals. The ECOWAS-led missions in Liberia and Sierra Leone between 1997 and 2003, the AU-led mission in Burundi between 2003 and 2004, and the AU mission in Sudan's Darfur region between 2003 and 2007 (all four eventually effectively taken over by the UN) revealed that, if the Security Council helps to mobilize resources and funds by external actors, and if there is a will on the part of the parties to disarm their factions, even a poorly resourced regional body can help stabilize conflict situations and save lives.

While the five permanent members of the UN Security Council often fueled conflicts and/or supported autocrats in Africa during the Cold War era, Council members have also sometimes played a more positive role in peacemaking efforts in post–Cold War Africa. Significantly, it took the support of Britain, the United States, and France—three Western "godfathers" and all veto-wielding permanent members of the UN Security Council—to establish a UN presence in their former spheres of influence. The UN mission in Liberia was directed by American diplomat Jacques Klein from 2003 to 2005, and Washington helped create a new Liberian army. In Sierra Leone, Britain sent eight hundred troops in 2000 to help stabilize a faltering UN mission, led international efforts to mobilize donor support, and used its permanent seat on the Security Council to increase the size of the peacekeeping force to twenty thousand—the largest UN peacekeeping mission in the world at the time. Likewise, France ensured the deployment of a UN mission to Côte d'Ivoire in 2004 and an EU force that helped stabilize parts of the DRC in 2003 and 2006. China also helped ensure that peacekeepers were deployed to South Sudan in 2005 and to Darfur in 2007. The role of the five permanent members of the Security Council is thus crucial to the creation and success of UN peacekeeping missions in Africa and beyond. However, with Africa and Latin America the only regions in the world without permanent membership on the Council, the need for the body to be democratized is urgent.

Establishing an Effective Division of Labor

It is important to emphasize that the UN Security Council has primary responsibility for international peace and security as enshrined in its Charter of 1945. The world body has, however, sometimes shifted its peacekeeping responsibilities to regional actors like the AU (Darfur and Burundi) and ECOWAS (Liberia, Sierra Leone, and Côte d'Ivoire) due to the reluctance of the Security Council, after *débâcles* in Somalia (1993) and Rwanda (1994), to sanction UN missions in Africa. The Council is yet to develop a strategic vision for engaging Africa's regional bodies and prefers to retain as much flexibility as possible to determine whether the interests of P-5 members are at stake rather than ensuring that viable peacekeeping missions are deployed where security needs are greatest. This volume's fifteen cases of UN peacekeeping in Africa offer important lessons for the future. There remains an urgent need for Western countries in particular to demonstrate a similar generosity to Africa as they have done in Bosnia, Kosovo, and East Timor. For example, in early 2000, while $2 billion was pledged for the reconstruction of what Egyptian UN Secretary-General Boutros Boutros-Ghali famously described as "rich men's wars" in the Balkans, barely $150 million was pledged for Sierra Leone's "poor man's war."

Based on these fifteen cases, there is a pressing need to establish a proper division of labor between the UN and Africa's fledgling security organizations, which need to be greatly strengthened by the UN Security Council. Rwanda's Arusha agreement of 1993, the DRC's Lusaka accord of 1999, and the Algiers accords of 2000 that ended the Ethiopia-Eritrea conflict all clearly revealed the military weakness of the OAU/AU, whose members lacked the resources to implement agreements they had negotiated without UN peacekeepers. In Sierra Leone and Liberia, the UN took over peacekeeping duties from ECOMOG in 2000 and 2003 respectively. The world body also took over the AU mission in Burundi and the ECOWAS mission in Côte d'Ivoire both in 2004, as well as the AU mission in Darfur in 2007. The UN Security Council has not done much to strengthen the capacity of regional organizations and to collaborate effectively with them in the field. The willingness of Western peacekeepers, who have both the equipment and resources, to continue to contribute to UN missions in Africa therefore remains important.

Although many UN processes have pledged support toward strengthening the peacekeeping capacity of Africa's regional organizations, this has often been more a case of rhetoric than reality. Since 1994, regular meetings have been held in New York between the UN and African and other regional organizations. These have tended to be "talk shops" in which the UN's chattering classes make empty declarations of intent in a charade of sound and fury that has signified nothing so far. In order to avoid the UN Security Council blocking peacekeeping interventions that are necessary to save lives and restore order in Africa, both the AU and ECOWAS have set up security mechanisms that controversially do not require prior UN authorization for action.[4] These regional bodies simply *inform* the UN after they have taken action. However, such actions could eventually weaken the UN's legitimacy in Africa as the body with primary responsibility for maintaining global peace and security.[5]

Western armies from the Netherlands, Canada, Denmark, and Italy contributed peacekeepers to the UN mission in Ethiopia-Eritrea in 2000 after years of retrenchment. The difficult experience of regional peacekeepers like ECOMOG, SADC, and the OAU in Liberia, Lesotho, Burundi, and

Comoros, as well as the near collapse of the ill-equipped UN mission in Sierra Leone, are all clear signs of the need for better-equipped and richer Western peacekeepers to continue to contribute to efforts to maintain peace and security in Africa. It is important that the Security Council not turn peacekeeping in Africa into an apartheid system in which the Africans and Asians spill most of the blood and powerful actors in the West pay some of the bills when they can be bothered. The Council's rhetorical support for "African solutions to African problems" often appears to many on the continent to be a cynical attempt to convert a Cold War battle cry by Africans to rid their continent of foreign meddlers into an excuse to abandon the UN's proper peacekeeping responsibilities in Africa.

But while the cases of Somalia (1993) and Rwanda (1994) signified to many the neglect of Africa by the UN Security Council, other cases provide examples of the potential of cooperation between the UN and Africa's regional organizations. The UN and the OAU eventually cooperated in the deployment of peacekeepers to Ethiopia-Eritrea, after the OAU had mediated an accord that the UN was asked to implement. In Ethiopia-Eritrea, as in Western Sahara and Rwanda, despite the OAU being the principal early mediators, when it came to deploying peacekeepers on the ground, the UN was called upon to keep peace due to the OAU's lack of logistical and financial capacity. The UN's peacekeeping efforts in Ethiopia-Eritrea and the crucial support of the United States and the European Union for the Algiers accords of 2000 demonstrate the importance of external actors to peace processes in Africa. In efforts to mediate an end to the conflict in South Sudan between 2002 and 2005, the United States and Britain (along with Norway) also provided political and military backing to IGAD's regional efforts. Regional actors in Africa still lack the financial, diplomatic, and logistical muscle of outsiders and must be generously supported.

After difficult experiences with ECOMOG in Liberia and Sierra Leone between 1993 and 2000, there is still great unease within the UN Security Council and Secretariat in New York about working alongside regional peacekeepers (especially within the UN Department of Peace-keeping Operations) There was, for example, much hostility directed against the continuing presence of Nigerian peacekeepers in Sierra Leone in 1999 within the UN Secretariat in New York due to a wish to have the world body clearly take over the mission. Many UN officials insisted on a reduced Nigerian role while overselling a new UN mission to Sierra Leoneans who were misled into believing that the Blue Helmets would be prepared to fight the country's rebels.[6] The same reticence was demonstrated by DPKO toward having a hybrid AU/UN force in Sudan's Darfur region in 2007 due to difficulties of a dual reporting structure. While I recognize the need for clear command and control and reporting structures, the UN must, however, be more sensitive about profound African apprehension at sacrificing blood and treasure in lonely peacekeeping theaters for many years, only to see a UN force belatedly riding in to steal the glory. The UN's peacekeeping efforts in Ethiopia-Eritrea and the crucial political support of powerful Western governments for the UN operations in Mozambique, Sierra Leone, Liberia, Côte d'Ivoire, and Sudan demonstrate the continuing importance of external actors to peacekeeping missions in Africa.[7]

In discussing the lessons of UN/ECOWAS cooperation in Liberia, Sierra Leone, and Côte d'Ivoire between 1999 and 2011, these interventions underlined the importance of an active Security Council role in subregional peacekeeping efforts. In Liberia, the UN played a limited but useful monitoring role to ECOMOG and oversaw the country's 1997 election. The UN also deployed a peacekeeping mission to Liberia in 2003 that was still there in 2011. In Sierra Leone, the UN played a similar military monitoring role as in the first intervention in Liberia until it took over peacekeeping efforts from ECOMOG in 1999. In Côte d'Ivoire, the UN took over ECOWAS's peacekeeping responsibilities after a year in 2004. In the cases of Burundi and Sudan's Darfur region, the UN effectively took over the AU's peacekeeping responsibilities in 2004 and 2007 respectively, "rehatting" many of their soldiers with Blue Helmets as it had done in the three West African cases. Such innovative divisions of labor are important to sharing the burden of peacekeeping in Africa. With the announcement by the AU commission in 2010 of the establishment of an African Standby Force (ASF), to be composed of five subregional brigades,[8] it will be important that the deployment of this force is closely linked to the UN's own peacekeeping efforts. The ASF could help act as a bridging force in African theaters, as ECOMOG did in Liberia before a larger UN force was deployed in 2003. UN peacekeepers in Sierra Leone, the DRC, South Sudan, and Darfur often took over six months to deploy most of their contingents; thus deploying the ASF could be sensible in these cases. As the Prodi report on peacekeeping in 2008 suggested, the UN Security Council should fund these missions and then take them over after six months.[9]

The UN Security Council's adoption of a regional approach to conflict management in Africa is also a positive step. The security complexes of all five African subregions examined here were highly interdependent. In North Africa, the Western Sahara issue was linked to a historical rivalry by Morocco and Algeria to secure leadership of the Maghreb region; in the Great Lakes, the Congo crisis was linked to the civil wars in Burundi and Rwanda, which drew armies, refugees, and rebels into a complex web of conflicts; in Southern Africa, liberation movements, governments, and rebels in Namibia, Angola, and Mozambique were involved in a struggle against apartheid South Africa; in West Africa, the conflicts in Liberia, Sierra Leone, and Côte d'Ivoire spread into each other's territories through rebels, arms, and refugees; and on the Horn of Africa, the two conflicts in Sudan were linked to those in Ethiopia-Eritrea, Somalia, Chad, and the

Central African Republic, with regional governments often supporting rebels against each other's regimes.

The UN office that was established in West Africa in May 2001 and the cooperation between UN missions in Liberia, Sierra Leone, and Côte d'Ivoire was repeated through the International Conference for the Great Lakes in November 2004 and August 2009, in which the UN sought to promote a regional approach to the conflicts in the region in partnership with the AU, regional governments, civil society actors, and foreign donors. Further efforts in this regard involved cooperation between UN missions in Burundi, the DRC, and Sudan and the UN's cooperation with IGAD in the Horn of Africa. These all represent potentially positive steps in ensuring that the links that fuel regional conflicts are effectively addressed. However, it must be noted that these efforts have not yet translated into genuine regional approaches on the ground, as institutional rivalries and entrenched national thinking still remain pervasive within individual missions.

Another important issue that must be addressed in the area of relations between the UN and Africa's regional organizations is the proliferation of mediators in cases such as Côte d'Ivoire, Burundi, the DRC, Liberia, and Sudan. This situation often complicated peacemaking efforts and encouraged warring parties to engage in "forum shopping," which sometimes allowed them to play off special envoys against one another and made the resolution of these disputes more complicated. It is important that either the UN or a regional body lead and coordinate future peacemaking efforts.

Multilateralizing Hegemony

The third key peacekeeping lesson from our fifteen cases is for the UN to find ways of harnessing the important military and financial capacity of local hegemons like Nigeria and South Africa into more multilateral efforts under a UN umbrella. Africa's two Gullivers must be tied into a web of mutual interdependence with other Lilliputian states in the region. The two ECOMOG interventions in Liberia and Sierra Leone demonstrated the importance of Nigeria to peacekeeping efforts in West Africa.[10] Despite continuing fears expressed by several ECOWAS states and numerous commentators of a bullying Nigeria clumsily rampaging through West Africa like a bull in a china shop, Nigeria appears to be an important presence to the success of subregional peacekeeping initiatives.[11] In Liberia and Sierra Leone, Nigerian-led ECOMOG forces were able to overcome their logistical shortcomings to protect Monrovia and Freetown from being overrun by rebels in 1992 and 1999 respectively. The Nigerians had also been able to repel Charles Taylor's NPFL from Monrovia in 1990 and to restore the elected president Ahmed Tejjan Kabbah to power in Freetown in 1998.

The mission in Côte d'Ivoire has been sustained by the presence of 4,600 French troops (reduced to nine hundred by 2010) backed up by eight thousand UN peacekeepers. France is, however, unlikely to be a more natural and reliable hegemon in West Africa than Nigeria. Pax Nigeriana, though, faces both opportunities and obstacles in a post–Cold War era. The country's enormous political and socioeconomic problems and the aversion of Nigerian public opinion to future costly interventions may prove to be major constraints for elected civilian governments as opposed to the military brass hats who launched interventions into Liberia and Sierra Leone. Nigeria withdrew 8,500 of its peacekeepers from Sierra Leone by 2000 and insisted that the UN take over the Nigerian-led mission in Liberia in 2003 after three months as a condition for deploying, illustrating the growing frustrations of the West African Gulliver with carrying a disproportionate burden of regional peacekeeping. Most ECOWAS countries, however, no longer question the need for Nigerian leadership but rather its penchant for a unilateral diplomatic style that often offends the sensibilities of smaller, poorer, and weaker states. Nigeria must learn to speak softly, even as it carries a big stick.

South Africa played a peacekeeping role similar to that of Nigeria in leading the UN mission in Burundi and contributing substantially to the mission in the DRC. The country also led peacemaking efforts in both countries that resulted in peacekeeping missions being deployed to Burundi and the DRC. South Africa's three postapartheid presidents—Nelson Mandela, Thabo Mbeki, and Jacob Zuma—were all involved in some of these efforts. In a short decade and a half, South Africa went from being the continent's most destabilizing force under apartheid to becoming its most energetic peacemaker.[12] But like Nigeria, South Africa also showed its frustrations at the burden of regional peacekeeping, insisting that the UN take over the AU force in Burundi in 2004. As the most unequal society in the world in 2010 (in terms of the Gini coefficient), with massive socioeconomic inequalities, South Africa is likely to focus greater attention on its own domestic affairs in future. However, Tshwane (Pretoria) must also be encouraged to continue to contribute to peacekeeping efforts on its own continent, particularly as—like Nigeria—it seeks a permanent seat on a reformed UN Security Council.

Dealing with Spoilers

The fourth lesson from our fifteen UN peacekeeping cases is that there is a strong case to be made for developing strategies to deal with "spoilers" like Somalia's Mohammed Farah Aideed, Angola's Jonas Savimbi, Liberia's Charles Taylor, Sierra Leone's Foday Sankoh, and Rwanda's *génocidaires* who were determined to see the UN fail and attempted to ensure its withdrawal from their countries by attacking its peacekeepers. The economic, political, and legal sanctions of the sort that were imposed on Taylor in

Liberia and Savimbi in Angola would seem appropriate in such cases. The post–Cold War innovation of establishing UN panels to "name and shame" countries and leaders that are supporting rebels could also be a useful tool for the UN to seek to achieve compliance with peace accords, as long as such reports are based on meticulous research and information. The economic sanctions imposed by the UN Security Council on Savimbi in October 1997 and Taylor in May 2001 appear to have made a significant contribution to ending the wars in Angola, Liberia, and Sierra Leone.

The two cases of Liberia and Sierra Leone particularly underline the importance of developing effective strategies and sanctions to deal with subregional spoilers like Charles Taylor and Foday Sankoh. In both cases, warring factions killed and kidnapped ECOMOG and UN peacekeepers and stole their weapons and vehicles. In both cases, peacekeepers were deployed with no peace to keep and with recalcitrant warlords determined to use violence to force the withdrawal of peacekeepers. It is difficult not to take decisive action under such circumstances, and the UN Security Council should consider, when appropriate, mandating peacekeepers to take enforcement action against spoilers and imposing carefully targeted economic, political, and legal sanctions of the sort that were successfully applied to the Revolutionary United Front in Sierra Leone and Charles Taylor in Liberia. European, North American, and Asian commercial firms also played a negative role in supporting Liberian and Sierra Leonean warlords through the illicit export of natural resources and minerals from both countries. In devising sanctions against factions or subregional states, the Council should consider the actions of these firms and, if necessary, punish them. The same approach should apply in the DRC, where countries such as Rwanda and Uganda were fingered in looting the country's resources and Western, Chinese, and South African firms were also accused of involvement in this illicit trade.

Led by Britain and the United States, the Security Council imposed economic and travel sanctions as well as an arms embargo on Charles Taylor's regime in May 2001. Though ECOWAS leaders opposed these sanctions at the time, the punitive measures appear to have had a major impact in ending the arms-for-diamonds trade between Taylor and the RUF. They weakened his regime tremendously and thus helped to end the wars in Liberia and Sierra Leone. The opposition of West African leaders to sanctioning Taylor's fueling of conflicts in the subregion and the granting of political asylum to the Liberian president by Nigeria in 2003 underlined the traditional reluctance of the continent's leaders to punish each other. While Taylor's autocratic rule and war crimes in Liberia are indefensible (though the Security Council met with the former warlord in Monrovia during its visit to the region in October 2000), US pressure saw Nigeria hand Taylor over to the Special Court in Sierra Leone in April 2006. Such selective, self-interested efforts at punishing warlords—apparently based on Washington's concerns of an alleged link, reported by a *Washington Post* journalist, between Taylor-backed RUF Sierra Leonean diamonds and Al-Qaida in the US global "war on terror"—are, however, unlikely to contribute to boosting the credibility of the evolving international criminal justice regime.[13] Sudanese leader Omar al-Bashir was also indicted for war crimes in Darfur by the Hague-based International Criminal Court in March 2009. This action was extremely unpopular with most African governments and some analysts as it was widely felt that only African actors were being targeted by the ICC despite its global mandate. It must, however, be noted that two African governments—Uganda and the DRC—had themselves referred cases to the Court.

In Angola, the UN Security Council imposed sanctions on the country's diamond exports in October 1997 in a bid to weaken rebel leader Jonas Savimbi's funding base. A UN panel of inquiry complemented this approach by working hard to "name and shame" countries such as Zaire (now the DRC), Congo-Brazzaville, Togo, and Burkina Faso that were suspected of providing military support to the Angolan warlord. But there were also several occasions when positive inducements rather than punitive sanctions were used against difficult warlords. Mozambican rebel leader, Afonso Dhlakama, was provided with about $20 million between 1992 and 1994 to transform his guerrilla movement into a political party and to cover other expenses. In Burundi, Pierre Nkurunziza's rebel group was brought into the transitional government in March 2004 before he went on to win presidential elections a year later. In the DRC, a transitional government in July 2003 brought Joseph Kabila together with former rebel groups until elections in 2006. Even Liberia's Charles Taylor and Sierra Leone's Foday Sankoh had earlier been brought into transitional governments in 1995 and 1998 respectively, though neither changed his war-mongering ways.

Selecting Effective UN Special Representatives

The fifth key lesson from our fifteen cases is concerned with the quality of diplomats serving as UN special representatives. This can be important to the success of peacekeeping missions, as the examples of Aldo Ajello in Mozambique and, eventually, Olu Adeniji in Sierra Leone demonstrated. Less skillful special representatives can, on the other hand, make a difficult situation worse as appears to have been the case with Jonathan Howe in Somalia, Jacques Roger Booh-Booh in Rwanda, and to a lesser extent Rodolphe Adada in Sudan's Darfur region. But it is important to note that adroit diplomacy alone is insufficient to achieve peacekeeping success, as the case of the martyred Alioune Blondin Beye demonstrated in Angola. While personalities do matter in peacekeeping, our fifteen cases demonstrate that it is the will of the parties to implement agreements and the consistent support of regional and external actors (particularly the UN Security Council) that are the most important factors in determining the success of UN peacekeeping missions in Africa.

* * *

Having assessed five key factors for peacekeeping success in Africa, I conclude with some further reflections on Africa's continuing peacekeeping challenges. The Brahimi Report of August 2000 had sought to strengthen the UN's peacekeeping capacity and suggested innovations such as preapproving funds for peacekeeping missions, improving the rapid deployment of civilian personnel to UN missions, and strengthening communication between headquarters in New York and the field. A decade later, the UN had only implemented some of these recommendations and peacekeeping continued to have an improvised character, driven largely by the political interests of the five permanent members of the UN Security Council. The Security Council did not accept Brahimi's recommendations to build sustained political and financial support to launch peacekeeping missions. The Council also declined to implement Brahimi's recommendations to establish standby brigades and to strengthen the UN's planning and analytical capacity. UN peacekeeping missions are also still often in desperate need of night-vision equipment, modern communication tools, naval vessels, and military helicopters.[14] The deployment of missions to Burundi, South Sudan, and Darfur between 2004 and 2008 certainly did not follow many of Brahimi's recommendations on rapid deployment and being able to say no to powerful members of the UN Security Council.

One of the key problems that emerged from these "third generation" peacekeeping missions after 1999 was the reluctance of national governments to put their own troops in harm's way, even when missions had Chapter VII peace-enforcement powers and mandates to protect civilian populations. This resulted in serious problems for UN missions in Rwanda, Angola, Sierra Leone, the DRC, South Sudan, and Darfur. In all these cases, peacekeepers were sent into theaters with no peace to keep and denied important equipment such as helicopters, leaving them vulnerable to attacks by warring parties, which often occurred, sometimes with fatal consequences. The key non-African contributors to UN peacekeeping on the continent also remain Asian countries such as Bangladesh, Pakistan, and India, whose soldiers do not have the equipment of richer Western nations. While Africa is grateful for the solidarity shown by these Asian countries, it is also important to capacitate UN peacekeeping contingents deployed to the continent. The emergence of China—the world's second-largest economy by 2010 and a permanent member of the Security Council—as a major investor in, and importer from, Africa has been much remarked on.[15] Beijing deployed about 1,800 troops to African peacekeeping efforts between 1999 and 2007. With a rapidly modernizing army, Africans must urge China to match its economic interests on the continent with peacekeeping support. However, with Beijing having more strategic interests closer to home, one should also not exaggerate its stomach to play a disproportionately burdensome peacekeeping role in Africa.

The peace-enforcement actions undertaken by UN peacekeepers in the DRC (alongside the Congolese army) also raise serious questions about the impartiality that had always guided UN peacekeeping since the Suez crisis of 1956. UN missions now operate in more difficult civil war environments with multiple factions that are often mutating. These situations do not involve the separation of two willing belligerent countries that was envisaged when peacekeeping started. However, enforcement actions by UN peacekeepers could seriously compromise their efforts and lead to attacks against their troops. Such strategies must thus be carefully calibrated and attempts made not to appear to be taking sides by fighting with armed groups, particularly central governments against which other factions are rebelling. In such cases, UN peacekeepers should act as autonomously as possible with a clear and achievable mandate in cases in which spoilers have previously been clearly identified and sanctioned by the UN Security Council.

One of the key challenges of UN peacekeeping in Africa and beyond is how to judge the success of peacekeeping. UN peacekeepers have been in Western Sahara for two decades, failing to organize a self-determination referendum but halting sixteen years of previous fighting. Three million people have died in the DRC since 2000 despite the UN's presence, but many would agree that the situation would have been even worse without the international peacekeepers whose military presence and civilian officials helped to organize the country's first democratic elections in forty years in 2006. Similarly, the UN's presence in Sudan's Darfur region since 2007 has not stopped the deaths of thousands of Darfuris, but few doubt that the killings have been slowed by the UN's presence, and many Darfuris find the deployment of UN peacekeepers important to curbing some of Khartoum's excesses and ending this dispute. The same arguments of the UN's legitimizing and stabilizing effect can be made in Liberia, Sierra Leone, and Côte d'Ivoire, despite serious political, military, and financial shortcomings.

The UN must, however, not underestimate the great damage that the Congo crisis in the 1960s did to its reputation in Africa, resulting in no deployment of any UN missions on the continent for twenty-five years. Following the death of Congolese prime minister Patrice Lumumba under the noses of UN peacekeepers in 1961, the suspicions of socialist liberation movements and regimes in Namibia, Angola, and Mozambique toward the UN were clearly evident. More recently, governments in Côte d'Ivoire, the DRC, Burundi, and Chad have all sought to assert their sovereignty by reducing the role of the UN in their countries. The world body must be conscious that several African governments hosting its peacekeepers have calculated that the presence of its peacekeepers is more trouble than it is worth. Some UN officials are also considered to be ignorant, pampered, overpaid, and insensitive bureaucrats who are living off the misery of war-torn countries. The cases of child sex abuse scandals involving its peacekeepers that have been reported have further damaged the UN's image in Africa. The world body would do well to take these complaints to heart in deploying future missions on the continent.

Finally, it is important to bring this conclusion to an end by once again noting Africa's immense conceptual and practical contributions to the birth, development, and growth of UN peacekeeping over the last five and a half decades. The Suez mission in 1956 was the first-ever armed UN peacekeeping force, while the Congo crisis in 1960–1964 provided the first case of UN peace enforcement. The multidimensional peacekeeping operations of the post–Cold War era were ushered in by the Namibia mission in 1989–1990, while further innovations have been seen in the cooperation between the UN and ECOWAS in Liberia, Sierra Leone, and Côte d'Ivoire between 1993 and 2004, with the AU in Burundi in 2004, and with the hybrid mission with the AU in Sudan's Darfur region that started in 2007. Three Africans—UN Secretaries-General between 1992–2006, Egypt's Boutros Boutros-Ghali, Ghana's Kofi Annan, and Algeria's Lakhdar Brahimi—were also instrumental in shaping much of the UN's post–Cold War peacekeeping architecture. Sudanese scholar-diplomat Francis Deng provided much of the early intellectual thinking that shaped the concept of the "responsibility to protect." With regard to UN peacekeeping on the continent, it is perhaps appropriate to end this study with the immortal words of Pliny the Elder, the philosopher-soldier of the Roman empire, who famously observed "Ex Africa semper aliquid novi": there is always something new out of Africa.

Notes

I thank Patrick Cammaert and Paul Williams for their useful comments on an earlier draft of this chapter.

1. Salim Ahmed Salim, "The OAU Role in Conflict Management," in Olara Otunnu and Michael Doyle, eds., *Peacemaking and Peacekeeping for the New Century* (Lanham, MD: Rowman and Littlefield, 1998), p. 246.

2. On the concept of "spoilers," see Stephen Stedman, "Spoiler Problems in Peace Processes," *International Security* 22, no. 2 (Fall 1997): 5–53.

3. I thank Paul Williams for helping me to nuance this point.

4. See Adekeye Adebajo, "Prophets of Pax Africana: Africa's Security Architecture," in Adekeye Adebajo, *The Curse of Berlin: Africa After the Cold War* (New York: Columbia University Press, 2010), pp. 31–52.

5. See Musifiky Mwanasali, "The African Union, the United Nations, and the Responsibility to Protect: Towards an African Intervention Doctrine," *Global Responsibility to Protect* 2, no. 4 (2010): 388–413.

6. See James Jonah, "The United Nations," in Adekeye Adebajo and Ismail Rashid, eds., *West Africa's Security Challenges: Building Peace in A Troubled Region* (Boulder: Lynne Rienner, 2004), p. 331.

7. I thank General Patrick Cammaert for helping me to nuance the points in this paragraph.

8. See Solomon A. Dersso, "The Role and Place of the African Standby Force Within the African Peace and Security Architecture," Institute for Security Studies, Tshwane, South Africa, Paper 209, January 2010.

9. UN General Assembly, Report of the Special Committee on Peacekeeping Operations, A/64/19, 22 February–19 March 2010.

10. See Adekeye Adebajo, "Mad Dogs and Glory: Nigeria's Interventions in Liberia and Sierra Leone," in Adekeye Adebajo and Raufu Mustapha, eds., *Gulliver's Troubles: Nigeria's Foreign Policy After the Cold War* (Scottsville, South Africa: University of KwaZulu-Natal Press, 2008), pp. 177–202.

11. This view was confirmed by Ahmedou Ould-Abdallah, UN special representative for West Africa, during an interview in Dakar, Senegal, 5 June 2006.

12. See, for example, Adekeye Adebajo, Adebayo Adedeji, and Chris Landsberg, eds., *South Africa in Africa: The Post-Apartheid Era* (Scottsville, South Africa: University of KwaZulu-Natal Press, 2007); Chris Landsberg, *The Diplomacy of Transformation: South African Foreign Policy and Statecraft* (Johannesburg: Pan Macmillan, 2010).

13. See A. Bolaji Akinyemi, "The Taylor Saga: A Clash of Civilisations," *New African*, no. 451 (May 2006): 20–23; Ali A. Mazrui, "A True Citizen of the World," interview, *AU Magazine* 1, no. 4 (June–August 2005), p. 17.

14. UN Department of Peacekeeping Operations and Department of Field Support, *A New Partnership Agenda: Charting a New Horizon for UN Peacekeeping* (New York: United Nations, July 2009), pp. 11, 24, and 32.

15. See, for example, Kweku Ampiah and Sanusha Naidu, eds., *Crouching Tiger, Hidden Dragon? Africa and China* (Scottsville, South Africa: University of KwaZulu-Natal Press, 2008); Chris Alden, Daniel Large, and Ricardo Soares De Oliveira, eds., *China Returns to Africa: A Rising Power and a Continent Embrace* (London: Hurst, 2008); Garth le Pere, ed., *China in Africa: Mercantilist Predator or Partner in Development?* (Johannesburg: Institute for Global Dialogue and South African Institute of International Affairs, 2006); Robert I. Rotberg, ed., *China into Africa: Trade, Aid, and Influence* (Washington, DC: Brookings Institution, 2008); Ian Taylor, *China's New Role in Africa* (Boulder: Lynne Rienner, 2009).

Bibliography

Abi-Saab, Georges. *The United Nations Operation in the Congo 1960–1964*. Oxford: Oxford University Press, 1978.

Aboagye, Festus. "Towards New Peacekeeping Partnerships in Africa? The OAU Liaison Mission in Ethiopia/Eritrea." *African Security Review* 10, no. 2 (2001): 19–33.

Aburish, Saïd K. *Nasser: The Last Arab*. London: Gerald Duckworth, 2005.

Adebajo, Adekeye. *Building Peace in West Africa: Liberia, Sierra Leone, and Guinea-Bissau*. Boulder: Lynne Rienner, 2002.

———. *The Curse of Berlin: Africa After the Cold War*. New York: Columbia University Press, 2010.

———, ed., *From Global Apartheid to Global Village: Africa and the United Nations*. Scottsville, South Africa: University of KwaZulu-Natal Press, 2009.

———. *Liberia's Civil War: Nigeria, ECOMOG and Regional Security in West Africa*. Boulder: Lynne Rienner, 2002.

———. "Nigeria: Africa's New Gendarme?" *Security Dialogue* 31, no. 2 (June 2000): 185–199.

———. "Selling Out the Sahara? The Tragic Tale of the UN Referendum." Occasional Paper Series, Institute for African Development, Cornell University, Spring 2002.

Adebajo, Adekeye, Adebayo Adedeji, and Chris Landsberg, eds. *South Africa in Africa: The Post-Apartheid Era*. Scottsville, South Africa: University of KwaZulu-Natal Press, 2007.

Adebajo, Adekeye, and David Keen. "Sierra Leone," in Mats Berdal and Spyros Economides, eds., *United Nations Interventionism 1991–2004* (Cambridge: Cambridge University Press, 2007), pp. 246–273.

Adebajo, Adekeye, and Raufu Mustapha, eds. *Gulliver's Troubles: Nigeria's Foreign Policy After the Cold War*. Scottsville, South Africa: University of Kwazulu-Natal Press, 2008.

Adebajo, Adekeye, Mark Paterson, and Jeremy Sarkin, eds. Special Issue: Africa's Responsibility to Protect, *Global Responsibility to Protect* 2, no. 4 (2010).

Adebajo, Adekeye, and Ismail Rashid, eds. *West Africa's Security Challenges: Building Peace in a Troubled Region*. Boulder: Lynne Rienner, 2004.

Adebajo, Adekeye, and Helen Scanlon, eds. *A Dialogue of the Deaf: Essays on Africa and the United Nations*. Johannesburg: Jacana, 2006.

Adebajo, Adekeye, and Chandra Lekha Sriram, eds. *Managing Armed Conflicts in the 21st Century.* London: Frank Cass, 2001.

Adebo, Simeon Ola. *Our International Years.* Ibadan: Spectrum, 1988.

Adedeji, Adebayo A., ed. *South Africa in Africa: Within or Apart?* London: Zed, 1996.

Adelman, Howard, and Astri Suhrke, eds. *The Path of a Genocide: The Rwanda Crisis from Uganda to Zaire.* New Brunswick, NJ: Transaction, 1999.

Adibe, Clement. "The Liberian Conflict and the ECOWAS-UN Partnership." *Third World Quarterly* 18, no. 3 (1997): 471–488.

African Development. Special issue on "Youth Culture and Political Violence: The Sierra Leone Civil War." *African Development* 22, nos. 2 and 3 (1997).

Ajello, Aldo. *Brasiers d'Afrique: Mémoires d'un Émissaire pour la Paix.* Paris: L'Harmattan, 2010.

Akokpari, John, Angela Ndinga-Muvumba, and Tim Murithi, eds. *The African Union and Its Institutions.* Johannesburg: Jacana, 2008.

Alao, Abiodun, John Mackinlay, and 'Funmi Olonisakin. *Peacekeepers, Politicians, and Warlords: The Liberian Peace Process.* New York: United Nations University Press, 1999.

Alden, Chris, Daniel Large, and Ricardo Soares De Oliveira, eds. *China Returns to Africa: A Rising Power and a Continent Embrace.* London: Hurst, 2008.

Amnesty International. *Chad: "We Too Deserve Protection."* London: Amnesty International, July 2010.

Ampiah, Kweku, and Sanusha Naidu, eds. *Crouching Tiger, Hidden Dragon? Africa and China.* Scottsville, South Africa: University of KwaZulu-Natal Press, 2008.

Anyidoho, Henry Kwami. *Guns over Kigali.* Accra: Woeli Publishing Services, 1999.

Appiah-Mensah, Seth. "The African Union Mission in Sudan: Darfur Dilemmas." *African Security Review* 15, no. 1 (2006): 2–19.

———. "AU's Critical Assignment in Darfur: Challenges and Constraints." *African Security Review* 14, no. 2 (2005): 7–21.

Autesserre, Séverine. *The Trouble with the Congo: Local Violence and the Failure of International Peacebuilding.* Cambridge: Cambridge University Press, 2010.

Bah, Alhaji M. S., and Festus Aboagye, eds. *A Tortuous Road to Peace: The Dynamics of Regional, UN, and International Humanitarian Interventions in Liberia.* Tshwane: Institute for Security Studies, 2005.

Barber, James, and John Barratt, *South Africa's Foreign Policy, 1948–88: The Search for Status and Security.* Cambridge: Cambridge University Press, 1990.

Baregu, Mwesiga, and Christopher Landsberg, eds. *From Cape to Congo: Southern Africa's Evolving Security Challenges.* Boulder: Lynne Rienner, 2003.

Barnett, Michael. *Eyewitness to a Genocide: The United Nations and Rwanda.* Ithaca: Cornell University Press, 2002.

Bathily, Abdoulaye. "La Crise Ivoirienne: Elements pour Situer ses Origines et ses Dimensions Sous-regionales." *Democracy and Development* 3, no. 2 (2003): 93–99.

Bekoe, Dorina A., ed. *East Africa and the Horn: Confronting Challenges to Good Governance.* Boulder: Lynne Rienner, 2006.

Bellamy, Alex J., and Paul D. Williams. *Understanding Peacekeeping.* Cambridge, UK: Polity, 2010.

Bentley, Kristina, and Roger Southall. *An African Peace Process: Mandela, South Africa, and Burundi.* Cape Town: Human Sciences Research Council, 2005.

Berdal, Mats, and Spyros Economides, eds. *United Nations Interventionism, 1991–2004.* Cambridge: Cambridge University Press, 2007.

Bolton, John. *Surrender Is Not an Option: Defending America at the United Nations and Abroad.* New York: Threshold, 2007.

Boutros Boutros-Ghali. *Unvanquished: A US-UN Saga.* New York: Random House, 1999.

Buzan, Barry. *Peoples, States and Fear: An Agenda for International Security Studies in the Post–Cold War Era,* 2nd ed. Boulder: Lynne Rienner, 1991.

Carter, Gwendolen M., and Patrick O'Meara, eds. *African Independence: The First Twenty-Five Years.* Bloomington: Indiana University Press, 1986.

Chipman, John. *French Power in Africa.* Oxford: Basil Blackwell, 1989.

Chopra, Jarat. "A Chance for Peace in Western Sahara." *Survival* 39, no. 3 (Autumn 1997): 51–65.

Cilliers, Jakkie, and Greg Mills, eds. *From Peacekeeping to Complex Emergencies: Peace Support Missions in Africa.* Johannesburg: South African Institute of International Affairs and the Institute for Security Studies, 1999.

Clapham, Christopher. *African Guerrillas.* Bloomington: Indiana University Press, 1998.

Clarke, Walter, and Jeffrey Herbst, eds. *Learning from Somalia: The Lessons of Armed Humanitarian Intervention.* Boulder: Westview, 1997.

Cockett, Richard. *Sudan: Darfur and the Failure of an African State.* New Haven, CT: Yale University Press, 2010.

Cohen, Herman J. *Intervening in Africa: Superpower Peacemaking in a Troubled Continent.* New York: St. Martin's, 2000.

Crocker, Chester, Fen Osler Hampson, and Pamela Aall, eds. *Herding Cats: Multiparty Mediation in a Complex World.* Washington, DC: United States Institute of Peace, 1999.

Dallaire, Roméo. *Shake Hands with the Devil: The Failure of Humanity in Rwanda.* London: Arrow, 2004.

Damis, John. *Conflict in Northwest Africa: The Western Sahara Dispute.* Stanford, CA: Hoover Institution Press, 1983.

———. "Morocco and the Western Sahara." *Current History* 89, no. 546 (April 1990): 165–168.

———. "Western Sahara Conflict: Myths and Realities." *Middle East Journal* 37, no. 2 (Spring 1983): 169–179.

Davenport, Rodney, and Christopher Saunders. *South Africa: A Modern History,* 5th ed. London: Macmillan, 2000.

Davies, J. E. *Constructive Engagement? Chester Crocker and American Policy in South Africa, Namibia and Angola, 1981–1988.* Oxford: James Currey, 2007.

Deng, Francis M. *Protecting the Dispossessed: A Challenge for the International Community.* Washington, DC: Brookings Institution, 1993.

———. *Sudan at the Brink: Self-Determination and National Unity.* New York: Fordham University Press, 2010.

———. *War of Visions: Conflict of Identities in the Sudan.* Washington DC: Brookings Institution, 1995.

Deng, Francis M., Sadikiel Kimaro, Terrence Lyons, Donald Rothchild, and I. William Zartman. *Sovereignty as Responsibility: Conflict Management in Africa.* Washington, DC: Brookings Institution, 1996.

Dersso, Solomon A. "The Role and Place of the African Standby Force Within the African Peace and Security Architecture." Paper 209. Institute for Security Studies (ISS), Tshwane, South Africa, January 2010.

De Waal, Alex, ed. *War in Darfur and the Search for Peace.* London: Justice Africa, 2007.

De Witte, Ludo. *The Assassination of Lumumba*. London: Verso, 2001.

Diehl, Paul F. *International Peacekeeping*. Washington, DC: Johns Hopkins University Press, 1994.

Diehl, Paul F., and Daniel Druckman, *Evaluating Peace Operations*. Boulder: Lynne Rienner, 2010.

Durch, William, ed. *The Evolution of UN Peacekeeping: Case Studies and Comparative Analysis*. New York: St. Martin's, 1993.

Dzinesa, Gwinyayi A. "A Comparative Perspective of UN Peacekeeping in Angola and Namibia." *International Peacekeeping* 11, no. 4 (2004): 644–663.

———. "Postconflict Disarmament, Demobilization, and the Reintegration of Former Combatants in Southern Africa." *International Studies Perspectives* 8, no. 1 (2007): 73–89.

Eden, Anthony. *Full Circle*. London: Cassell & Company, 1960.

Ellis, Stephen. "How To Rebuild Africa." *Foreign Affairs* 84, no. 5 (September/October 2005): 135–148.

———. *The Mask of Anarchy: The Destruction of Liberia and the Religious Dimensions of an African Civil War*. London: Hurst and Company 1999.

Evans, Gareth. "When Is It Right to Fight?" *Survival* 46, 3 (2004): 59–84.

Ferguson, Niall. *Empire: How Britain Made the Modern World*. London: Penguin, 2004.

Finnegan, William. *A Complicated War: The Harrowing of Mozambique*. Berkeley: University of California Press, 1992.

First, Ruth. *South West Africa*. Baltimore: Penguin, 1963.

Fortna, Virginia Page. *Does Peacekeeping Work? Shaping Belligerents' Choices After Civil War*. Princeton, NJ: Princeton University Press, 2008.

Fortna, Virginia Page, and Lise Morjé Howard. "Pitfalls and Prospects in the Peacekeeping Literature." *Annual Review of Political Science* 11 (2008): 283–301.

Furley, Oliver, ed. *Conflict in Africa*. New York: Tauris Academic Studies, 1995.

Furley, Oliver, and Roy May, eds. *Peacekeeping in Africa*. Brookfield, VT: Ashgate, 1998.

Gaddis, John Lewis. "International Relations Theory and the End of the Cold War." *International Security* 17, no. 3 (Winter 1992–1993): 5–58.

Gambari, Ibrahim. *Theory and Reality in Foreign Policy Making: Nigeria After the Second Republic*. Atlantic Highlands, NJ: Humanities Press International, 1989.

Goulding, Marrack. *Peacemonger*. London: John Murray, 2000.

———. "The United Nations and Conflict in Africa Since the Cold War." *African Affairs* 98, no. 391 (April 1999): 155–166.

Harbeson, John W., and Donald Rothchild, eds. *Africa in World Politics: The African State System in Flux*. 3rd ed. Boulder: Westview, 2000.

Hargreaves, J. D. *Decolonization in Africa*. London: Longman, 1988.

Hawkins, Virgil. "History Repeating Itself: The DRC and the UN Security Council." *African Security Review* 12, no. 4 (2003): 47–55.

Hirsch, John L. *Sierra Leone: Diamonds and the Struggle for Democracy*. Boulder: Lynne Rienner, 2001.

Hirsch, John L., and Robert B. Oakley. *Somalia and Operation Restore Hope: Reflections on Peacemaking and Peacekeeping*. Washington, DC: United States Institute of Peace, 1995.

Hodges, Tony. *Angola: From Afro-Stalinism to Petro-Diamond Capitalism*. Oxford: James Currey, 2001.

――――. *Western Sahara: The Roots of a Desert War.* Westport, CT: Lawrence Hill, 1983.

Horne, Alistair. *A Savage War of Peace: Algeria 1954–1962.* New York: New York Review of Books, 2006.

Hoskyns, Catherine. *The Congo Since Independence, January 1960–December 1961.* London: Oxford University Press, 1965.

Howard, Lise Morjé. "UN Peace Implementation in Namibia: The Causes of Success." *International Peacekeeping* 9, no. 1 (Spring 2002): 101.

――――. *UN Peacekeeping in Civil Wars.* Cambridge: Cambridge University Press, 2008.

Howe, Herbert. "Lessons of Liberia: ECOMOG and Regional Peacekeeping." *International Security* 21, no. 3, (Winter 1996/1997): 145–176.

Hume, Cameron. *Ending Mozambique's War: The Role of Mediation and Good Offices.* Washington, DC: United States Institute of Peace, 1994.

Hurd, Douglas. *Memoirs.* London: Abacus, 2004.

Institute of International Affairs. *South African Yearbook of International Affairs 2000/2001.* Johannesburg: South African Institute of International Affairs, 2000.

International Commission on Intervention and State Sovereignty. *The Responsibility to Protect: Report of the International Commission on Intervention and State Sovereignty.* Ottawa: International Development Research Centre. 2001.

International Crisis Group. "Darfur: Revitalising the Peace Process." Africa Report no. 125, April 30, 2007.

International Peace Institute. "Peace Operations." IPI Blue Paper no. 9. Task Forces on Strengthening Multilateral Security Capacity. New York, 2009.

Iyob, Ruth, and Gilbert M. Khadiagala. *Sudan: The Elusive Quest for Peace.* Boulder: Lynne Rienner, 2006.

Jacquin-Berdal, Dominique, and Martin Plaut, eds. *Unfinished Business: Ethiopia and Eritrea at War.* Asmara: Red Sea, 2004.

James, Alan. "The Congo Controversies." *International Peacekeeping* 1, no. 1 (Spring 1994): 44–58.

――――. *Peacekeeping in International Politics.* Basingstoke, UK: Macmillan, 1990.

Jan, Ameen. "Peacebuilding in Somalia." IPA Policy Briefing Series. New York, July 1996.

Joffé, George. "Sovereignty and the Western Sahara." *The Journal of North African Studies* 15, no. 3 (September 2010).

Jonah, James O. C. *What Price the Survival of the United Nations? Memoirs of a Veteran International Civil Servant.* Lagos: Evans Brothers, 2006.

Katjavivi, Peter H. *A History of Resistance in Namibia.* Paris: United Nations Educational, Scientific and Cultural Organization, 1988.

Keen, David. *The Benefits of Famine: A Political Economy of Famine and Relief in Southwestern Sudan, 1983–1989.* Princeton, NJ: Princeton University Press, 1994.

――――. *Conflict and Collusion in Sierra Leone.* New York: Palgrave, 2005.

Keller, Edmond, and Donald Rothchild, eds. *Africa in the New International Order: Rethinking State Sovereignty.* Boulder: Lynne Rienner, 1996.

Khadiagala, Gilbert, ed. *Security Dynamics in Africa's Great Lakes Region.* Boulder: Lynne Rienner, 2006.

Khadiagala, Gilbert, and Terrence Lyons, eds. *African Foreign Policies.* Boulder: Lynne Rienner, 2001.

Lamin, Abdul Rahman. "The Conflict in Côte d'Ivoire: South Africa's Diplomacy, and Prospects for Peace." Occasional Paper no. 49. Institute for Global Dialogue, Johannesburg, August 2005.

Landsberg, Chris. *The Diplomacy of Transformation: South African Foreign Policy and Statecraft.* Johannesburg: PanMacmillan, 2010.

———. "Exporting Peace? The UN and South Africa." *Policy: Issues and Actors* 7, no. 2 (April 1994).

Large, Daniel. "China and the Contradictions of 'Non-Interference' in Sudan." *Review of African Political Economy* 35, no. 115 (March 2008): 93–106.

Lawless, Richard, and Laila Monahan, eds. *War and Refugees.* London: Pinter, 1987.

Lemarchand, René. *The Dynamics of Violence in Central Africa.* Philadelphia: University of Pennsylvania Press, 2009.

le Pere, Garth, ed. *China in Africa: Mercantilist Predator or Partner in Development?* Johannesburg: Institute for Global Dialogue and South African Institute of International Affairs, 2006.

le Pere, Garth, and Nhamo Samasuwo, eds. *The UN at 60: A New Spin on an Old Hub.* Midrand, South Africa: Institute for Global Dialogue, 2006.

Louis, William Roger. *Ends of British Imperialism: The Scramble for Empire, Suez and Decolonization.* London: I. B. Tauris, 2006.

Louis, William Roger, and Roger Owen, eds. *Suez 1956: The Crisis and Its Consequences.* Oxford: Oxford University Press, 1989.

Lowe, Vaughan, Adam Roberts, Jennifer Welsh, and Dominik Zaum, eds. *The United Nations Security Council and War: The Evolution of Thought and Practice Since 1945.* Oxford: Oxford University Press, 2008.

Luck, Edward C. "Sovereignty, Choice, and the Responsibility to Protect." *Global Responsibility to Protect* 1, no. 1 (2009): 10–21.

MacQueen, Norrie. *United Nations Peacekeeping in Africa Since 1960.* London: Pearson Education, 2002.

Magyar, Karl, and Earl Conteh-Morgan, eds. *Peacekeeping in Africa: ECOMOG in Liberia.* New York: St. Martin's, 1998.

Malan, Mark, ed. *Whither Peacekeeping in Africa?* Monograph no. 36. Tshwane: Institute for Security Studies, 1999.

Malan, Mark, and Joao Gomes Porto, eds. *Challenges of Implementation: The UN Mission in the Democratic Republic of the Congo.* Tshwane: Institute for Security Studies, 2004.

Malan, Mark, Phenyo Rakate, and Angela McIntyre. *Peacekeeping in Sierra Leone: UNAMSIL Hits the Home Straight.* Tshwane: Institute for Security Studies, 2002.

Malaquias, Assis. "The UN in Mozambique and Angola: Lessons Learned." *International Peacekeeping* 3, no. 2 (Summer 1996): 87–103.

Malone, David M., ed. *The UN Security Council: From the Cold War to the 21st Century.* Boulder: Lynne Rienner, 2004.

Mamdani, Mahmood. *Saviours and Survivors: Darfur, Politics, and the War on Terror.* Cape Town: Human Sciences Research Council, 2009.

Marchal, Roland. "Horn of Africa: New War, Old Methods." Africa Report, no. 8 (October–December 2007): 47–50.

Martin, Harriet. *Kings of Peace, Pawns of War.* London: Continuum, 2006.

Martin, Ian. *Self-Determination in East Timor.* Boulder: Lynne Rienner, 2001.

Mazrui, Ali A. *Towards A Pax Africana: A Study of Ideology and Ambition.* Chicago: University of Chicago Press, 1967.

Mbaya, Kankwenda, ed. *Zaire: What Destiny?* Dakar: Council for the Development of Social Science Research in Africa, 1993.

Meisler, Stanley. *United Nations: The First Fifty Years.* New York: Atlantic Monthly Press, 1995.

Melvern, Linda. *A People Betrayed: The Role of the West in Rwanda's Genocide.* London: Zed Books, 2000.

Minter, William. *Apartheid's Contras: An Inquiry into the Roots of War in Angola and Mozambique.* London: Zed, 1994.

Mwanasali, Musifiky. "The African Union, the United Nations, and the Responsibility to Protect: Towards an African Intervention Doctrine." *Global Responsibility to Protect* 2, no. 4 (2010): 388–413.

Neethling, Theo. "Whither Peacekeeping in Africa: Revisiting the Evolving Role of the United Nations." *African Security Review* 18, no. 1 (March 2009).

Negash, Tekeste, and Kjetil Tronvoll. *Brothers at War: Making Sense of the Eritrean-Ethiopian War.* Oxford: James Currey, 2000.

Nowrojee, Binaifir. "Joining Forces: UN and Regional Peacekeeping, Lessons from Liberia." *Harvard Human Rights Journal* 18 (Spring 1995): 129–152.

Nujoma, Sam. *Where Others Wavered: The Autobiography of Sam Nujoma.* London: Panaf, 2001.

Nzongola-Ntalaja, Georges. *The Congo: From Leopold to Kabila.* London: Zed, 2002.

O'Brien, Conor Cruise. *To Katanga and Back: A UN Case History.* London: Hutchinson, 1962.

———. *The United Nations: Sacred Drama.* London: Simon and Schuster, 1968).

O'Brien, Donal B. Cruise, John Dunn, and Richard Rathbone. eds. *Contemporary West African States.* Cambridge: Cambridge University Press, 1989.

Olonisakin, 'Funmi. *Peacekeeping in Sierra Leone: The Story of UNAMSIL.* Boulder: Lynne Rienner, 2008.

———. "UN Co-operation with Regional Organizations in Peacekeeping: The Experience of ECOMOG and UNOMIL in Liberia." *International Peacekeeping* 3, no. 3 (Autumn 1996): 33–51.

Olukoshi, Adebayo, Omotayo Olaniyan, and Femi Aribisala, eds. *Structural Adjustment in West Africa.* Lagos: Nigerian Institute of International Affairs, 1994.

Organization of African Unity. *The International Panel of Eminent Persons to Investigate the 1994 Genocide in Rwanda and the Surrounding Events,* July 2000.

Otunnu, Olara, and Michael Doyle, eds. *Peacemaking and Peacekeeping for the New Century.* Lanham, MD: Rowman and Littlefield, 1998.

Ould-Abdallah, Ahmedou. *Burundi on the Brink, 1993–95: A UN Special Envoy Reflects on Preventive Diplomacy.* Washington, DC: United States Institute of Peace, 2000.

Paris, Roland. *At War's End: Building Peace After Civil Conflict.* Cambridge: Cambridge University Press, 2004.

Pazzanita, Anthony G. "Morocco Versus POLISARIO: A Political Interpretation." *The Journal of Modern African Studies* 32, no. 3 (1994).

Pazzanita, Anthony G., and Tony Hodges. *Historical Dictionary of Western Sahara,* 2nd ed. Metuchen, NJ: Scarecrow, 1994.

Powell, Kristiana. "The African Union's Emerging Peace and Security Regime: Opportunities and Challenges for Delivering on the Responsibility to Protect." Institute for Security Studies, Monograph Series no. 119, May 2005.

Prunier, Gérard. *Darfur: A 21st Century Genocide.* Ithaca: Cornell University Press, 2008.

―――. *From Genocide to Continental War: The "Congolese" Conflict and the Crisis of Contemporary Africa.* London: Hurst & Company, 2009.

―――. *The Rwandan Crisis: History of a Genocide.* New York: Columbia University Press, 1995.

Pugh, Michael, and Waheguru Pal Singh Sidhu, eds. *The United Nations and Regional Security: Europe and Beyond.* Boulder: Lynne Rienner, 2003.

Quaison-Sackey, Alex. *Africa Unbound: Reflections of an African Statesman.* London: André Deutsch, 1963.

Rikhye, Indar Jit. *Military Adviser to the Secretary-General: UN Peacekeeping and the Congo Crisis.* New York: St. Martin's, 1993.

Rogier, Emeric. "MONUC and the Challenges of Peace Implementation in the Democratic Republic of Congo." Report on the Institute for Security Studies International Expert Workshop, Tswhane, 17–19 September 2003.

Rotberg, Robert I., ed. *China into Africa: Trade, Aid, and Influence.* Washington, DC: Brookings Institution, 2008.

Sahnoun, Mohamed. *Somalia: The Missed Opportunities.* Washington, DC: United States Institute of Peace, 1994.

Said, Edward W. *Reflections on Exile and Other Essays.* Cambridge, MA: Harvard University Press, 2002.

Saxena, S. C. *Western Sahara: No Alternative to Armed Struggle.* New Delhi: Kaliya, 1995.

Shubin, Vladimir. *The Hot "Cold War": The USSR in Southern Africa.* London: Pluto, 2008.

Sørbø, Gunnar, and Peter Vale. eds. *Out of Conflict: From War to Peace in Africa.* Uppsala: Nordiska Afrikainstitutet, 1997.

Soyinka, Wole. *Interventions,* vol. 2. Ibadan, Nigeria: Bookcraft, 2010.

Srinivasan, Sharath. "Minority Rights, Early Warning and Conflict Prevention: Lessons from Darfur." Minority Rights Group International report, September 2006.

Stedman, Stephen. "Spoiler Problems in Peace Processes." *International Security* 22, no. 2 (Fall 1997): 5–53.

Synge, Richard. *Mozambique: UN Peacekeeping in Action 1992–1994.* Washington, DC: United States Institute of Peace, 1997.

Taylor, Ian. *China's New Role in Africa.* Boulder: Lynne Rienner, 2009.

Taylor, Ian, and Paul Williams, eds. *Africa in International Politics: External Involvement on the Continent.* London: Routledge, 2004.

Thornberry, Cedric. *A Nation Is Born: The Inside Story of Namibia's Independence.* Windhoek: Gamsberg Macmillan, 2004.

Urquhart, Brian. *A Life in Peace and War.* New York: W. W. Norton, 1987.

Uvin, Peter. *Life After Violence: A People's Story of Burundi.* London: Zed, 2009.

Vines, Alex. *RENAMO: Terrorism in Mozambique.* Bloomington: Indiana University Press, 1991.

Vogt, M. A., and A. E. Ekoko, eds. *Nigeria in International Peacekeeping 1960–1992.* Marina, Lagos: Malthouse, 1993.

Wai, Dunstan M. *The African-Arab Conflict in the Sudan.* New York: Africana, 1981.

Williams, Paul D. "Into the Mogadishu Maelstrom: The African Union Mission in Somalia." *International Peacekeeping* 16, no. 4 (August 2009): 514–530.

Williamson, Richard W. "Sudan and the Implications for Responsibility to Protect." The Stanley Foundation Policy Brief, October 2009.

Woodward, Peter. *The Horn of Africa: Politics and International Relations*. London: I. B. Tauris, 2003.

———. *Sudan, 1898–1989: The Unstable State*. Boulder: Lynne Rienner, 1990.

World Bank. *Post-Conflict Reconstruction: The Role of the World Bank*. Washington DC: The World Bank, 1998.

Young, Crawford, and Thomas Turner. *The Rise and Decline of the Zairian State*. Madison: University of Wisconsin Press, 1985.

Zacarias, Agostinho. *The United Nations and International Peacekeeping*. London: I. B. Tauris, 1996.

Zartman, I. William, ed. *Collapsed States: The Disintegration and Restoration of Legitimate Authority*. Boulder: Lynne Rienner, 1995.

———. *Ripe for Resolution: Conflict and Intervention in Africa*. Oxford: Oxford University Press, 1989.

Ziai, Fatemeh. "Keeping It Secret: The United Nations Operation in Western Sahara." *Human Rights Watch Middle East* 7, no. 7 (October 1995).

Zoubir, Yahia, and Daniel Volman, eds. *International Dimensions of the Western Sahara Conflict*. Westport, CT: Praeger, 1993.

Index

About the Book

Nearly half of all UN peacekeeping missions in the post–Cold War era have been in Africa, and the continent currently hosts the greatest number (and also the largest) of such missions in the world. Uniquely assessing five and a half decades of UN peacekeeping in Africa, Adekeye Adebajo focuses on a series of questions: What accounts for the resurgence of UN peacekeeping efforts in Africa after the Cold War? What are the factors that have determined the success, or contributed to the failure, of the missions? Does the mandating of so many peacekeeping missions signify the failure of Africa's regional security organizations? And, crucially, how can a new division of labor be established between the UN and Africa's security organizations to manage conflicts on the continent more effectively?

Adebajo's historically informed approach provides an in-depth analysis of the key domestic, regional, and external factors that shaped the outcomes of fifteen UN missions, offering critical lessons for future peacekeeping efforts in Africa and beyond.

Adekeye Adebajo is executive director of the Centre for Conflict Resolution in Cape Town, South Africa. He obtained his doctorate from Oxford University, where he studied as a Rhodes Scholar. His numerous publications include *From Global Apartheid to Global Village: Africa and the United Nations, A Dialogue of the Deaf: Essays on Africa and the United Nations, Building Peace in West Africa: Liberia, Sierra Leone, and Guinea-Bissau*, and *The Curse of Berlin: Africa After the Cold War*.